WITHDRAWN FROM COLLECTION

FORDHAM UNIVERSITY LIBRARIES

Journal of
Don Francisco Saavedra de Sangronis

Don Francisco Saavedra de Sangronis
by Francisco José de Goya y Lucientes, 1798
Courtauld Institute Galleries, London (Lee Collection)

Journal of
Don Francisco Saavedra de Sangronis
during the commission which he
had in his charge from 25 June
1780 until the 20th of the
same month of 1783

Edited and introduced by
Francisco Morales Padrón

Translated by
Aileen Moore Topping

University of Florida Press
Gainesville

Copyright 1989 by the Board of Regents
of the State of Florida

Printed in the U.S.A. on acid-free paper.

Library of Congress catalog information appears
on the last page of this book.

✽

The University of Florida Press is grateful to the Program for Cultural Cooperation between Spain's Ministry of Culture and North American Universities for financial support for the publication of this book.

The press also acknowledges with thanks the assistance given by three scholars to the work of annotation and translation that Aileen Moore Topping was prevented by death from completing. James A. Lewis and Allan J. Kuethe graciously reviewed her work at late stages of the book's production, contributing materially to the completeness of its annotations and the precision of its language; Francis C. Hayes verified her translation against the Spanish-language transcription prepared by the editor, Francisco Morales Padrón.

The maps reproduced in this volume were all photographed from the collections of the University of Florida Map Library. The press gratefully acknowledges the expert assistance of Dr. Helen Armstrong, curator of maps, University of Florida Libraries.

✽

University Presses of Florida is the central agency for scholarly publishing of the State of Florida's university system, producing books selected for publication by the faculty editorial committees of Florida's nine university presses: Florida A&M University Press (Tallahassee), Florida Atlantic University Press (Boca Raton), Florida International University Press (Miami), Florida State University Press (Tallahassee), University of Central Florida Press (Orlando), University of Florida Press (Gainesville), University of North Florida Press (Jacksonville), University of South Florida Press (Tampa), University of West Florida Press (Pensacola).

Orders for books published by all member presses should be addressed to University Presses of Florida, 15 NW 15th Street, Gainesville, FL 32603.

Contents

List of Maps
vi

Introduction
by Francisco Morales Padrón
vii

Journal of
Don Francisco Saavedra de Sangronis,
1780–1783
1

Glossary
by Aileen Moore Topping
xxxix

Index
xlv

Maps

Regni Mexicani seu Novae Hispaniae ... (ca. 1750)
20–21

Jamaica (1817)
52–53

Kingston Harbor (1782)
57

Isola Cuba (1763)
102–103

Nova Hispania, Nova Galicia, Guatimala (n.d.)
110–111

Carte de l'Isle de Saint Domingue (1764)
136–137

Mexico (1754)
236–237

Editor's Introduction

Editor's Introduction
Francisco Morales Padrón

THE AGE in which Don Francisco Saavedra de Sangronis lived was one of the most interesting in the history of Spain and of the world because in it lay the foundations of modern times. This Sevillano lived from the middle of the eighteenth century (he was born in 1746, the same year as Goya) through the first two decades of the nineteenth (he died in 1819). He was thus a contemporary of Cabarrús, Jovellanos, Cavanillas, Olavide, Feijóo, O'Reilly, Juan Bautista Muñoz, Cadalso, Aranda, Campomanes, Gálvez, Floridablanca, and four kings descending from Ferdinand VI to Ferdinand VII, with Charles III and Charles IV in between, and of Pitt, Catherine II, Clement VIII, Napoleon, Clive, Voltaire, Schiller, Mozart, Goethe, Hegel, Marie Antoinette, Malthus, Joseph II, Frederick II, Cook, Bougainville, Kergulen, Sir Walter Scott, Beethoven, Chateaubriand, Mme de Staël, Goldsmith, and Humboldt. These Europeans watched the liquidation of their nations' American empires and saw the dawn of a new Europe, especially of a new Spain. Spain began in 1808 a chaotic era in which its empire was lost. It would not end until 1868 with the deposition of Isabella II.

In Saavedra we have a man of the upper class but with roots and broad connections at other levels. He is an excellent example of a product and exponent of an age, providing us a view of both his inner world and his perception of the milieu surrounding him. He was privileged to observe the struggle for power begun by the bourgeoisie in 1810, a revolutionary process rooted in eighteenth-century doctrine. Saavedra was born in Seville, a city that in the middle of the eighteenth century—when Jovellanos went there at the age of twenty-four in 1763—was the most important center for the thought of the Enlightenment, thanks to Don Pablo de Olavide, its great advocate.

The eighteenth century was an enterprising time, as Saavedra's career illustrates. Much of what was done then remains today; other reforms that were planned were never realized. Spain discarded its static character, although it continued to be, as it is today, a land of contrasts. Its tremendous poverty seemed to undermine any realization of economic reforms that might have let new political and religious ideals come forth. Reformers censured an idle nobility, a flourishing but ineffectual bureaucracy, and the presence of as many as 200,000 professional beggars as the causes of the country's social problems. Although some reforms brought about economic betterment, they did not motivate a fairer distribution of wealth. The reformers identified with the state, so their reforms were not made in a revolutionary way, as V. Palacio Atard ably points out.

Spain in the eighteenth century did not hold a notable place in the field of science. It was the age of the *dilletanti*, "*los eruditos de violeta.*" Physiocracy; humanitarianism, with the reform of workhouses and courts; administrative reforms; polemics between the "new man" and the defender of the past inimical to change; illusions produced by the foreign (a logical development after the decadent seventeenth century); blind faith in education (reform from above, education from below), which would permit altering economic conditions under which practical concerns could be pursued; theaters, bullfights, *tertulias*, balls, academies, the periodical press—this was Saavedra's Spain, which became that of Charles III (on which America also had an influence) and of Ferdinand VII, who governed a nation in crisis.

The Man Saavedra

A SPANISH thinker has written, "What happens to a man today happens to him in that form and in that fashion because another thing happened to him yesterday, and so successively, and we do not understand what is happening today if we are not told the tale of what happened yesterday and the day before, because that is the key and the cause of the present." We find this to be particularly true of Saavedra. An understanding of his life and his experiences, especially his Hispanic-American period, requires a knowledge of his earlier years, those between his birth and 1780—formative years that shaped and supported the years of maturity.

At ten years of age Saavedra went to Granada to be educated. When he was two, his father had died, and his mother had remarried; at eight he had begun to study Latin grammar in the Colegio de Santo Tomás. In Granada he was a student in the Colegio de Sacromonte (1756),[1] where, as usual, he felt that they considered him cleverer than he was. This "difference between true and apparent merit is one of the keys of my life," he confessed. Doubtless he was mistaken, but chance meetings with specific persons favorably impressed by him— especially Alejandro O'Reilly and José de Gálvez—determined his course on more than one occasion during his life.

At seventeen he was graduated as *licenciado* and doctor. He was strongly attracted to the military, the deployment of forces, and the history of Rome. He translated Cicero and Livy, wrote poetry, forming his style by reading Mariana, Saavedra, Solís, Feijóo; he must have had a superb memory. His family situation had given him the opportunity to manage the affairs of his stepfather, but he had chosen to remain in Granada.

In 1766 he was twenty years old and living in Seville in the home of a sister. He read the classics and French and looked

---

1. In 1590 in the present Colegio Mayor located in the upper Sacromonte neighborhood, men working in the woodland came upon a tunnel and some Latin inscriptions referring to the martyrdom of a Christian there. In order to commemorate this, the archbishop Don Pedro de Castro, in 1595, founded a collegiate church with its own abbot and canons and adjacent university college. It was a large, solid building that communicated with the "Santas Grutas" at the transept of the temple. Apparently this foundation never prospered, and by the middle of the nineteenth century it was totally in ruins (from *Recuerdos de un viaje por España*, Madrid, 1849).

Editor's Introduction

after his property. He was made a member of the Academy of Buenas Letras.[2] At almost the same time that the Jesuits were expelled, he decided to be ordained in Minor Orders.[3] Taking advantage of the presence in Cádiz of a bishop who was en route to the Indies, he moved to that city and received the first orders. This was not an impediment to his going to the opera and to the bullfights, where he admired Pepe Cándido.[4]

That same year he took the competitive examinations for the position of prebendary of Cádiz; he did not win it, but he was very impressive, so much so that a lady threw a *décima*

---

2. He was recommended to become honorary académico on 6 February 1767; he was accepted on 13 February and took the oath on 20 February. The title of the discourse given by Dr. D. Francisco de Saavedra in the Academia de Buenas Letras on 27 February 1767 was "The Year of Christ's Death Cannot Be Determined by the Prophecy of the Weeks of Daniel."

3. Minor orders:

Doorkeeper: The bishop gives the doorkeeper a key. His job is to open and close the doors of the church, to admit the deserving and refuse the unworthy.

Lector: The bishop gives the lector the books of readings. His office is to read the psalms and lessons from the pulpit, instruct the people in the doctrines of faith, and bless the bread and fresh fruits.

Exorcist: The bishop gives the exorcist the book of exorcisms. He has the special power to bless the obsessed. (Today this order may not be carried out without the special permission of the bishop.)

Acolyte (altar boy): The bishop gives the acolyte a candelabra with its candle snuffed out and some empty cruets. His job is to assist the subdeacon in the solemn mass, take the cruets to the altar, and light the candles.

(N.B.: In the modern discipline, these exercises may be carried out by laity, except that of the exorcist.)

4. Pepe Cándido was born in Cádiz and left in the home of the Espósitos de Santa María del Mar in that city on 30 November 1734. His teacher was Lorencillo; according to the critics of his time, he stood out more for his courage and willpower than for his skill. He originated the *salto al testuz* and killing with the dagger. He fought bulls in Seville in 1762, 1764, and 1771. He died on 24 June 1771 in the Puerto de Santa María, as a result of a wound received in the bullring the previous day, in which in order to *hacer el quite* [to attract the bull's attention away from a man in danger] for a picador named Coriano, he fell immobile to the ground; whether from a blow on the head or as an effort to escape from the bull is not known. The fact is that the bull then attacked him and threw him

Editor's Introduction

into his cap. It appeared that his career was to be an ecclesiastical one. But in Cádiz not only did he become acquainted with the Academy of Marine Guards; he also saw the ship on which the Viceroy Marqués de Croix was going to Mexico and the frigate on which Governor Bucareli was sailing to Buenos Aires. He also witnessed the formation of the entire Regiment of Zamora, feeling so much pleasure that the experience became "the first spark of his military vocation."[5]

His Andalusian perspective—Seville, Granada, and Cádiz—was broadened when he moved to Madrid. The religious-ecclesiastical object of this journey was interrupted and frustrated when, at the age of twenty-one, he fell in love, albeit platonically, with an actress and wrote a tragedy inspired by Voltaire's *Marianne*. Lurking in his imagination was his desire to be a military man, and the life he led was more appropriate to his age than to his intended estate. With a friend he frequented the residence of some girls who lived in the famous house of Tócame-Roque in the *barrio* of Barquillo.[6] One night, he and a

---

quite a distance. He is buried in the Prioral del Puerto. He is the first celebrated bullfighter whose tragic death is recorded; he was called "El Incomporable" and was considered one of the great fighters of the eighteenth century.

5. Don Carlos Francisco de Croix was of Flemish origin, native of Lille (in Flanders), a soldier with excellent character for command and government, belonging to the best of the Flemish nobility. He had served in Italy under Gages and afterwards as military governor of Galicia. From there he was called urgently to Madrid, to receive the news of his appointment as viceroy of Mexico (23 August 1766). He left Cádiz in a Spanish ship and took 69 days to reach Veracruz. The transfer of command from Cruillas occurred in Otumba.

Francisco de Paula Bucareli y Ursúa was the son of Luis Bucareli Henestrosa y Ribera and Ana María Ursúa. He was born in Seville, was Comendador de Almendralejo of the Order of Santiago, which he entered 29 May 1745, lieutenant general of the Reales Ejércitos, governor of Buenos Aires, viceroy and captain general of Vatavoa, and gentilhombre de Cámara of Charles III. He was the brother of the viceroy of Nueva España [Mexico]. The reason for his departure, mentioned by Saavedra, was to become governor of Buenos Aires.

6. The Casa Tócame-Roque was a famous historic building of Madrid destroyed by fire at the end of the eighteenth century. Located on Bar-

Editor's Introduction

drunken friend, were arrested by the famous police force created by the Conde de Aranda.

Two weeks' imprisonment encouraged his military aspirations. In the detention quarters he became acquainted with the colonel of the Regimiento Inmemorial del Rey [the King's Immemorial Regiment], the Conde de Fernán Núñez, whose house at Ecija he would visit in August 1768 in order to present his papers soliciting admission as a cadet. To do so required that he first go to the Ayuntamiento in Córdoba to investigate his genealogy in the papers edited by Ambrosio de Morales. The genealogical curriculum now in the Ayuntamiento of Seville is undoubtedly the copy he made in Córdoba in order to demonstrate his linkage with the surnames Pérez de Saavedra, Arias de Saavedra, Narváez de Saavedra, Marqués de Quintana, etc.

Life, which from time to time brought Saavedra contact with persons able to influence the direction of his career or unexpectedly introduced a subject or a problem with which he would later be associated, now destined him to meet on this trip to Andalusia Don José Espelius, the lieutenant of engineers commissioned by Olavide to study the navigability of the Guadalquivir River between Seville and Córdoba. (Saavedra would be named president of the Guadalquivir River Company in 1814.)

At the age of twenty-three, on returning to Madrid, he met Don Alejandro O'Reilly. It was the time of "the second year of masquerades, a diversion invented by the Conde de Aranda to distract the public from other preoccupations, but which greatly disturbed the minds of the young." With the attention to detail that characterizes his diaries, Saavedra described the ten *reales* a day promised him by his sister, his emotional separation from his mother, the books he packed in his luggage (Caesar, Jenofont, Vegetius, Horace, Sallust, Livy, Plutarch, Tacitus), and his preparation for the entrance examinations for the military. At

---

quillo Street at the Belén corner, this huge building contained around sixty families, among whom frequent and scandalous quarrels occurred. It was a typical tenement house, the fame of which inspired literary themes such as a work of Fernández y González which bears the building's name. On occasion it would be hostile to law and custom because of the dubious morality of some of the families gathered there.

the time he attained the rank of sublieutenant his mother died. O'Reilly left for Louisiana to put down the insurgency there, and Saavedra left for Valencia on 6 October 1769.

In Valencia operas, excursions, dances, and fêtes so overtaxed him that in 1770 he suffered from bloody vomiting followed by a burning fever, which obliged him to go to Seville to recuperate. There he had several casual love affairs; he felt his poetic inclination reborn, and he became the intimate friend of the Conde de Aguila, Jovellanos, and others. Because he did not yet know his native city well, he decided to visit it in a leisurely fashion while clearing up the matter of the property inherited from his parents. His mother had left jewels at Granada and an estate called El Coral in Utrera, which had seventy-four *aranzadas* (an aranzada was 4,756 square meters) of very old olive groves and twelve of neglected vineyards, as well as a quantity of casks and kettles for making brandy. He liquidated everything, paid debts, ordered an excellent wardrobe, bought books, and had 11,000 reales left over.

His vacation was interrupted by the rumor of war with Great Britain over the Malvinas (the Falkland Islands). He returned to his post, passing through Ecija and Cartagena, whose fiestas and amusements he describes in his diary. The five months in Cartagena must have been a continual fiesta, because he counts them among the happiest of his life. When the threat of war receded, his regiment moved to Alicante. He devoted the ensuing months to memorizing the poetry of Metastasio and to his affection for belles lettres.

Back in Valencia in June 1771, he cultivated the friendship of Gregorio Mayáns[7] and began to study violin and drawing. Although his military duties prevented him from completing these studies, his artistic inclination and "principles of good

---

7. Gregorio Mayáns y Siscar was born in 1689 in Oliva (Valencia) and studied in Barcelona, Valencia, and Salamanca. In Valencia he was catedrático de código and canon from 1723. He brought to light many rare books and, because of this, Philip V appointed him palace librarian, a position he retained until 1740; in that year he retired to his native village in order to dedicate himself to his favorite studies. He published many works, excelling in those of a juridical nature and in his zeal to purify the

Editor's Introduction

taste" would remain with him. With a festive gathering of friends he celebrated his twenty-fifth birthday, enjoying himself greatly.

By this time O'Reilly had returned from Louisiana, famous and more powerful than before, although some were criticizing him for having killed M. Lafrenière, instigator of the uprising against Governor Antonio de Ulloa. O'Reilly prevented the Conde de Fernán Núñez from taking Saavedra on a journey through Europe, alleging that it would curtail his career. Saavedra no longer received an allowance from his sister; his income was limited to the 240 reales per month of his pay. This was not enough to satisfy his living expenses, so he devoted himself to translating, not being the kind of person to gamble or borrow.

When the Catalonians grew restive over the imposed levies of *quintas*, Saavedra's regiment was moved to Tortosa, where he continued translating, hunting hares, and attending social gatherings. To deal with smuggling on the frontier, his regiment made yet another move, which allowed him to pass through Barcelona, where he was impressed by the "industrious activity that prevails in its interior." Earlier he had thought that the mouth of the Ebro River required an artificial port; now he concluded that Spain would be a very opulent country if it had four regions like Catalonia and ten cities like Barcelona. From Gerona he took a trip to the other side of the Pyrenees, recording the incidents of the journey, until orders from O'Reilly obliged him to set out for Madrid in January 1773. He delivered translations of Bossuet to a client and, via Albacete, reached Madrid on 5 February.

O'Reilly had planned to create a military academy at Avila, and he sought Saavedra's opinion on it. From that time on, Saavedra enjoyed O'Reilly's favor and was invited to his house, where he went almost every evening, "paying court to him and to the countess, who also was very kind to me." His connection with O'Reilly was fateful in a decisive and far-reaching fashion, because their later estrangement, after the Algiers expedition, would alter the course of Saavedra's life.

Spanish language.

In the meantime Saavedra translated Guibert's *Treatise on Tactics*.[8] On 15 April the Academy of Avila was inaugurated, and he describes its ambience, curriculum, and so forth. He had a secretary to whom he dictated. Already he was taking the walks that in his old age he would recount, even their distances. Each evening at eight o'clock he went to bed to read and write, at ten had his supper, and then went to sleep. He awakened at five o'clock in the morning and worked until nine, when he went to the academy. He had one table for his work and another for dictating to his amanuensis.

In March of 1775 rumors began to circulate about the concentration of troops in Cádiz, Cartagena, and Barcelona, readying to punish the emperor of Morocco, who had attacked Melilla. Saavedra, who had not yet been under fire, begged O'Reilly to keep him in mind in case of any action. O'Reilly made an appointment with him in Madrid, and, as on other occasions, Saavedra made the journey with Don Bernardo de Gálvez, a man to whom he would later be linked by "a friendship that was in some way the basis of his early good fortune."

O'Reilly revealed to him the plan of the expedition against Algiers, of which Charles III did not approve, and Saavedra studied it. The British king George III was alarmed by these preparations (the discord with the American colonies was beginning at that time) and demanded to know their objectives. The ministry informed him of their purpose, the British communicated it to Gibraltar, and from there a Jewish informant traveled to Algiers to relay the plans to the king of Algiers. When the Spaniards arrived, the Moors were ready for them.

---

8. Conde de Guibert Jaime Antonio Hipólito was a French military writer, born in Montauban in 1734, died in Paris in 1790. He commanded campaigns in Germany and in 1766 distinguished himself for his courage in Corsica. In 1787 he was named member of the Administrative Council of the Department of War, and it is said that he died of annoyance at not having been elected deputy in 1789. His *Essai Général de Tactique* (London, 1772; Paris, 1804) received general applause, but because of certain indiscrete passages, he had to leave France and was given a magnanimous welcome by Frederick the Great. Back in France in 1775, he took part in the reorganization of the army in accordance with principles of his Prussian model.

Editor's Introduction

At the end of April 1775, when, coincidentally, the Infanta Carlota Joaquina was born, the Spanish forces finished preparations for the expedition; Saavedra and O'Reilly joined in Cartagena in May. Saavedra gave a detailed description of the forces that sailed on 27 June and reached Algiers between the twenty-ninth and the thirtieth. The punitive invasion was a disaster. Saavedra, wounded in one leg, narrated fully the military action and his break with O'Reilly, which took place in the Puerto de Santa María. Saavedra had previously gone from Algiers to Alicante, the Chafarinas (which he examined with O'Reilly by order of the king), and Melilla. Here he met for the first time Don Francisco de Miranda, then a lieutenant of the Regiment of the Princess, who was to create "so much clamor in the world" and incur "such varied fortunes."[9]

O'Reilly had been named captain general of Andalusia. In a letter, Saavedra, half jokingly, half seriously, had recounted to a friend the disaster of Algiers. The letter was stolen and came into O'Reilly's possession, and he no doubt waited for an opportune moment to make use of it. Saavedra continued in O'Reilly's administrative office, "but reluctantly," because he knew that he no longer enjoyed the favor of his superior.

---

9. In the edition from the *Archivo del General Miranda* (Caracas, 1929–50, 24 vols.), we read in vol. 4, pp. 352–53 and 385:

My esteemed friend:
I had the opportunity to speak to my inspector about you and to tell him what I learned of your talent and circumstances during the brief time in which I had the pleasure of seeing you in Melilla.

This gentleman is charitable, patriotic, strongly inclined to protect the young people who promise to be useful to the nation; however, due to one of those strange situations so frequently found in royal courts, his credit and his influence are so limited that he scarcely could suggest to the Sargentías Mayores of the provincial units persons with whom he wishes to conduct the remainder of his work.

These kinds of appointments in the militia can't suit you or any other man of recognized merit because they offer no opportunity to excel and consequently offer little hope of rising to a higher rank. Most of those who came to the militia from the army, either because of annoyance with their officers in command or with the injustice of seeing others ranked higher,

Editor's Introduction

find that because of the character of these corps they can not rise farther, becoming fretful and disgusted. If some day my inspector has the power that corresponds to his capacity, cogency, and military knowledge (a change that may come any day), I assure you sincerely that he will have in his favor the distinction that he deserves. It is likely that he will respond to the letter he received from you in July in the arriving mail. He has not written until now because he did not know your regiment or assignment.

I am no help in many ways, but if my words, my travel, and my connections can be of assistance, count on me; I hope to see you well placed.

Madrid, September 20, 1776.
I kiss your hand.—Your obedient servant,
Francisco Saavedra

To Señor Don Juan Miranda (vol. 2, f.133, Oy 4-1780)
Dear friend Miranda: I think that the determination that the inspector will have for you will be to send you to a fortress for two months and also give you a reprimand. They told me about this matter in such a way that it causes me to doubt its certainty somewhat; nevertheless, keep it in mind and be prepared. It is unfortunate that all men of talent must frequently navigate against the wind; yet it seems to me that time spent in adversity is not time lost philosophically. I wish you better luck than you currently have; then you will see how sweet it is to tell of past troubles—especially when, not having been deserved, they teach us lessons which providence gives us. In misfortune even more than in prosperity remember that you have a friend in

Saavedra

(Oy, 28-1780)
My friend and master: I esteem you by inclination and from acquaintance; far from bothering me, it will always be a pleasure to have occasion to help you. Tomorrow, no later, I will find out what can be the status of your file in the War Department, and I will use on your behalf very bit of my limited influence—which never would be better used than for a man of worth and true friend such as yourself.

Francisco de Saavedra

Señor Don Francisco de Miranda
Dear friend Saavedra: I give you infinite thanks for the fine and thoughtful remarks with which you favored me in your letter of the second of last month, products of a noble and generous spirit. The aforesaid dossier has already been sent according to the *Rl. orn.* which I copy below. I don't

Finally, O'Reilly summoned Saavedra one evening to discuss the letter. Saavedra answered "firmly that it was not to be wondered at that he should say confidentially to a friend what he had said to him [O'Reilly] openly when this event was reported to the king." With regard to certain harsh passages in the letter ("this haughty and miserable being, who believes that the whole universe was created for his service, does not hesitate to destroy thousands of his fellow human beings over a few square inches of land, more or less"), he explained that they alluded to man in general, not to O'Reilly. (Bernardo de Gálvez, himself a participant at Algiers, composed a ballad about the expedition, as he had a "special taste for music.")

With good reason Saavedra feared that O'Reilly was "generous enough in not damaging his enemies, but incapable of promoting those whom he did not regard as his friends and even his adherents." In order that his presence not constitute an irritant, Saavedra requested leave and transfer. In Cádiz he saw the last fleet, commanded by Don Antonio de Ulloa, that would sail for the Indies, and he enjoyed the Spanish, Italian, and French theaters (the French being best, supported by the powerful Gallic colony). Returning to the Puerto de Santa María at the end of December, he received his transfer immediately. He left for Seville to await publication of the list of the Algiers promotions, suspecting that O'Reilly had not included him on it; he decided that if "he were excluded from so ordinary a promotion, [he would] depart for Madrid and ... solicit a militia adjutancy, for which he had initiated procedures in advance."

Saavedra arrived in Seville as 1775 ended. He liquidated the "odds and ends" of the hacienda El Coral in order to meet the expenses of his new enterprise. He went to the theater, which still retained vestiges of the brilliance Olavide had given it, and frequented the tertulias of Jovellanos. At the end of January

---

write to tell you of the case because you are not instructed in the details, nor do I have the necessary audacity for it.

Finally, if you have the opportunity to investigate what the resolution is which the inspector is to send me, I would be ever so grateful, for we do not have Urcas's letter here.

[This rough copy is Miranda's: vol. 2, fol. 207, verso.]

* xx *

1776 he was visited by Bernardo de Gálvez, who was en route to Madrid, and learned from him of the death of Don Julián de Arriaga, minister of the marine and the Indies, and about the subsequent division of the ministry. Don José de Gálvez, one of Bernardo's uncles, had been given the Ministry of the Indies.

Saavedra was then thirty years old. He had been separated from O'Reilly, but another influential man had crossed his path. Don Bernardo offered to introduce him to his uncle, and Saavedra felt a premonition of what such a friendship would mean. He confessed, "I can swear that from this point on my heart told me that fortune was calling me in this direction, although it did not come true until more than two years later, when I had already renounced hope."

In mid-February the *Gazette* published the Algiers promotions list; Saavedra's name did not appear, but it did include names of men who had not disembarked to fight in Algiers or who had pretended to be wounded in order to re-embark. The list hardened his resolve to seek opportunity "without hesitating or looking backward."

Granada, however, was still the pivotal city in Saavedra's life. His aunt lived there, he had been educated there in part, and he went there now to collect some of his mother's things. The city was in commotion because of two cases being heard in the Audiencia, upon which Saavedra expounded at length. One case was against a famous bandit who was defended by a lawyer whose pleadings were very much within the philosophy of the era. The other involved some friends of Saavedra, including the prebendary Don Juan de Flores, implicated with others in the falsification of pieces found in the excavations of the Alcazaba.

The court in Madrid was Saavedra's next stopping place. His life was becoming more complicated, and step by step he was drawing closer to the New World. Among his new friends was the minister of war, the Conde de Ricla, whose house at Aranjuez he frequented, also becoming acquainted with other important persons. Among old friends, he encountered Don Ramón de Guevara, his English master, whom the Academia de la Historia had just commissioned to translate William Robertson's *History of America*. Saavedra assisted a little in this translation, "but the government, influenced by interests more personal than political, prohibited the copy and the original." "Certainly," said Saavedra, "no foreigner has spoken more truthfully than Robertson about our conquests in America; but in some notes of his history he gave a great eulogy to Campomanes, and this was an unpardonable sin to some of those who were governing then and who did not care for this magistrate."(10)

At the beginning of June, before leaving Madrid for Avila, Don Bernardo de Gálvez presented Saavedra to his uncle Don Miguel, counselor of war. Although Saavedra had obtained an adjutancy, he managed to postpone taking his place in the assigned post and to remain instead with the inspector of militias, Don Martín Álvarez, as an aide attached to the Secretariat of Inspection. Don Bernardo soon returned; the king made him first colonel of the Fixed Regiment of New Orleans and later governor of Louisiana. Don Bernardo introduced Saavedra to his uncle Don José, minister of the Indies, and Saavedra dined in the minister's house more than once. The Gálvezes were at

---

10. Edmundo O'Gorman, concerning the prohibition from publication of the book by William Robertson, *The History of America*, relates in his book *La Idea del Descubrimiento de América* (Mexico, 1951), that it was suppressed by the minister Gálvez on 9 December 1778, a suspension later confirmed by the king. It was said that the book was offensive to Spain.

According to O'Gorman, this was not the reason. He says that Casria has demonstrated that Gálvez's order arose from political considerations, since the international situation was such that it made Spain a hostile power toward England.

According to Ballesteros, when the publication of the work was prohibited, it was because of the general conditions in Europe. It was the time when war against England was being prepared and the Spanish would attack Gibraltar. It was not an opportune time to publish an English book. Furthermore, in 1770, Father Reynal had published his *Historia filosófica y política de los establecimientos y comercios de europeos en las dos Indias*, wherein he had attacked the Inquisition harshly as well as the Spanish colonial system.

It was necessary to answer the diatribes of Reynal and to correct the errors of Robertson. According to Ballesteros, this was the prime reason for entrusting Juan Bautista Muños with the preparation of a true and documented history of the Indies.

their political apogee: José, the *visitador* of Mexico (1765–71) and now minister; Matías, president of Guatemala and later viceroy of New Spain; Miguel, counselor of war; and Bernardo, son of Matías, who had been commandant of the frontiers of Mexico until 1770 and who would, like Matías, become viceroy of New Spain.

For Spanish politicians the American world had two key theaters. One was the Río de la Plata and the Colonia del Sacramento, which the Portuguese were attempting to penetrate, but the expedition of Don Pedro de Cavallos was leaving at that time. "It was one of the best organized and best provisioned enterprises that has been prepared in Spain," declared Saavedra. The other was North America; the estrangement between England and her North American colonies would produce certain results, predicted Saavedra: the colonies would seek independence; France would support them; and France would drag Spain into the conflict.

Having obtained a three months' leave from his adjutancy, Saavedra went to Granada, drawn there by a desire to visit his aunt and his old friends, to improve his health, and to gain a thorough knowledge of "the antiquities of that town which was always his favorite." He was in the city of the Darro River from July to September, returning to Madrid on 3 October 1776, when there was still talk about the presence of the French fleet at Cádiz. It had arrived in August and was said to be on maneuvers, but actually it was a division of the fleet that the French were preparing with great secrecy to assist the rebelling North American colonials.

Saavedra's friends in Granada had suggested his suitability to be appointed major of the Militias of Granada, "but luck, or rather, providence—which while taking me through extraordinary paths never has granted me what issued from them, and later has given me much more than I deserved—placed a large obstacle in that pathway." He returned to the Secretariat of Inspection, but providence was pushing him toward the New World.

The Conde de Fernán Núñez, having returned from his journey through Europe and been named ambassador to Lisbon, offered Saavedra the post of secretary of the Spanish embassy in Portugal. He accepted and, predictably, endeavored to learn everything about Portugal, with whom relations were strained because of tensions in the Río de la Plata region. He began associations with Don José Moñino, who had arrived from Rome in order to direct the Ministry of State, with Don Tomás de Iriarte, who assisted him greatly, and with Iriarte's brother, who managed the Secretariat of Ministry of State. Saavedra consulted Don Matías Gálvez and Don Miguel de Gálvez and informed them of his concerns about his career. They listened indifferently to the news of Saavedra's appointment as embassy secretary; they had made their own plans for Saavedra, as he was informed by Don Miguel. Indeed, on the recommendation of Don José de Gálvez, Charles III granted Saavedra a post in the Secretariat of the Ministry of the Indies with a salary of 20,000 reales.

The dilemma was enormous: on the one hand, an appointment with the Gálvezes as sponsors, on the other, the embassy secretariat in Lisbon, with the Conde de Fernán Núñez behind him. Saavedra decided to stay with the Gálvez family and was named official, fourth grade, of the Secretariat of the Ministry of the Indies. On 20 August, Don José de Gálvez welcomed him and as soon as they were alone told him that "he found himself engulfed in one of the most difficult businesses that had come up in a long time; and that he was counting on me to assist him in the arduous enterprise for which he was responsible, because its aim was to deregulate [Latin] American commerce." Gálvez calculated that the experiment in freedom that the Caribbean islands had enjoyed since 1765 had greatly advanced the development of Cuba and Catalonia.

Saavedra knew nothing about economic matters and he told Don José so, but the latter handed him a series of papers and told him that "for business of primary importance in which it is necessary to depart from ordinary norms, he placed a higher value on virile and alert reason than on misapplied experience, incapable of shaking off the yoke of preconceptions." Saavedra devoted himself wholeheartedly to the task and, amid great opposition, overcome only by Gálvez's strength of character, the Regulation of the Free Trade was promulgated. During this

Editor's Introduction

process he learned enough to see the truth of something he had heard Ensenada say in Medina del Campo, that "in Spain it would never be possible to undertake a fundamental reform while all the Ministries were not united in one hand."

The queen of Portugal was resident in San Idelfonso at that time, conducting frequent conferences with her brother Carlos in which "the spirit of the Marqués de Pombal surely existed still." To Saavedra's mind an extremely disadvantageous peace was made with the Portuguese to which "the condescension of Charles III toward his sister contributed no less than did the want of vision of our Cabinet."

While the negotiations were still in progress, there arrived from Lisbon, sent by Fernán Núñez, a man named Cantofer, a native of Madrid who had enjoyed favor in Pombal's ministry. He was acquainted with the commerce of the Orient and the foreign establishments there and had been an adviser to Caravello in the revitalizing of trade in Goa and Macao. Moñino and Gálvez listened to Cantofer and then charged Saavedra to meet with him and see if it was possible to organize a plan of commerce with India and China through a company or through individual investors. But these talks and plans were interrupted by the sudden peace with Portugal. Cantofer expressed his bitter disappointment; nevertheless, the information he supplied and the work he did became the basis of the Company of the Philippines.[11]

The war had already spread rapidly. In the Orient the British captured Pondicheri. In the New World, the principal theater, the French took Tobago, Dominica, and Granada, and successes and failures alternated. Saavedra observed

> Spain, who could neither tolerate the retention by the English of the absolute control of the seas they had arrogated to themselves, nor contemplate without misgivings the independence of the

---

11. In the work of Mª Lourdes Díaz-Trechuelo concerning *La Real Compañía de Filipinas* (Seville, 1965), we find no mention of these prefatory remarks or antecedents that Saavedra cites.

Anglo-Americans next door to her richest possessions, remained neutral in a war in which her interests were as though counterbalanced; and this neutrality was sustained with the greatest tenacity by her ministers. At last, the ambassador of France, the Comte de Montmorint, who was lying in wait for an opportunity to catch Charles III alone, said to the King, "Your Majesty is the Abraham of the House of Bourbon, and Heaven is offering to you the decisive moment to avenge the great injuries which it has suffered at the hands of Great Britain: unite, Your Majesty, the great maritime forces you have ready with those of France, and England will be humiliated in this campaign." King Charles III, who needed little to rekindle his resentment against the English, resolved at that moment to join France and to break with England.

Despite the fact that Spain had a respectable armada composed of forty-two ships-of-the-line (thirty in Cádiz and twelve in Ferrol), England could not believe that the country having the most possessions in America "would decide in favor of the side which aspired to erect an independent power there." So disbelieving were the British that they let Spain finish her preparations, send orders to America, and choose the most propitious moment.

A manifesto that Saavedra helped to prepare was communicated to the authorities in America on 20 May 1778 and proclaimed in Spain on 21 June, while the plan to be followed was being studied. It was argued that from Cádiz twelve warships with 6,000 men could descend unexpectedly on Jamaica. But the French point of view won out—to join the fleets in order to attack Great Britain and put an end to the conflict. Part of the Spanish fleet joined the French; four vessels and some frigates were sent to the Islas Terceras to intercept a rich English convoy coming from the Orient, but they did nothing, even though the British passed almost in sight of them.

The British, meanwhile, although surprised by the unexpected Spanish declaration and joining of French and Spanish forces, were able to protect Jamaica with only twenty-four warships; they made their island secure, conserved their forces, and saved

Editor's Introduction

their convoys. In January, taking advantage of the fact that the major part of the fleet was wintering in Brest, the British routed Don Juan de Lángara's force of twelve warships off the Cape of Santa María.

These failures convinced the Spanish government that "the gigantic projects of France were fantasy" and that the war was going to last longer than had been supposed. For that reason it was decided to prepare a respectable force for the Indies. But there was a scarcity of funds. A *junta* of ministers and councilors of state was called, and almost all present believed it necessary to raise taxes. Gálvez consulted Saavedra on the matter, and the latter's opinion pleased the minister so much that he was asked to put it in writing. In his report Saavedra argued that (1) the greatest tax a king can impose on a people is war; (2) war makes domestic products fall in price and foreign products rise; (3) if at such a juncture taxes are imposed, the country is oppressed; (4) the prudent thing is not to raise taxes but to lower them and to borrow the sums that ordinary income cannot provide. "When peace is made, conditions change: domestic products rise, foreign ones fall—that is the moment to raise taxes in order to liquidate the loans that have been negotiated." Although this opinion was well received, taxes were raised by one-third, though it was never possible to effect this increase.

The war did not cause much dislocation. Spain continued to open *consulados* (merchant guilds) and abandoned or changed many duties. Never was commerce so prosperous in Spain as in the interval between the promulgation of the Regulation for Free Trade and the declaration of war. Had Spain remained neutral, her commerce could have profited enormously. But "everything was turned upside down by the impolitic and inopportune war, which, although less unfortunate in its events than any of the previous ones, served only to disturb the spirits of our colonies with the example and to create a formidable enemy to the rear of our most opulent possessions." Saavedra's judgment or prophecy was the same as that of Aranda.

The principal "business" of the war fell to Saavedra as a responsibility of the secretariat. There he devoted himself, among other things, to extracting and putting into order for consideration the reports made by the brigadier of engineers, Don Agustín Crame, resulting from his tour of the fortifications between the Orinoco and Veracruz.[12] Crame had made illustration of them all, specifying what was worth preserving and what to dismantle. Saavedra speculated that this useful work would probably be conserved permanently in the Archivo General de Indias.

Late in 1779 and early in 1780 the king was given an account of Crame's studies, the authorities of the Indies were informed of Crame's campaign plans, and forces were prepared for America. In April 1780 an expeditionary force of twelve ships-of-the-line and five frigates left Cádiz escorting a convoy of merchant vessels and 7,000 men.

Don José Solano commanded the naval forces, and Lieutenant General Don Victorio de Navía led the land forces. In April news arrived of the capture of several British strongpoints by Governor Gálvez, among them Baton Rouge. For this victory he was promoted to field marshal and was ordered to take Pensacola, a point from which the English were carrying on much contraband trade in the Gulf of Mexico.

In June, word arrived that Gálvez had taken Mobile on the way toward Pensacola. The officer bearing this news also communicated the motives and difficulties attendant on the expedition against Pensacola, the scarcity of resources in Havana, and the discord prevailing in the high command. In light of the international situation, Don José de Gálvez calculated that the principal theater of the war would be North America and that what was needed there was a man "who, being well informed about the European situation and the cabinet's plans and not being tied down by a command or employment which fixed him in any one place, should be present in the military juntas and communicate in person the thoughts of the court, bring the leaders into agreement, confer with the generals of the allied nations, dispose the remittances of funds from one place to

---

12. Many of these maps drawn by Crame are in the Archivo General de Indias. Those relative to Venezuela are described in F. Morales Padron and J. Llavador Mira, *Mapas, planos y dibujos sobre Venezuela existentes en el Archivo General de Indias* (Seville, 1964–65).

another, and go freely wherever his presence was required by necessity or the good of the public cause."

On 22 June, Gálvez described this need to Saavedra, who instantly volunteered his services. On the same day Gálvez consulted Moñino; the two having the same opinion, the matter was referred to the king, who authorized the project and the appointment.

The Commissioner Regius

SAAVEDRA RECEIVED instructions and orders directed to the president of the Junta de Generales established in Cuba and to the Treasury of Havana. The junta was commanded to respect Saavedra's instructions as if they came from the king himself; the treasury was instructed to provide the royal commissioner with any funds he might request. The instructions set forth a program of American action: in order of priority, to capture Pensacola, to remit rapidly to Spain all funds possible, to assist the president of Guatemala to expel the English from Nicaragua, and, in collaboration with the French, to conquer Jamaica.

Saavedra left Aranjuez on 25 June 1780, reached Coruña on 3 July, and sailed for America on 21 August. He had already started his first journal. Aboard the frigate *Diana*, which formed part of a Franco-Spanish convoy, the commissioner, who was barely thirty years old, was about to experience an authentic adventure. Early in the voyage, at the latitude of Lisbon on 30 August, a storm caused some vessels to collide and lose their masts. On 12 September, off Madeira, the convoy was divided; the *Diana* proceeded alone by decision of her captain, who was interested in taking on liquors in the Canary Islands, and in this way she was saved from a hurricane that destroyed the rest of the ships. On 9 October the *Diana* left the storm behind and on the fifteenth entered Cumaná, where news had arrived about a Franco-British encounter. Thinking that the British might be patrolling the waters between Jamaica and South America, the captain decided to sail north through the channel separating Puerto Rico and Santo Domingo, then south in search of Baracoa (Cuba). They set sail on 28 October and on 9 November encountered an English warship—the *Pallas*—which pursued and shelled them until the *Diana* was forced to surrender. Thus did Saavedra become a prisoner of the English, who, ignorant of his identity and mission, took him to Jamaica with the other prisoners. Needless to say, Saavedra had necessarily disposed of all his compromising papers.

On 15 November 1780 they anchored in Kingston, Jamaica, where Saavedra remained until 2 January 1781. During these weeks he formed important and lasting friendships, studied and observed the island's aspects that attracted him, recorded his observations in his journal, and collected a good index of intelligence and useful references for his mission. Still concealing his identity, he professed to be an official who specialized in economic matters. Among the friends he made was Mr. Berry, secretary to Governor Dalling, who obtained for him a license to depart.

On 22 January 1781 Saavedra entered Havana via Trinidad. So, tardily (he had sailed from Coruña almost seven months earlier), did his mission really begin. He quickly discovered that the Spanish leaders did not all share the same views, that Monteil, the commandant of the French naval force, was displeased because his advice was not taken, that the Spanish troops were few (7,500 men) and in poor condition, that hospitals were lacking, that the warships of the fleet appeared to be unserviceable, that sailors were deserting, that the royal treasury was complaining about enormous debts, and that provisions were scarce.

Seeing that the Spanish commandants held differing points of view, Saavedra quickly took stock of the situation and convened the Junta de Generales on 10 February 1781. The leaders decided that the expedition to Pensacola was their first objective; the expedition against Jamaica was postponed until the following year. As soon as Pensacola was taken, the funds in Havana (4 million pesos) would be sent to Spain, and reinforcements would be sent to Guatemala. The twenty-eighth of February was fixed as the date for the departure of the forces for Pensacola, and several vessels sailed on that date under the command of Bernardo de Gálvez.

Editor's Introduction

The Capture of Pensacola

SAAVEDRA REMAINED in Havana working toward his objectives. In Pensacola the English had fortified themselves in three small forts on heights overlooking the town. The principal fort, Red Cliffs (Barracas Coloradas), dominated the entry channel. Gálvez himself boarded the brigantine Gálveztown and gave the order to enter the harbor; it did, with such good fortune that not one enemy shot reached it. The rest of the fleet, with the same luck, followed.

Saavedra's preparations in Havana were interrupted by an alarming report. At the end of May, an English fleet had been sighted sailing toward Cape Antonio. Without doubt, he thought, it was bound for Pensacola with reinforcements. A Franco-Spanish expedition commanded by Field Marshal Juan Manuel de Cagigal was organized to reinforce Gálvez at Pensacola. Saavedra himself embarked with the expedition when it sailed on 9 April. On the twenty-first the reinforcements joined the men who were laying siege to Pensacola.

Saavedra—who must have had access to the log of a pilot—narrates in great detail the incidents of the crossing from Havana to Pensacola. This scrupulous, detailed narration went on until 8 May when, unexpectedly, the English fort Half Moon was blown up by a Spanish cannonball. In the diary entries from 21 April to 8 May, Saavedra developed a detailed account of the siege of Pensacola superior even to that in Gálvez's diary. Saavedra's entries refer to the various encounters that ensued, the many deserters, and the arrival of an emissary on 25 April from Governor Peter Chester for the purpose of making an agreement not to destroy the town and to limit the encounters to the three British forts.

After the unexpected explosion of Half Moon Fort, the attackers did not give the besieged time to react but almost immediately occupied the bulwark and prevented the two other forts from using their artillery. The victory over the English had come at a critical moment, for the Spanish were running short of cannonballs. The English proposed the suspension of hostilities and capitulation, but Gálvez replied that capitulation must take effect first. General John Campbell accepted the Spaniard's demand and commissioned his nephew to discuss the articles of surrender, by which Pensacola and West Florida passed into the hands of Spain. On 9 May the articles were signed, and at three o'clock that afternoon Gálvez, with two companies of grenadiers, occupied Pensacola.

At the conclusion of his North American mission, Saavedra was appointed intendant of Caracas. As the head of the Intendencia he encouraged the development of agriculture, established an experimental garden for the acclimatization of plants from other regions, and ordered the construction of quarters for troops and buildings for the royal officials and the courts and the preparation of a statistical report on the country.

Saavedra returned to Spain in 1788 and a year later was granted a place on the Supreme War Council. Not much is known about this period of his life, but he probably continued to perform as one among many public functionaries and bureaucrats in the capital. In 1797 he was appointed minister of finance. Spain is indebted to him for the creation of the Banks of Amortization, which established the basis of a credit system.

In March 1798, Saavedra became minister of state—first in an interim capacity, then officially—and left finance. It is easy to imagine, although he does not say so, that enemies opposed him continually. In addition, he had a serious illness that forced him to request retirement. The king granted him a place on the Council of State and permitted him to retire to Andalusia to recover his health. Little is known about this period of his life. But events in 1808 drew Saavedra out of retirement and placed him again in the forefront.

When the French invaded Andalusia in 1810 and the Central Junta was dissolved, Saavedra presided for six days over the Junta of Seville; he succeeded in reunifying the Central Junta in Cádiz. Nine months later, like so many others, he was obliged to take refuge in Ceuta for safety. He then began to edit his journals. He returned to Seville in February 1813 and took on duties as president of the Guadalquivir River Company, established to improve the channel of the river, develop its lands, and organize the navigation of steamships. He also presided over the Economic Society and the Academy of Medicine and busied himself with several free schools in Triana—his own idea, supported by the state. He died on 25 November 1819 and was buried in the sacramental chapel of the church-convent of La Magdalena, where Las Casas was consecrated bishop.

Saavedra's Diaries

DURING HIS 1780 mission in America and later from the beginning of the Napoleonic invasion, Saavedra wrote a series of journals. He also left an unfinished autobiography entitled *Los Decenios* (*The Decades*). They all form part of the Saavedra Archive, made up of some fifty *legajos* of heterogeneous content, preserved in the Casa-Residencia of the Jesuit Fathers of Granada. This material, some of it in Saavedra's own handwriting, is of great value because this genre of historiography is rare in Spain.

Saavedra's mission to the Indies is collected in his first journal, of which there are several differing versions:

1. A version in clear, elegant penmanship, i.e., a fair copy, that begins with some reflections about English politics and includes his study of the history, economy, and society of Jamaica made after his capture on the high seas (2 January 1781) and during his subsequent confinement on the island. It ends with his departure from Jamaica. The first sections of this transcription and translation are taken from this account.

2. A version in clear, elegant penmanship that begins on 25 June 1780; it is more abridged overall than version 1 but in certain parts more extensive. It ends on 21 April 1781, reviewing the days of that month very briefly.

3. A version that begins on 26 June 1780 and ends on 28 April 1781. The text is almost identical to version 2, but it has marginal additions that have been used already in version 1.

4. The complete journal, which includes the study on Jamaica and ends on 15 February 1783.

5. The so-called *Decenios*, with a version similar to version 4 but ending in 1786.

Saavedra's *Journal of the Mission to America* is unique in

Editor's Introduction

Spanish historiography of that period. It does not constitute an official report; rather it is the personal vision of a politician-traveler observant of details and given to recording them. Our version of this journal is formed from version 1 complete, an excerpt from version 4, the "diario," and years six and seven of the *Decenio* 4 that is found entirely in a fair copy and bound with the *Decenios*.

The Battle of Pensacola: A Comparison of Accounts

IN COMPARING Saavedra's journals with the books *The Battle of Pensacola* by N. Orwin Rush and *Bernardo de Gálvez in Louisiana* by John Walton Caughey, it must be remembered that neither of the two North American historians knew of the existence of the Saavedra journals. This is not surprising: the journals have not been published, nor are they in the Archivo General de Indias of Seville. Caughey refers to and makes use of the correspondence between Saavedra and José de Gálvez, available in the Archivo de Indias de Seville (Indiferente General 1578). Letters that Saavedra wrote to José de Gálvez on 12 February, 2 March, and 7 April 1781 are cited in footnotes in chapters 11 and 12; they refer to the preparation for the battle and the battle itself (Caughey, pp. 188, 193, 195, 198, 203, 206). Although Rush knows and cites Caughey's work, he does not mention Saavedra nor does it appear that he consulted Saavedra's letters to Gálvez.

In the narration of the battle, the three versions have much in common; the two American historians used the diary of Gálvez, which necessarily coincides with that of Saavedra on the events that occurred but has a different focus. For Caughey the emphasis is on Bernardo de Gálvez, to whom he assigns the role of hero of the battle; the chapter on the battle is entitled "Yo solo," the motto that Gálvez ostentatiously displayed on his escutcheon following the battle to commemorate his heroic action of entering Pensacola Bay alone. Rush principally uses a technical approach to the battle, culled from the Spanish diaries and the correspondence of the English authorities. His version

Editor's Introduction

differs more from Saavedra's journal than does Caughey's. For Saavedra, conforming to his general practice, it was most important to record his participation in everything that was happening, and he describes everything that concerned him in great detail. For that reason it is not surprising that he devotes much more attention to the preparation of the reinforcement expedition than to the battle itself.

There are some concrete instances in which certain discrepancies appear. First, all three versions contain descriptions of the differences between Gálvez and Calvo de Irazábal (the latter had refused to enter the port, fearing the fire of the English batteries installed on the Red Cliffs). They all narrate how Gálvez boarded the *Gálveztown*, of which he had complete command, hoisted the commandant's flag, and forced his passage, running through enemy fire without damage (Rush, p. 9; Caughey, p. 204). Saavedra tells us nothing more about the friction between the fleet and Gálvez; the others declare that friction persisted until the end and that there was a general lack of cooperation (Rush, pp. 28, 29; Caughey, pp. 204, 210).

Second, Saavedra mentions an interesting fact not noted in the other versions: the scarcity of cannonballs and of war matériel in general on the Spanish side. He relates that on 6 May, Gálvez confided to him that there remained enough for only two days; that he was going to assault the Half Moon Fort by escalade; and that although he was paying the soldiers two reales for each enemy ball they recovered, the effort was not sufficient. This scarcity is especially important if considered in relation to the quantity of ammunition captured from the English, for it demonstrates that the Spanish victory at Pensacola was a stroke of luck.

A third important difference is seen in the citations of the number of forces attacking and defending Pensacola. On 22 April 1781 the day after Saavedra's arrival at Pensacola, he tells us that Gálvez's forces had 7,806 men, including 1,617 in Cagigal's detachment, 1,505 seamen, and 275 Frenchmen, who had been sent from Cuba as reinforcements. Caughey estimates Gálvez's forces at about 7,000 (p. 208). Rush's numbers are much larger: he cites a report from General John Campbell to Sir

* xxxv *

Henry Clinton dated 12 May 1781 in which the forces that attacked Pensacola are estimated at between 9,000 and 11,000 soldiers, 500 artillerymen, and 14,000 seamen (p. 106). He also says that the French numbered at least 2,000 and probably 4,000 (p. 34n). Saavedra's and Caughey's versions seem more likely to be accurate, since the English general may have been trying to explain away his own surrender.

As to the numbers of the forces that defended the stronghold, there is virtual unanimity. Saavedra mentions 1,625 men (not counting blacks or Indians), 101 women, and 123 children (10 May). Caughey describes the forces that defended Pensacola as 2,500 men but includes in that number 300 armed blacks and 600 hunters and inhabitants (p. 187). Rush gives an approximate number and indicates the discrepancies regarding the number of English and Spanish casualties in the accounts of Gálvez and Campbell (pp. 32–33).

In reference to the war matériel that the English had in Pensacola, the three versions coincide closely. Saavedra mentions 143 cannons, 1 mortar, 6 howitzers, 40 swivel-guns, 2,150 fusils, and a great number of balls, sacks of grapeshot, and cartridges. Caughey counts 143 cannons, 4 mortars, 6 howitzers, 40 swivel-guns, 2,142 guns, 8,000 gun-flints, 298 barrels of powder, bombs, balls, cartridges, and bayonets (p. 212). Rush says exactly the same, taking these numbers from Gálvez's diary (p. 34).

Saavedra's journal, then, is an important document for confirming what happened at the Battle of Pensacola and for clarifying some doubtful points. Because he was a little removed from those who were fighting, he could observe the events with greater impartiality. His journal does not contain an exaggerated eulogy of Gálvez; it even perhaps gives preference to other leaders like Ezpeleta and Girón, who have been neglected by other historians.

The Other Journals

APART FROM the journals concerning America and the Indies, Saavedra has left us many others, all transcribed and some already studied or used:

Editor's Introduction

1. Journals of the years 1811 to 1819 (nine volumes).
2. Journal of the Guadalquivir River Company.
3. Medical journal from 28 December 1805 to 25 November 1812.
4. Journal of the operations of the Junta of Seville from the beginning of the Revolution (brief).
5. Journal as president of the Sociedad Patriotica (brief), 1817–18.
6. Journal concerning the charitable institutions of Seville (brief), 1816–27.
7. Journal of the operations of the Regency from January to October 1809.

The totality of this material is a rich source for students of Spain and Seville at the beginning of the nineteenth century. Some of it has been used in three dissertations for the licenciatura: *Perdida de la isla de Trinidad* (1966), by Josefina Pérez Aparicio; *Los Rusos en America* (1966), by Enriqueta Vila; and *Don Francisco de Saavedra, segundo intendente de Caracas* (1973), by Angel López Cantos.

Journal of
Don Francisco Saavedra de Sangronis

Journal of
Don Francisco Saavedra de Sangronis
during the commission which he had in his charge from 25 June 1780 until the 20th of the same month in 1783[1]

ENGLAND found herself engaged in a civil war in an effort to retain possession of her North American colonies, who had already proclaimed themselves independent, when France, suspected up to that time of having aided those colonies secretly, openly declared herself their protector by revealing on 13 March 1778 through her ambassador in London, the Marquis de Noailles, that she had just concluded a treaty of alliance and trade with them.[2]

This step, although cloaked with all the subtleties of the language of diplomacy so that it would not appear to be a provocation, was viewed in the British Parliament as a formal rupture of the peace, and soon afterward the two nations began hostilities.[3]

In the beginning, Spain, who could neither tolerate the re-

---

1. The period actually recorded in this journal is 25 June 1780 to 15 February 1783. The commission referred to ended on 20 June 1783, when Saavedra was appointed intendant of Caracas. [Tr.]

2. France and Spain had been assisting the North American colonists secretly since 1776. Spain's aid had been sent at first by way of France. The capitulation of Burgoyne at Saratoga prompted Louis XVI of France to recognize the independence of the United States, and on 4 May 1778 the Continental Congress ratified two treaties with France, one of alliance, one of trade. See Juan Francisco Yela Utrillo, *España ante la Independencia de los Estados Unidos* (Lérida, 1925), 2:9–10. [Tr.]

3. Hostilities between France and England began with the indecisive Battle of Ushant on 27 July 1778, between a British fleet of thirty ships

tention by the English of the absolute control of the seas that they had arrogated to themselves, nor contemplate without misgivings the independence of the Anglo-Americans, remained neutral in a war in which her interests were as though counterbalanced. In the end, the reiterated importunities of the Court of Versailles resolved her ambivalence, and early in May of 1779 Spain decided to join France and to break with England, who had recently spurned her offer of mediation.[4]

Despite the fact that the Spaniards had armed a respectable fleet, the British cabinet never believed that the nation that possessed the most dominions in America would decide in favor of the party that aspired to erect an independent power there; lulled by that misapprehension, they gave Spain time to complete her preparations, to choose the most propitious moment to declare her intention, and even to send beforehand orders to her overseas dominions.[5]

In fact the declaration of war against Great Britain was communicated to the principal officials of the Indies on 20

---

commanded by Admiral Keppel and a French fleet of equal strength commanded by Admiral the Comte d'Orvilliers. [Tr.]

4. When in 1777 the Conde de Floridablanca succeeded the Marqués de Grimaldi as the foreign minister of Charles III of Spain, he hoped to continue indirect aid to the United States and to remain aloof from the conflict. On 20 January 1779, through the Spanish ambassador Almodóvar, he proposed mediation by the Spanish monarch in the hope that Great Britain would move to prevent Spanish diplomatic and military intervention by ceding Gibraltar to Spain. George III's refusal was reported to the Spanish court on 16 March 1779. [Tr.]

5. On 18 May 1779 the Spanish court sent notification to colonial officials that war was to be declared against England (José de Gálvez to the governor of Louisiana, 18 May 1779, no. 124, Archivo General de Indias, Papeles Procedentes de Cuba, legajo 569, hereinafter AGI:Cuba, followed by the legajo number). The royal order of 18 May was received by Diego José Navarro, governor of Havana, on 17 July. Navarro wrote an urgent letter to the Spanish observer and unofficial agent to the Continental Congress Juan de Miralles asking for news "especially if the Congress plans to proceed to conquests of the territories bordering on Louisiana" and urging Miralles "to accelerate and promote with the Congress as soon as possible the conquest of San Agustín de la Florida" (Diego José Navarro to Juan de Miralles, 19 July 1779, AGI:Cuba 1281). [Tr.]

[Introduction]

May of that year, and it was solemnly proclaimed in Spain on 21 June.[6] During this interval the plan of operations to be adopted was discussed. Some expressed the opinion that twelve warships should immediately be detached from the great fleet that had been made ready at Cádiz and, transporting five or six thousand soldiers, should descend unexpectedly upon Jamaica, which was unguarded. But the system proposed by the French prevailed, that the fleets of the two nations should be integrally combined so as to overpower England with one blow, with so formidable a preponderance of forces as to put an end to the war in a single campaign.[7]

The English, although surprised by the Spaniards' unexpected declaration, found means of freeing themselves from the storm that threatened them. They protected their island against an anticipated invasion, removed their fleet from danger, drew their convoys together, and in January of the following year, taking advantage of the opportune circumstance that the greater part of our maritime forces had remained to winter in Brest, surprised and routed the fleet of Don Juan de Lán-

---

6. The French foreign minister, the Comte de Vergennes, urged Spain to enter the war, promising the recovery of Gibraltar, Florida, Minorca, and, if possible, Jamaica. As early as February 1779 the French minister plenipotentiary in Philadelphia had informed the Continental Congress that Spain probably would declare war, and the Congress had formed a committee to study the possible consequences of that action. On 12 April, France and Spain concluded the Convention of Aranjuez, in which they pledged themselves to continue the war until Gibraltar was secured for Spain. The declaration of war was made on 21 June, and it was announced in Havana on 22 July (Navarro to Miralles, 22 July 1779, AGI:Cuba 1281; Navarro to Bernardo de Gálvez, 18 July 1779, AGI:Santo Domingo legajo 2082, hereinafter AGI:SD followed by the legajo number). [Tr.]

7. Both of the Bourbon kings aimed at weakening England's maritime supremacy and at revenge for humiliations suffered in earlier wars. In other respects their aims were divergent. France wanted to invade England; Spain was unwilling to send to the north from Cádiz the warships requested for that purpose, because protection of the arrival of the fleet and preparation for the siege of Gibraltar were of paramount importance. Spain considered unwise the French strategy of dividing the French fleet, one part to be sent to the North American continent and the other to the West Indies. [Tr.]

Journal of Don Francisco Saavedra de Sangronis

gara[8] off the Cape of Santa María, and brought relief to Gibraltar, which was blockaded by land and sea.[9]

These events disabused our cabinet of illusions and convinced them that the war would be one of greater duration than they had confidently believed at the beginning, and they resolved to send to America considerable forces, which would protect our possessions or attack those of the enemy according to the circumstances.[10] To this end, in the month of April

---

8. Juan de Lángara y Huarte (1736–1806), a seaman, was born in La Coruña. From 1776 to 1778 he was captain of the *Poderoso*, flagship of the Marqués de Casa Tilly in the expedition against the Portuguese in Brazil. In 1779 he fought Rodney's twenty-one warships and ten frigates at Gibraltar, although he had only eleven warships and two frigates, and he was forced to surrender four of his vessels. In December 1779 he became a fleet commander, and in February 1780 he was given command of the combined Spanish and French fleet. Before joining the campaigns against England in 1779, he had sailed around Africa and Asia and had promoted scientific expeditions. He fought against France in 1793 and became secretary of the navy and member of the Council of State. [Ed.]

9. Sir Jeffrey Amherst was given the responsibility of guarding the British Isles against any attempted invasion. Admiral George Rodney, in an engagement off Cape Vincent on 16 January 1781, captured or destroyed seven of the eleven ships of Lángara's fleet and was able to relieve Gibraltar. On 12 April, Admiral Derby brought additional supplies to Gibraltar. [Tr.]

10. Saavedra, who had just turned thirty-three, before commenting on this expedition, expressed in *Decenios (Decades)*, his autobiography, some interesting opinions on the neutrality of Spain and the shifting of this attitude through the intervention of the ambassador of France: "Spain —whom it suited neither that the English should continue their maritime hegemony which they had arrogated to themselves, nor that she look without grave concern upon the independence of the Anglo-Americans, neighbors to her richest possessions—remained neutral in a war in which she found herself between two equally strong self-interests; and Spain's ministers maintained her neutrality with tenacity. Finally, the Count of Monmoriet [sic], who kept his eye pealed for a favorable occasion when the cabinet of St. James desired to drop their mediation, succeeded in catching Charles III alone and said: 'Your Majesty is the Abraham of the House of Bourbon, and Heaven now offers you the decisive moment to avenge the great harm you have received from Great Britain; unite the great maritime forces you have provided and England will be humbled in

[Introduction]

of 1780, twelve ships-of-the-line commanded by Fleet Commandant José de Solano and 7,000 soldiers commanded by Lieutenant General Don Victorio de Navia sailed from Cádiz bound for Havana.[11]

In June of the same year it was learned that Don Bernardo de Gálvez, governor of Louisiana, had captured the stronghold of Mobile.[12] The officer who brought this news informed the minister of the Indies about the state of affairs in America, the causes that up to that time had prevented the projected expedition against Pensacola, the scarcity of funds that existed in Havana, and the nature of the discord that reigned among the leaders there.[13]

Because events were making it look as if the Indies must be

---

this campaign.' Charles III, who needed little urging to revive his resentment of the English, resolved at that moment to join with France and break with England; and he resolved it so strongly that his ministers could not dissuade him either as a group or singly." [Ed.]

11. José de Solano y Bote had served earlier as governor of Venezuela, captain general of Santo Domingo, and president of the Real Audiencia de Santo Domingo. After Spain's declaration of war against England in 1779, his fleet joined the French fleet, commanded by Admiral the Comte d'Orvilliers, in closing English ports. In February 1780 he sailed for North America, convoying transports carrying 12,000 men for the campaigns in America. He took part in the capture of Pensacola and afterward was made commander-in-chief of the navy in America. Lieutenant General Victorio de Navia came with Solano as commandant of the Army of Operations. He was relieved of his command by a royal order of 12 February 1781 and was succeeded by Bernardo de Gálvez. [Tr.]

12. See note 68 below. This news was brought to Spain by Lieutenant Manuel González of the Regiment of Spain. [Tr.]

13. After the capture of Mobile, Bernardo de Gálvez wished to move at once against Pensacola, which had been his principal objective since the declaration of war. Deterred by intelligence reports of British reinforcements of Pensacola, and confused by disagreements concerning the relative advantages of proposed campaign plans, the captaincy general delayed preparation of the forces necessary for the Pensacola expedition. Gálvez went in person to Havana to obtain the men and ships he needed. See Francisco de Borja Medina Rojas, S.J., *José de Ezpeleta, Gobernador de la Movila, 1780–1781* (Seville: Escuela de Estudios Hispano-Americanos de Sevilla, 1980), 395–400.

the principal theater of war, Don José de Gálvez believed that there was needed an individual there who, being well informed about the situation in Europe and the plans of the ministry, and not bound by a command or employment that kept him in any one place, should be present in the military juntas; he also should personally inform them of all deliberations in Madrid, bring the leaders to a meeting of minds, confer with the general officers of the allied nations, arrange for the remittance of funds from one place to another, and go freely wherever necessity and the good of the cause required his presence.[14]

---

14. José de Gálvez (1720–87), born in Macharavialla (Málaga), studied law in Salamanca and Alcalá. While a lawyer at the French Embassy and secretary to Grimaldi, he was appointed visitador (investigative minister) for New Spain in 1765. The reforms that he brought about there in the treasury and the army were remarkable. It was his responsibility to expel the Jesuits and to strengthen the missions in California at the same time that he fortified the Hispanic North by establishing military headquarters for the interior provinces. Appointed Marqués de Sonora and minister of the Indies, it fell to him to establish free trade and to set up consulates and the system of intendencias. A determined supporter of the rebellion of the thirteen colonies, he fostered the Solano expedition. [Ed.]

Gálvez presented the following memorial to the king:

Sire

The conquest of Jamaica is the most important and splendid objective which Your Majesty's armed forces can undertake in this war, but its execution is attended by difficulties which can be surmounted only by a plan of attack in which many circumstances are combined with exactitude.

It is essential that the Spanish forces be joined in Guarico with the troops and warships which the Most Christian King is to place there at Your Majesty's orders, that without an instant's delay the expedition be executed at the opportune and precise time when it is known that the Negroes of Jamaica are putting into practice the uprising they have promised, that a diversionary action is being made against the British forces in the Leeward Islands and the colonies threatening the French at Saint Christopher or Saint Lucia, and by the revolutionaries at New York or Savannah. It will also be necessary that, if Pensacola is already under Your Majesty's dominion, we make some movements feigning designs against San Agustín de la Florida.

[Introduction]

I was serving at that time as official of the secretariat of the Ministry of the Indies, and I was in charge of military and commercial affairs of those departments.[15] On 22 June the minister communicated to me the idea above, and I instantly volunteered to execute the commission, if he considered me fit to accomplish it. That same day he discussed the matter with the minister of state,[16] and, the two ministers being in agreement, a report was given to the king, who authorized the project with his approval.[17]

I made ready with the haste demanded by the urgency and

It is very difficult, if not impossible, to treat this matter in writing in such a way that all who are to take part in it will join unanimously in its execution with the necessary energy. Orders, no matter how clear and forceful they may be, are always subject to interpretations or misunderstandings and never fail to give apparent pretexts for disobedience or delay. It happens also that when one treats with official papers a matter to which many persons must contribute, rarely does there fail to occur a breach in the secrecy which is always useful but in the Jamaica enterprise is absolutely necessary. A good example of this is the expedition against Pensacola, which, although its execution was ordered by the clearest and most forceful orders, has been delayed for more than a year with great risk to its outcome, and for at least four months the English have known that our armed forces were going to execute it. (José de Gálvez to the king, undated, AGI:Indiferente General legajo 1578 [hereinafter cited as AGI:Ind. Gen. followed by the legajo number]). [Tr.]

15. In 1705 two departments were set up, war and treasury. In 1714 were added departments of state, justice, the navy, and the Indies (the New World). These departments, the work of the Bourbon reforms, were like ministries. [Ed.]

16. José Moñino, Conde de Floridablanca, in 1777 became a minister in the cabinet of the Marqués de Grimaldi, who had initiated aid to the American Revolution in 1776. In April 1777, Floridablanca succeeded Grimaldi as prime minister. He continued the assistance, but, fearful of the effect on Spanish colonies, he opposed recognition of the independence of the United States. [Tr.]

17. José de Gálvez's memorial elicited this response: "The King being informed has resolved with very particular satisfaction that Don Francisco de Saavedra go to Havana on the next mail packet, and that he then go on to the other parts of America where necessary, carrying the confidential orders which are to be sent to Generals Navia and Navarro, with the

gravity of the commission, and in the meantime the orders I was to carry were issued. These orders were only two: the first, addressed to the president of the Council of General Officers [*Junta de Generales*] ordered to be formed in Havana for the planning of military operations, advised that credence and compliance be given in the junta to whatever I might say, as if my words were orders of the king communicated by his ministers; the second stated that whatever funds I might request were to be furnished by the treasuries of the Indies for the objectives which His Majesty had communicated to me.[18]

I was instructed orally that the principal objectives I must promote were the following: (1) that the expedition against Pensacola to expel the English totally from the Gulf of Mexico

---

corresponding credential to accredit him with them and the other leaders with whom he must treat the important matters of the war and the conquest of Jamaica, etc." (to José de Gálvez, 22 June 1780, AGI:Ind. Gen 1578). [Tr.]

18. Saavedra carried the following confidential order to the governor of Havana: "Army Captain Don Francisco de Saavedra, official of my Secretariat of State for the Universal Office of the Indies, will deliver with this royal order to Your Excellency and to General Victor de Navia the confidential orders I gave him on the 19th instant concerning the expedition which must be executed against Jamaica. And because it is not easy to explain in writing all the attendant causes which intervene in order for the enterprise to be executed and performed without loss of time, the King has resolved that this individual go to instruct Your Excellency and the other general officers orally about his royal intentions, as Saavedra is perfectly informed about the present state of Europe, the interests of the belligerent powers, and the war office of my secretariat of which he is in charge.

"For these and many other reasons, His Majesty desires that Your Excellency and the other voters of the Junta hear him in the Junta and give to him the same credence and assent as if it were I speaking in his royal name; that after the corresponding resolutions and provisions are taken, consistent with the importance of the matters, according to the state in which the prior conquest of Pensacola is found, he go to Guarico or Martinique to confer with the French generals and plan the enterprise of Jamaica; that he also go to West Florida, where Don Bernardo de Gálvez was, and to the other places necessary, later joining the expedition against Jamaica if he can, and being given for these purposes all the assistance and

[Introduction]

be executed; (2) that as much money as possible be sent to Spain without delay, under an escort calculated to be adequate for their security; (3) that assistance be sent to the president of Guatemala[19] to enable him to drive out the enemies from the various places they were occupying in that province; (4) that our land and sea forces united with those of the French undertake the conquest of Jamaica, or any other important operation the circumstances might dictate.

I agreed with the minister of the Indies that during the performance of my commission no precise amount should be fixed for the expenditures I must make, except that all expenses would be defrayed in the name of the king, and for that I was given an open order.

25 June 1780

After I was given the royal orders by the minister of the Indies and an official paper from the minister of state addressed to the administrator of mail-packets in Coruña, I left Aranjuez for Madrid, without telling anyone the true object of my journey.

26 June 1780

In Madrid I made various preparations for the journey, which I began at ten o'clock in the evening in a stagecoach, accompanied only by my servant.

From the descent from the Guadarrama Pass as far as Galicia, the roads, although badly neglected, are tolerable because for the

---

funds he may need and request, for which Your Excellency will secretly communicate a copy of this order to the intendant of the army there, and make it known in the Junta so that all the general officers will obey it with the understanding that His Majesty so commands. I inform Your Excellency of this his sovereign resolution for your punctual and effective compliance" (to the Governor of Havana. José de Gálvez to Navarro, 27 June 1780, AGI:Ind. Gen. 1578). [Tr.]

19. Matías de Gálvez, later viceroy of New Spain, a brother of José de Gálvez and the father of Bernardo de Gálvez. [Tr.]

most part the terrain is level. There is a good stretch of road constructed without regard to cost from Villafranca del Bierzo to the middle of the Zebrero hill; from there to Betanzos the road is abominable, and I do not know how there can be a vehicle that dares to undertake it. The inns of this highroad are generally dirtier and less well furnished than those of the rest of Spain.

Nothing notable occurred in this short journey, which I completed in seven days.

3 July 1780

At nightfall on 3 July I entered La Coruña. Immediately I went to see the administrator of mail-packets, Don Bernardo Caro García, to whom I delivered the written order of the minister of state. In it he was ordered to make ready without losing a moment the swiftest mail-packet there and to arrange my embarkation on it. While this was being done I remained hidden, first in a kind of lodging-house and later in a private home, not allowing myself to be recognized by anyone at all.

12 July 1780

By 12 July they had readied the frigate *Diana*, about whose speed they told me marvelous tales. The weather was favorable for our departure, so I sent my luggage to the vessel, ready to go aboard myself as soon as the signal we had agreed upon was placed on the highest point of the mast. But the frigate made no attempt to move, despite my importunities, because it was rumored that an English fleet was cruising off Cape Finisterre, lying in wait for a French convoy escorted by a ship-of-the-line and two war frigates which, shortly before my arrival in La Coruña, had taken refuge in El Ferrol and was awaiting larger forces in order to put out to sea.

18 July 1780

On the eighteenth, two ships-of-the-line and two frigates

18 July 1780

arrived from Brest, and all that day they remained at the mouth of the port of El Ferrol, plying to windward. We believed that they were waiting for the blockaded convoy and that in fact the latter would immediately set sail for Martinique, which was its destination. I embarked on the morning of the nineteenth and remained on board until four o'clock in the afternoon when I went ashore again, having seen the warships and frigates put into El Ferrol and being convinced that neither the convoy nor the packet would go out at that time.

Almost every day I urged the administrator to hasten our departure, but he obstinately insisted that there were enemy forces at Cape Finisterre, that the mail-packet could not undertake the voyage without great risk, and that it ought to take advantage of the protection of the French convoy, which would set sail without delay.

This detention displeased me greatly, both because the nature of my commission demanded that every instant be employed usefully and because delaying the sailing so much would necessarily bring the vessel into port in America in the hurricane season. I pointed out this fact to Madrid, whence orders for the mail-packet to go out without delay were sent repeatedly, but all the orders were fruitless.

12 August 1780

On 12 August the 110-gun French warship *Invincible* arrived at La Coruña, with a 36-gun frigate, and on the following day both put into El Ferrol. However, I had occasion to go on board the warship that same evening and to examine it at leisure.

The convoy could not sail from El Ferrol except with a northeast wind, and west winds prevailed for many consecutive days.

My long delay gave me an opportunity to acquaint myself with the condition of La Coruña, to examine its environs, and to put into writing my observations. This town, not long before reduced to the most miserable conditions, commenced to prosper after the declaration of free trade with the Indies[20] and the es-

---

20. The Regulation of Free Trade (1778) granted to thirteen Spanish

tablishment of the maritime mail service.⁽²¹⁾ In the short period of fifteen years its population has doubled, its agriculture has increased greatly, and its industry has made rapid progress. Formerly only poverty was to be seen there; today there are many moderately rich commercial houses, the neighboring lands are well cultivated, and more than 2,000 families live comfortably, employed in weaving cloth and making shirts, stockings, gloves, and several other kinds of thread and linen products for the trade with the Indies.

It would not be difficult to establish here another profitable branch of industry, to wit, that of preserving meats by salting. The meats of Galicia are as good as those of Ireland, and our salt is abundant and the best in Europe. After the declaration of war there was in this port a great scarcity of salted meats from the north, and the captains of the mail-packets were obliged to be personally responsible for the provision of this commodity for their voyages. As a consequence, the meats were good but very expensive because of the high price of salt.

The suburb of La Coruña, more extensive and of a better appearance than the body of the city, is almost all new. I counted more than twenty houses of good size that were being built all at one time. This rapid growth is one of the many miracles that commerce performs, and it brings to mind the reason for the decadence and desolation that sadden the traveler when he traverses the Castillas.

The port of La Coruña is located at $43\frac{1}{2}°$ north latitude. The fort of San Antonio on the northern bank and that of San Diego on the southern bank, a long half mile distant from each other, frame and defend its entrance. The anchoring ground stretches inward to the west and northwest three-quarters of a mile. A large number of ships-of-the-line cannot be harbored in it without the greater part of them being exposed to swells from the north and northwest, which are very violent there. For frigates

---

ports the right to trade freely with a number of American localities. [Ed.]

21. On 24 August 1764 were passed the "Provisional Rules Governing Maritime Mail between Spain and her Western Colonies [the Indies]," establishing a regular monthly mail boat between Spain and the New World. [Ed.]

12 August 1780

and ships of lesser burden it is an excellent and safe anchorage.

It was decided to establish the maritime mail service in this port. I do not know what political reasons there could have been for not adding this branch to the Royal Navy, which would have supported it at very little cost and would have found in it a constant opportunity for training its officers. Even under present conditions, the mail service would be much improved if the necessity of defraying its expenses with the proceeds from freight did not compel it to build ships more suitable for cargo than for speed. There are nonetheless some swift mail-packets, and the experience of the many that fall into the hands of the enemy in time of war has caused a change in the system of construction, sacrificing to speed some percentage of profitability. These vessels go out well-provisioned and well-manned. Their officers are for the most part experienced seamen, although somewhat more dominated by the mercantile spirit than their calling permits.

Six leagues from La Coruña by land, and three uncomfortable leagues by sea, is located the naval department of El Ferrol. Its basin, docks, arsenals, and other works breathe magnificence. But there occurs to one at once the doubt as to whether it was proper to employ so much treasure in a port that never could serve as a point of rendezvous for great fleets and where entrance and exit are subject to a single wind.

There are in Spain few monuments of antiquity that so much attract the attention of the curious as does the tower of Hercules, situated one mile to the northwest of La Coruña upon a large rock, which rises above the sea high enough to be visible from far away.

Its shape is a square thirty-six feet long, in whose interior, in order to reinforce the structure, there is inscribed a cross of the same material and of the same thickness as the walls of the exterior square, which are two yards thick. The height of the tower, without counting the superimposed cupola where the lantern is, is 124 feet. The tower is divided into three stories of varying height, and each one of them has a door, which formerly opened onto an exterior stairway or ramp that surrounded the structure in the form of a spiral, of which only vestiges remain on the walls. It is not easy to deduce at what time the ramp was demolished. The certainty is that in the past century the lack of it was remedied by breaking the arches so as to clear the way up through the interior for a wooden staircase, which exists today and by which one climbs with great discomfort to the top.

A little more than three yards from the foot of the tower, on the side that faces eastward, there is a rock with a Roman inscription. On the upper part of the rock there are indications that it once served as a pedestal for a statue, which probably was a statue of Mars, for it is dedicated to that deity by an architect named Sevius Lupus, apparently a native of Aqua Flavie, today called Chaves.(22)

A thousand fabulous stories have been spoken and written about the antiquity of this tower, attributing its construction to Hercules and other personages of legendary centuries. The truth is that none of the geographers prior to the fourth century of the Christian era such a monument. All signs are that it was built to serve as a beacon to the vessels that plowed these seas. This being so, as sound criticism persuades one to believe, it cannot be prior to the time of Caesar, an era in which the inhabitants of La Coruña, then Brigantium, were in a state of barbarism similar to that of the American natives when the New World was discovered. Most probably this structure is from the time of Trajan, who left in Spain and in other places in the Roman dominions so many monuments dedicated to the benefit of the public. If the inscription on the rock is contemporary with the structure, as seems credible, one can draw from it a creditable deduction that both are after the reign of Vespasian. The appellation of Flavio was given to Chaves and to several other towns by reason of respect for or flattery of the Emperor Vespasian and his two sons, who were of the Flavio family.

Today this tower serves as a lighthouse or beacon, as it did in the beginning, and it is hoped that an effort will be made to repair it, so that so useful a monument may not perish, for no

---

22. It is believed that this quadrangular lighthouse tower was ordered constructed by Trajan. Its architect was Caius Sevius Lupus, who dedicated the work to Mars. Restored in the eighteenth century, it is what remains of the Roman port of Brigantium at La Coruña. [Ed.]

[21 August 1780]

matter what was the epoch of its construction, it has resisted almost intact the injuries of at least eighteen centuries.

At ten o'clock in the morning of 21 August, the wind changed to the northeast. At noon the French convoy began to go out from the river mouth at El Ferrol. Immediately the *Diana* fired the signal for weighing anchor. I went aboard without delay, and by two o'clock in the afternoon we had already set sail together with the frigate *Tucumán* and the packet *Tenerife*, mail-packets for Buenos Aires and the Canary Islands. The convoy was composed of seven ships-of-the-line, three of them Spanish, five frigates, one cutter, and sixty-two merchantmen. One corvette and three transports carrying troops were bound for Sénégal; the rest were bound for Martinique. The *Diana* was armed with twenty-two 6-caliber guns on deck and had a crew of 105 men.

Having joined us as passengers were Don Manuel González, lieutenant of the Regiment of Spain, who had brought the news of the capture of Mobile and was now returning to his corps; one artillery lieutenant who was bound for La Margarita; one chaplain and two harbor pilots from the crews of the packet-boats of Havana, whom the English had brought to Europe as prisoners; two boatswains, one of them from Genoa and the other a creole, who also had been taken to Europe as prisoners; a page of the minister of the Navy Don Pedro Castejón who was going to Havana;[23] a person employed in the revenue service of Veracruz; and finally one native of Cádiz, now a resident of Cuba and a navigator by profession.

On the following day we rounded Cape Finisterre, and we sailed southward without incident, although the winds were variable and very light.

On the night of the thirtieth, when we were on the parallel of Lisbon with a fresh east wind, there came a sudden contrasting wind from the southwest. It caught the convoy unprepared, and some vessels ran afoul of each other; as a result three merchant vessels were dismasted before dawn; the *Diana* found herself threatened by a warship that was bearing

---

23. The reference is to Don Pedro González de Castejón (1720–83), secretary of state and navy. [Ed.]

down upon her; there was, as happens on such occasions, much confusion and shouting, but we came out of the difficulty without calamity.

The convoy was under careful observation for two days while the damaged merchant vessels were repaired.

On 12 September we sighted the island of Puerto Santo and later the island of Madeira. That evening the convoy was divided. The warships headed toward Cádiz; the merchantmen, under escort of the two frigates *Cérés* and *Inconstante*, proceeded toward their destination; and we, with the mail-packets for the Canary Islands and Buenos Aires, set our course for Tenerife.

It surprised me that although there had been delivered to the captain of the *Diana* at the time of our departure from La Coruña an order which he was to open when twenty leagues at sea, in which the minister of state advised him that he was to be at my orders, not only did the captain not consult me about what we should do, he did not even acknowledge being aware of such instructions. I was equally discreet, to avoid disputes.

It seemed most prudent that the *Diana* take advantage of the protection of the French convoy as far as Martinique, proceed from there to Guarico,[24] where the war frigates were to go without stopping, and set a course then for Havana by way of the old channel, where only lightly armed pilfering corsairs cruise, against which the *Diana* had more than enough armament. So thought the pilots and the passengers, but the captain was unwilling to follow this suggestion, and subsequent events attested to the accuracy of his decision. For although it is true that while following the French convoy we were less exposed to capture by the English, it is also true that the furious hurricane that laid waste the Isles de Barlovento [Windward Islands] that year would have caught us off Martinique, where the greater part of that unfortunate convoy perished.

On the fifteenth, while still thirty leagues at sea, we sighted the peak of Teide,[25] and on that evening we drew near to the

---

24. The aboriginal name of Cap Haitien, the French Cape, on the island of Hispaniola, or Saint Domingue to the French. [Tr.]

25. A peak on the island of Tenerife, 3710 meters high, considered to be

[15 September 1780]

island of Tenerife, but we could not enter the port of Santa Cruz until the following morning. We obtained fresh provisions and water, and the ship's officers loaded a good quantity of spirits, especially brandy. All the passengers went ashore, but I remained on board, so as not to risk being recognized and to avoid conjectures about the object of my voyage.

There we had news by a Catalonian vessel that the combined fleet commanded by Don Luis de Córdova had captured off the Azores an English convoy of many richly laden ships bound for Jamaica and the East Indies.[26]

At that time an epidemic of smallpox, which had carried off many people of all ages, was afflicting the Canary Islands. This contagion, exterminated in that country for a period of thirty-four years, had been reintroduced a few months earlier by a sufferer who disembarked from a mail-packet, and, after ravaging quickly all the island of Tenerife, it was devastating the other islands.[27]

At dawn on the eighteenth we set sail with a fresh east wind. On the following day the mail-packet for Buenos Aires left us, and we lost sight of a Latin American brigantine, which had gone out from Santa Cruz with us. We began to experience the east winds called *Alisios*, or *brisas*, the trade winds that constantly refresh the regions of the torrid zone.

On the twenty-second we crossed the Tropic of Cancer, and among the seamen there was the festivity customary on such occasions.

---

the highest in any Spanish territory. [Ed.]

26. Córdova commanded a combined French and Spanish fleet of sixty-eight ships. In the English Channel he captured the 74-gun *Ardent*; in August 1780 off the Cape of Santa María, he captured a convoy of fifty-five English ships as well as the war frigates escorting them, which later in the Spanish fleet were called *Santa Balbina*, *Santa Paula*, and *Colón*. In 1781 in the English Channel, he captured another convoy of twenty-four sails. [Tr.]

27. The vaccine-carrying expedition of Francisco Javier Balmis reached the Canary Islands on 9 December 1803 and Caracas in 1804; the observations that Saavedra made about vaccines were added later to the original diary (see entry for 15 October 1780). [Ed.]

REGNI MEXICANI
seu
NOVÆ HISPANIÆ,
LUDOVICIANÆ, N. ANGLIÆ,
CAROLINÆ, VIRGINIÆ, et PENSYLVANIÆ,
nec non
INSULARUM ARCHIPELAGI MEXICANI
IN AMERICA SEPTENTRIONALI
accurata Tabula
exhibita
A IOH. BAPTISTA HOMANNO
Norimbergæ

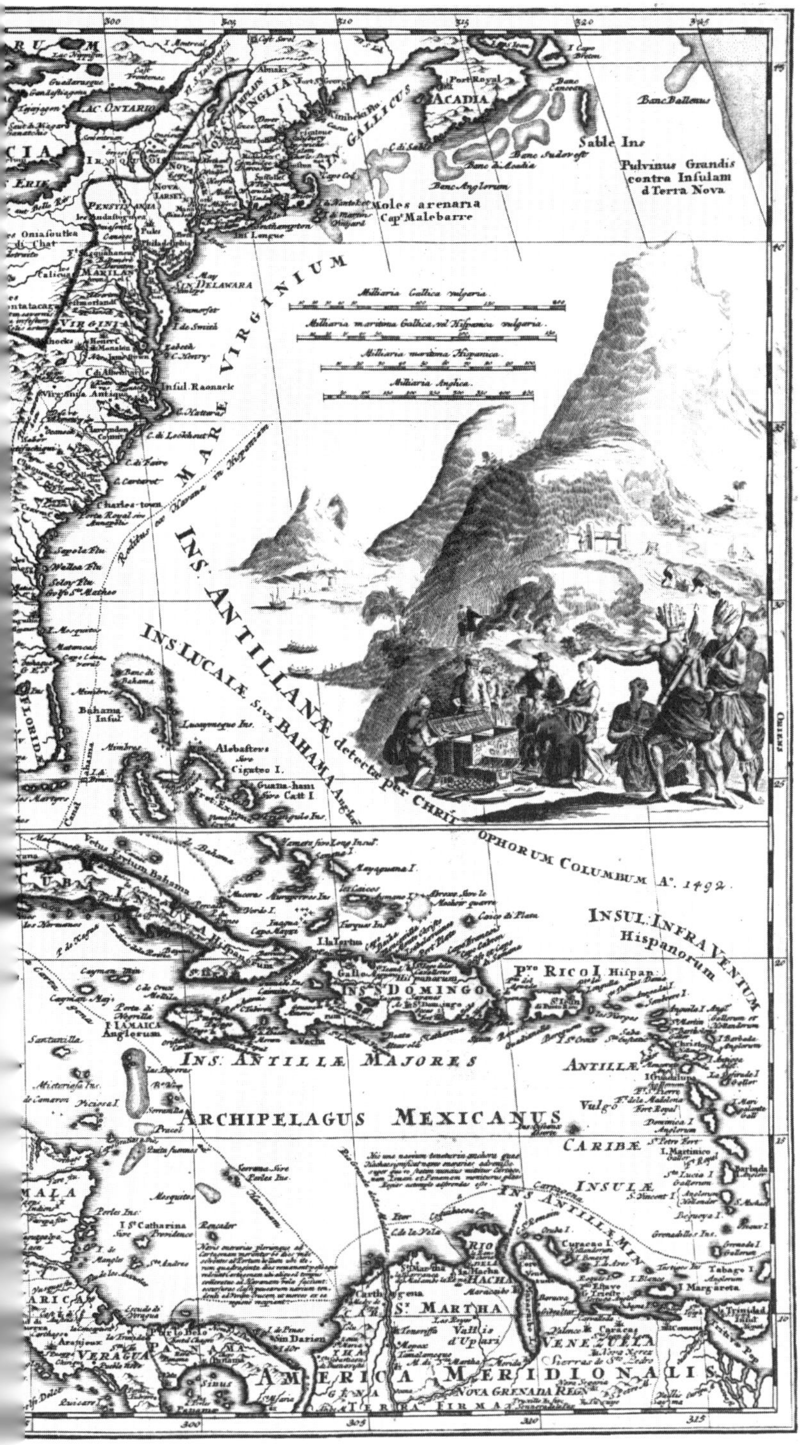

The navigation was uneventful. Rarely did we fail to make from forty to fifty leagues in a day's run. We marveled at the tranquillity of those seas and the constant serenity of the winds. On 3 October we began to perceive a certain change. A succession of stubborn calms set in, interrupted only by brief light breezes. It was excessively hot. Dense clouds began to cover the sky, which lost the placid aspect that delights and reassures the navigator in all the Gulf of Las Damas.[28] There were frequent thunderstorms, and the pilots believed they saw signs that predicted the proximity of a fierce squall.

9 October 1780

Our course was set for Cumaná, where we were to leave the correspondence for the province of Tierra Firme[29] before proceeding to the Bay of Jagua on the southern coast of the Island of Cuba, which was the prescribed course of the mail-packets during the war. We were at 10 degrees of latitude, 100 leagues from the island of Trinidad, more or less, when there bore down upon us a violent hurricane which lasted forty-eight hours without intermission. The wind ran the entire compass, with violent gusts, and amidst the repeated sudden changes of the winds, which prevented the use of the sails, we were at the point of striking the masts, because the frigate lost its equilibrium with the enormous weight of the artillery that it carried over the hatches, and it moved heavily in the swells.

At intervals we ran well, at other times we had to heave to constantly. The sea became frightful, and the darkness of the sky, together with the repeated flashes of lightning that were seen to the northeast, made us believe that the storm was dis-

---

28. So-called because of the ease of navigation in the Canaries-Indies route, by contrast to the Gulf of las Yeguas (Peninsula-Canaries): Gonzálo Fernández de Oviedo y Valdés, *Historia General y Natural de las Indias* (Madrid: Real Academia de la Historia, 1851–55), bk. 1, chap. 9. [Ed.]

29. Thus the Spaniards baptized northern South America, today Venezuela and Colombia. It was considered continental rather than insular territory. [Ed.]

[12 October 1780]

charging its greatest force off the Windward Islands.

After the weather had become calm, on the morning of the twelfth, we sighted Trinidad. Sixty leagues before reaching this island on the southwest side, we noted a change in the color of the water, and we found a depth of 100 fathoms, which diminished gradually up to the land. We were uncertain whether this sandbank began along the island or from Tierra Firme, which is nearby and is very low there. The bottom is of clean sand, without a single stone in all the extent and without any reef whatever. On that same night we rounded the eastern end of Trinidad called Galera [Point], passing between this island and the island of Tobago, which are apparently five leagues apart.

In the afternoon of the following day we sighted the Bocas de los Dragos [Dragons' Mouths],[30] high rocks that form channels of varying widths through which part of the waters of the Orinoco and other deep streams flow out of the Golfo Triste [Gulf of Paria], dashing very rapid currents in several directions. Showers or thunderstorms were incessant. We had to lower the sails continuously, which in so rough a sea was very fatiguing.

At dawn on the fourteenth we were off the coast of Paria in the province of Cumaná. As the great depth of those waters permits sailing rather close to shore, we distinguished the ports of Río Caribe and Carupano, and hugging the coast we observed several small vessels that appeared to be engaged in contraband trade. We confirmed that surmise by questioning one of them, which was forced by cannon shots to come alongside. Its master guided us to Pampatar, a port on the island of Margarita, where we anchored that evening.[31]

The artillery lieutenant who traveled to that destination as a passenger on the *Diana* disembarked there, and we took on a harbor pilot for Cumaná, which is ten leagues distant. The sight

---

30. Channel between South America and the island of Trinidad, discovered by Columbus on his third voyage (1498). [Ed.]

31. The island of Margarita, eighteen miles from the coast of Venezuela, was discovered by Columbus in 1498. It became an important colonial pearl-fishing center. [Tr.]

of the island of Margarita brought to mind the first discoveries and conquests of Spaniards in that New World. This island is to us a symbol of that history in which it once played a role as distinguished as its present role is miserable.

15 October 1780

We set sail well after dawn. From Margarita to Cumaná one navigates always along a sandbank four or five fathoms deep, full of exquisite fish of many varied species. Within sight of the coast of Araya and not very far from it, there came alongside the frigate a canoe full of Indians, who were bringing fish, plantains, and other fruits. The strangeness of their appearance had a not inconsiderable effect upon those of us who saw those miserable people for the first time, and we conjectured about the impression they must have made upon the first discoverers.

Early in the evening we cast anchor in Cumaná. Immediately Don Manuel González, who was the nephew and namesake of the governor of that province, went ashore. He returned to the ship on the following morning and took me ashore to the home of his uncle, who treated us splendidly, not allowing us to lodge elsewhere.

The change of climate and food did not affect me in the least, although it was the season of calms and was very hot. My servant Don Ignacio García was attacked by a disease endemic in those countries which rarely spares foreigners. It is commonly called *el Bicho*, is accompanied by a great variety of fevers and pains, and if neglected can be fatal, but it is easily cured with cold sour beverages and by applying sections of lemons to the rectal orifice.

I remained in Cumaná twelve days, during which I went over all the town and its environs and saw everything worthy of attention there. I endeavored to learn about the political and military conditions of the province, and from what I observed, as well as from what I was told by experienced and intelligent persons, I formed some ideas.

Located at 10°28′ north latitude, Cumaná is fertile and healthful. Its mild climate and beautiful flora made Columbus believe

[Cumaná]

that Paradise was not far distant.[32] The province is 200 leagues long by 40 leagues wide, and it borders on the provinces of Guayana and Caracas. Its conquistadors named it Nueva Andalucía [New Andalusia], alluding to its fecundity and temperate climate, but it has kept the name of Cumaná, which the natives gave it. It is watered by many rivers, some navigable; those that carry most water are the Tigre, the Guarrapiche, and the Areo, which flow into the Gulf of Paria and the Orinoco River, whose west bank belongs in part to this province. The capital is situated on the shores of the Manzanares, a river of medium size, but accessible to launches of considerable capacity; it divides the capital into two parts that are joined by a pontoon bridge. The population of the capital is 1,500 citizens; that of the whole province, including the district of Barcelona, scarcely amounts to 8,000 of all classes. The terrain is variegated, with mountains and plains, and therefore is suitable for different kinds of cultivation.

Today the province barely produces articles of primary necessity for the subsistrence of its inhabitants, and about 4,000 *fanegas* of cacao per year, which maintains a weak export trade. It could produce four times as much cacao, much indigo, coffee, cotton, and other produce if its agriculture were not in a deplorable state. Many causes contribute to this evil: the scant population that supplies few farm workers; the scarcity of lands, as almost all the good lands are occupied by the missions and *doctrinas* [missionary parishes] of the Indians, in whose hands they are unproductive, while the *criollos*, confined to limited space and the poorest land of the province, cannot increase their industry; the monopolistic trade of the Guipuzcoana Company, sole seller of manufactured articles and sole buyer of produce, and therefore sole arbiter of all prices; the monopoly of tobacco, salt, and rum, which deprives trade of the most abundant and most consumed products; and finally, contraband trade, the fruitful source of evils, an inevitable result as much of the political condition of the province as of its geographical location.

Under certain restrictions the inhabitants are permitted to ex-

---

32. In fact this is what Columbus thought during his third voyage (August 1498). [Ed.]

port mules and meats to foreign islands; the mules come from the province of Caracas but are easily brought out through Barcelona and the Guarrapiche River. Meat is abundant in all Tierra Firme, especially on the shores of the great rivers that empty into the Orinoco. If this trade were soundly based, it would bring great prosperity to these provinces and would make all the non-Spanish islands dependent on the Spanish dominions for the most necessary articles, since those islands, because of their intensive cultivation, lack lands on which to raise any kind of cattle. It is highly probable that the way trade is now conducted in Cumaná will bring more loss than gain.

In the capital there are a few moderately prosperous commercial houses. I doubt that the worth of the richest comes to 1,000 pesos. The other inhabitants are poor, and, unfortunately, the lack of opportunity to enrich themselves makes them unwillingly idle. As long as the Barcelona Company had a license to send some shipments here, trade was somewhat revived and contraband diminished, while four or five Catalonian houses established here had a fair run of business, but they are now heading for ruin.[33]

The Spanish families settled here since ancient times cling stubbornly to notions of their nobility, despite the few means they have with which to maintain it; but this prideful concern has produced one good effect, preventing them from mixing with the various colored races that have vitiated Spanish blood in other parts of America.

The women are graceful, fecund, and industrious. They generally dress well, although modestly, and they devote themselves zealously to the management of their households and estates. The men are tractable, and if one knows how to deal with them one can make profitable transactions. There is much fraud there, however, due for the most part to the abun-

---

33. In the first part of the eighteenth century, through the initiative of the new dynasty, commercial companies were established. The first one was in Caracas (1728), the last one in the Philippine Islands (1785). The Barcelona, or Catalonian, company was begun in 1755. See R. Hussey, *The Caracas Company* (Cambridge: Harvard University Press, 1934; Spanish version, Caracas, 1962). [Ed.]

[Cumaná]

dance of lawyers who, not finding in so poor a country opportunities to practice their profession honorably, stir up litigation and the fires of discord and live at the expense of the tranquillity of their fellow citizens.[34]

In the environs of Cumaná, and in the very suburbs of the town, live the Indians called Gualiquiries, about whose strength and fortitude in every kind of labor extraordinary tales are told. Above all, their endurance in rowing in the difficult voyage that the mule-traders' boats must make in order to go to Martinique causes amazement. Not less marvelous is their frugality amidst such arduous work. These indisputable facts give the lie to the widely held idea of the laziness and weakness of the Indians and show that these defects ought not to be attributed to their physical constitution, as the first conquistadors believed, but to many political and moral causes. The kings have granted to the Gualiquiries very liberal privileges for having contributed at various times to the defense of the province against enemy incursions.[35]

The seas that bathe these coasts abound with fish; but the monopoly on salt, which caused its price to rise from two to ten reales per *arroba*, has destroyed the salting industry that they used to have here to supply salted fish to Caracas and some foreign islands, whose gross profit was worth in many years more than 40,000 pesos. The abandonment of fishing, which has been the inevitable consequence of that monopoly, damages shipping so much that Margarita, which in other wars was the seedbed of corsairs that made the English possessions tremble, in the present war has not one armed ship.

Almost from the time of the discovery of America the island of Margarita was important because of the many beautiful pearls that were gathered on its shores and on the neighboring islets of Coche and Cubagua, but about two centuries ago this rich harvest was lost, exhausted by the disorderly greed with which it

---

34. From the sixteenth century on, some people—Vasco Núñez de Balboa, for example—demanded that lawyers be forbidden entrance to newly discovered lands because they sowed discord. [Ed.]

35. The Gualiquirie Indians, located near the Orinoco River at the source of the Caura, were first evangelized by the Jesuits in 1732. [Ed.]

was practiced in the beginning.[36] However, frequently pearls are found in the common oysters gathered in these areas, and I myself, dining in the home of the commanding officer of the troops of Cumaná, Don Pedro Moreno, found in one oyster as many as twenty-four small pearls.

Earthquakes are frequent here, especially in years of little rainfall. In 1768 there was a violent one that flattened rather substantial buildings. In order to guard against the effects of this calamity, they build houses of reinforced wood covered with a light coating of a material they call *bajareque*,[37] a kind of mud mixed with dried grasses and lime, which hardens quickly and resists the strongest tremors.

In the middle of the last century a smallpox epidemic occurred in Cumaná which wreaked havoc, so much the more severe because the effects of this illness were completely unknown there. The urgency of a danger that did not respect any age caused the people of Cumaná to resort to banishing those who were stricken with smallpox to some houses in the country, which they call pest houses, cutting off all communication with them that could spread the contagion. In that way they succeeded in extinguishing the disease, which is almost completely forgotten there. At about the same time the province of Caracas suffered a similar attack, and there they instituted inoculation, which had already begun to be used in Europe. Inoculation cut short the danger but did not completely exterminate it.

It is debatable which of these two methods was the wiser. The extermination of smallpox seems more advantageous to the public, but if it is not universal, there remains the danger that if the infection is once introduced, its ravages may be much greater; moreover, it deters individuals who have not had this illness from any communication with countries where they fear contracting it. This is the case of the people of Cumaná, who do not dare to go to Caracas for fear of being exposed to smallpox. Inoculation, at the price of a slight indis-

---

36. Cf. Enrique Otte, *Las Perlas del Caribe* (Caracas: Nueva Cádiz de Cubagua, 1977). [Ed.]

37. *Bahareque, bajareque:* canes and mud. [Ed.]

[Cumaná]

position, protects the person who undergoes it from the risk of a dangerous illness, but it is prejudicial to the public because it feeds and propagates the contagion, keeping in existence the root from which it originates. Nothing would be better than its extinction, if inoculation were universal and all nations agreed on it at the same time. Inoculation would benefit the individual without harm to the community if it were permitted in country hospitals with the precautions necessary to prevent the spread of the contagion. I venture to express these reflections foreign to my profession because the scene of the events inspires them, and perhaps they can be fruitful.

The city of Cumaná is not defensible against an enemy who attacks it with a force of middling strength. In several places hills rise above the city, and it is open to the sea and the land. Its only fortification is one battery with eight guns, open at the gorge, at the mouth of the Manzanares River, and two small forts located on high ground, built it seems in the time of Charles V to contain the incursions of the Caribs and other bellicose Indians of those regions. One of these forts is falling down. The forts have some small-caliber artillery, most of it old, the most important piece being a long bronze 8-caliber culverin cast in Lima in the middle of the sixteenth century.

Four leagues from Cumaná, on the other shore of the Gulf of Cariaco, an arm of the sea that penetrates more than ten leagues inland,[38] can be seen the ruins of the Castillo de Araya, demolished thirty years ago by order of Madrid. Its purpose was to guard the salt mines that abound on these coasts. Its cost, which amounted to 40,000 pesos annually, was consigned to the treasury of Mexico, and the vestiges of it, which we went to examine, attest that it had been too important a fortification to have deserved its fate.

In Cumaná there are four companies of veteran troops with their commandant, one militia artillery company with veteran officers, and other militia companies of colored people. Although Cumaná offers few means of defense, an enemy can penetrate the interior of the country only with difficulty,

---

38. Araya Peninsula (Venezuela). [Ed.]

provided that the governor knows how to occupy the heights that overlook the coast and to take the necessary steps to withdraw to them. The capital is not defensible, but its poverty does not offer much incentive to the greed of an invader who wants to take out of it at least the cost of his expedition.

On the fourth day of my sojourn in Cumaná, there began to arrive reports of the destruction caused by the most recent hurricane in the Windward Islands. The governor had a letter from the general of Martinique that painted in vivid colors the distress of that island, where the storm had destroyed towns, obliterated plantations, and sunk or dashed against the coast a great number of ships, and he requested assistance in the form of food. The same news, even sadder if possible, came from Saint Eustatius, Antigua, Guadeloupe, and Barbados.

Amidst the general consternation caused by these disasters, one event that was reported in Cumaná with the appearance of authenticity afforded some consolation. It was said that the English had been preparing on Santa Lucía a 40-gun frigate and other smaller armed ships with 500 soldiers in order to take possession of Trinidad, because the commencement of development there was beginning to arouse their suspicions and had made them aware of the importance of a settlement so advantageously located; but the hurricane had destroyed the frigate and had undone the preparations that had been made for the expedition.

The source of this intelligence was investigated, and the report was found to be well enough based that it should not be taken lightly. Consequently the governor of Cumaná, in order to guard against any unexpected sudden attack, sent to Trinidad immediately a company of experienced troops, a few artillerymen, and the meager assistance he could afford. It is certain that that island is for its geographical position alone, apart from other advantages, one of the most important points of Spanish America. In possession of Trinidad the English or any other powerful nation would in a short time become masters of the Orinoco, and through it would dominate the provinces of Cumaná, Caracas, and Maracaibo, being able to go on navigable rivers almost as far as the gates of Santa Fé. It is to

[Cumaná]

be feared that the acquisition of this island is one of the objectives of Great Britain in the present war, or in another in which she is not so hard-pressed. Hence either there should be no thought of developing it and it should be kept as insignificant as it was for three centuries, or it must be put in a respectable state of defense at once.[39]

During the twelve days we were in Cumaná the frigate was boot-topped, as it was very dirty, fresh water was taken on, and the supply of food was renewed. In some places there was a rumor that after the French fleet had withdrawn from the Windward Islands, the English fleet had gone back to Jamaica. The course assigned to the mail-packets during the war ran between Jamaica and Tierra Firme. It appeared to the captain of the *Diana* that if the enemy forces were so close by, they probably had established cruising stations to intercept Spanish ships in a passage that was as important as it was much frequented; fearful of a fatal outcome if he followed the prescribed course, the captain asked that a junta of pilots and bar pilots experienced in those waters be called. The governor presided over the junta, in which the course of our voyage was discussed. It was resolved that the least hazardous course was to pass between Puerto Rico and Santo Domingo, proceed northward as far as 24 degrees, enter the channel between the Caicos and Mogarra [Mayaguana], go down to Baracoa, leaving there the official papers from Madrid, then follow the Old Channel to Havana.

These matters having been settled, and the frigate being ready, we set sail from Cumaná on 28 October. With us as passengers were Don José de Cartas who, after having been for three years the auditor of that province, was going to be auditor of Havana and was taking his family with him; two ecclesiastics, one of them a Capuchin who, while bound for Louisiana in the convoy of Don José Solano, had been captured by the English, taken to Barbados and sent to Cumaná;[40] and another was an observant

---

39. The British plans, intuited wisely by Saavedra, provided England the means of capturing Trinidad in 1797. See Josefina Pérez Aparicio, *Pérdida de la Isla de Trinidad* (Sevilla, 1966). [Ed.]

40. Two abortive expeditions had set out from Havana to attack Pensacola since Solano's arrival from Spain on 20 February 1780. The Capuchin

of the missions of Píritu.[41]

From the Capuchin, who was quite well informed, I learned of the events experienced by the convoy above: its arrival at Martinique; the successful union of our fleet with that of the French, despite the advance warning of its arrival received by the English; the many men who had fallen ill during the voyage, some of whom had remained in the Windward Islands; and the setting out for Havana of all the convoy except for some other ship which, like his, had become separated and had fallen into the hands of the enemy.

As far as the vicinity of Puerto Rico not one sail that could cause alarm was sighted, but at various intervals we did indeed encounter masts, planks, chicken coops, a yard with a scrap of sail, a big piece of a keel, a part of the side of a ship with a gunport like that of a ship-of-the-line, and other fragments of vessels, doubtless the plunder of the great hurricane that had spread ruin through those seas.

6 November 1780

At dawn we rounded the Mono and the Monito, small but high islets situated in the middle of the channel that runs between Puerto Rico and Santo Domingo. Near noon we discovered ahead of us many vessels that appeared to be sailing in a convoy. We put about immediately, and simultaneously the largest of those ships we had sighted detached itself from the convoy and came in pursuit of us. After a period of four hours it seemed to me that the ship was gaining on us considerably. Others were of a contrary opinion, prejudiced perhaps in favor of

---

must have been in the convoy that left Havana on 7 March and returned on 21 May of that year "without having accomplished anything because it had not appeared possible to the commander of the squadron to silence the forts which defend the said port." See John Walton Caughey, *Bernardo de Gálvez in Louisiana, 1776–1783* (Berkeley: University of California Press, 1934; reprint, Gretna, LA: Pelican Publishing Company, 1972), pp. 187–88, quoting Saavedra to José de Gálvez, 16 February 1781, AGI:Ind. Gen. 1578. [Tr.]

41. Píritu is located on the Caribbean coast of Venezuela. [Tr.]

[9 November 1780]

our frigate, which had never seemed to me as swift as it was reputed to be, and before long they were made aware of their error.

At seven o'clock on the morning of the ninth, when we thought we were near the Caicos, a large ship to leeward was spotted from the topmast. At first it did not alarm us, but soon its maneuvers gave rise to some misgivings. The captain climbed to the crosstree with his spyglass and ascertained at least that it was a frigate larger than the *Diana* and that by all signs it was cruising in that area. We took flight, heading into the wind as far as possible. The other frigate did the same and was gaining on us as much as a league to starboard without having succeeded in overtaking us, despite her visibly superior speed.

Finding no other recourse, the captain decided to abandon the course, and at nine o'clock in the evening we began to fall off to leeward little by little; but our pursuers, favored by the bright moonlight, perceived all our maneuvers with spyglasses in the night, and at a distance they set about to cut us off. At ten-thirty they were upon us. They approached us at once and told us in English to lower the longboat into the water; when we refused to do it, they lowered their own, but a short time later they took it back without using it. The frigate was flying the long English flag, and from that fact as well as from the number of gun-ports and the many people who could be discerned on deck, I soon deduced that she was a war frigate, although most of our people took her for a corsair.

After having examined us for a long time, they wondered what nation we belonged to (because on the one hand we had raised a Spanish flag and on the other we were making use of a seaman who spoke their language well, they supposed us to be Englishmen who had come out from New York). The frigate came astern, fired one cannon shot at us for the purpose of indicating to us, as we learned later, that we were to follow in their wake until daybreak. The cannonball passed overhead, but we, believing that shot to be the beginning of hostilities, replied with six shots from the stern guns. At once the frigate came along the weatherside, and at little more than the distance of a pistol shot we fired broadsides at each other. The frigate passed ahead of us, keeping up a lively fire and advanced somewhat. When that was seen by our seamen, they began to shout that we must attack her, that she was about to escape.

Up to that time we had been lying to, so as not to be hindered by the maneuver during the combat, but at this point we set all the sails and steered straight for the enemy, and at maximum range we fired for a long time.

It was two o'clock in the morning, and our frigate was considerably damaged. It appeared that the opponent was in little better condition, and so we separated, each to repair the damages sustained. Our mainmast was split, the halyards and many of the shrouds were cut, and the side was open in several places at the waterline.

10 November 1780

We spent the rest of the night in making our repairs, but at first light we steered toward the enemy, who in the beginning shunned our encounter and, trusting in their ship's speed, sailed around us, with the purpose (as we were told later) of preventing our resistance by demonstrating ostentatiously that they were twice as strong as we. Nevertheless, we remained in the posture of awaiting her, and with both frigates lying to, scarcely the distance of a rifle-shot apart, a fierce combat was joined.

The *Diana* resisted as much as her strength permitted, but the enemy's fire was much livelier and the caliber of her artillery twice as great. Our mainmast was almost sprung, the yard of the main-topsail chopped off, the fore-topmast broken, the side penetrated in several places to the extent of taking on fifty inches of water per hour, and, although the *Diana* had a stout parapet of old cable and rope yarn taller than a man, which protected the crew from the effects of the grapeshot, there were many wounded. In these circumstances the captain, who had been wounded on the head by a shell splinter, ordered that the boxes of correspondence be thrown overboard, and at nine-thirty o'clock in the morning he struck the flag. A short time later, when the enemy's longboat was already coming very close in or-

10 November 1780

der to take possession of our vessel, I threw into the sea the orders and confidential papers that I carried, weighted with a 12-pound cannonball. Everyone on our frigate conducted himself well and, even knowing the decided superiority of the antagonist, surrendered unwillingly.

The longboat came alongside carrying two officers, eight soldiers, and fifteen sailors. The naval officer named Mr. Cunningham spoke to us courteously on behalf of his captain, especially so to the wife of the auditor Cartas. He told us that we had fought against the British frigate *Pallas*, a 40-gun ship with a crew of 260 men, which had had four men killed and ten wounded, her side pierced in several places, much rigging cut, and the foremast split from side to side near the top-rigging, so that if the caliber of our artillery had been greater, in all likelihood we should have dismasted her, and we could at least have escaped.

The captain of the *Pallas* was named Thomas Spry, the son of an admiral of the same name who in the war of '45 commanded part of the British forces in the East Indies. He treated us generously, giving back to the passengers everything that belonged to us and not allowing our trunks to be touched. Some of us lost a large part of our luggage, however, due to the disorder of our own crew.

At nine o'clock in the evening Lieutenant González and I were transferred to the *Pallas*. Mr. Spry, who spoke French very well, received us courteously, invited us to supper at his table, and gave us a comfortable stateroom. But that same night there occurred a misadventure that disturbed in great measure our relief at having fallen into the power of so urbane an officer.

It happened that after the *Diana* was surrendered, our sailors, overheated and thirsty, flung themselves into the hold, opened several casks of wine and brandy, and became unrestrainedly drunk, so that when the English arrived to take possession of the ship, they found our sailors almost mutinnous. The sailors uttered horrible shouts, threatened to assassinate the Englishmen, threw knives at the sentries, slapped a pilot's face, insulted the chaplain, sacked the storeroom, and committed a thousand other excesses. Mr. Cunningham, apprised of the origin of this disorder, calmed our men as well as he could, and because it was not feasible to subdue them with the few men he had brought to the *Diana* he proceeded to transfer them to the *Pallas*. There, fearing the effects of their turbulence, after taking their knives away from them, the English confined them for that night in a kind of storeroom where, as the captain assured me, they had on other occasions had as many as 130 men. On the following morning the sentries went to take them out, and found twenty-one of them dead. Actually thirty-six appeared to be dead, but the captain, a very humane man, made all possible efforts to revive them, and fifteen recovered consciousness. The rest were not lowered into the sea until after twenty-four hours had passed, when they were all unquestionably dead.

It seems that the storeroom was really small, that although two barrels of water had been placed in the room for the sailors they spilt the water fighting over who was to drink first, and that the sentry stationed at the door did not inform the captain of hearing any noise or outcry whatever, as he had been ordered to do. The fact is that our crew had not eaten nor drunk water in all the previous day, and that they had exerted themselves incessantly throughout the combat, and it can be conjectured that, exhausted by fatigue, inflamed by brandy, and thrown together in a hot place, either they died of dehydration or they could not breathe the air.

On the following day we passengers returned to the *Diana*, and after both frigates had repaired the damages suffered in the engagement, both set sail for Jamaica. We followed in the wake of the *Pallas*; only Mr. Cunningham, one marine guard, and fourteen seamen had remained aboard our frigate.

On the thirteenth a sail was sighted ahead of us. The *Pallas* gave chase and recognized it as an English mail-packet. That night La Inagua was sighted by the light of the moon, and we set our course to pass through the channel that divides the islands of Cuba and Santo Domingo.

At the entrance of this channel, not far from the headland of Maísí, three sails were sighted; the *Pallas* recognized them as merchant vessels going from New York to the English islands.

At dawn on the fifteenth we rounded Morant Point, which

[15 November 1780]

forms the eastern extremity of Jamaica. We followed the coastline without losing sight of it, and at four o'clock in the afternoon we cast anchor in Kingston Bay. This bay forms a great cove more than four leagues in circumference, which is entered by way of a narrow channel bordered on each side by reefs and dominated by a fort with eighty 24- and 36-caliber guns, situated on the tip of the tongue of land upon which is located Port Royal. Vessels have to pass half a musket shot away from this battery, presenting to it first the bow and then the side.

On the other side of the entrance channel, a cannon shot away from Port Royal, there is a hill about fifty yards high on whose brow is built the battery of the Apostles, so-called because it has twelve heavy-caliber guns.

The shape of the bay approximates that of a bow to which the tongue of land that is stretched out from the body of the island serves as a string. The island is flat and sandy. It is two leagues long and in places does not reach a width of 200 *toises* [see glossary]. In the center of the bow there is a fort named Augusta, which is equipped with much artillery, more than 100 cannons. It defends the channel through which must pass vessels that go to Kingston, the commercial center of Jamaica, situated one league from there on the same bay.

In Port Royal there is a navy yard of the king near which warships cast anchor. I counted as many as fourteen ships-of-the-line at anchor there, eleven of them completely dismasted. I inquired the cause of this damage and learned that thirteen of those ships and some frigates, having gone out to escort a convoy until it sailed out of the Bahama Channel, were struck, on their return voyage to Jamaica, at 24 degrees of latitude, by a hurricane so violent that all of them almost perished; all were badly crippled, and eleven had to come back with jury masts.

There was no news of the *Stirling Castle,* a 74-gun warship and one of the thirteen, and it was thought to have been lost. Indeed that was true, for while running before the storm the ship crashed against the reefs of La Plata, and only eleven seamen and one marine guard escaped in a section of the ship that had broken off and kept floating backward and forward at the will of the waves for fifteen days. Fatigue, thirst, and hunger took the lives of nine of the men one by one, and those who survived nourished themselves by sucking the blood of those who had just expired. A French boat picked up the two remaining men in this lamentable condition. One of them was the marine guard. He arrived at Jamaica on our tenth day there.

16 November 1780

Cartas, González, and I went to Kingston to seek lodging. We had hardly stepped on shore when two Englishmen of respectable appearance, one of whom spoke Spanish tolerably well, came to meet us. They greeted us courteously, took us to dine in their house, and promised to have comfortable lodgings ready for us the next day. Those persons were named Mr. Fitch and Mr. Allwood, and they had some commercial connections with the Compañía de Negros de la Havana, where Allwood had been several times.[42] We returned to the *Diana* in the evening.

On the seventeenth we passengers went ashore in the longboat of the *Pallas* with Mr. Spry, who invited us to dine in the house of a friend of his named Robinson. In the afternoon we appeared before the commissioner of prisoners, Mr. Newil, to whom we gave our word of honor to conduct ourselves in accordance with the laws of the country, and we then took up residence in a house which Allwood had ready for us. Although distinguished prisoners usually went to live in Spanish Town, the capital of the island, General Dalling, the governor, at Spry's

---

42. In the Peace of Utrecht in 1713, Britain was granted the *asiento* or contract for the exclusive privilege of supplying African slaves to the Spanish Indies, which contributed to English domination of Spanish American trade. In 1750 by the Treaty of Madrid, Spain gained the asiento. During the period of the American Revolution, the Aguirre Aristegui Company of Cádiz exercised the contract by royal appointment. The director of the company in Havana was Gerónimo Enrile Guercía (Juan de Miralles to José de Gálvez, 13 April 1778, AGI:Cuba 1281; Marqués de la Torre to Enrile Guercía, 30 April 1776, AGI:Cuba 1227). Allwood, a factor of the company, was later accused of conspiracy in the shipping of contraband goods from Jamaica to Havana and was imprisoned in Havana. [Tr.]

[17 November 1780]

request, permitted us to remain in Kingston, where we had met such a good reception.[43]

19 November 1780

Don Juan de Ayusa, governor of the Castillo de San Juan de Nicaragua, Lieutenant Don Pedro Brizzio, and Ensign Don Antonio Antonioti came from the capital to visit us. These officers had been taken prisoner in the capture of that fort. They recounted to us their really extraordinary adventures and the history of the unsuccessful English expedition to Lake Nicaragua.[44]

This was the favorite topic of conversation on the island at that time. The British Ministry had confidently believed that by this enterprise they would realize their long-held desire to open a communication between the Atlantic and Pacific oceans. Briefly, the plan consisted of entering by way of the San Juan River, which rises from Lake Nicaragua and empties into the northern sea on the Mosquitos coast, taking possession of that lake, founding a settlement on the island of Ometepe, which is in its center, and by means of a navigable canal cutting the intervening space of little more than four leagues from the southern extremity of the lake to the Gulf of Papaguaya on the southern sea.[45]

The plan was devised by a certain Smith who, after having lived amidst the Mosquito Indians for many years and having therefore examined the shores of the lake as well as the south-

---

43. John Dalling was appointed to the post of lieutenant governor of Jamaica in 1767 and became governor in 1777. He sent expeditions to Honduras and Nicaragua and sent reinforcements to Pensacola for a proposed attack on New Orleans. [Tr.]

44. As a consequence of Spain's adherence to the Franco-American Alliance (1779), Great Britain organized an expedition against Nicaragua. Major Polson and Captain Horace Nelson landed in San Juan del Norte (April 1780) and captured Castillo Viejo in the interior, which they had to abandon in January 1781. [Ed.]

45. The idea of a canal that would link the two oceans was conceived of as early as 1524 by Charles I (Emperor Charles V), who had the area surveyed.

ern coast, had made very detailed maps of those lands. I myself saw his maps in Spanish Town, by a fortuitous circumstance, as I shall tell later.

The expeditionary force destined for this objective was formed in Jamaica. It consisted of a 50-gun warship, four 36-gun frigates, and several transports with 3,000 troops, good artillery and plenty of ammunition, all commanded by Colonel Polson, a very reputable officer.

They reached the port of San Juan, where the river of the same name empties into the sea. They proceeded in armed boats up to the fort, situated twenty leagues from the mouth of the river and 400 yards from its western bank. If they had then proceeded without interruption to Lake Nicaragua, the enterprise likely would not have failed; but they tarried in order to take the fort, which against all expectations managed to resist for nineteen days, with only fifty men and lacking in ammunition, food, and even water. During this interval, the governor found a way to send intelligence about his plight to the president of Guatemala. Comprehending the enemy's plan, the latter, by forced marches with as many men as he could assemble, occupied the mouth of Lake Nicaragua, which is by its nature impregnable. Therefore, when the English, after the fort was surrendered, undertook to take possession of the lake, they found that the Spaniards had anticipated them, and, not being able to force the entrance, they had to fall back.

In those operations the English lost more than two months, during which the insalubrity of that climate, the most deadly in the universe, demonstrated all its horrors. An epidemic of putrid fevers attacked the troops, and it did not spare the crews of the ships at anchor in the port. Both were soon reduced to fewer than one-fourth their complement, and the survivors, in order not to suffer the same fate, had to reembark precipitately and set sail, abandoning, in the port of San Juan and on the banks of the river, artillery, ammunition, some war vessels, and many transports.

The prisoners from the Castillo de San Juan, reduced to the three officers above, one engineer officer, one artillery officer,

19 November 1780

and forty soldiers, were taken to Jamaica on a shabby merchant vessel. Because of calms and foul weather they had a long and difficult voyage. They arrived at Savanna la Mar, a port of the aforesaid island, on the eve of the great hurricane. Ayusa, Brizzio, and Antonioti refused to go on to Kingston by sea because they were suffering from scurvy. They went ashore that same day, and before dawn on the following morning they set out to go overland to Kingston. They had not traveled two leagues when the hurricane struck with such violence that the town of Savanna la Mar was submerged, with all its inhabitants. The ship that was carrying the prisoners was shattered into a thousand pieces within the port itself, without anyone escaping from it, and the three officers, who, by remaining on the ship or by not leaving the town so quickly, would have suffered the same disaster, were saved by unheard-of good luck.

They had lost all their luggage in the wrecked ship, and they were almost destitute, but the English treated them with esteem in which, in spite of enmity, a sense of fairness defers to excellence, considering, and with reason, that their good defense of the fort of San Juan was the principal reason for the failure of that enterprise. The English attributed their misfortune to the bad leadership of Colonel Polson, who had fruitlessly lost precious time before a fort of little importance, which could have been blockaded effectively with 100 men, instead of proceeding at once with the bulk of his army to take possession of Lake Nicaragua, which was the chief objective of their expedition and was undefended at that time.

The inhabitants of Jamaica regretted this disappointment all the more because they had contributed more than 600,000 pesos for the expenses of the expedition. The pain of having sacrificed so much money uselessly, and of seeing frustrated their joyous hopes that so vast a theater would be opened up to commerce, had divided the island into factions; their fervor had spread to the principal leaders, and from minds had passed to the public papers, where they satirized each other with all the license and lack of decorum that the spirit of party inspires in republican governments.

21 November 1780

Cartas, González, and I went to Spanish Town to call on Governor Dalling and to thank him for the favor he had done for us. This city is three leagues from Kingston. The road is a beautiful highway built with some elevation above the terrain, which in the rainy season becomes very muddy. Midway there is a drawbridge over a deep ravine and to the right a 12-gun battery which dominates this essential avenue from the sea to the capital.

Spanish Town under the name of Santiago de la Vega was also the capital of the island under the Spaniards;[46] of that time only feeble vestiges remain. In Spanish Town reside the governor, who is at the same time the captain general, the military staff, the tribunals, and the parliament. The town is large and well situated. Government House, located on a rectangular plaza, is a grandiose and dignified edifice of spiraled brick whose front has a granite column of Doric architecture. Opposite this structure is the Governor's Palace, tolerably comfortable and spacious, whose entrance is embellished by a peristyle of six great columns of white marble in Ionic style, quite magnificent in themselves but disproportionate to the rest of the building.

The governor received us courteously and invited us to dine. He spoke at length about Havana. He had taken part in its capture in the year '62, serving in the corps of engineers. We were joined at dinner by several officers of the troops who were then garrisoned in Jamaica, among them Milord Harrington, a brother of the Duke of Manchester, a nephew of the Duke of Richmond, and a grandson of Lord Bolingbroke, the famous minister of the time of Queen Anne.

Don Pedro Brizzio introduced me to the secretary of the government,[47] and we had a long session with him. The subject of the Nicaragua expedition came up. He had been one of

---

46. See Francisco Morales Padrón, *Jamaica española* (Seville, 1952), for the history of this island under Spanish sovereignty (1493–1655). [Ed.]

47. Edward Berry, who later signed the permit for Saavedra's departure from Jamaica on the French cartel vessel *Alexandre*, Captain M. Camus.

the most ardent promotors of that enterprise, and after its failure the most violent outcries of the public had been directed against him. Therefore he heatedly entered a conversation in which his self-esteem was so concerned. I told him that communication between the northern and southern seas did not seem to me as feasible as it was thought to be and that, laying aside the opposition of the Spaniards, it was probable that in the nature of the terrain would be found obstacles difficult to overcome in opening the canal from Lake Nicaragua to the Gulf of Papaguaya as envisioned by Smith. Instantly, he produced the plans of the whole project, in order to defend it against criticism as being chimerical and to demonstrate to us the easy communication between the two oceans. In fact, if the maps were accurate, the project was well planned, and its accomplishment did not seem impossible, but I understand that Spanish engineers, after examining the same places, have formed the opposite opinion.

That seemed to me a good opportunity to hint something to the secretary about my freedom. I told him that not being a military man I was therefore not subject to exchange, that I hoped I would be given a passport of asylum so that I could go to the Spanish possessions on the first flag-of-truce ship available. He answered that he would mention it to the governor, that although an exchange of prisoners had not been established with Havana he did not think there could be any difficulty about my departure, and that when an opportunity was presented the passport would undoubtedly be granted to me.

This was a business that I had to handle delicately, because from certain things heard from the crew of our own frigate the English had come to suspect that I was going to Havana with important commissions, and there were even some who thought I was an officer in disguise. In this situation discovery would expose me to a long detention on that island, and to conceal myself more than was necessary was to give substance to their suspicions and perhaps to fall onto the very reefs I was trying to avoid.

I chose, therefore, a middle but well-considered course, so that in no case should they catch me in a contradiction. To several persons who approached me with artful curiousity to inquire about my profession and destination, I answered ingenuously that I had served for twelve years in the army of Spain and had attained the rank of captain, that later, retired and without military status, I had been engaged by the Ministry of the Indies in some mercantile affairs, and that at the moment I was going to Havana and New Spain commissioned by that same ministry to confer about several matters concerning trade and mines which, regarded politically, I added, ought to be considered as relating to European industry in general.

There is no deceit more efficacious and less hazardous than half the truth, and on this occasion that was verified completely, because the English learned later that I had been an officer, that I was employed by the Ministry of the Indies, and that I was going to Havana as a commissioner; but, finding this intelligence in accord with the information I had given them, they went no further in their suspicions, and they permitted me to depart freely at the first opportunity, which I took great care not to waste.

22 November 1780

We went to dine in the home of Mr. [Nathaniel?] Watts, a well-educated Irishman, a hydraulic engineer by profession. He had built the docks of Antigua and was employed in Jamaica on the works of Port Royal. He spoke Spanish very well. He was in Havana when the English captured it; after its restitution he remained there for two years, and he designed the water mill for sawing wood that has been built there. In his company was a youth named Jemelin, the son of a deceased English physician who had settled and married in Havana.

23 November 1780

Occasionally there came to see us a Jew whose name was Aaron Enríquez, an old man of good character and singularly expert on the American trade. From him I acquired several

23 November 1780

useful facts which are found in this journal. He showed us the synagogue, a building of little architectural interest. He took us to the home of a wealthy associate of his named Jacob Bernal, who gave for us a splendid feast which was attended by many officers and other distinguished persons of the country. Enríquez appreciated Spanish books, and I gave him several that I was carrying. He gave me a translation of the Psalms in Spanish verse done in the last century by a rabbi of Jamaica and printed in London. I found in it nothing contrary to our religion but indeed much to admire in the great variety of meters that the author employed and in the skill with which he handled the Castilian language. I doubt that there is a single copy of this book in Spain. I presented it through the good offices of Don Ignacio de Hermosilla to the Real Academia de la Lengua.[48]

The Jews receive good treatment among the English. In Jamaica there are many of them, and some live opulently; they are the agents of the contraband trade with the Spaniards, for which their knowledge of the Spanish language gives them great aptitude.[49]

24 November 1780

Accompanied by Captain Spry we went to visit Vice Admiral Peter Parker,[50] commandant of the naval forces there, who was living in a country house two leagues distant from Kingston, located on a pleasant hill from which Port Royal can be seen and where it is easy to be in communication with

---

48. The Real Academia de la Lengua was established by Philip V on 3 October 1714 to oversee the purity of the language. [Ed.]

49. These were Sephardic Jews, a name given to the Jews from the Iberian, North African, and Middle Eastern countries. See W.N. Hargreaves-Mawdsley, ed. and trans., *Spain under the Bourbons, 1700– 1833, A Collection of Documents* (Columbia: University of South Carolina Press, 1973), 138–44. [Tr.]

50. In 1776 Parker commanded the fleet that sailed from England to the colonies in February. He was with Clinton and Cornwallis at their defeat in Charleston in June and commanded the squadron that convoyed Clinton to Newport in December 1776. He was military commander of Jamaica under Governor Dalling in 1779–81.

the fleet by means of signals. We dined there in the company of several naval officers.

Immediately after dinner, in what is the true social hour of the English, there was a conversation concerning the corsairs from the island of Cuba, who are known in Jamaica as *picarones*, and the admiral said he marveled that the Spanish government authorized with royal letter of marque those veritable thieves who practiced a sort of larceny condemned among civilized nations. He and the others related several strange stories about these corsairs, against whom I had heard in Kingston the most violent imprecations.

The true motive for the hatred with which the English regard these men is the irreparable damage they cause. For the most part they go out from the port of Trinidad, which is situated on the southern coast of the Island of Cuba. Their vessels are canoes, each holding three or four men at most. Their weapons are nothing more than the machete that each man carries, and their provisions only a scant store of round cakes made of cassava. They make the crossing to the northern coast of Jamaica in one night. If a canoe capsizes, which happens frequently in that turbulent channel, they resolutely plunge into the water, lift the canoe and set it right, bail out the water, and proceed. Generally they try to reach the coast by night; they know the coast well because they are smugglers in peacetime and corsairs in time of war. They hide their canoes in a creek or hidden sloping bank, and they hide themselves within the palisades of the plantations. They lie in ambush there, awaiting the footsteps of the Negroes, whose capture is the chief incentive of their cupidity, and although the Negroes may come that way in greater number than their own, the picarones hurl themselves upon them unexpectedly, machetes in hand. The Negroes, either because they regard the picarones with terror or because they know that slaves find better treatment among the Spaniards, never put up any resistance; they do not dare to open their lips, nor do they have the courage to take flight. They immediately throw themselves upon the ground and let themselves be manacled and led to the canoes; a corsair, upon having five or six of them tied up, happily returns to his point of departure.

24 November 1780

The picarón is pernicious if he is successful in his attack, but he is much more so if he is captured. As he has a license as a corsair, he must be treated as such. Commonly he is taken to Kingston and confined with the other prisoners in a great tower that overlooks the sea. The picarón, either by diving into the water from some window or by bribing some sentry, can manage to escape within a few days. Relying upon a knowledge of the country and of the language, which his practice of smuggling has afforded him, he seduces some Negro domestic servants; together they steal some boat or launch, and he goes with the Negroes to Cuba, where he immediately sells them as slaves, although he had promised them freedom. Some have been so bold as to penetrate by swimming at night to the longboats that warships have on the stern, to throw into the water the sailor on duty, who usually is drunk, to cut the cable, and to go away with the longboat, carrying off eight or ten Negroes. The English relate these exploits endlessly. Their theme is that a convention should be made between the nations so that every corsair who does not go armed with a certain number of guns or carry an adequate crew be treated as a pirate.

On the twenty-sixth we went with Mistress Fitch and other ladies to lunch in the home of Colonel Orwell. He had arrived in Jamaica a few months before with his wife in the convoy of Commodore Walsingham, which brought six regiments, but the climate of the island had caused such a frightful loss among them that, according to the account they gave us there, that force was already reduced by more than half. European troops generally suffer greatly in the torrid zone, but especially the English, either because they come from more northern lands or because they make a more intemperate use of strong liquors.

We went to a public ballroom in the evening. This building is a copy of the Vauxhall of London, and although it is built of wood, it has an elegant appearance and considerable capacity. It is elliptical in shape, supported by pilasters of Corinthian design. The middle room, site of the balls, is covered by a vaulted ceiling which is pleasingly painted. On the sides are two elevated galleries for the musicians. A spacious corridor for the comfortable passage of the people who attend the functions encircles the salon. There are areas for various kinds of games or diversions and other areas where every kind of food and drink is served. The principal room is painted in white with strokes of different colors, so that it appears to be made of marble, and the reflections of the illumination create a beautiful effect. One enjoys there a decorous freedom without disorder, because any excess is corrected promptly. A brilliant company was present that night. The ladies were beautifully adorned, especially the European ladies who had come in the latest convoy, and they were numerous, because English officers seldom fail to be accompanied by their wives. At midnight we retired, having dined well and had an amusing evening.

On the morning of the twenty-eighth we saw the 74-gun warship *Ramillies* pass in front of the city, going to be watered. It is the ship that left England escorting the convoy that Don Luis de Córdova captured off the Azores. Because of its speed the *Ramillies* escaped from several other Spanish and French ships that pursued it, and it arrived at Jamaica with another vessel that had managed to escape. The captain immediately was brought before a court-martial, and his trial was still in progress at that time. Everyone said that the best thing that could possibly happen to him would be that he would be relieved of his command for having proceeded negligently or at least with audacious presumptuousness. The loss of such a convoy had caused great perturbation of mind on that island and had ruined many of its merchants.

In imitation of England, there are in Kingston many good cafés or inns, which are called taverns there. On 30 November we were given a great banquet in the principal tavern by Colonel Dalrymple, who was making a pompous display of affection for Spaniards, no doubt because he had become rich by plundering their trade. In fact he commanded the expedition that captured the fort of Omoa and the vessels loaded with indigo that were in the harbor there, from which his share in the distribution of booty was more than 100,000 *pesos fuertes*. He undertook that operation on his own authority, without order or commission from his government. He happened to be in the English settlements on the coast of Honduras, and there he learned that

[30 November 1780]

the fort at Omoa was poorly garrisoned. He assembled a body of volunteers, few of whom were soldiers, sailed toward the fort, landed near it without being observed, scaled it by night in an unguarded place, surprised the few who defended it, and captured it almost without loss. It made me very sad to learn that a group of idlers had succeeded in taking a fortress whose construction had cost the Spanish Treasury more than 1.5 million pesos.[51]

4 December 1780

Rare was the day when I did not go in search of a flag-of-truce ship that could take me to Havana. One of this type had just come from Cuba; it was the property of a citizen of Kingston named Barry Burke. I went to see him, and although he voiced a desire to make a second voyage, I understood that he would need much time to prepare it, because his funds were limited and his health poor. Nonetheless, we agreed that he would begin to make his preparations; if in the meantime an earlier opportunity was presented I should avail myself of it, and he would remain to conduct other prisoners of the many who were there.

In the evening we went to the theater. It is a well-planned wooden structure with accommodations for a considerable number of people. Its shape is a semi-ellipse, its arrangement, with negligible difference, like that of French theaters; the decorations are mediocre, although very costly for that place. A work by Shakespeare was presented. The actors were army officers and the actresses professional performers. Outstanding among the former were Colonel Orwell and a sergeant major who would inspire envy in the most accredited professional. This is not odd among the English, who do not regard the theatrical profession as discreditable and who number acting among the refinements of good breeding.

There are in that country, as in all those British dominions,

---

51. See Troy S. Floyd, *The Anglo-Spanish Struggle for Mosquitia* (Albuquerque: University of New Mexico Press, 1967), chap. 10. [Ed.]

eccentric persons. Our experience with Mr. Green is a confirmation of this fact. He was one of the rich men of Jamaica, a member of the Parliament, and highly esteemed by the public. He frequently passed by our house. We were accustomed to go out to an exterior gallery to take the air. Although we greeted him many times, he never returned the courtesy, nor did he turn his head to look at us. We judged him to be a fierce and unmannerly republican who regarded other men with scorn, but what was our surprise when one day our friend Mr. Watts brought us the key to Mr. Green's house, with a note from him. He told us that his esteem for the Spanish nation was as great as was his hatred for the French; that from our comportment he had comprehended that we were men of merit and distinction; that his character, shy and averse to ceremony, did not permit him to disclose his feelings by any personal expression; that he was retiring to the country for several months but leaving with Mr. Watts the keys of his house, where he had a good supply of excellent wines, beers, hams, butter, and other victuals much esteemed there, as well as a good library of English books and a collection of exquisite prints; that we were to take freely as much as we pleased, with the understanding that we should cause him great displeasure if he found upon his return that we had not accepted his offer with complete freedom.

We responded to this message in courteous terms, refusing to avail ourselves of an offer that we had no reason to accept, but Mr. Watts told us that if we did so, considering Mr. Green's temperament, he was capable of returning from his country house to challenge us, taking our refusal for mistrust. In the end we felt obliged to accept some bottles of Madeira wine and some excellent beer, and I accepted several English books, among them Blackstone's *Commentaries on the Law*, and some prints by Robert Strange.

The subject that most occupied the attention of the inhabitants of Jamaica at that time was the fate of the colonies to the north. Some thought that they would be subdued and others that they would remain independent, but I noted with wonder that most of the Jamaicans were anti-American, it being true that the natural order of things and the analogy of their respective situations appeared to demand that they prefer the party that even in the mother country itself had numerous adherents. But whether it was because of a failure of understanding or because of suggestions from the ministerial faction, they obstinately insisted that if England lost her domination of the colonies, those colonies would forever be subject to the influence of France.

The English are extremely prone to talk about political matters, and this mania, exalted on that occasion by the grandeur of the circumstances, approximated a kind of frenzy. In all gatherings the question of the colonies was , and it took over the conversation. I heard, therefore, an enormous amount of talk about the subject; I read a great variety; I confirmed my judgment as well as I could, reduced to a very few and very clear ideas. England committed two capital errors with her colonies.

The first error was to give them an occasion for rebellion by trying to subject them to the decrees of a Parliament in which, contrary to the spirit of its own constitution, they did not have representatives. The second was to attempt to subdue them by force, without calculating the resistance with which they would oppose that force or realizing that 3 million men united in their refusal to be subjugated cannot be subdued, especially when they have the ocean as a barricade. But another, no less important error of England, which has become of transcendental importance to almost all the cabinets of Europe and has given a motive for the present war, has been the belief that the loss of the colonies can seriously damage British power.

I imagine that the insurgent thirteen colonies now risen in rebellion will in the end be independent and that the same thing would occur even if such powerful protectors as they have had not intervened in their behalf; but I believe that without them the English will be as much stronger than before as France would be even if she lost her islands, and as Spain would have been had the great states of the House of Burgundy not joined her. Harm will come to England not from the reduction but rather from the amplitude of her dominions, the immensity of her commerce, and the ravenous extravagance that accompanies it, incompatible with patriotism and the virtues that guarantee

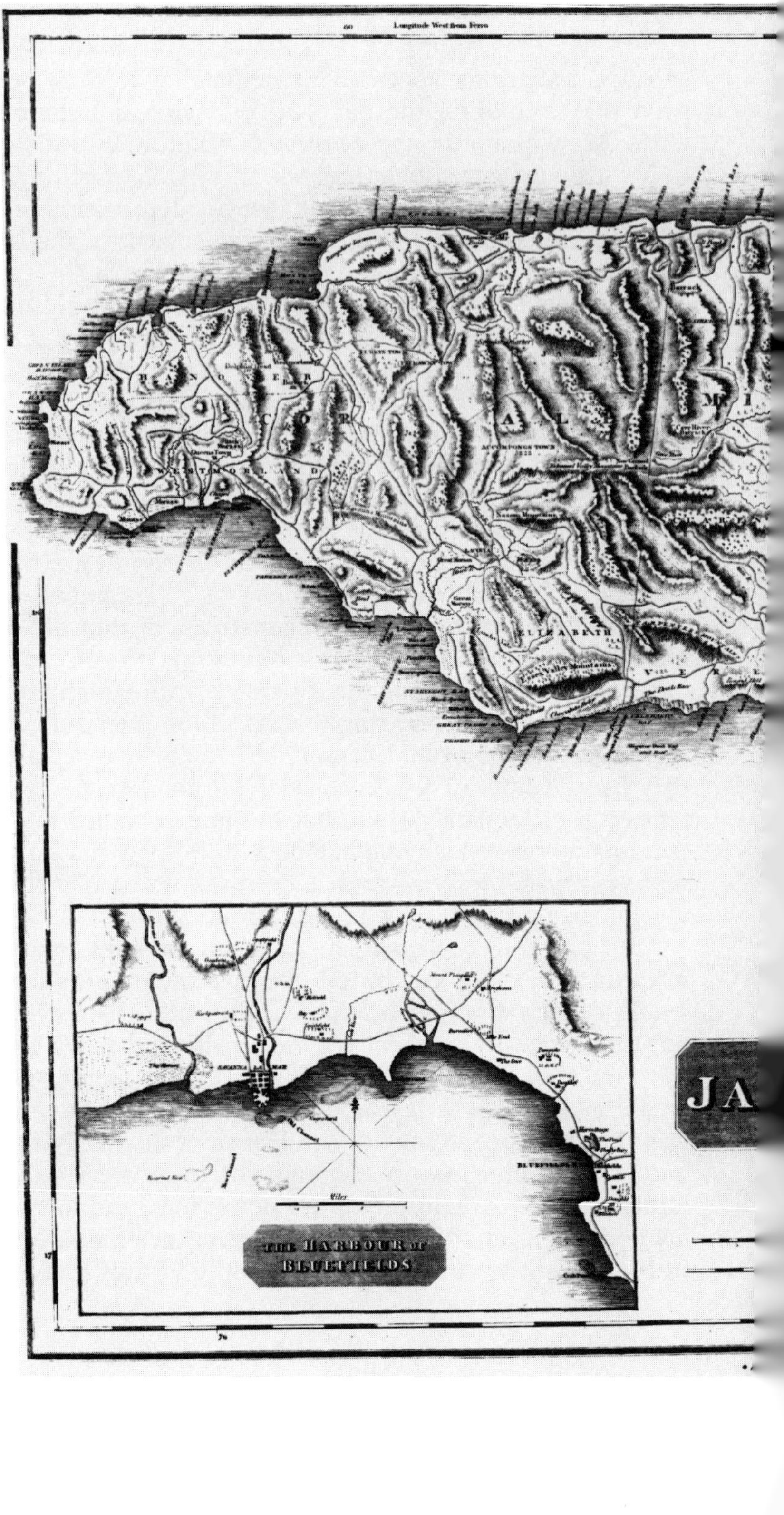
60
Longitude West from Ferro
H A N O V E R
C O R
W E S T M O R L A N D
ELIZABETH
ACCOMPONG TOWN
Queens Town
Savanna
Miles
THE HARBOUR OF BLUEFIELDS
70

62

the stability of republics. What is not being thought about at present, what ought to occupy the whole attention of politics, is the great upheaval that in time the North American revolution is going to produce in the human race.[52]

6 December 1780

Within sight of Kingston is a high mountain on whose slopes several pleasantly situated country houses are to be seen. Innumerable small brooks flow down from the summit, now forming natural cascades, now crossing meadows, and there are such groves as the happiest imagination could conceive. The differences in altitude, causing equal variety in the temperature, afford throughout the year flowers, fruits, and vegetables native to the most distant regions. The English are devoted to the pleasures of rural life; they spend a good part of the year in the country, and there are opulent families who seldom go to the cities. The society offered by this assemblage of people in such delightful places closes the door on the boredom that solitude produces.

Mr. Watts took me to spend a couple of days on one of those estates. It was three leagues distant from the port and at an elevation of 400 toises above sea level, according to observations made with the barometer. One felt there an agreeable coolness such as that of a beautiful May day in Europe. The house was elegant and comfortable without ostentation. There were separate quarters for the slaves, corrals, a dovecote and aviary, fenced paddocks, stables, and other rural buildings. It was a dwelling almost of pure recreation, but on the plantation they cultivated some coffee, cotton, malagueta pepper, and other kinds of spices, from which they derived a profit sufficient to maintain the estate. The cultivated area covered about half a league, divided among English-style gardens, meadows, groves, and cultivated land. Three streams that flow through the plantation carry enough water to irrigate the greater part of it.

---

52. Saavedra, like the Count of Aranda, foresaw the pragmatic value of the revolution of the English colonies in America. [Ed.]

6 December 1780

The house is set on a low hill from which on one side the gaze is lost in a limitless sea, and on the other side it overlooks Kingston and all its environs as far as several leagues inland. The owners treated us courteously, and I remember having passed few days in my life as enjoyable.

After many efforts, I lost hope that a cartel ship would be available soon to take me to Havana, and in order not to waste time while I must remain in Kingston, I set about composing a description of the island of Jamaica. With this in mind, I read many books that treat the subject, examined some good papers in manuscript form, and consulted several talented persons experienced in different branches of study. The danger that they might take me for a spy prevented me from acquiring exact maps, but nonetheless I used an excellent general map of the island and a detailed chart of the port of Kingston and its environs and fortifications.

At first I planned to write about the natural history of the island, and I had already collected some materials that were furnished to me by my friend Mr. Watts, who was very learned in the subject; but I desisted from that intent as soon as there fell into my hands the magnificent work written on the same subject by Sir Hans Sloane, printed in London in two volumes in folio, in which any interested person will find more than I could say.[53] Therefore I limited myself to writing a description of the geographical, military, and political situation of the island. As I had available enough material and more than enough time to meditate, it turned out somewhat more diffuse than what is permitted by the boundaries of a journal.

Geographical Description of Jamaica

This island is situated between 17°44' and 18°34' north

---

53. Sir Hans Sloane, English physician and naturalist, was a personal physician to George II, president of the Royal Society, and president of the Royal College of Physicians. His collection of botanical specimens, as well as over 50,000 books and manuscripts, formed a beginning of the British Museum. He wrote in Latin a catalogue of the plants of Jamaica and published an account of his stay there.

latitude and between 75°51' and 78°22' longitude west of the meridian of London.

Its position is at 112 leagues to the southeast of the North American continent, 18 to the south of the Island of Cuba, and 80 to the southwest of the Island of Santo Domingo.

According to the latest measurements taken with considerable accuracy, the island is 170 English miles long and 70 miles wide at its widest point. Its shape is oval; it widens in the middle and narrows at each end, so that it seems to end in a point. A high range of mountains, running from east to west, inaccessible in many places and rugged everywhere, divides the island into two almost equal parts. The southern half is more craggy and barren, the northern more fertile and level and therefore more cultivated.

The island is watered by about a hundred rivers, most of them small and none navigable. There are crystalline brooks without number and some thermal springs. No settlement lacks running water, all the fields are well irrigated, and more than half of the sugar mills are worked with water power.

The temperature is very hot in the plains, temperate on the slopes of the mountains, and cold on the peaks of the mountain range. The east winds constantly moderate the heat of the sun from eight o'clock in the morning until nightfall, and the land winds, which originate in the mountains and follow the directions of the coves and creeks, cool off the nights so much that in some places they make the night air injurious.

The climate is generally healthful, more so on the east and north than on the west and south, but the excesses of concupiscence and gluttony, more dangerous in the torrid zone than in the temperate zones, have given to the island the reputation of being the sepulcher of Europeans. Those who live on the island with moderation prolong their lives to an advanced age, with fewer discomforts than in cold climates.

The rains there, as in all countries situated below the tropic of Cancer, begin in May and end in October. It rains almost every day but seldom for longer than an hour, in which short period fall torrents of water, causing great havoc at times. In the months of August and September there are frightening thunder-

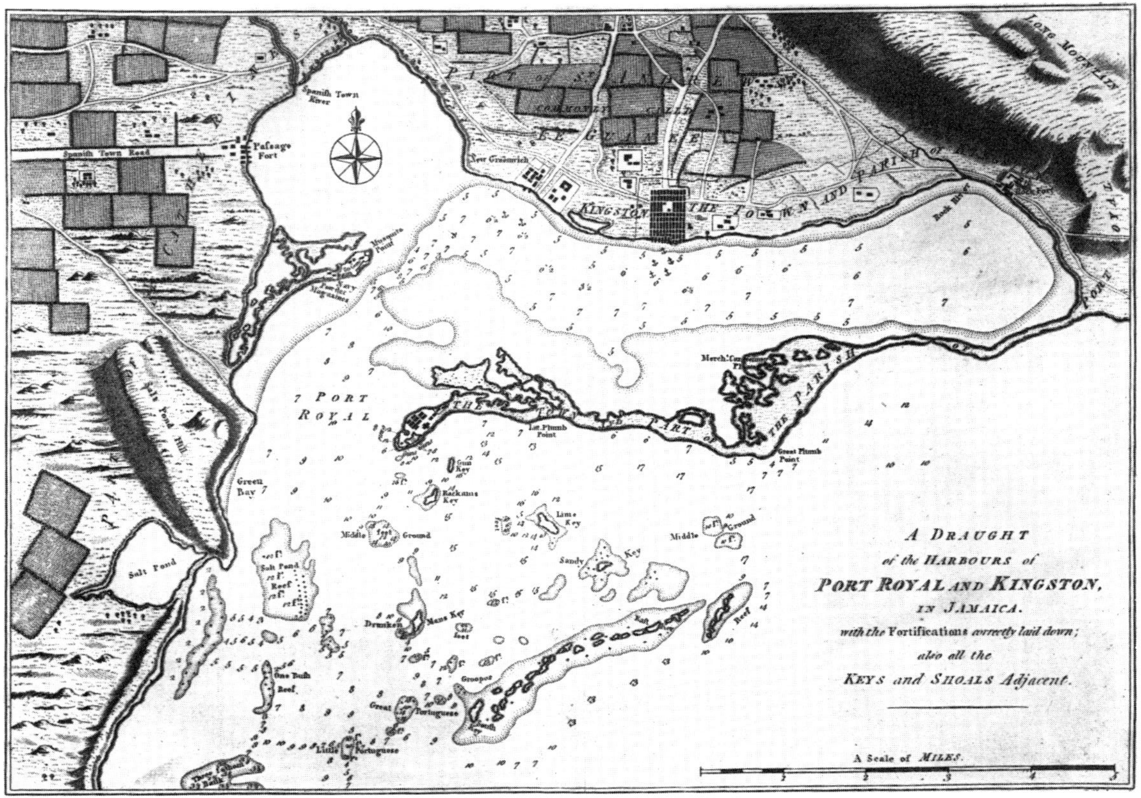
A DRAUGHT
of the HARBOURS of
PORT ROYAL AND KINGSTON,
IN JAMAICA.
with the Fortifications correctly laid down;
also all the
KEYS and SHOALS Adjacent.
A Scale of MILES.
LONG MOUNTAIN
Spanish Town River
Passage Fort
Spanish Town Road
New Greenwich
KINGSTON
THE TOWN AND PARISH OF
Rock Fort
Mosquito Point
PORT ROYAL
Green Bay
Salt Pond Hill
Salt Pond
Lit. Plumb Point
Great Plumb Point
Gun Key
Rackams Key
Middle Ground
Lime Key
Sandy Key
Salt Pond Reef
Drunken Mans Key
One Bush Reef
Great Portuguese
Little Portuguese
Groopos
Reef

storms and in many years hurricanes, which lay waste the towns and obliterate the crops.

Jamaica is very liable to earthquakes, especially in the vicinity of the mountains of Palenque, which are the highest. Rare is the year when no earthquake is experienced, but the big ones come from one century to another.

The island has many good ports. On the east side there is only the bay of Manchioneal, which, although safe and a good anchoring ground, is not much frequented because its environs are barren and uninhabited.

Rounding the eastern headland, called Morant Point, one finds on the southern coast a port of the same name which is very good but is difficult to enter. At a short distance from Port Morant is Morant Bay, which is more useful. On the stretch of coastline that runs from there to Kingston, which is about fourteen leagues, there is shelter only for very small vessels.

The port of Kingston is the principal and best harbor of the entire island; its capacity is immense, and at least half of the island's produce is shipped through it. There are countless warehouses filled with as many European and Asian articles as might be desired. The town is very beautiful. The houses generally are built of wood, many of them of beautiful appearance, with porticos and portals that imitate marble so perfectly that in some the illusion can be detected only by touch. These houses are brought in numbered sections from England itself, and before the war there were many such in her colonies to the north.

Five leagues to the west of Kingston is Old Harbour, where many merchant vessels congregate. It is a good port, but it has a difficult entrance, which is its only defense.

About twenty leagues beyond is Black River Bay, which is frequented by many small vessels. It is protected on the north and east by winds but open in the center.

The port of Savanna-la-Mar has low water, and its surface at the entrance is dangerous because of many sandbars and reefs. It is the worst port on the island, but much shipping is done from there because the neighboring lands are extensively cultivated.

The western coast of the island, whose extremity is formed by

Negril Point, is very narrow, and there is only one port on it, named Orange [Bay], where seven or eight vessels are loaded each year.

The first port on the northern side is the bay of Santa Lucía [Lucea Harbour], safe and spacious. One poor battery defends its entrance, and considerable shipping goes through the port.

Nine leagues to the east is the excellent port of Montego Bay, capacious, a good anchoring ground, defended by a 12-gun battery. Inland from it is the town of Barnett, through which is exported about one-fourth of all the produce of the island.

Beyond is Saint Ann's Bay. Its entrance is difficult; however, it loads fifteen or sixteen ships annually for the mother country. This place is notable for having been the port at which Columbus arrived in his first discovery of the island, and he named it Santa Gloria because of its delightful situation.

The last port on the northern coast is Port Antonio, excellent for its natural advantages but less frequented than apparently it ought to be, perhaps because it is not so near the plantations for convenient loading of produce. It has a small fort garrisoned by a detachment of veteran troops. At the mouth of the port there is an islet that is rather well situated for defense. It is one of the places in Jamaica through which an invasion, especially an invasion by the Spaniards, might be feared.

The Military State of the Island

The principal military force in Jamaica is concentrated in the port of Kingston, protected from all winds, large enough to shelter numerous fleets and convoys, and made impervious to capture by the considerable forts and batteries that guard its entrance and the many reefs and sandbars that confine ships to a channel so narrow that it barely affords the precise space required for the passage of a ship.

One fort is Fort Charles, constructed on the extremity of that tongue of land that forms the port and encloses it on the south side. The shape of the fort is an irregular quadrangle closed at the gorge, with bastion, moat, and stockade. On the side that faces the sea it has sixty guns, according to the number of embrasures that I myself counted, which are said to be of 36-caliber; furthermore, on the western side aimed at the channel, there is another small, level battery, covered so as to be bombproof, with twenty 24-caliber guns. Inside the fort are quarters and magazines which are said not to be bombproof. The Spaniards had a fort in the same place, the only building to survive the earthquake and inundation that in the year 1692 devastated the famous city of Puerto Real. The Spanish *castillo* forms a part of the present-day Fort Charles.[54] Its walls, built of extremely hard stone, are thick, and its foundations rest on the only firm terrain to be found on that isthmus.

This fort guards the entrance to the port and renders it impregnable. In order to proceed up the channel, a vessel must come within musket range of one of the façades of its bastions. Next, as it approaches even closer to the fort, the ship's side is exposed, and it is also exposed on the wing to shots from a kind of salient angle of the same bastion and on the bow to shots from the Battery of the Apostles. As the channel is so narrow, any ship dismasted or sunk in it would obstruct the passage.

Upon rounding the promontory of Port Royal, still within the narrow channel, one sees on the left the Apostles, a battery of twelve 36-caliber guns, solidly built on the slope of a rugged acclivity. It overlooks the anchoring ground of the warships and crosses its fire on one side with that of Fort Charles and on the other with that of Fort Augusta. During the war the English have placed on the same hill another temporary battery with an equal number of guns but superior to the guns of the Apostles, in order to intensify their fire at so important a point.

Following the coast on the west side, with some declination toward the north, one finds Fort Augusta, an irregular shape approximating a quadrangle. It mounts almost 100 heavy guns; it is enclosed on all sides; it has hornworks with their ravelins in front which can be attacked from the land; it has capacious quarters, and it is believed that its works are mined.

---

54. Saavedra says *del día*, which means present-day, modern. [Ed.]

The terrain that surrounds the fort is subject to flooding, and it would be necessary to conduct an attack by way of a narrow tongue of land which is dominated by the Battery of the Apostles.

In the center of the bay is the city of Kingston, open on all sides and without fortification. There is only one battery with four 4-caliber guns near the quarters, intended more for the drilling of troops than for any defensive purpose.

To the southeast of Kingston is the Castillo de Rockfort, built on a height above the road that must be used in going to the city from that side. Rockfort interrupts the road and then follows a wall cutting into the hillside; it is so rugged that every step is dangerous. The shape of Rockfort is an irregular square; it mounts thirty guns, and it dominates the place where warships go for watering. The port of Kingston has two channels, the first for entering with an east wind, or brisa, the second for going out with the west or land wind. Having taken the entrance channel, one steers to the west until one is carried past the headland of Port Royal, then luffs to the northwest and later to the north. The channel passes in front of the Battery of the Apostles and Fort Augusta at a distance of 200 toises. Having sailed past this latter fort, one enters the great inlet of Kingston Bay, which can accommodate thousands of ships anchored near the town itself. The exit from this port is narrow also, between reefs, standing toward the south, following a channel somewhat farther from Fort Charles than is the entrance channel but still within range of its artillery.

There are several other forts on the coasts of this island in Saint Ann's Bay, Port Maria, Port Antonio, Savanna-la-Mar, Bluefields Bay, and Morant Bay. Most of them, and some others situated in the interior, are of little importance and are not in the best of condition. That is not true of the fort that overlooks the road that leads from Kingston to Spanish Town and guards the deep ravine over which there is a drawbridge. Its location is strategic. It is well maintained; its artillery is of bronze 12-caliber guns, and in case of an invasion it would be extremely useful.

It is said that the English are fortifying a strategic place called Saint Thomas, in the center of the island, where they plan to make an encampment in case they are attacked by the Spanish and French with superior forces; from there they hope to be able to send assistance to wherever it is needed or to have a safe retreat in case of a misadventure.

Troops

There is no fixed number of veteran troops on the island; instead, they are sent from England as required. Before the expedition to Lake Nicaragua there were 2,700 men brought from Europe; as a result of that unsuccessful enterprise they were reduced by at least one-half that number. A short while afterward 6,000 men arrived in the convoy of Commodore Walsingham; their number has been greatly diminished by the illnesses with which the torrid zone greets Europeans. At present one can say with assurance that the number of veteran troops now in Jamaica does not amount to 4,000 men.

There are militias of infantry and cavalry on the island. In each parish or judicial district (of which there are nineteen), all whites capable of bearing arms are enlisted as militiamen; thus in each of the two branches of militia there are one, two, or three companies with their commandants and other officers. These militias are seldom assembled, and therefore they entirely lack discipline.

In Kingston there is one militia company of grenadiers, seven of fusiliers, and one of artillerymen. These companies do not have fixed components but can be computed at eighty men each.

The cavalry militia is distributed into three divisions called eastern, central, and western, which are commanded by three colonels. As each man is free to serve in the militia corps of his choice, there are more who prefer the cavalry to the infantry, especially among those who live in country places where all have horses. Therefore it can be estimated that the cavalry numbers no fewer than 3,000 men. In Kingston there are two cavalry companies, one of them made up of mulattoes.

The staff of the island is composed of nine major-generals,

one adjutant general, two lieutenants, and one quartermaster, who usually is an engineer.

At this time, in order to attack Jamaica one needs 15,000 men and a fleet superior to the one the English have. The port of Kingston cannot be forced; therefore it is necessary to choose between two plans of attack. The first is to disembark in the bay of Old Harbour, eighteen miles to the lee side of Kingston, which affords space and shelter to warships and transport vessels, and proceed from there with the army toward Kingston, taking possession of the heights that overlook the port on the west side, capturing from the rear the Battery of the Apostles and then attacking Fort Augusta. In this way Kingston and Spanish Town fall at the same time, making it possible to take possession of Rockfort and Port Royal, which cannot be reinforced. The second plan is to disembark on the peninsula of Port Royal itself on the south side and to direct the first attack against Fort Charles—possession of Fort Charles would bring with it possession of the port and of the two towns above—and next to assault the Battery of the Apostles and Fort Augusta, which can then be easily blockaded.

If the enterprise is undertaken in the month of December, which leaves an interval of five months until the beginning of the rainy season, the first plan is preferable and safer. If it is done in the month of March or later, the second plan must be hazarded. In any case, it will be advisable to hasten the operations, because the effects of the climate will carry off more cautious persons than the enemy's fire will kill among the reckless.

It is also possible to disembark on the north side of the island, especially in Port Antonio, whose location is useful for an advantageous attack and affords an excellent position for the army to be sheltered from danger. But the distance from there to Kingston is twenty leagues. The English would block the roads, and their cavalry would harass the troops in their march. Nonetheless, one must consider that once in possession of the northern side of the island, the Spaniards would be masters of the greater part of it.

Political Situation of the Island

Writers do not agree as to the origin of the name Jamaica. Some believe that it is the ancient name given to the island by the natives before the arrival of the Spaniards. Others think that its discoverer called it San Tiago or San Jaime [Saint James] and that the name Jamaica is a corruption of the latter.[55]

The island was discovered by Admiral Christopher Columbus on 14 May 1494 on his second voyage, but he made no settlement there. Nine years later, returning from Veragua, he was forced onto the coasts of Jamaica by a storm; he managed to save himself and his men, but as his vessels had been dashed to bits on the reefs he was obliged to remain there for a year, sustained by the assistance afforded him by the unguarded hospitality of the natives. In the year 1503, Juan de Esquivel established the first settlement on the island with seventy men whom he brought from Santo Domingo by order of the second Admiral Don Diego Columbus.

Within a few years Jamaica's population increased rapidly, and five towns of some importance were found on it: Sevilla on the west side, and there the Collegiate Church was built; Melilla on the north coast; Oristan on the south coast; Vega on the same side of the island, three leagues inland; and the port of Cognai, where Port Royal is today.

One must conjecture that the Spaniards, disappointed because there were neither gold nor silver mines on this island, applied themselves to cultivating the land and established plantations of agricultural produce, especially cotton and cacao, which flourished in the beginning but later were ruined. Their decline can be attributed to two causes: first, the frenzy that took hold of the inhabitants of the islands for moving to the realms of Mexico and Peru, the fame of whose riches enticed them with more flattering, although perhaps less solid, hopes; second, the debility of the Indians, whose weak consti-

---

55. *Yamaye* is what the indigenous name of the island (Xamaye) sounded like to the Spanish ear; Columbus had given it the name Santiago during his second voyage (1493); that is what the Crown wished to call it in 1511, but the attempt was unsuccessful. [Ed.]

tution, accustomed to the idleness of nomadic life, could not endure the continuous and persistent labor of lucrative agriculture. The extermination of the Indians was followed by the importation of African slaves, but African slaves could not fill the void left by the Indians in a country whose scant means made acquisition of the slaves impossible.

From the lack of field laborers came the abandonment of the plantations and from this the destruction of the towns, a catastrophe escaped only by Santiago de la Vega and the port of Cognai. The population of the whole island was reduced to about 3,000 souls, including both free men and slaves; its agriculture diminished to the proceeds from a little cacao and its trade to the occasional sale of some provisions to ships that happened to pass near its coasts.

Such was the condition of Jamaica in the year 1655, when the English commanded by Admiral Penn and General Venables took it. The Spaniards, devoid of means with which to resist the superior force that attacked them, fled with their slaves to the mountains, fortified themselves in the crags, and remained there until, stripped of all hope of reinforcement, they managed to move to the island of Cuba. The Negroes, fearful of returning to slavery, refused to follow them and remained hidden in the most inaccessible parts of the mountain ranges; dominated by the maroon Negroes from this rugged refuge, they became not less feared but also famous for the tenacity of purpose with which, in the course of more than a century, they were able to preserve their freedom.[56]

Once the English were in possession of Jamaica, there began to spring up among them the dissensions and political parties that were agitating their homeland at that time. Instead of devoting themselves to the cultivation of their new acquisition, they were at the point of watering it with their blood; in the end there would have been victims of this spirit of discord if,

---

56. The rugged central region of Jamaica is inhabited by the maroons, called *marrons* by the French and *cimarrones* by the Spanish, the runaway slaves who fled when the British took the island in 1655. For many years they fomented frequent rebellions against white colonists. By a treaty in 1739 they were granted lands of their own and virtual independence.

after their conquerors had departed, fortune had not given them as their governor General Dudley, a man of eminent qualities who knew how to reconcile them, get rid of the most disorderly and attract useful settlers, and lay the foundations of the future prosperity of the island.

However, the government was purely military until 1682, when a civil constitution was established on the model of that of the mother country. Supreme authority resides in a Parliament composed of representatives elected by the towns in a manner almost identical to that which is followed in England for the election of members of the House of Commons. The governor presides over it in the name of the king. In it the subsidies to support the public offices are voted, the accounts are examined, and the other measures relative to the well-being of the colony are discussed.

English laws are completely in force in Jamaica, and the greater part of the lawsuits that occur are decided according to them. But because in many cases those laws would be incompatible with the local circumstances of a place so remote from the countries for which they were made, an effort was made early to modify them to fit the situation and climate of the island by forming a sort of municipal code of laws, which has contributed greatly to the development of the island. In the code are treated the distribution of lands, the formation of new towns, the arrangements of the jurisdictions, the treatment of slaves, the improvement of agriculture, and the protection of trade.

Among other wise laws in this code there are three very notable ones which undoubtedly have contributed greatly to the development of the colony, but I have no notice that they have been adopted by any other of the nations established in the New World.

In order to persuade the citizens to defend the island without being dissuaded by the fear of losing their possessions, the first law provides that all damage caused by the enemy to the properties of private individuals be remedied by the state and that, if the public treasury of the colony is not sufficient to cover it, the amount is to be apportioned in shares among all citizens.

The second law is favorable to the population. It orders that every captain of a ship that brings to Jamaica a man who cannot pay for his passage is to receive by way of a usual gratification one pound sterling, in addition to another special gratuity according to the place from which the man came, that is to say, eight pounds if from England or Scotland, six if from Ireland, four if from the American continent, and two if from the other islands.

Not less notable than the two laws above is a third made in favor of the agricultural class. When a planter cannot pay his debts, his possessions are sold in a juridical sale at public auction, according to the just evaluation which has been made of them, and the proceeds are divided among the creditors by quota. If the debts exceed the value of the plantation, the debtor is solvent, free of all obligations when he delivers the property. If the value of the plantation exceeds that of the debts, the surplus proceeds are returned to the debtor. This law, which at first glance gives the impression of being unjust and biased, assures good faith between creditors and debtors. It makes the former prudent, so as not to risk their fortunes blindly to someone who can betray their trust under the protection of a law that favors him. It obliges the latter to be heedful in the fulfillment of their contracts, sure that in each creditor they have a sentinel who scrutinizes their conduct closely. Whether it be the effect of this law or proceeds from another cause less well known, the fact is that nowhere in the New World are there made so many advance payments of funds, nor are there fewer insolvent debtors, than on this island.

Jamaica has owed its prosperity not only to good laws but also to a series of fortunate events. The obstacle that most retards the development of new colonies is the lack of funds with which to make the enormous preliminary investments that the land requires before it will free its treasures, and Jamaica obtained these funds by measures that the most perspicacious policy could not foresee. At the time of the conquest the buccaneers were beginning their famous forays. They made the island a depository of rich booty from Spanish possessions, and in this way there came to the island enormous sums of money that gave the first impetus to agriculture and trade.

The extermination of these celebrated pirates at the end of the seventeenth century seemed to deprive Jamaica of the riches that fertilized it, but at almost the same time the Portuguese undertook to provide Negroes to the Spanish dominions and, lacking the funds sufficient to conduct this vast business by themselves, they turned to English merchants, who carried it on in their name. The shipments of Negroes destined for this trade stopped first at Jamaica, and from there they were distributed on the continent and the islands. This afforded to the inhabitants of Jamaica interchange with Spanish colonies and means for instituting a great contraband trade, which during the calamitous epoch of the War of Succession reached its final period.

In the Peace of Utrecht [1713] the English obtained the exclusive purveying of Negroes in the dominions of Spain by the asiento,[57] and under the protection of the license granted to the stipulated ship "of Registry," they appropriated much of the profits made by this method. Although in the year 1732 the asiento and registry were nullified, the English still retained control of contraband trade because of the many connections they had formed with Spanish possessions and the accurate knowledge of their coastlines they had acquired.

With the great wealth obtained by the ways above, the inhabitants of Jamaica purchased many slaves, cleared the fertile lands of the island which had been untouched up to that time, availed themselves of the courses of the rivers for working mills and for irrigation, and perfected their agriculture, making it produce an immense abundance of food and profit which fed a vast trade with their mother country.[58]

Jamaica was already one of the most flourishing colonies of

---

57. By Article 42 of the Treaty of Utrecht, Spain conceded to Great Britain permission to send annually to the Spanish Indies a boat of 500 tons of merchandise that might be sold; likewise they were granted the right to import 144,800 Negro slaves annually for twenty-five years. The privilege was given to the Compañía de la Mar del Sur. [Ed.]

58. For a study of Jamaican agriculture in the eighteenth century see Richard B. Sheridan, "The British Sugar Planters and the Atlantic World, 1763–1775," in *Eighteenth-Century Florida and the Carribean*, ed.

the New World when, in the middle of this century, the war that was declared at that time came to augment the sources of its prosperity. Rich with the spoils from France, who was defeated in all parts of the world, the English merchants made new advance payments and loans to the planters of the island who, emboldened by the discouragement of their rivals, eagerly profited from the good opportunities afforded them by the fortunes of war.

The peace concluded in 1763 could not stop the impetus given to agriculture by the contingencies of the war, which were like the sea that violently seizes the land in some places and relinquishes it in others, and the productions of the island increased by one-third more than they had been up to that time.

A succinct idea has been given of the progress of Jamaica up to its present state. Let us now see what its present condition is, surveying briefly the branches that make up this totality called the public welfare.

Population

It has been said that at the time when the English conquered Jamaica there were on it no more than 3,000 souls, about half of them free and the other half slaves. Fifteen years later a census was taken, and 7,900 of the former and 8,000 of the latter were found. In 1734 the whites did not exceed 7,644, and the slaves numbered 86,558. In 1746 there were 10,000 whites and 112,428 slaves. In 1768 the whites exceeded 17,900 and the colored people 167,000. In 1775, the date of the latest census, there were found 18,500 whites, 3,700 free Negroes or mulattoes, and 190,914 slaves. At present it is said that there are more than 20,000 whites and 200,000 slaves.

In the year 1755 there remained on the island no towns except Santiago de la Vega and Cognai. The English kept both, changing only their names, the former to Spanish Town, the latter to Port Royal.

Samuel Proctor, pp. 11–14 (Gainesville: University Presses of Florida, 1976). [Ed.]

Spanish Town, located on a beautiful plain on the shore of the Cobre River, which is the deepest on the island, is one mile long and almost one-half mile wide. It contains about 600 houses, 4,000 white inhabitants, and 3,000 slaves. The captain general and the Parliament reside in it, which makes it the capital of the whole colony. Hardly a vestige remains of the time of the Spaniards, and all signs indicate that there was no building there worth preserving.

Port Royal grew marvelously after the conquest; but on 7 July 1692 there occurred in Jamaica a frightful earthquake accompanied by a terrible hurricane, which demolished the towns, pulled down entire mountains, and threatened to destroy the entire island. It discharged its greatest fury on Port Royal. All the houses were leveled, and most of the land on which the town stood sank and was submerged beneath the waves. According to contemporary accounts, 13,000 persons perished in this catastrophe. Those who survived took refuge at first on high ground, but hardly had they recovered from the fright caused by such a formidable phenomenon when they began to rebuild the town, making use of the land that had remained free of the sea, creating a smaller town, but a town with so sinister a destiny that in the year 1702 it was totally consumed by conflagration. Then the English government ordered the Jamaicans to abandon a place that seemed to be condemned by God to desolation and moved the town and all its inhabitants to a place where is now found Kingston, which in a short time became the trading center of all the island. There remained in Port Royal only the fort, which had withstood the tremors of the earthquake and the ravages of the fire, and a sort of shipyard for the careening of warships.

Kingston, built directly on the seashore on a wide plain, not far from the neck of land running out into the sea at Port Royal, occupies about one and one-half miles of terrain from north to south and one mile from east to west. It contains 1,700 houses. The number of its white inhabitants exceeds 6,000, and there are 1,200 free coloreds and 5,000 slaves. Not included in this count are transients, who number in the thousands because of the many merchant ships and warships that are always in that port.

There are several other towns on the island, especially on the coasts, of good size and numerous population. One of the largest and richest was Savanna-la-Mar, destroyed this very year by the famous October hurricane. Its rebuilding is being planned at present, and the government and all the other towns are lending their support to the project.

Jamaica is divided into three counties, Middlesex, Surrey, and Cornwall, which contain nineteen parishes or jurisdictions and thirty-three towns. Outside the towns are many plantations, country houses, and vacation homes, so that the whole island with the exception of the most rugged places looks like one continuous settlement. There are many fenced cattle ranges with cultivated pastures where the cattle are fattened rapidly, and from them the inhabitants are supplied meats as excellent as those of Ireland. The towns are connected by hard roads built without regard to cost, which in many places cross the high mountain range that divides the island, so that there is not on the whole island a moderately large property whose produce cannot be carried on wheels to the seacoast.

Agriculture

The great development that England has fomented in her own agriculture for the past two centuries could not fail to spread to her colonies. Agriculture would have prospered in them even without this powerful motivation, because the abundance of good lands in those settlements, the low price at which land could be acquired, the privileges and assistance with which the government favors new colonists, and the natural freedom that the immense distance from the mother country affords them influence their progress so powerfully that they overcome all the difficulties that might retard it.

These causes have operated in all the colonies of the New World, but more forcefully and quickly in some than in others, in proportion to whether the assistance that has been dispensed for their benefit has been greater and whether the number of obstacles they have found in the ordinances of their respective governments or the circumstances of their local situations has been lesser. Although the laws of the English nation (which in no deliberation loses sight of its commerce) have been favorable to the prosperity of all its colonies, those of North America have prospered more rapidly than have the islands, because the produce cultivated in North America has given an opportunity for the lands to be better distributed than in the islands; there the sugar plantations, which form the principal part of their agriculture, demand that each planter occupy great areas, making impossible the division of the land into small portions, and each plantation absorbs enormous investment.

However, it can be stated that in the English islands lands have been distributed as equitably as their constitution permitted, two principal causes having intervened to prevent as much as possible that many lands be amassed in few hands. The first is that there has never been permitted the establishment of entailment or primogeniture, and therefore not only are inheritances divided among all the sons of the families but each one of them can transmit his portion in the form he thinks proper. The second is that lands that are not cleared and cultivated within a certain time, even though they have an owner, are declared irremissibly to be vacant, and ownership of them is transferred to another owner who will make better use of them.

The proximity of the Spanish islands has also contributed not a little to the prosperous cultivation of Jamaica, because the importation from Santo Domingo or Cuba of as many animals as they need for their food supply, farm labor, cartage, and other domestic uses has made it unnecessary for the Jamaicans to keep uncultivated the extensive lands needed by domestic animals for grazing.

According to the calculation of a very judicious and observant man who was for a long time employed in the government of Jamaica, this island contains 3,800,000 acres of land. The mountains, lakes, rivers, glades, roads, towns, and other portions that cannot be dedicated to cultivation occupy 1,728,431 acres. The government has successively distributed 1,671,569 acres that are cultivated or are about to be so. There remain, therefore,

400,000 useful acres to be distributed, and this part of Jamaica can be developed. I have been told that since these observations were made a good part of these uninhabited lands have been tilled or cleared for pastures, and I have not been able to ascertain how many remain uncultivated, although well-informed persons calculate them as more than 200,000 acres.

Because most of the distributed lands have been cultivated intensively for more than a century, many of them are now exhausted, and this circumstance diminishes the profits of the planters, partly because production is less abundant, partly because it forces them to use more costly and frequent fertilization. The English supplement this deficiency in part with the perfection of their cultivation and by minimizing the cost of all farm laborers and animals with the use of good machinery. They open many irrigation ditches from the rivers, at times raising the water to extraordinary heights, and they lose no opporunity to employ water power, an agent as beneficial as it is powerful, to assist or to supplement the strength of men.

Let us see which products have made Jamaica important from the time of its discovery and today constitute its riches and fame.

Cacao

The first product cultivated by the English in Jamaica was cacao, as the Spaniards had left several nurseries of young cacao trees. This lasted only until those trees grew old, and whether the English did not succeed in replanting them, as some people think, or whether they were unwilling to expend their efforts on a product that had little consumption in the mother country, as is more believable, the fact is that for a long time now not one cacao bean has been picked on the whole island.

Indigo

Shortly after the conquest the English applied themselves to the cultivation of indigo; this crop began to prosper extraordinarily, but the English Parliament caused its total ruin by imposing a heavy tax on it. Confronted by this disappointment, Parliament tried to revive it by several measures. First indigo was freed from all taxes. Later a premium was granted to shipments of indigo brought to England from Jamaica. But the remedy came when the illness was no longer curable, and it served only to cause new damage, because greed for such a premium immediately incited the inhabitant of Jamaica to export indigo from the French islands clandestinely and to take it into the ports of Great Britain as the production of their own soil. This fraud continues to be practiced today. Therefore, any entries of indigo to be found in the export statistics of Jamaica can be viewed as imaginary, or at least doubtful.

Cotton

The Spaniards cultivated cotton from the time of their first settlement on the island. Herrera says that by the year 1510 the cotton of Jamaica was reputed to be the best that had been found in the New World up to that time, and that cloth made of it produced lucrative profits for the residents of the island.[59] This crop perished with the others when the Indian race was extinguished, but it revived in the hands of the English, who have never ceased to promote it. It is a profitable crop because it is cheap to plant, it does not require much labor, poor sandy and rocky soil useless for other crops can be used for it, and the universality of its consumption assures its expeditious sale. Today Jamaica produces 7,000 to 8,000 quintales [see glossary] of prepared cotton.

Ginger

Ginger is a crop peculiar to the torrid zone. It is found in

---

59. Antonio de Herrera y Tordesillas, *Descripción de las Indias Occidentales. Historia General de los Hechos de los Castellanos en las Islas y Tierra Firme del Mar Océano*, 7 vols. (Madrid: Nicolás Rodríguez, 1729–30.) [Tr.]

all the Antilles, and the Indians, particularly in Jamaica, made frequent use of it as a special sedative for the stomach. The Spaniards adopted it for the same purpose, and the English have given it a wider usage, applying it to all the uses which pepper has today. The low price of pepper diminished the consumption of ginger, but its cultivation was continued in Jamaica, whence 3,000 quintales are shipped to England annually.

Tabasco Pepper (Grain of Paradise)

The pepper of Jamaica, also called *malagueta*, or allspice, was not cultivated on this island until the year 1668, when some settlers from Barbados brought it here. It is an aromatic shrub whose leaves exhale strong fragrance. It is grown easily in all parts of the Indies situated below the tropics, but nowhere save in Jamaica has it become a useful article of trade. Jamaica produces an average of six to seven quintales of this spice each year; from England it is shipped to the other European markets.

Coffee

At one time it was believed that coffee was a crop belonging exclusively to Arabia Felix.[60] The Dutch carried it from Moka to Surinam a short while after the English ceded that settlement to them in 1670, and from there it spread to the Antilles. The crop has had its greatest development among the French. The English also brought it to their islands, but, not having adopted it as a national beverage, they did not cultivate it with as careful attention as did their rivals. Jamaica, however, produces from 18,000 to 20,000 quintales of coffee per year, of a quality somewhat inferior to that of Martinique.

---

60. An ancient division of Arabia, in the southern part, sometimes restricted to Yemen.

Sugar

Sugar is the principal product of the Caribbean islands. The English did not cultivate it in Jamaica until the year 1670, when the first sugar plantation was begun by Thomas Modyfort, who rose by his merit and service from simple farmer to the general command of the island. At that time the buccaneers were at the height of their fame, and the settlers of Jamaica, principal participants in their successful piracy, following the example and persuasion of their governor, invested the rich spoils taken from the Spaniards in the development of sugar plantations. They founded mills, bought slaves, and extended the cultivation of sugar so widely that within a short time it constituted their principal wealth. They utilize not only the sugar, which is the most valuable product of the cane, but also the syrup to make spirits in an inferior grade, called *tafia*, and, when purified to a certain point, rum, consumed in great quantity in the British dominions. Today an average of 1 million quintales of sugar per year are exported from Jamaica, most of it unrefined or brown, as well as 4 million bottles of rum and 300,000 bottles of syrup.

Various other products shipped from Jamaica to England swell the exports from this colony but do not really originate there. Such are, for example, 5,000 quintales of logwood brought from the coasts of Campeche and Honduras, a great quantity of tortoise shells from the keys that surround the island of Cuba on the southern side, and various precious woods, most of which originate in the Spanish colonies.

The value of all the products mentioned above, estimated at their usual price, amounts annually to almost exactly 10 million pesos fuertes, as seen in detail in the attached list [Table 1, p. 75]:

These are the products that Jamaica supplies to the export trade. In addition it produces all those of primary necessity for the subsistence of its inhabitants. There are abundant harvests of corn, yucca or cassava, plantains, yams, Spanish sweet potatoes, and other plants indigenous to the torrid zone, which form

Jamaican Crops — Sugar

[Table 1.]

Quantities	Product	Value	Pesos fuertes
1 million quintales	sugar	@ 8 ps per q	8,000,000
4 million bottles	rum	@ 6 reales [vellon] per bottle	1,200,000
3 million bottles	syrup	@ 6 rs	30,000
7,000 quintales	cotton	@ 30 ps per quintal	210,000
6,000 quintales	malagueta pepper	@ 3 ps per quintal	54,000
18,000 quintales	coffee	@ 15 ps per quintal	270,000
3,000 quintales	ginger	@ 14 ps per quintal	42,000
Other minor articles evaluated in bulk			200,000
		Total	10,006,000

the major part of the food of the slaves and the poor. There are many farms or orchards which produce an abundance of vegetables and fruits of the kinds peculiar to those regions as well as those from temperate climes which have been successfully acclimatized there by dint of industry and care.

There are no sheep or goats in Jamaica, as they do not thrive in the intense heat of the islands. The only fresh meat consumed there from cattle is brought from the Spanish dominions and fattened in cultivated pastures, their fattening being one of the branches in which English agriculture excels and is worthy of being imitated in other New World countries which, with better advantages, never succeed in producing such excellent meat.

Neither is there in Jamaica any breeding of horses, but the inhabitants have a great number of horses brought from different places, especially from New England, where they grow strong, robust, and swift. They serve for hauling, riding, carriages, of which there are few, and light gigs, which are used widely.

A few mules are found there, and the continent and Spanish islands provide them. Their use is limited in Jamaica, because horses are used for hauling, and where there is no water power to turn the machinery, the sugar mills are worked by oxen as in Havana and only rarely by mules as in Guarico and Martinique.

In general it can be stated with assurance that in Jamaica agriculture has acquired all the perfection compatible with its political and geographical circumstances; one of the causes that has most effectively contributed to this end is the great extent of its trade, which, as we shall see, has prospered at the same pace as have the products that feed it.

Commerce

All the nations that possess dominions in the New World have subjected them in their foreign trade to a monopoly more or less restrictive and therefore more or less adverse to their progress. Any regulation that diverts trade from the natural course it would follow if left entirely free establishes a sort of monopoly; this monopoly, under whatever form it is disguised and even though at first sight it promises to be advantageous, when followed in all its gyrations and connections, is found in the end to be damaging not only to the country that suffers from it but also to the nation that expects to grow rich from its profits.

The monopoly exercised in the Indies by the European nations has assumed various forms at different times and in different colonies at the same time, according to the degree of prosperity or enlightenment of the mother countries. In some places trade has been controlled by exclusive companies, in others, limited to fleets that went out at specific times; in many, all New World trade, both import and export, has been limited to a single European port, and all have prohibited other nations from trading with their respective dominions, conducting it themselves exclusively and not permitting their products to be shipped directly except to the ports of the mother country. In almost all the colonies this exclusion has been unlimited, and in only some has it been limited to a certain class of products.

Trade with the English colonies was absolutely free to nationals and foreigners from 1620 until 1660, at which time it was made subject to the exclusive privilege of the companies of London and Plymouth; this privilege ended in the Revolution of 1688. Part of the earlier freedom was granted only to the English themselves, and the going out and return of the vessels employed in trade was even limited to British ports. This restriction in regard to return voyages was limited to those products of America specified in the famous Navigation Act;[61] those products, called "enumerated products," they were honey, coffee, cocoa, tobacco, pepper, whalebone, raw silk, skins, indigo, logwood, and naval stores. Articles not listed remained free to be carried directly from the colonies to the ports of any nation in the world, although subsequently this freedom was successively reduced to only the countries south of Cape Finisterre.

Among the products not enumerated in the Navigation Act, or excluded from it by other later acts, that therefore enjoy in the English colonies greater freedom for their trade than in any other settlements of the New World are grains of every kind, wood for construction, fresh or salted meat, fish, rum, and sugar. The last two articles constitute the principal wealth of Jamaica. By this method there was opened to them a market much wider than they could have obtained had they been limited only to that of England, and in the opinion of many politicians it is one of the principal causes of the prosperity and growth of its commerce.

It is true that sugar was not counted among the unenumerated products until 1731 and that from that time up to the present it has reaped little benefit from the exemption that this situation gave it. This was because the great consumption of this commodity in Great Britain and the facility of shipment from Jamaica have not necessarily encouraged shipment directly to other nations in search of the profitable price easily obtained in the English market. But it [free trade] has encouraged the colonists to give free rein to their industry,

---

61. Laws of Navigation, from 1651, reserved for England a monopoly on the transportation of colonial products and regulated imports favoring English products. [Ed.]

sure that come what may in domestic or foreign markets they will not lack good sales. Rum is the most important article of the trade carried on by the New World colonists on the coasts of Africa. On their return voyages they bring the Negroes who constitute the principal foundation on which the agriculture of these islands is built.

The enumerated articles produced by the English colonies suffer the same restrictions at the ports of their mother country as those of all the other European settlements in the New World, but even in England these products have obtained particular advantages that have compensated in great part for their restriction. First, all of them are exempt from duties upon their export from the colonies, and only some products require very low duties upon their arrival in the ports of Great Britain. Second, a good price has been assured for them by imposing heavy duties on the same products brought from foreign countries. Third, their transshipment to other ports of Europe has been encouraged by returning, upon their departure from England, the duties paid on their arrival. Recently premiums have been granted for some of these products when brought to the mother country, and in fact this is done with raw silk, hemp, linen, indigo, and naval stores.

It can be seen from the above that all the products of Jamaica enjoy absolute freedom from duties at the time of their exportation from the colony; that in addition to this exemption, indigo, lumber, pitch, tar, and other maritime products reap the benefit of a premium upon their arrival in England; and that sellers of sugar and rum are absolutely free to seek their best price in almost all markets of the world.

Such are the advantages that the products of English America enjoy in the market. England has also treated her colonies very generously in regard to the merchandise they import for sale. This merchandise is either the product of her own industry, that is, produce harvested in Great Britain or articles manufactured in her factories, or the articles and products of foreign industry. In the colonies nothing is exacted from either: those of the first category are free of all kinds of duties, trade them as you please; those of the second class pay at their entrance into England duties in such proportion as to prevent their causing damage to products of the country or its factories. But the greater part of these duties is returned to those who reexport the products to other countries, and although this kind of restitution, called "drawback," was granted originally to the reexportation of foreign articles to other nations independent of Great Britain, the practice extended from the beginning to those articles that are brought from her own colonies; they have enjoyed this benefit for almost a century, until the year 1763, when it was abridged but not curtailed completely by the 4th Act of George III.

One consequence of this freedom of trade and exemption from duties enjoyed by the English colonies is the facility of importing and distributing goods in all of them without their merchants being subject to the registry, delays, examinations, and other fiscal precautions that burden the trade of other nations. Consequently they have reaped benefits equivalent to a great reduction of costs, because in commerce time is money, and every formality that retards it is a sort of tax that encumbers it.

Merchant ships arrive at Jamaica, unload as they please with the least possible loss of time, load in the same way, and do not count on more delays in estimating the costs of their expeditions than those inseparable from all maritime trade. The customhouses hand over the export licenses and accept as valid those for imports upon the presentation of only the invoice of the trader. Goods move about freely on sea and land, without any interruption of their natural flow. Merchants do not fear smuggling because the lowering of taxes and the flourishing condition of their factories have guarded against it, and thus they avoid the fatal effects of the fear of fraud, perhaps more dangerous to trade than fraud itself.

In Kingston, in addition to several public wharves, each moderately rich commercial house has its own wharf annexed to its warehouses, located for the most part on the seacoast. All these wharves are made of wood over pilings and are therefore inexpensive and easily repaired. I counted as many as forty of this kind. Vessels of 200 tons burden and greater can come alongside them. This convenience together with good capstans enable the vessels to load and unload with indescribable speed. I myself saw a convoy of 250 sails load in three days, and all that haste was needed so as not to give time for news of its departure to be carried to the enemy colonies who could send forces to intercept it.

Although, as has been seen, the commerce of the English colonies enjoys as much freedom and protection as seemed compatible with their dependency, there are certain points in which their inhabitants appear to be less than satisfied with the provisions of the British Parliament. Such are, for example, those that discourage the bleaching and refining of sugar, obliging the Jamaicans by an indirect but efficacious method to ship it in the state they call raw. A quintal of dark or brown sugar weighing 112 pounds pays today upon entrance into England only six shillings, two pence, the equivalent of about twenty-seven *reales vellon*, while the same amount of refined sugar pays four pounds, two shillings. These enormous duties with respect to refined sugar amount to an absolute prohibition established in favor of the refiners of the mother country.

It is true that, like all the resolutions relating to the trade of the colonies, those duties were inspired by the preponderance of merchants in the House of Commons, which became more favorable to the merchants than to the colonists and in not a few cases sacrificed the progress of overseas dominions and even the general good of the nation to the spirit of commercialism. If all the provisions issued by England in behalf of her colonies are examined in the light of reflection, it will be found that in the last analysis the principal purpose was not to foster the colonies as much as to secure in them a profitable monopoly for her merchants. Despite its destructive tendency, this policy has retarded but has not been able to impede the prosperity of the colonies, because in newly settled countries as fertile as those in the New World each small stimulus they receive produces gains so considerable that in the end the pernicious influence of restrictions is nullified.

Indeed, restrictions have been even less effective in English settlements than in the others of the New World, because the immense extent of trade of their mother country, the soundness of its factories, and the enormous amounts of capital that industry and navigation concentrated in England all make it impossible for the wealth of the center not to be reflected to the ends of the British Empire.

The value of the European goods that are brought from England to Jamaica corresponds, with little difference, to the value of the produce of the island and to that of the contraband trade that it carries on with Spanish and French possessions. This will be discussed later. Consequently it is calculated that in an average year it amounts to eleven to twelve million pesos fuertes, the greater part of which proceeds from the articles already mentioned and the rest from the silver and gold furtively removed from Spanish dominions. In spite of these rich returns, the inhabitants of the island owe great sums of money to the people of the mother country because of the large advance payments that have been sent from time to time to Jamaica for its development. However, this debt is smaller in Jamaica than in other New World settlements, for the reason that many of the large plantations belong to citizens of the mother country, who supply all necessities at their own expense, and also because of the rich colonists who pay their debts promptly. These two circumstances have in part freed this colony from the heavy yoke of usury with which the merchants in other dominions oppress the farmers and do not allow them to prosper.

This trade annually involves 60,000 tons distributed in more than 300 ships of different burdens. Some say that the tonnage amounts to 100,000, and in fact that has happened on extraordinary occasions, but after a detailed investigation I came to the conclusion that in any ordinary year 100,000 is an exaggeration.

Contraband Trade

It is sad to have to report violation of the law by people who live amidst fortunate surroundings. But the fact is that not only has Jamaica become rich by legal trade but that contraband trade with the Spaniards has also contributed to its wealth.

Smuggling reached its zenith at the beginning of this century as a result of the *Asiento de Negros* and because British domination was introduced on the coasts of Guatemala and Campeche, but for some years it has declined rapidly, being at present reduced to one-third of what it was then. The persons best informed about the trade of the island assure me that at that time the annual income from smuggling amounted to, or exceeded, four million pesos and that today it probably reaches hardly one and one-half million.

This decline results from several causes. In the opinion of the experts one of the principal causes is the freedom of trade with the islands of Cuba, Santo Domingo, and Puerto Rico granted in the year 1765 and later extended to all Spanish America.[62] They believe that the fraud would be much less if certain kinds of foreign manufactured goods that are consumed in great quantity in our possessions, and are simply not to be found in our factories, were not prohibited; these are printed fabrics, silk stockings, threads, and china, articles to which almost all the illicit trade of Jamaica is now limited.

It is worthwhile to reflect that this island has enjoyed its greatest growth since the time when contraband trade with the Spaniards began to decline. This fact, which appears inexplicable at first glance, conforms with the most solid principles of the science of economics and demonstrates that capital employed in illicit trade, although it momentarily produces astonishing profits, suffers such enormous losses that in the long run it contributes much less to public prosperity than would the same capital if it were invested in any kind of legitimate trade or industry. So it happens that the rich inhabitants of Jamaica, convinced of these ideas by long experience, finally abandoned a risky and hazardous though lucrative traffic, in which many were the victims of their greed; instead they devoted themselves exclusively to the sound labors of agriculture and the untroubled trade with their mother country.

---

62. After the British occupation of Havana (1762), Spain, in view of the English control of the Antilles, decreed the abolition of annoying formalities, lowered imports, and established a maritime mail system with the purpose of favoring insular trade. [Ed.]

Contraband Trade

Indeed there are today few reputable traders on this island who permit themselves to be seduced by the chimerical profits of clandestine trade, and the Jews, especially the less rich ones, are the only ones who perpetuate it.

There is also considerable illegal traffic with the French colony on the island of Santo Domingo, and over this practice there exists a certain tolerance on both sides which almost places it in the order of legal commerce. The English bring into Guarico flour, Negroes, and Asiatic goods and take out in turn wine, tea, indigo, and some manufactured articles of luxury. In this contraband trade profit and loss are reciprocal, and if the balance of profit tips a bit toward one side, it is to the side of the French.

By one of the many contradictions that are produced by political egoism, no nation has shown itself to be as rigorous as the English against contraband trade that could damage it, and none has sustained with more unjust tenacity contraband trade that could be profitable to it. One cannot read without horror of the severe punishments with which the English government has endeavored to restrain the fraudulent exportation of certain articles and the importation of others. At diverse times exporters of wool were punished by death or by mutilation of the left hand or at least by perpetual exile and the total confiscation of their properties. Fortunately, these punishments, like all those not proportionate to the intrinsic gravity of the crimes, have rarely been enforced, but they demonstrate the bitter zeal with which Great Britain has always defended the laws of her commerce and industry, whether well or badly calculated.

Amidst this severity, and despite the reciprocal justice that nations owe to each other, the English nation has openly authorized affronts to other nations. She has maintained costly settlements on Tierra Firme and its environs that could serve only as a support for the fraud of her subjects; she formerly sustained by force of arms and with the protection of her Royal Navy the clandestine trade that the English of Jamaica conducted with Spanish dominions, and if she does not do the same today, it is due to the propagation of information about the economy that has disabused the trading nations of the idea that contraband is a sure road to riches.

Industry

If England has been more liberal than other nations on various points in which her prosperity was inseparable from that of her colonies, she has on the contrary shown herself to be more restrictive than any other in all branches in which this identity of interest did not exist. All the benefits of the English system go to those products of the Indies that come from the hand of Nature without the intervention of any labor except what is necessary to prepare them for exportation. Any finishing or subsequent manufacture has been proscribed with all the avarice inspired by commercial jealousies. We have seen how with an enormous increase of taxes they have discouraged in their islands the bleaching and refining of sugar. Mills for the fabrication of all kinds of textiles, and even mills for manufacturing iron, steel, and any other metal, are absolutely forbidden. It can be stated with certainty that in Jamaica, and it happens in the other English islands as well, only those crafts without which the simplest society cannot subsist are permitted. Everything is brought from the mother country: worked silver, ready-made clothing, boots, ladies' fashions, furniture of every kind, and even the wooden houses in which the people live.

Other nations have been more generous with their New World dominions in this regard, and most of all the Spanish nation, in whose possessions every kind of craft for the making of necessities and even luxuries is permitted and encouraged. This freedom is so extensive that in the realms of New Spain, Santa Fé, and Peru there are commonly many factories with substantial output that satisfy a great part of their needs and deprive Spanish commerce of some markets of quickest sale and greatest profit. This is a part of a truth about which perhaps I shall speak more fully in the course of this journal—that is to say, that the Spanish government has treated its colonies more liberally than has any other European government, although the very immensity and dispersion of its colonies, and many other

Industry in Jamaica

causes, have frustrated in practice the effects of its good intentions.

If then we understand by the word *industry*, as commonly used, that aggregate of factories, crafts, and mechanical arts that are confined to cities and can properly be called urban industry, there is no doubt that in Jamaica it has made very little progress; to express it better, in Jamaica it has depended, and now depends totally, upon the industry of the mother country. But if we limit ourselves to speaking about rural industry—that is, about the efficacious aids that the application of the arts and sciences lends to the cultivation and preparation of the arts and skills both practical and theoretical that today constitute the rustic economy of the colonies—we shall in general point out enough to make intelligible how the English have succeeded in taking out of the small lands of their American islands, many of them unproductive, the abundant wealth of productions that has been mentioned.

When the work of the fields is directed by a blind routine and left to the stupidity of day laborers, it cannot be thought of as dependent on the arts and sciences, and its advancements are slow and incidental. Imbued with this truth, the inhabitants of Jamaica have for a century made a profound study of agriculture; they look upon it as a difficult and complicated science, they inform themselves about all the branches of physics that are related to it, they make frequent experiments in the quality of the lands, the different strata that constitute them, and the kind of culture that each crop requires. Thus they have rendered fruitful terrain that seemed sterile and have perpetuated the fertility of other land which by the law of nature ought to have been already totally exhausted. Observation and analysis have taught them to correct the luxuriant fertility of certain places, refining the dense or grossly abundant soil[63] of some lands, and invigorating the slow vegetation of others; now by means of moisture, now by the free circulation of air, the two most powerful agents of plant life, now with an opportune mixture of sand, loam, and clay, the kinds of soil that compose the superficial

---

63. Saavedra says *sucos*, which means muddy soil. [Ed.]

layer of the American islands. It would be never-ending to enumerate all the recourses that art, study, and thought have taught the good farmers of Jamaica, to enable them take out of their fields all the profit that nature aided by industry can yield.

An unvarying observation repeated by many learned men is that variations of the barometer are almost imperceptible in all lands of the torrid zone that have only a slight elevation above sea level, and that there the utility of the land and the density of the atmosphere are almost uniform. As a result, only those fruits native to subtropical regions can be cultivated in the plains, and generally in the Indies islands the lowlands are devoted to the production of sugarcane. But in proportion as the land rises above sea level, the atmosphere becomes rarefied, the barometer varies, and the earth lends itself to the production of other crops that appear to belong to different climes.

To take advantage of this diversity of temperatures so as to adapt to each the crops that correspond to it is the work of a very refined agriculture, and in this regard the efforts of the settlers of Jamaica are so much more admirable inasmuch as the mountains in the regions of the torrid zone are more resistant to cultivation than in other parts of the globe. In Jamaica, and almost the same is true of the other islands and many places on the American continent, the terrain near the sea, and at times in the interior, is extended in spacious prairies and then suddenly is interrupted and broken by high and rugged mountains, out of which during the rainy season fall fierce torrents, which carry off the whole layer of topsoil and leave exposed the armature of living rock that forms the skeleton of our globe.

Two peculiar causes make these effects more forcible there than in any part of the Old World: the first is that the rains are more violent; the second, that the soil is more friable. As long as the hills remain uncultivated, the impenetrable density of underbrush and thickets resists the action of the water, or when it causes some damage, the leaves and fragments of the plants quickly repair the ravages. But as soon as the land is cleared and the soil broken up and separated by cultivation, the water, not encountering any obstacle to contain its violence, carries off in a short time the vegetative and fruitful crust, injuring the terrain to the point of rendering it useless.

Against this powerful effect of the physical nature of the land, the settlers of Jamaica have set up all the recourses of ingenuity, skillfully fighting against a harsh and obstinate nature and defeating it by dint of the most incessant activity. Emulating the Creator, they have prescribed limits to the rivers, confining them to determined and precise beds; they have corrected the sterility of a worn-out and exhausted soil by covering it with soil carted from afar. In these ways they have succeeded in filling, with luxuriant plantations of coffee, cotton, corn, and other plants, the gently sloping hills and even those that appeared to be so rugged as to be intractable. They have transplanted to the tropics the fruits, vegetables, flowers, and other products of the temperate zone and have converted into healthful and pleasant orchards and gardens the briery woods that since Creation have remained impenetrable to the rays of the sun and, surrounded by a pestilent and deadly atmosphere, had turned away all efforts of human industry.

But in order to achieve a flourishing agriculture, it is not enough to prepare and fertilize the land, obliging it to repay with interest the sweat of the farmer. It is necessary later to prepare the produce either for immediate use or for faraway trade, and indeed the most valuable products of the Indies require a particularly careful preparation before they can be consumed or shipped. The cost of this finishing would enormously increase the price of this produce, making it unsalable, if the settlers had not found methods of economizing the costly work of men and animals, either by taking advantage of the resources of nature or by availing themselves of the help of machinery.

In Jamaica more than half of the sugar mills are run by water power, and only in mills that have not found a way to avoid it are animals used for the purpose. Lately they have devised windmills for grinding the cane, and at present they are experimenting with them, although I was not able to ascertain exactly the result of an investment whose profitability is still regarded as problematical. In the same category must be placed the application of steam engines to the operation of sugar mills, about which some articles have been written recently; I do not know whether they have also conducted any experiments.

Since the ninth and tenth centuries, when the Arabs brought the cultivation of sugar to Spain, among other branches of oriental skills, not one single step has been taken toward perfecting the production of an article that custom and caprice were imperceptibly converting into a staple commodity. All the machines and tools employed in the preparation of sugar passed from the coast of Granada to the Canary Islands, and from the Canaries[64] to the Indies in the same condition in which Spain had received them from Arabia. The sugar mill consisted, as originally, of three round wooden presses or logs which, no matter how hard they were when they began to compress the cane, successively diminished their pressure as the cylindrical shape was lost. The animals that put into motion the sugar mill were placed on the same level on which the mill was set and pulled on an inclined line, the pulling losing its force as it departed from the horizontal plane. The juice from the cane was cooked and purified on ordinary stoves after it had been pressed out of the cane. The wood fire increased notably the cost of the operation. After the sugar coagulated, it was dried by the sun, spread out in great patios and exposed to damage and loss caused by rain.

After having learned the cultivation of sugar along with the other products of America from the Spanish, the English and French, after imitating them for a long time without any particular progress, have in the past few years made considerable improvements in the handling of this and other crops. This was an inevitable result of the great advances made in the two nations in the natural and exact sciences, whose beneficent

---

64. From the Canary Islands came pigs, bananas, sugarcane, and the first techniques for the sugar industry (G. Fernández de Oviedo, *Historia General y Natural de las Indias*, bk. 4, chap. 8, bk. 8, chap. 1). [Ed.]

The Sugar Industry

influence has spread to the whole sphere of the accomplishments and operations of human industry. Guarico and Jamaica are the two colonies that claim the inventions and the perfection of their uses.

In the sugar mills the wooden presses were converted into cylinders of iron or bronze, some smooth and others fluted or grooved, but so well proportioned that while the compression is increased by the accuracy of the form, it is at the same time made more permanent by the hardness of the material. Around the sugar mill and at a proportionate distance they contrived to raise a circular plane three or four yards high and wide enough so that from it the animals that move the machinery can pull it on an almost horizontal line. To cook and purify the syrup, they invented what they call smelting stoves, which are fed with only the bagasse or residue of the cane left after the pressing, and they avoid the expense of wood, which is so important that it is calculated to amount to almost one-eighth of the total value of the crop. They dry the sugar in chambers constructed for the purpose with such skill that they gradually provide the precise heat for perfection of the operation. They have also invented very good machines for the extraction of *aguardiente* and rum, for the cutting and baling of cotton, and for many other uses which it would be too tedious to mention. In short, physics, chemistry, mechanics, and other practical and experimental sciences have contributed with their inventions to the perfection of the economy and the efficiency of rural operations in the colonies referred to above, uniting for their development the latest efforts of human reason with the primary purpose which the Creator of Nature made known to man.

Royal Revenues

Among the European possessions in the New World only those of the Spanish and Portuguese have contributed immediately to enlarge the public treasuries of their respective metropolises, aiding them in peacetime with sums of money more than sufficient to defray expenditures made on their behalf and maintaining in wartime the great armaments needed for their defense. The other nations have required of their colonies only the necessary costs of sustaining their civil governments and the small military establishments calculated as indispensable for their domestic tranquillity.

This was the case of the English islands and the English settlements on the American continent. Although Great Britain proposed as her objectives in the two wars begun in 1739 and 1755—to maintain the contraband trade that the Jamaicans practiced with the Spanish dominions in the first, and to extend the boundaries of her northern colonies at the expense of the possessions of France in the second—the immense expenditures laid out in the wars were entirely from the revenues of the mother country; for this reason her national debt spread beyond 300,000 pesos fuertes, without her colonies having contributed one single real toward the repayment of so enormous a sum, or even the interest on it. From this practice arises the fact that taxes in the English settlements in America are so low that they do not even equal the tithe that is paid to the Church in Spanish and Portuguese colonies and make up only a small portion of their public contributions. Sound proof of this is that the northern English colonies, composed of thirteen large provinces and a population of three million, paid, before the turbulence that now agitates them, less than £100,000 sterling with which all the costs of their government were defrayed.

Seen from this angle, the English system has been more beneficent to the colonies than that of the other nations mentioned; but considered relative to the whole British Empire, it has lacked the distributive justice that characterizes the provisions of a wise government. In the final analysis, their system has sacrificed immense wealth and burdened all classes of the state with the weight of an intolerable debt, not in order to develop their colonies, as it appears at first glance, but in order to assure in them a profitable monopoly for British merchants.

When the Peace of Paris was concluded in 1763, England realized the extent and the imprudence of a loss that no longer concealed the false hopes of the triumphs she had just purchased so dearly. She tried to correct then the political error she had committed in the beginning and to make all parts of the English Empire sustain proportionately a burden that up to that time had been distributed with so much inequality. She began to try this new system in her northern colonies. They naturally resisted an innovation that they considered contrary to their rights. The English Parliament resorted to force in order to support a measure that was considered equitable but that had been decided upon late, and this conflict of interests, maintained on the one side with all the constancy that the desire for independence inspires and handled by the other side with more heat than polity, was the true origin of the shaking off of the yoke of British domination by the Anglo-Americans and of the present war which, whatever its outcome, will certainly cost England more than any previous one.

Jamaica, in the matter of taxes, remained as it always had been. These taxes include only those necessary to support the civil government on the island, a small military establishment adapted more to domestic police duty than to defense, and some public works of common utility. In a calculation made over a period of five years, from 1770 to 1775, the taxes do not exceed 200,000 pesos fuertes in an average year.

These sums are voted annually in the parliament or general assembly of the island, which at the same time distributes them for the purposes designated, trying to arrange always that they weigh as lightly as possible on agriculture, commerce, and articles of primary necessity. Generally this means taxes on houses, on articles of pure luxury, and on imported foreign beverages, to which is generally added a light head tax on Negroes, which in extraordinary cases is doubled or tripled. For each of the nineteen parishes of the island the parliament names a tax collector, who collects these public contributions with the premium of 2 percent for his work and responsibility. He remits them to the receiver or treasurer general, who is always in Spanish Town and is paid 5 percent of all the money he administers.

Although England herself supplies the costs of the protection and defense of her colonies, on certain important occasions the colonies contribute voluntarily so as to mitigate in part this heavy expense to the mother country. For example, an assessment was levied among the rich citizens of Jamaica to defray the costs of the expedition to Lake Nicaragua which amounted to £100,000 sterling, and they also contributed large sums for the repair and enlargement of the fortifications of Kingston.

The taxes mentioned above are not always paid in specie but often are paid in paper currency. For comprehension of this circumstance peculiar to the economic system of the Indies, one must explain in a separate article how, not having mines, and coins not entering the colonies from the mother country, they contrive the supply of money or currency indispensable to the circulation of funds.

1 January 1781

Until this day there was not available any ship that could take me to Spanish territory. Finally, by paying well for it, I was able to persuade a French flag-of-truce ship to carry me to one of the ports on the southern coast of the Island of Cuba. My passage being assured, I solicited my passport from the governor and the commissioner of prisoners. I said farewell to Cartas and González, who planned to depart on the ship which Mr. Burke was preparing. With two ecclesiastics, the three officers from Nicaragua, and other prisoners, I embarked that same night on the French cartel ship, a very sorry looking brigantine. At midnight the man who was to serve as our harbor pilot swam out to the ship. He was one of the corsairs from Trinidad, who had managed to escape from prison.

2 January 1781

We set sail at dawn. As we passed in front of the battery of Port Royal, a launch came alongside with a naval officer who inspected the ship, examined the list of crew and passengers, and let us continue our voyage. The inspection was superficial; while it was in progress I was rather uneasy, fearing that they might discover our pilot, who was hidden in the ballast, and that we should be in a sad plight. It was almost calm that day, and we moved away from Jamaica very little.

3 January 1781

Before dawn the northeast breeze began to freshen, and it blew all day. We approached the Island of Cuba in the district of Trinidad at twilight. Not being able to put into the port before dark, we tacked back and forth until daybreak.

4 January 1781

At noon we cast anchor in the Río Guainabo, one league from Trinidad to the west. Don Bernardo Ogaban, one of the prisoners who was on the cartel ship and who knew the country, immediately sent a message to Don Manuel de Lara, tax collector of the area, informing him of our arrival. Lara instantly sent horses for all of us, gave us dinner in his house that evening, and found lodging for us to stay in while our journey to Havana was being arranged.

A slight indisposition detained me for ten days in Trinidad where, although I was well treated by the people, I had to endure the unavoidable discomfort of eating only cassava, because nothing else was available. I wondered whether to undertake the journey overland to Havana, ninety miles away by a bad and lonely road, or to go by sea to Batabanó, whence there is an overland route of only fourteen leagues to Havana. To save time and to escape the tropical heat to which I was not yet accustomed, I chose the latter course, which was not without danger and discomfort.[65]

16 January 1781

I embarked that night in an open launch, the only vessel I could charter for Batabanó. At eleven o'clock in the evening we put out to sea from the Río Guainabo. As far as the vicinity of the Bay of Jagua, a distance of some thirty leagues, the coastline is high and mostly precipitous. This passage is called Canarros, and the crosswinds there are dangerous. Besides the fact that the boat was uncomfortable, we were so crowded in it, the three of-

---

65. In what we call Version 3 of the diary there are annotations for January 5, 6, and 16, which do not pertain here. [Ed.]

ficers from Nicaragua, two servants, two seamen, and I, that we could not budge, and at every movement we feared the boat would capsize.

17 January 1781

At noon, unable to endure the sun, which was directly overhead, we put into a river called San Juan, ten leagues to windward of Jagua. It was deep enough for a brigantine, the water clear, the banks verdant. In the shade of some enormous cedars we tranquilly ate several fish caught by the seamen as we watched.

We set out again. Soon a deep calm descended which lasted until dawn, but with faint breezes and use of the oars we ran nine leagues.

18 January 1781

The first light of dawn brought a fair light wind, and at seven o'clock we were off the Bay of Jagua. Although the sun was very hot and the wind had moderated, I wanted to reach the entrance to see as well as possible one of the most beautiful and capacious ports that I believe there must be in the universe. Perhaps some time they will consider placing stocks for the construction of warships there, since in addition to its unalterable tranquillity, the bay has the advantage that the most enormous cedars moisten their branches in the sea around its whole circumference, which in my opinion is not less than four leagues. The forests are virgin, and they extend for vast distances inland; therefore the conveyance of wood to the bay would be cheap, whereas to bring wood into Havana is already expensive because of distances. The only inconvenience that the Bay of Jagua presents at first sight is the difficulty of fortifying it, because its mouth is open very wide.[66]

Once past this bay, in order not to encounter some corsair,

---

66. The present-day Bay of Cienfuegos is a great commercial port and the site of a naval base of the Revolutionary Navy. [Tr.]

we entered a labyrinth of keys and narrow channels accessible only to a boat such as ours, which did not draw three full feet of water. Not without reason they have given to this inland waterway the name of Los Jardines [The Gardens].[67] The keys are flat islands of land very little above sea level, full of verdure and leafy growth. They are innumerable, of various sizes, and the largest I saw was probably not more than two *varas* long. Between them are narrow channels of varying depth but never deeper than one fathom, and at times not two feet deep. They are scattered in picturesque formations: here, they form a second channel which looks like a deep river bordered by cool groves of poplar trees; there, they widen into an immense basin a league or more in diameter surrounded by leafy forests. The bottom is clean and clear, and one can see fish, which are abundant. We ran aground frequently, but because there was no danger, and by jumping into the water a man could free the boat at once. I considered it quite worthwhile as a way to see the most beautiful views a poetic fancy could imagine.

At twelve o'clock, already bothered by the heat, we landed on a key, where we prepared our meal. We spent two hours there, protected by the shade of thick branches, but not without considerable anxiety, because on other keys we had seen several crocodiles, a kind of lizard of a yellowish color. Although smaller than the alligator, to whose family they belong, they are swifter and more voracious. We proceeded that afternoon and throughout the night with a favorable light northeast wind.

19 January 1781

At dawn we caught sight of Batabanó, where we landed at eight o'clock in the morning. It is a kind of open beach with a good anchoring place but with no protection except the keys, which are to windward and leeward there, leaving the front clear. It has no more than ten feet of water. On the seashore is located a circular battery built of palm logs and sand, in which

---

67. "The Garden of the Queen" was what Columbus called a group of keys covered with green vegetation on his second voyage (1493). [Ed.]

are mounted six 12-caliber cannons. There was there at that time a detachment of fifty men of the Permanent Regiment of Havana. There is no town, large or small, in Batabanó, nor any building save a guardroom for the troop and a poor tavern where liquors and some foodstuffs are sold. We were lodged there that night and the following day because they had no horses ready to carry us to Havana; they had to go elsewhere to find them.

21 January 1781

We left Batabanó, rode eight leagues, and spent the night in some farm buildings.

22 January 1781

We reached Havana at midday on the twenty-second, but I remained until nightfall in the suburb of Christo, outside the walls of the stronghold, and at eight o'clock in the evening I went to see Don Bernardo de Gálvez.[68] He had already been notified by Madrid of my coming, and as he was unaware that the English had captured me, my tardiness had caused him anxiety. I related my adventures to him and explained the purpose of my journey; he reported to me the condition of

---

68. Bernardo de Gálvez (1746–86), nephew of José de Gálvez (the powerful minister of the Indies) and son of Matías de Gálvez (viceroy of New Spain), followed a military career, winning recognition in the war with Portugal and on the frontier of New Spain fighting against the Apache Indians (1769). He participated in the expedition of Algiers in 1775 and returned to New Orleans in 1776 as colonel of the Regiment of Cantabria. Appointed interim governor and captain general of Louisiana by a royal order of 19 September 1776, he took office on 1 January 1777 at the age of thirty-one, and was made permanent governor in July 1779. As governor of Louisiana he continued the assistance of the American patriots begun by his predecessor Luis de Unzaga y Amezaga. After receiving word in August 1779 of Spain's declaration of war, Gálvez captured three English posts on the Mississippi River—Manchac, Baton Rouge, and Natchez —and by the end of September he had achieved complete control of the lower Mississippi. His next objective was Mobile, which he took on 14 March 1780. [Ed.]

things there, and I described to him the method I proposed to follow for the accomplishment of my commission. This conference lasted until eleven o'clock in the evening, and as it was then too late to go to see the governor, I left that for the following day.

23 January 1781

At eight o'clock in the morning I called on the governor, who at that time was Don Diego Navarro.[69] He received me cordially and handed me a confidential letter from Madrid. It contained a duplicate of the credentials and the other confidential orders that I had thrown into the sea at the time of my capture. As the content of my credentials was merely to show who I was and the object of my journey, and to order that in the junta of general officers promotion was to be given to him whom I should name personally, by word of mouth, I was able to describe to the governor the situation in Europe, the sovereign's desire for them to operate more vigorously in the Indies, and the necessity for moving forward with the projects from Madrid. As the governor was well intentioned, although somewhat weakened by his great age, he manifested with the most animated expressions his fervent desires that the orders of His Majesty be complied with as promptly as possible.

Next I went to see Don Victor de Navia,[70] commanding general of the Army of Operations, Don Juan Bautista Bonet,[71] commandant of the Navy Department, Field Marshal

---

69. Diego José Navarro García de Valladores had had a distinguished military career before he succeeded the Marqués de la Torre as governor of Havana and captain general of the Island of Cuba in 1777.

70. Lieutenant General Victor de Navia, bringing an army of 7,000 men, left Cádiz for Havana in April 1780 in the fleet and convoy of Admiral José Solano. In Havana he commanded the expeditionary force called the Army of Operations. He was relieved of his command in February 1782 by a royal order and was succeeded by Juan Manuel de Cagigal.

71. Lieutenant General Juan Bautista Bonet, naval commandant at Havana, was accused of inaction and delay in furnishing the ships and reinforcements needed by Bernardo de Gálvez in order to proceed against Pensacola after his capture of Mobile. Bonet was reprimanded by the king

Don Juan Manuel de Cagigal,[72] and the fleet commanders, Don José Solano and Don Juan de Tomasco. With Don Bernardo de Gálvez they constituted the junta of general officers over which the governor presided, and Don Antonio del Valle, the secretary of the Havana government, acted as secretary.[73] Later I went to the house of the intendant of the army, Don Juan Ignazio de Urriza,[74] who told me that he had arranged lodging for me in the home of the treasurer of the army, Don Ignacio Peñalver, one of the richest individuals of the island and one of the most generous and benevolent persons I have known in my life.

At that time there was in Havana a French fleet, commanded by the Chevalier de Monteil,[75] composed of three 74-

---

(José de Gálvez to Diego José Navarro, 20 April 1780, AGI:SD 2082) and relieved of his command by royal order of 12 February 1783 (AGI:Ind. Gen. 1578). [Tr.]

72. Juan Manuel de Cagigal was born in Santiago de Cuba, the son of a Spanish army officer who was later viceroy of New Spain. Cagigal, a brigadier, took part in the siege of Gibraltar in 1779. He was sent from Cádiz to Havana with the Regiment of Navarra, which arrived in Havana in April 1780. In 1781 he served in the Pensacola expedition under Bernardo de Gálvez. On 12 February 1782 he was named governor of Havana and captain general of the Island of Cuba. In April–May 1782 he led an expedition against the Bahamas. He was succeeded in office by Luis de Unzaga on 29 December 1782, having been removed because of alleged complicity in the importation of contraband goods. He was cleared of the charges in Spain in 1799. [Tr.]

73. Antonio Ramón del Valle, captain of engineers, served as secretary of the government of Havana throughout the period of the American Revolution. Governor Navarro called him "my secretary for confidential matters," and it was del Valle to whom all reports regarding expenses and shipping were sent by the agents in Philadelphia, Juan de Miralles and Francisco Rendón (AGI:Cuba 1227, passim). [Tr.]

74. The efficiency and integrity of Juan Ignazio Urriza and his "honourable disposition of mind" are mentioned elsewhere in this journal, as is the importance to the allied cause of the confidence and trust that the people of Havana had in him. [Tr.]

75. The Chevalier de Monteil had come to the West Indies with a fleet and convoy that left Brest in early February 1780 under the command of the Comte de Guichen and arrived at Martinique on 22 March. De

23 January 1781

gun warships named *Palmier, Destin,* and *Intrépide;* the 60-gun warship *Triton;* the frigates *Andromaque* and *Licorne* with 36 and 22 guns, respectively; the 14-gun brigantine *Levrette;* and the 18-gun cutter *Serpent*. This fleet had come to Havana in fulfillment of a promise made to us by France to place at our disposition for the defense of our possessions four ships-of-the-line and a regiment of troops,[76] who were already in Spanish Santo Domingo. The warship *Palmier* was being careened, and the *Intrépide* was being prepared for careening. The frigates and the cutter were cruising off Cape San Antonio. I went that same afternoon to see the Chevalier de Monteil and had a long conversation with him relative to the operations of the war and to conditions there. Later I went to pay my respects to the Reverend Bishop,[77] having been told that he was in a village called San Juan, two leagues from there, and on the following day he wrote me a letter filled with cordial sentiments.

My primary concern was to inform myself fundamentally about the condition of our land and sea forces, the amounts of money on which they could rely, and the current state of their preparations.

The army numbered fewer than 4,000 men, including the corps that could be added from the garrison of Havana. The convoy commanded by Don José Solano had suffered greatly, both from the long voyage and from the crowded conditions in which the men were distributed in the ships, the scant quantity and poor quality of the food, and the greed of the merchants who, in order to have more space in which to load their merchandise unrestrictedly, had shipped a niggardly sup-

---

Guichen proceeded in August to the French Cape with 2,000 troops for use by the Spaniards. He left the cape in mid-August with orders for Cádiz, leaving behind nine ships-of-the-line with Commodore the Chevalier de Monteil, who had brought four warships, two frigates, and three smaller vessels to Havana. [Tr.]

76. In 1779 Spain joined France in a family pact of anti-British policies and support for the North American rebel colonies. [Ed.]

77. Santiago José Echevarría y Elguzúa, bishop of Santiago de Cuba. See Michael V. Gannon, *The Cross in the Sand* (Gainesville: University of Florida Press, 1967), 89.

CARTA ESATTA
rappresentante l'
ISOLA di CUBA
estratta dalle Carte
del Sig.r Poppler

ISOLE DI BAHAMA O LUCAYOS

PASSO SOPRA VENTO

GIAMMAICA

ply of water. There were many soldiers and not a few sailors. The army reached Havana sick and greatly diminished in numbers, in August, that is, in the rainy season and in subtropical heat. There were no quarters in which to place the men. It was necessary for them to be piled into the vaults of the narrow and poorly ventilated fortifications, and as these fell far short of containing all of them, it was decided to build a kind of covered barracks or sheds on the parade ground, a humid place and therefore [no] more healthful. With several corps housed there, violent outbreaks of dysentery, putrid fevers, and other illnesses began to occur and in a short time carried off great numbers of men.

This calamity could not be cut short until the army resorted to lodging the men in the dry, spacious, and well-ventilated cloisters of the convents. All of the religious communities offered their comforts for the relief of the army, and they even contributed insofar as they were able to care for the men.

Neither were there hospitals in Havana to treat so many patients. The Belamites and the religious of San Juan de Dios took under their care as many as their infirmaries would hold, but it was necessary to use for the same purpose many private homes scattered throughout the town and its environs, where the care, being divided and necessarily little supervised, gave carte blanche to many abuses harmful to the men and the treasury.

Even when the troops arrive in America during the cool season, after a not particularly difficult voyage, their health is affected adversely, and it seems that much of this is due solely to the change in climate. What must have happened, then, when they were faced with a combination of casualties all lethal? Of about 7,000 men who left Cádiz, not 3,000 remained; furthermore, many staff officers had died, and it would have been impossible to undertake anything if the garrison of Havana, which was composed of two European regiments, one of them regularly based there and lacking its full complement, had not been robust, acclimated, and even experienced in warfare.

In the incidence of illnesses the fleet had suffered only a little less than the army. It had experienced many desertions, how-

23 January 1781

ever, so that 3,000 sailors were missing. The warships were very dirty, four of them were dismasted, all were in need of repair and some of careening. In the navy yard there were no masts, no military stores, not even pitch.

The army commanded by General Navía had brought only six siege guns, and these were exposed to the elements on wooden rollers on the beach below the Morro, because there was no covered area in which to protect them. It is a remarkable thing that in Havana, where from the year '63 more than 12 million pesos had been spent on fortifications, there should be neither quarters, nor hospital, nor armory even for artillery of medium capacity. The present century had censured Philip II for not having built one yard of paved road from Madrid to the Escorial, after having spent 12 million *ducados* on that monastery to which he used to go frequently, and for enduring the discomfort of being stuck in the mire almost every year.[78] I do not know how future centuries will judge the lack of quarters and hospitals in the most important stronghold of America, which requires 10,000 soldiers to garrison its forts.

According to information given me by the intendant, the Treasury of Havana was in very bad condition also. At the moment it did not have 1 million pesos on hand, and it owed debts of 3 million, of which at least enough to promise future profits must be repaid promptly, so as not to lose the public confidence. It is true that a little earlier the *flota*[79] had arrived from Veracruz carrying the funds that must go to Spain, probably about 4 million, but that was an inviolable deposit to

---

78. El Escorial (San Lorenzo del Escorial), a monastery, a palace, and the pantheon of Spanish kings, is fifty-seven kilometers from Madrid. It was built (1563–84) by Philip II to commemorate the victory over the French at San Quentin in 1557. [Tr.]

79. Fixed trade routes protected Spanish-American merchant vessels. In theory two fleets sailed from Spain every year. One of them, the New Spain fleet, or *flota*, sailed to Veracruz and from there to Havana for the return voyage to Spain. The flota of 1778 carried cargoes of indigo, copper, and grain, with silver worth some twenty-two million pesos. See Francisco de Solano, *Estrategia Española y Conflictividad en el Mar de las Antillas durante la Guerra de Independencia Norteamericana*, in *Cardinales de Dos Independencias* (Mexico: Fomento Cultural Banamex, A.C.,

which the treasury could not have recourse except in the direst need. Ever since they learned in Havana about the declaration of war, they had clamored there for funds from Mexico, but up to that time they had been sent only 1 million pesos for the navy and 700,000 for the army, and this is less than would have been adequate in time of the most widespread peace.

The store of food was scant also. In Veracruz there were great stores of packaged flour, vegetables, and meats, but the merchant vessels did not dare to bring them because of the danger of corsairs, and warships were few and slow and had many ports of call. The Anglo-Americans had supplied this need as much as possible, for in fewer than eight months they had brought to Havana in their light crafts as many as 100,000 barrels of food, but this was a precarious assistance which depended on the degree of vigilance of the English privateers. Moreover, thirty pesos had been paid for each barrel of flour, and in this way almost 3 million pesos had been exported to the Northern Colonies. If, seen from one point of view, this seems a bad thing, seen from another it contributed to the happy success of the North American Revolution, for this succor of money reached the colonies in circumstances so critical that without it their lack of specie and the discredit of their paper currency would perhaps have made it impossible for them to continue their resistance against the British forces.[80]

With so little money it had not been possible to make much progress in military operations in Havana. Nevertheless, in the month of October of last year the expedition against Pensacola had gone out, but on the third day after its departure

---

1978), 103. [Tr.]

80. Juan de Miralles, a native of Spain and a prosperous merchant established in Havana, was sent from Havana in December 1777 by Governor Diego José Navarro in fulfillment of a royal order to observe the activities of the Continental Congress and the progress of the war. He and his successor, Francisco Rendón, sent cargoes of food and naval stores as an excuse to remit reports. Temporary licenses were granted permitting the regular importation of foodstuffs from the United States. These regula-

from Havana, it had been frustrated by a great hurricane which overtook and scattered fleet and convoy and dismasted four warships. Many of the vessels returned laboriously to Havana, others went to Campeche, some to Louisiana, one 36-gun frigate was dashed to pieces on the coast of Yucatán, two transports perished on the coasts of the savage Indians. The Pensacola expedition was not executed until five months later, and when I arrived in Havana the preparation for it was well under way; but, as will be seen later, the land and sea forces assigned to it were very disproportionate to the forces with which Pensacola could oppose it.

The flota was being made ready to go out for Spain, but they were only beginning to load merchantmen; opinions as to the time of its departure were divided, because it had not been decided how many ships from the fleet would escort it and because the orders from Madrid were difficult to understand.

The governor of Guatemala, attacked by the English in Nicaragua and threatened in other areas, was begging for an urgent reinforcement of ships and troops. Some assistance of food and money had already been sent to him, but it was inadequate to supply his needs.

There was disagreement between the general of the land forces and the naval commandant, and among the general officers of each service, as could not fail to happen where each chief, seeing that the projects are superior to the means, argues in favor of the enterprise to which his personal glory is linked. The general of the army wished to have under his orders the greatest possible force in order to execute the attack on Jamaica, if the arrival of the reinforcements promised by Madrid and Paris made it possible to employ them in that enter-

---

tions were in effect until January 1784, when they were abrogated by Spain. Trade between the United States and Cuba helped not only to supply the Spanish and French armed forces but provided virtually the only currency in specie obtained in the North American colonies before the arrival of Rochambeau's French army in July 1780 (Francisco Rendón to José de Gálvez, 1 May 1784. AGI:Cuba 1354). [Tr.] [See also James A. Lewis, "Nueva España y los esfuerzos para abastecer La Habana, 1779–1783," *Anuario de Estudios Americanos* 33 (1976):501–26.]

prise. Don Bernardo de Gálvez sought to take to Pensacola a force great enough to prevent endangering the success of an expedition that would decide his fortune and the fame he expected to win from his sponsors and rivals. The governor of Havana was unwilling to acquiesce to any plan that would leave inadequately garrisoned the important post he commanded. The commandant of the Navy Department was inclined to conceal the bad condition of the ships and the impoverished state of the arsenal and did not want the expeditionary force to exceed a size proportionate to his facilities. The generals who had to command the fleet in any enterprise wished to go into action promptly with the greatest possible number of warships.

In this situation, neither could the interests of all be reconciled, nor could the various projects from Madrid be considered to be practicable at the same time, nor was it possible to execute them successively within the same year. In the subtropics of America a campaign season begins in November and ends in May, when the season of rains, storms, and illnesses begins. It was already January. For execution of the Pensacola expedition, even if it were to go out that very day, three long months would be required for the departure, the duration, and the return. The voyage from Havana to any Windward port where we must be based in order to attack Jamaica would require one month. According to the most trustworthy sources, the forces with which the French were to assist us could not be in America until June. The reinforcements we were expecting from Cádiz would be delayed even longer. In this situation it was indispensable that our plans for the year be limited to the most urgent and most feasible operations, such as the already prepared expedition against Pensacola, the reinforcement of Guatemala, which could not be postponed, and the dispatch of the fleet with the funds that were so anxiously awaited in Spain. The Jamaica expedition must necessarily be left for the following campaign, and I proposed to go to Mexico in the interval to solicit the necessary funds.

This plan was the most judicious and indeed the only one permitted by the circumstances. The difficulty lay in its being made acceptable to the generals who, not having to take part in

23 January 1781

the Pensacola expedition, would have to remain idle, to their displeasure, until the next campaign. On the whole it seemed to me that I ought to proceed to initiate preparations for all land and sea forces to be made ready at once to go to be based in the Windward Islands, so as to be ready to begin the attack on Jamaica as soon as the season made that possible, maintaining in the meantime a state of readiness with respect to the English, so that they could not undertake any attempt against our possessions.

Unfortunately, Havana, which had been made the center of our forces, is not suitable because of its geographical location for waging an offensive action against the English islands in time of war; it can only defend the Gulf of Mexico. Although we have many possessions to windward, none has the capacity to receive a considerable expeditionary force. Therefore our court had chosen Guarico as the port of rendezvous for the Jamaica enterprise.

It was indispensable also, in order to avoid the perplexity and procrastination that produce discord, that I gain for myself the goodwill of the general officers, not with artifices or intrigues, whose natural result is distrust, but with a frank and impartial policy.

Such was the plan of conduct I proposed for myself, after having learned, with the exactitude permitted by the pressure of time, about the state of things there and having talked about them frankly with each chief individually.

31 January 1781

On this day the governor summoned me to his house to tell me that he was going to call a junta of general officers for the next day and that I should make my presentation in it as we had agreed. He discussed with me which seat I should occupy in the junta, and I said any seat the members might assign to me, that I should never argue about protocol and should be honored to occupy any place, even the last, in so distinguished a gathering.

NOVA HISPANIA,
NOVA GALICIA,
GVATIMALA.

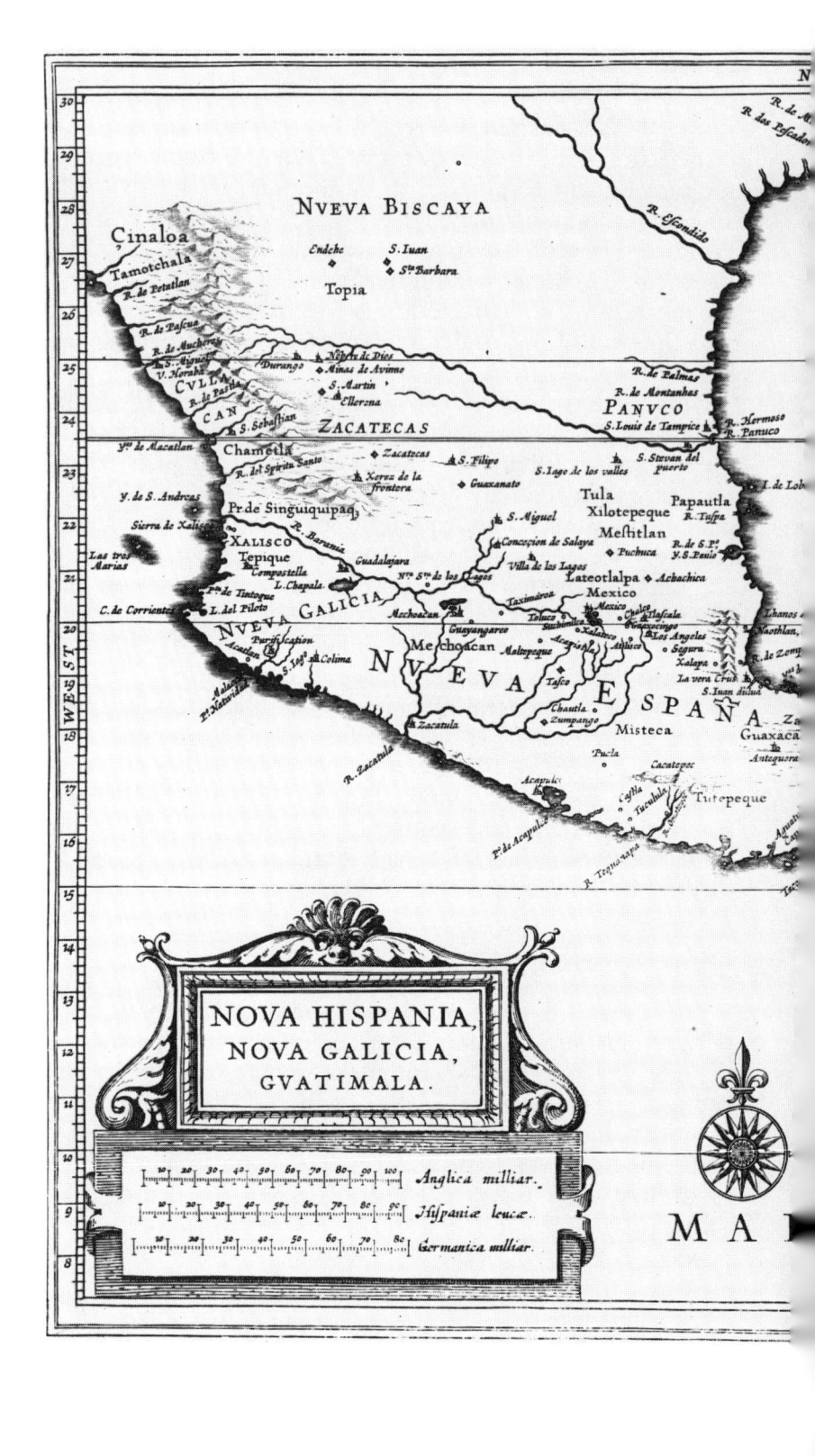

Map

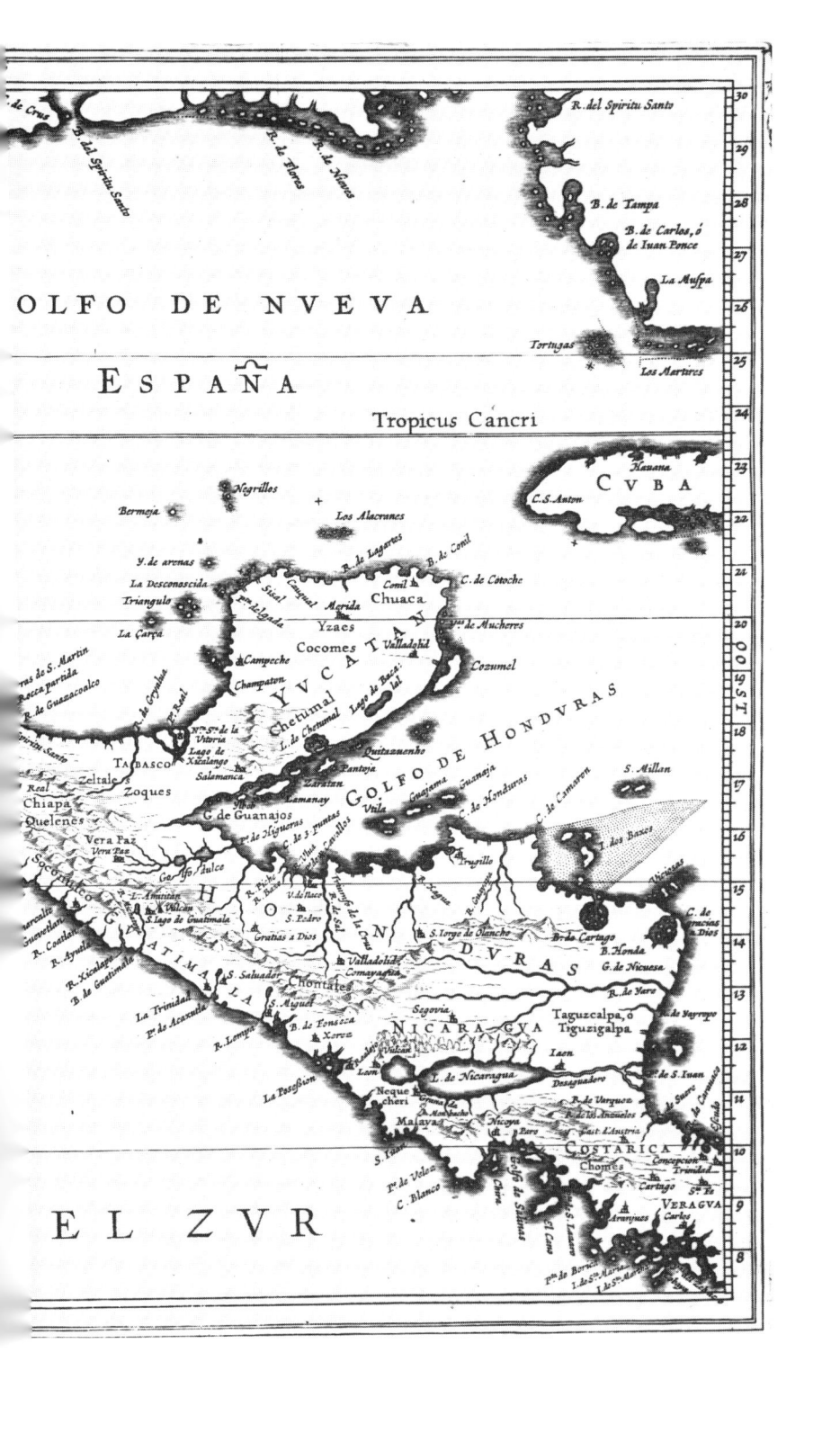

Golfo de Nueva España · *Tropicus Cancri* · *El Zur*

Labels visible on the map include: R. del Spiritu Santo, B. de Tampa, B. de Carlos ó de Iuan Ponce, La Aufpa, Tortugas, Los Martires, Havana, C. S. Anton, Cuba, Negrillos, Bermeja, Los Alacranes, Y. de arenas, La Desconoscida, Triangulo, La Garça, R. de Lagartos, B. de Conil, C. de Cotoche, Sisal, P.ta de Mucheres, Chuaca, Merida, Yzaes, Cocomes, Valladolid, Cozumel, Campeche, Champaton, Yucatan, Chetumal, L. de Chetumal, Golfo de Honduras, Tras de S. Martin, Boca partida, R. de Guazacoalco, R. de Coyuba, N.S.ra de la Vitoria, Lago de Xicalango, Salamanca, Tabasco, Zeltales, Zoques, Real, Chiapa, Quelenes, Vera Paz, Socomlco, Suchitepec, Xicalapa, Ayutla, R. Xicalapa, B. de Guatimala, Golfo Dulce, L. Amatitan, Vulcan, S. Lago de Guatimala, Gratias a Dios, Guatimala, La Trinidad, P.to de Acaxutla, S. Saluador, S. Miguel, B. de Fonseca, Xerez, R. Lempa, La Poseßion, Neque cheri, Malaya, S. Iuan, P.to de Velas, C. Blanco, G. de Guanajos, P.ta de Higueras, Lamanay, Pantoja, Zaratan, Quitzaneneho, Honduras, V. de Nacos, R. Piche, S. Pedro, Pexenge de la Cra, Comayagua, Valladolid, Chontales, Segovia, Nicaragua, Iaen, Leon, L. de Nicaragua, Desaguadero, Nicoya, Golfo de Salinas, El Caño, Guajara, Vtila, C. de Honduras, Trujillo, S. Iorge de Olancho, B.a de Cartago, B. Honda, G. de Nicuesa, R. de Yare, Taguzcalpa ó Tiguzigalpa, R. de Verguca, Past. d'Austria, Costarica, Cartago, Chomes, Concepcion, Trinidad, S.ta Fe, Veragua, Carlos, Aranjuez, P.to de Borica, I. de S.ta Maria, S. Millan, los Baxos, S. Camaron, C. Camaron, C. de Gracias a Dios, P.to de S. Iuan, R. de los Angeles.

1 February 1781

The junta met, the governor read my order of credentials,[81] I was invited to enter, and they gave me a seat between Señor Navía and Naval Commandant Bonet. I told the members that the king desired the operations of the war to be executed with the greatest vigor, as the only means of achieving a prompt and advantageous peace, and that those operations be limited to the four principal ones: (1) the attack on Pensacola so as to close the Gulf of Mexico to the enemy, (2) aid to the president of Guatemala to enable him to dislodge the enemy from the lands they had occupied on the coasts of that province, (3) dispatch of the fleet to Cádiz so that it would be in the Azores Islands by the time when, according to royal orders, the combined fleets of France and Spain would be awaiting it there, and (4) stationing our army and naval forces on the French Cape, as Madrid advised, in order to attack Jamaica after meeting with the French wherever the circumstances demanded.

All the voters said they were ready to execute the royal intention, but that because the basis of all the enterprises must be a knowledge of the forces and supplies that could be counted on for their execution, they agreed that the commanding generals of the army and navy should give a report, each for his own department, of the number of troops, crews, and ships that could be assigned for these objectives, and that at the same time the intendants of the army and navy be asked to give a report of the foodstuffs they could provide, in order to make an accurate calculation of what could be undertaken.

Then the present state of the preparations for the expedition against Pensacola was discussed. The generals wrangled over what maritime forces the expedition ought to take. I reminded the junta that from very recent intelligence it was known that there had gone out from Jamaica, bound perhaps for the Gulf of Mexico, three 40-gun frigates and one 50-gun

---

81. José de Gálvez to the governor of Havana, 24 June 1780 (confidential), AGI:Ind. Gen. 1578. [Tr.]

1 February 1781

warship, that if the expedition carried no guard except the 36-gun frigate *Clara* and some other small armed vessel as had been decided, it would be going out recklessly, and I stated that I felt that the junta ought seriously to contemplate this point and its consequences. In fact, the matter was discussed for a long time, and in the end it was decided that the 64-gun warship *San Román* and the 36-gun frigate *Cecilia* should be added to the expedition. Bonet undertook to convey to their captains the corresponding order. With this the junta adjourned.[82]

2 February 1781

On the following day I went to see the intendant of the army. We talked about the provision of victuals for the expeditions contemplated, and he said he had on hand all the provisions needed for the troops to be sent against Pensacola and that with some difficulty he could further provide without delay enough food for 4,000 men for a period of three months. He explained to me in detail the poverty of the Treasury of Havana, the scant assistance that New Spain had sent, and the plans he had in mind for unforeseen emergencies. His principal resource rested on the confidence which the people of that country had in his trustworthiness, and he wanted to keep that confidence by repaying immediately, to the extent possible for him, the sums that those citizens had recently supplied to the treasury, even though it might be necessary tomorrow to borrow from them an equal or larger amount. This honorable disposition of mind of Intendant Urriza got us out of enormous difficulties on numerous occasions.

That afternoon I had a conference with Bonet about the condi-

---

82. In this junta Bernardo de Gálvez expressed his deep concern for Louisiana, particularly for Mobile. He asked that because of the news that three 40-gun British frigates had sailed from Jamaica bound for the Gulf of Mexico, and a report that the English had occupied Dauphin Island, the reinforcements for Mobile planned in a previous junta be convoyed by the warship *San Román* in addition to the two frigates destined for the convoy (Junta de Generales, La Habana, 1 February 1781. AGI:SD 2083 B). Gálvez's discourse in this junta is quoted by Medina Rojas, 659–60. [Tr.]

tion of the fleet. He assured me that he could not make ready more than twelve warships and some frigates but that these would be ready before the end of February.

3 February 1781

The junta met. In it were presented a report in which the intendant of the army set forth the provisions and money he could supply, and a similar report from the commandant of the navy. From them it was evident, among other things, that there was sufficient flour, but that because of the lack of ovens it was difficult to convert it in advance into hardtack as quickly as was necessary in order for it to be cold at the time of embarkation so as to prevent spoiling. Various methods for remedying this defect were proposed in the junta, among others that of making new ovens, and obtaining the assistance of the bakers who were on all of His Majesty's ships. I undertook to discuss the matter with Intendant Urriza.

Next there was a long deliberation about the number of warships that could be made ready. The naval commandant repeated what he had said earlier, that only twelve could be got ready. Solano and Tomasco insisted that, with various expedients, as many as fourteen could be prepared, but after a quarrelsome debate, nothing was decided.[83]

Later the junta resolved that in order better to conceal from the public the purpose for which the warships were being fitted out, the funds of the fleet recently come from Veracruz should be brought ashore. For that purpose, this precaution seemed useless to me, but it could cause little disadvantage to the departure of the fleet when it was ready, and it was prudent that all the warships be disencumbered in case any unforeseen incident might happen. The incident proved that a proper precaution had been taken for a chimerical purpose.

---

83. Saavedra to José de Gálvez, 16 February 1781. AGI:Ind. Gen. 1578. [Tr.]

4 February 1781

I discussed with the intendant the equipping of new ovens, and he agreed at once that if possible four ovens would be added to those already existing and that they would be placed in the country for supplying the army, while those already in the stronghold would supply the navy.

No doubt it causes surprise to see that in a town of so great a population and concurrence of visitors as Havana there should be a shortage of ovens for baking bread, but it arose from a simple cause. Among various expedients that were proposed for paying for the uniforms of the militia of that island, the system adopted was to limit the making of bread to a small number of individuals who, in return for this business, would undertake to pay for the said uniforms. The annual cost of the uniforms was 12,000 pesos. By this method eight or ten bakers were authorized to exercise an unlimited monopoly, so much the more intolerable because it was based on the most essential commodity. Those bakers were arbiters of the price of the flour controlled by the commerce with Spain, and no other person could buy flour; they were also the arbiters of the price of bread, of which they were the only purveyors.

Very quickly this company acquired enough wealth to be above the law, to become formidable to the leaders, and to find a way to practice with impunity every kind of abuse. They harassed merchants to such a degree that they stopped bringing grain to that port, causing Spain to lose one of the most important branches of her trade. This abuse opened wide the door to a new order of greater abuses, because it was then necessary to permit the bakers to buy grains from foreign colonies, and within the protection of this traffic contraband trade abounded unrestrained. The public always ate expensive bread, at a price unrelated to variations in the price of flour, calculated by the penurious speculations of eight greedy monopolists, and the number of ovens was reduced to precisely that needed for the scant daily provision. [See James A. Lewis, "Anglo-American Entrepreneurs in Havana: The Background and Significance of the Expulsion of 1784–1785," in *The North American Role in the Spanish Imperial Economy, 1760–1819,* edited by Jacques Barbier and Allan J. Kuethe (Manchester: Manchester University Press, 1984), pp. 112–14.]

This afternoon I took a stroll with Don Bernardo de Gálvez. We talked at length about the Pensacola expedition, and he confided to me his plan of attack, which seemed to me well coordinated. But I was always of the opinion that the forces he was counting on were not adequate for the purpose, as the troops taken out of Havana together with those to be brought from Louisiana and Mobile to join them did not amount to 3,000 men, while the English had in Pensacola a garrison of two regiments of veteran troops experienced in war and the assistance of many friendly Indian nations and could be reinforced from Jamaica from one day to the next. The general knew better than I the insufficiency of his resources, but in order not to delay the launching of the expedition he did not dare to request more troops. I promised him that after his departure I should solicit some reinforcement of men and war vessels, especially if it were conjectured that the English were sending reinforcements to the stronghold.

5 February 1781

On the fifth the governor sent for me to tell me that a junta was to be held on the following day. At the same time he begged me to see if I could pacify a controversy that had arisen between Don Victor de Navía and Don Bernardo de Gálvez. The latter wanted the detachment of army troops destined for the Pensacola expedition to be turned over to him as the commanding officer of that enterprise, which he was, so that he could review and distribute the men, because from the moment they were embarked he would not see them together again before confronting the enemy. Navía looked upon this as a rebuff to his own authority and position, that a person other than himself should exercise any act of command over the troops of his army. There occurred to me instantly a method of cutting short this dispute, but I did not speak of it for the moment, so that its good effects should not be prejudiced by certain people who were fanning the flames of the dispute on one side or the other.

6 February 1781

There was a junta of general officers. In it Señor Navía proposed that we determine the number of warships that would go to Guarico, the number of troops to be transported on them, and the number of men destined to garrison them, so that he could know how many men would be transported on merchant vessels and could proceed to charter the requisite number of ships.

Bonet repeated his dictum that he could make ready only twelve warships—one warship for Pensacola, four for the fleet, and seven for Guarico—and four frigates, that in each case 200 men would go on each warship, and that no more than 400 were needed to fill vacancies in their garrisons. He said that he would if possible prepare more warships, which, although they would not for the present follow the fleet, would join it at a designated place.

Next a paper from the quartermaster general, Don Luis Huet, was presented,[84] which dealt with the funds necessary for the expeditions contemplated; it was resolved that the governor, the general of the army, Don Josef Solano, the intendant, and Don Luis Huet should discuss these matters separately and then give a report to the junta about whatever might require its attention.

On the morning of the seventh I learned that at eleven o'clock on the previous evening there had come letters that the packet boat from Spain had left on Cape San Antonio. I went to the governor's house and was given an envelope marked confidential, which contained only duplicates of the orders carried by the brigantine from Sepúlveda.

The minister [José de Gálvez] was insisting to the governor

---

84. Huet was an engineering officer. He prepared a "Plan of the town of Pensacola, and of Fort George and the adjacent fortifications, constructed for the defense of the plaza and the trench built by the Spanish forces in order to attack them. 15 May 1781."[Tr.]

that small vessels be sent rather often to inform our court about what was happening in those dominions, because the serious lack of news they were experiencing was giving the enemies an opportunity to contrive and to spread abroad in their gazettes news that was apt to alarm the nation. Accordingly, the governor and I talked about this essential point, and we agreed that every fortnight there should go out for Spain a swift vessel on which there always should go an officer or other trustworthy person who, in the event of being obliged to throw the official papers overboard, would be able to inform the ministry about events that had occurred.

I also talked about this important matter with the intendant, and he told me that he had a brigantine already prepared to serve as a mail-packet, that it could set sail as soon as the Pensacola expedition had departed, and that he would have vessels ready to perform the same in the future.

Next I pointed out to the governor and the intendant that it was necessary to send flag-of-truce ships to Jamaica, both for the relief of our unfortunate prisoners and for the purpose of acquiring up-to-date intelligence about the condition, forces, and plans of the enemies. They concurred with my way of thinking, and they introduced me to Don Pedro Ruiz, a man who had been employed several times already and had performed this kind of confidential assignment very well.

At nightfall, while I was in the house of Gálvez, there came to him by the packet boat from New Orleans news that our troops in Mobile had gallantly repulsed a surprise attack made by the English. Their account of the action was not accurate.

After the capture of Mobile by our armed forces, Don José de Ezpeleta, colonel of the Regiment of Navarra, remained there with 800 men and the provisions that could be collected.[85] Militiamen, Negroes, and mulattoes were sent there

---

85. José de Ezpeleta, colonel of the Regiment of Navarra, was Bernardo de Gálvez's major general at Pensacola. Later he served as captain general of Louisiana and West Florida and as a counselor of state (Medina Rojas, xlvii-lxxviii). He was captain general of Cuba in 1785–89 and viceroy of New Granada in 1789–97 (Allan J. Kuethe, *Military Reform and Society in New Granada* [Gainesville: University Presses of Florida, 1978]).

from New Orleans as well, to contain the forays of the several nations of warlike Indians who frequent the environs of that place. A fortified post was established three leagues to the west of Mobile in a place called The Village; it was to serve as an advanced post against the designs of the garrison of Pensacola, which is hardly twenty leagues away, and other precautions conducive to the security of that conquest were taken.

After several months had passed, Ezpeleta found himself in need of provisions and military stores, and he requested those together with some reinforcement of men from Havana. Don Bernardo de Gálvez was in Havana at the time, and he urged that Ezpeleta be sent some vessels loaded with provisions, weapons, and 500 soldiers, under the escort of the armed coastal vessel *Chambequín*. This small convoy arrived at the mouth of Mobile Bay and found that the water in the narrow channel that forms its entrance was very shallow. The harbor pilots examined the entrance and agreed that the *Chambequín* would be exposed to grave danger on entering but that all the other vessels could enter without the slightest risk. Despite this statement, the officer who commanded the convoy ordered it to go out to sea and sent it on to the Mississippi River, sixty miles west of Mobile; he himself returned with the *Chambequín* to Havana.[86]

It seems that the English in Pensacola learned of this misadventure and of how ill-provisioned Mobile was and, having determined to attack it, Colonel Waldes[87] and Naval Captain [Deans][88] planned that the former would go by land with thirty regulars and 400 Indians, while the latter, with two 24-gun frigates, would invest the port by sea.

---

86. José Fermín de Rada commanded the *Chambequín*.
87. Colonel Johann Ludwig Wilhelm von Hanxleden.
88. At the beginning of 1781 the British war vessels at Pensacola were the frigates *Mentor*, *Port Royal*, and *Hound* and the brig *Childers*. They were employed in cruising and in building the Royal Navy redoubt. *Hound* was sent out on 27 February to escort a merchant convoy to England; on 4 March she sighted Bernardo de Gálvez's expeditionary force, and the merchantman *Baltic* carried a warning to Jamaica. When Gálvez appeared off Santa Rosa Island, Robert Deans, captain of *Mentor* and

The frigates arrived, and in a surprise attack the enemy captured a detachment of twenty men and one officer who were on Dauphin Island situated at the mouth of Mobile Bay. The land forces approached the post called The Village on a stormy night; passing by the Negro encampment without being witnessed, they ran into a recently erected stockade of which they had no knowledge. It detained them temporarily, but, divided along the front and the sides, they invested the post from all directions.

Our troops were surprised by the first blows of so unexpected an attack, but they rallied quickly, and, separated into several groups, they repulsed the English, many of whom had already penetrated the moat and the stockade.

The English lost there the Waldes colonel and his aide, two grenadier officers and twelve men killed, and they had more than sixty wounded. On our side, one officer of the Regiment of Spain and four men were killed, and some mulattoes were wounded.

In The Village were stationed certain men commanded by Don Ramón de Castro, lieutenant of the Regiment of the Prince, who acted with great presence of mind, and forty militiamen from Louisiana. The English displayed much grief at the death of the Waldes colonel, who was said to be the best officer there was at Pensacola.[89]

---

senior naval officer at Pensacola, sent a warning to Admiral Parker by the brig *Childers*. After guns, powder, and all but twelve men had been sent ashore to be dispersed in the fortifications on land, *Mentor* was sent up what is now Blackwater River, where she was burned when the Spanish advanced inland. *Port Royal* was captured. See *Log of H.M.S. Mentor, 1780–1781*, introduction by Robert R. Rea, edited by James A. Servies (Gainesville: University Presses of Florida, 1982), 20–23.

89. For accounts of this action see J. Barton Starr, *Tories, Dons, and Rebels* (Gainesville: University Presses of Florida, 1976), 183–84; Medina Rojas, 544–46; Caughey, 194–295; and Ezpeleta to Bernardo de Gálvez, 20 January 1781, AGI:Cuba 1233.

8 February 1781

I urged the governor to dispatch a mail-packet to Honduras and to send on it one of the officers from the Castillo de San Juan de Nicaragua who had just arrived with me from Jamaica; being well informed about the plans and preparations of the English on that island, he could give much information to the governor of Guatemala. In fact, the governor decided that Subaltern Don Antonio Antonioti should embark on it, furnished with all the assistance he might need.

9 February 1781

I wrote to the governor, telling him that one of the objects of my commission was to help to get reinforcements to him promptly, that I had already taken steps to have assistance sent from Mexico, and that reinforcements of troops and war vessels would also go to him from Havana.

The engineer Don Luis Huet showed me the maps of Jamaica he had and the plan he had devised for an attack on that island. He also showed me the plan he had made for expelling the English from the San Juan River in Nicaragua and the coasts of that country. This officer had acquired much information, but some of it was inaccurate and some referred to earlier times. I told him my opinion candidly, and he heard it appreciatively.

I had already informed myself in detail about the present state of the warships of the fleet, the naval stores needed for their repairs, which of them were in the arsenal and which could be obtained elsewhere, and everything else pertinent to this matter.

By dint of my investigations I perceived that, in order to alleviate the critical condition of the navy, three things were needed: to win over with gentle persuasion and cunning Commandant Bonet, who was basically a good fellow but obstinate in the formalities of authority and irresolute in difficulties; to proceed in complete agreement with Don José de Acosta, commandant of the navy yard, and Don Alfonso de Cárdenas, the navy auditor, both of them intelligent and industrious men in whom Bonet had complete confidence; and to devise a way by which Intendant Urriza should lend to the navy various military stores that he had in his warehouses. These three objectives were achieved to my complete satisfaction with little effort. Bonet, discarding his natural slowness, quickly did what was proposed to him as necessary; Acosta and Cardenas worked with the greatest earnestness on the preparations for the fleet; and Urriza supplied to the navy a portion of planks, canvas, pitch, and other articles.

Nevertheless, I realized that it was impossible for all the seventeen warships that were in the harbor to be made ready, both because of the lack of seamen resulting from illnesses and desertions and because there were no masts for repairing the dismasted warships and frigates. Those warships that could be put in a state of readiness for useful service numbered at most twelve or thirteen.

11 February 1781

The Chevalier de Monteil had from our first meeting manifested an intense desire that we should get in touch frequently. He was an ingenuous and extraordinarily active man. He visited me almost every day, and he never failed to suggest to me how important it was that our fleet and his should go into action forthwith, so as not to waste time in a port so distant from the principal theater of the war. His vehement desire was that both fleets go to cruise off Jamaica, where the English had few maritime forces. I commended his good sentiments without committing myself to any agreement, and I endeavored to excuse the lagging behind that he noted in our preparations.

Because of a letter he had just received from the French Cape, he came to my house on the eleventh to notify me that the ships that he had in careening would be ready by the first of March, at which time it was absolutely imperative that he return to the Windward Islands to protect the commerce of their colonies, which were excessively harassed by the privateering of the English, and that unless I exhausted all my efforts, he was of the opinion that it would be impossible for the Spanish fleet to be in condition to set sail by the time he must depart.

At the same time he voiced to me confidentially certain complaints he had against the Spanish officers which he could no longer disregard, because even his subalterns were criticizing their indifference, and he believed that he had not been accorded the courtesies due his position. His principal complaint was based on the fact that he had not been invited to the military juntas which were held frequently, whereas the French had always included the Spanish general officers of the combined fleet in the juntas held in Brest. I placated him by explaining that up to that time only purely economic matters had been discussed —the kind of domestic business which all nations discuss behind closed doors in order to supply what is needed, as well as the funds and resources that can be counted on; that as soon as it was necessary to decide upon some enterprise or to form a plan of operations in which the combined forces would play a part, he would undoubtedly be one of the first called, especially inasmuch as the generals had a good idea of his capabilities and gallantry. With this, and with assurances of the continuation of my efforts for the prompt readiness of the fleet, he was satisfied and pleased.

12 February 1781

There was a junta on the eleventh. Its purpose was to determine how many troops would suffice for the garrison of Havana and what portion of the troops destined for it could be added to the army, as well as the artillery, weapons, and stores that they could contribute to it. Lists were presented of the troops on hand and the number needed by the stronghold in order to be properly garrisoned.

The number of effective men who remained at that time was 2,193, in which number were included 528 who must be ready to reinforce Gálvez in case he needed them; it was necessary also to give 450 men to the navy for garrisoning the warships, whose crews were much reduced in number.[90]

---

90. Bernardo de Gálvez had obtained the ships he requested, as well as

There was a discussion as to whether it was advisable to put the militia under arms and whether they even could be employed in overseas expeditions. There were long debates over these points, and, as it was already late, the junta was adjourned until the following day.

In the meeting held on the thirteenth it was resolved that 1,500 men of the veteran troops should remain in the stronghold and the rest added to the army of operations and that the three militia battalions should be called to active duty so as to complete the garrisons of the stronghold and the warships.

14 February 1781

A junta was planned, but the illness of the governor prevented it.

The Pensacola expedition now being ready, there came the critical moment in which Navía and Gálvez were at the point of a break over whether the latter should review and drill the army troops designated to go out under his command. There had been much caviling over a matter which to my mind was frivolous, and in spite of my repeated efforts at reconciliation, meddlers had exacerbated the spirits of both generals to the point that a public dispute was to be feared.

In order to forestall that, I talked that morning with each of them separately and communicated to them the method I had devised for settling the difficulty; both agreed to it. My method was that the troops be embarked at least one day in advance of the departure of the convoy, without Gálvez having exercised any act of command over the troops or having yet been recognized as commander-in-chief of that expedition; then after the troops were aboard the ships, General Navía should send a mes-

---

an increase in the number of troops he would take; he had practically achieved his objective of organizing a third expedition against Pensacola without disclosure of this intention in the juntas of general officers held up to that time. See Medina Rojas, 662–64; "Diary of the Operations of the Expedition against the Place of Pensacola, conducted by the Arms of H. Catholic M., under the Orders of the Field Marshal Don Bernardo de Gálvez," *Louisiana Historical Quarterly* 1, no. 1 (1917): 44–46. [Tr.]

14 February 1781

sage to Gálvez delivering to him command of the troops, as distinguished from the command of the ships they were aboard; later on the following day Gálvez should disembark the troops in the camp of Regla, on the opposite side of the harbor, and there do with them whatever he pleased. Actually it was done in that way that same afternoon so as not to give time for further discussions. The troops were embarked, then on the following afternoon were disembarked in Regla,[91] where Gálvez at his leisure announced himself as the commanding general of the expedition; next he reviewed, examined, disposed, and drew up troops completely on his own. This was the comic end of a dispute that could have brought tragic consequences.

On the eighteenth the king's mail-packet frigate set sail for Spain. On it I sent to Minister Gálvez an account of all the events of my voyage from Coruña, the state of things there, the forces that constituted the Pensacola expedition, and how near it was to its launching.[92]

19 February 1781

There was a junta in which the naval commandant read a paper whose substance was that by 10 March the fleet would be able to depart for Spain with the four warships required by royal orders; that the fleet of the Chevalier de Monteil would sail with it as far as the latitude of Bermuda, along with four more ships-of-the-line with the land troops that would be ready; and that the remaining three warships as well as the seven that were to be made ready would go to Guarico later with the rest of the expeditionary force. He added that he thought it proper to give a warning to traders immediately about the imminent departure of the fleet so that their cargoes could be made ready.

---

91. A point situated between the Bay of Havana and the end of Guanabacoa. [Ed.]

92. Saavedra to José de Gálvez, 16 February 1781, AGI:Ind. Gen. 1578. Saavedra kept in his files copies of all the letters written to Gálvez from Havana and Pensacola as well as the short letters from the minister acknowledging their receipt and assuring complete confidence. They are all in leg. 21 of his files. [Ed.]

In view of these two proposals, the junta resolved (1) that as many land and sea forces as possible be made ready, and, as soon as Madrid advised, as it had promised to do, of the sailing of the French fleet from Brest bound for the Windward Islands, the fleet as well as any part of the expeditionary force that might be ready would set sail, and (2) that an order be sent to the intendant so that, as soon as the Pensacola expedition went out, he would announce the imminent departure of the fleet; in the meantime he would make his prior preparations.

21 February 1781

I went to see Don Bernardo de Gálvez, who was already aboard the warship *San Román,* and we talked at length about the plan he had formed for the attack on Pensacola and about the means of reinforcing him frequently with provisions, ammunition, and the other things he might need. All was now ready for his departure, but the weather was not yet fit for sailing.

24 February 1781

The sky became cloudless, and the breeze was steady from the northeast. They fired the shot to signal weighing anchor, and the Pensacola expedition prepared to go out on the following day. That night the weather turned foul again with heavy cloudbursts and squalls.

25 February 1781

The expedition could not go out because of the foul weather. I went again to see Gálvez, who was distraught because of the delay of the departure. He had sent advance orders for the troops of New Orleans to join him on Santa Rosa Island, which is before the port of Pensacola; consequently he feared that the army, reaching the point of rendezvous before the arrival of the expedition from Havana and not having brought warships, would be captured by the English, who had two war frigates there.[93]

On the same night a brigantine from Louisiana put in with the news that an English frigate had pursued it in Tortuga Sound, whereupon the Chevalier de Monteil ordered the warship *Triton* and the frigate *Andromaque* to go out immediately in search of it.

27 February 1781

The above-mentioned warship and frigate being ready, they tried to sail today at dawn but could not because there was no land wind.

As the weather was now calm, the Pensacola expedition prepared to set sail on the following day. That afternoon I made my last visit to Gálvez, and I reiterated my promise to be on the alert to see that he would be reinforced with everything needed at the conclusion of his operation.

28 February 1781

At one o'clock in the morning, before the first rays of dawn, the *Triton* and the *Andromaque* set sail. At five o'clock the convoy for Pensacola began to go out, at eight o'clock all were already outside the harbor in orderly configuration, and at twelve o'clock they could hardly be seen. The convoy included the 61-gun *San Román*, the 36-gun frigates *Cecilia* and *Clara*,

---

93. On 22 February Ezpeleta received a letter from Bernardo de Gálvez dated 30 January, sent via New Orleans because of fear that Mobile Bay might be closed, advising that he would sail from Havana within ten or twelve days. Ezpeleta had to get ready without loss of time, embarking the artillery, ammunition, and what food he had. Gálvez expressed fear that Dauphin Island was in enemy hands and that communication between Mobile and New Orleans might be cut. He did not know whether he would enter Mobile, await Ezpeleta outside Mobile Bay, or go directly to Pensacola, sending orders for Ezpeleta to come overland to join him. Final orders indicating the point of rendezvous would be sent at sea (Bernardo de Gálvez to José de Ezpeleta, 30 January 1781, AGI:Cuba 1377; Medina Rojas, 669). [Tr.]

the 20-gun chamberquín *Andaluz*, the 18-gun packet boat *San Pío*, and thirty-two transport vessels on which were 1,300 soldiers, a train of military stores, and provisions.[94]

This same day the imminent departure of the fleet was announced.

I made the most diligent efforts to prevent those large merchantmen, which already had great cargoes of sugar aboard and which could not postpone their departure without serious loss to the shippers, from being designated to transport the troops who were to go to Guarico.

2 March 1781

A junta was called for the following reason: because the ports of the island had been closing for the imminent sailing of the fleet, fishermen and the boatmen who brought in firewood for the arsenal tried to go out and were not permitted to do so. Therefore the naval commandant sent an official protest to the governor, complaining that this order was causing delay in fitting out the fleet. In order not to be himself responsible for such a result, the governor called a junta, and in the meeting it was resolved that the prohibition against vessels going out from the port was not to include coastal fishermen and firewood carriers.

5 March 1781

I arranged with the governor that a settee [*saetía*, small packet] that was ready to go to Spain as a mail-packet, should set sail on the seventh, and he named Don Ignacio Acosta, a lieutenant of the permanent regiment of Havana, to go in charge of the official papers for the court.

This day a courier came from La Filipina with the report that a frigate armed with 20 to 24 guns, with all the appearance of being English, was about to double Cape Antonio. Immediately an order was given for the 36-gun frigate "O," the brigantine

---

94. Saavedra to José de Gálvez, 5 March 1781, AGI:Ind. Gen. 1578. [Tr.]

5 March 1781

Renombrado, and the French cutter *Serpent* to go out to see if they could find it.

La Filipina is a kind of watchtower, situated on the southern coast of the Island of Cuba on a promontory from which can be seen all vessels that attempt to round the headlands of Corrientes and San Antonio en route to the Gulf of Mexico. In time of war a detachment of dragoons is always at this port, and when some sizable vessel with indications of being an enemy craft is sighted, a dragoon rides posthaste to bring the news to Havana, some forty leagues away. No matter how swift the vessel may be, this gives enough time for ships to go out from Havana to intercept it, and this fact serves as a strong check on Jamaica, because it is very difficult for their trading vessels to pass between the eastern end of the Island of Cuba and the Island of Santo Domingo in search of the English Channel, or to pass between Caicos and Mayaguana; consequently they are obliged to double the Cape of San Antonio so as to sail through the Bahama Channel. For this reason, the maintenance of naval forces at Havana, and the alertness of their officers, can cause much damage to the commerce of Jamaica.

The coming of the English frigate promoted the supposition in Havana that it was probably the scout of a great convoy that was known to be in Jamaica preparing to go to Europe. This made the general officers uneasy, and they called a junta for the following day.

6 March 1781

At dawn the "O," the *Renombrado*, and the *Serpent* weighed anchor. The junta met at nine o'clock. M. de Monteil was summoned to it, as I had promised he would be. The latest intelligence from Jamaica was read, all of it coinciding with the reports that I had given. This intelligence confirmed that the English had a large convoy prepared and ready to go out from Jamaica and that with it would sail with jury-masts those warships dismasted by the great hurricane that could not be repaired there for want of masts. It was very unlikely that this convoy would go up as far as Point Morant in a season when the northeast winds were already very fresh; this left no alternative except to come by way of Cape San Antonio in search of the Bahama Channel. It was also unlikely that the convoy would be escorted by many warships, for the English, who were expecting the French fleet in the Windward Islands from one day to the next, could not detach from there more than two or three warships from their six or seven at most, including the four which had been fitted with masts in Jamaica. With these facts in mind, the matter was discussed in the junta, and it was resolved that a diligent effort be made to capture all the [enemy] warships and frigates if possible, that the silver and provisions that had already been loaded be removed from the warships of the fleet, and that at first notice of the sighting of the convoy they would go out to meet it.

7 March 1781

I went to the small town of Santiago, four leagues from Havana, to visit the bishop, who was taking the baths there.[95]

10 March 1781

At four o'clock in the morning the settee, as a mail-packet, set sail. I gave to Don Ignacio de Acosta, the officer charged with care of the pouches of official papers, a letter for Minister Don José de Gálvez, and I wrote the message on a separate piece of paper so that Acosta could commit it to memory and be able to deliver it orally in case he were obliged to throw the correspondence overboard.

I dined with M. de Monteil aboard his ship the *Palmier*. In the afternoon I went with several officers to see the fortification called La Cabaña, an immense work whose enormous cost exceeded 8 million pesos. Its defense requires sixty-nine men, and its indispensability, or even utility, many intelligent persons question.

---

95. The diocese of Havana was not established until 1785, so this bishop had to be the one from Santiago de Cuba. [Ed.]

11 March 1781

There was a junta to which the intendant of the army was summoned so that he could report the funds and means that could be counted on for the contemplated operations. He presented a statement of the condition of the treasury, the gist of which was that it had on hand 982,000 pesos, that it had obligations of 2,917,219 pesos that must be paid at once, and that therefore it was more than 1.9 million pesos in debt. There was no immediate hope that money would come from Mexico, so it was necessary either to make use of some of the funds of the fleet or to limit the preparations to what the scant faculties of this exhausted treasury could afford.

This point was discussed for a long time, and it was decided that the general of the army and the intendant should prepare an estimate of the expenditures necessary for execution of the plan of the operations contemplated and that there should be omitted from the project the part for which the means on hand, after all resourses had been exhausted, could not suffice.

In the afternoon I went to see the Morro. This fortress, built in the time of Philip II by the famous Antonelli,[96] is very well located for defense of the harbor. In the year '63 the English took it by surprise, after having lost many men in the assault. The place through which they surprised the fortress, difficult at that time, at present is inaccessible. Since that unfortunate event the defenses of the fortification have been augmented, and today it appears to be impregnable to any force with which it can be invested. The bad thing is that because of its particular location, Havana can be captured without bothering with the Morro or the Cabaña, which in the end will surrender to a blockade, once the stronghold is occupied by an enemy superior in maritime forces. This fact has prompted an increase in the number of fortifications in the environs of the city; a fortune has been spent in constructing them, and an army is needed to defend them. Nevertheless, that defect still exists, and according to the experts, it is possible to take pos-

---

96. See Diego Angulo Iniguez, *Bautista Antonelli: Las Fortificaciones Americanas del Siglo XVI* (Madrid, 1942). [Ed.]

session of the stronghold equally undeterred by the forts that surround it.

13 March 1781

A junta was held in which to read four representations from the Chevalier de Monteil; his purpose was to hasten the departure of the Spanish fleet in company with his own. The final petition proposed one of two methods by which to effect the prompt sailing of the two fleets: either that the fleet be detained and all attention be fixed on the dispatch of the convoy of troops who were to go to Guarico, or that the fleet go out with all the warships that were ready, that Monteil go with them as far as the latitude of Bermuda, and that the convoy accompany the rest of the warships when it was ready. There was a long conference concerning these proposals, and it was resolved that the members answer in writing two questions that had arisen: whether the fleet and convoy, before their departure, ought to await the notice that the king's orders were announcing that the French fleet had departed Brest bound for the Windward Islands; and which of the two ought to sail first, in case both could not go out at the same time.

14 March 1781

At four o'clock in the afternoon the governor sent for me to show me several letters and papers found on an English brigantine that was sailing from Jamaica to Pensacola; its crew, composed of Frenchmen, Spaniards, and Americans, had mutinied, and when in control of the ship had taken it into one of the roadsteads of the Island of Cuba. There was nothing whatever worthy of attention in the letters, as most of them referred to business affairs. Among several gazettes from Kingston, there were some in which the declaration of war between England and Holland was mentioned, as well as the arrival of Admiral Hood at the Windward Islands with eight ships-of-the-line and a large convoy of troops and the arrival at Jamaica of two warships and many merchantmen.

15 March 1781

I urged the intendant to make haste to send to Pensacola some reinforcement of provisions. This day the frigate "O," the *Renombrado,* and the *Serpent* came into the port; they had not been able to find the English frigate that had rounded Cape Corrientes.

17 March 1781

I was in the navy yard with Don Juan Bonet, who showed me the state of the fleet's preparations.

18 March 1781

There was a junta in which the voters presented in writing their votes on the points proposed on the twelfth of the month. In the end all agreed to respond to the Chevalier de Monteil, that he would be given at the end of the month the junta's definitive determination concerning the departure of the fleet and the convoy.

19 March 1781

The Chevalier de Monteil gave a reception aboard his ship for the general officers and distinguished persons of the city, which I attended. At five o'clock in the afternoon a dragoon came from La Filipina with the news that two English merchant vessels and one warship had been sighted going in search of Cape San Antonio. The general immediately called a junta of general officers, and as it appeared by the signs very probable that those vessels were part of a convoy that was behind them, the officers determined unanimously that one hundred soldiers be put aboard each Spanish warship and that the whole fleet go out on the following day.

20 March 1781

The French warships *Triton* and *Palmier* went out. The Spanish ships were about to do the same, but the wind changed suddenly and they had to wait until the next day.

21 March 1781

The warships began to sail at dawn, and at nine o'clock all were outside. The fleet was composed of fifteen ships-of-the-line, eleven of them Spanish and four French, two frigates, and another small ship. On the night of the nineteenth, the frigate *Andromaque,* the cutter *Serpent,* the schooner *Levrette,* and the brigantines *Caulican* and *Renombrado* had gone out and since then had been stationed in the keys which are called the Northern Keys [the Florida Keys], to warn the fleet about any enemy vessel they might discover.

As soon as all the vessels were beyond the Morro, the light squadron composed of three warships and two corsair frigates under the command of Don Juan de Tomasco advanced more than two leagues. The rest of the fleet assumed a formation in three columns. In the center column went the fleet's commodore, Don Juan Bonet; Don José Solano led the column on the right; and the one on the left was led by the Chevalier de Monteil. That evening, when the fleet was tacking, the French warship *Destin* ran afoul of the *San Francisco de Asís* and broke her bowsprit, which forced her to return to the port.

22 March 1781

All this day was employed in making naval maneuvers. The outermost ships at the edges of the fleet stretched from the Island of Cuba out to the middle of the channel that runs between that island and Tortuga Sound. The frigate *Andromaque* and the other scouting vessels came to report having reconnoitred the Northern Keys and all their environs without encountering any vessel whatever. In view of that, the general officers were called aboard the warship *Guerrero,* which was the flagship, to voice their opinions as to what ought to be done. Being on that same ship, I also attended this conference, somewhat like a junta, in which it was decided that the frigates be sent to reconnoiter the keys again, and that if by the following day there was no danger, we should return to the port.

24 March 1781

At nine o'clock in the morning the French schooner *Cerf* was caught sight of far away. It had been sent on the previous afternoon to reconnoiter a vessel that was in sight at a great distance. This schooner was coming leeward, firing cannon shots incessantly and flying a blue pennant on the masthead. Convinced that it was coming to report some important news, and seeing that it would be slow in arriving because of being well to leeward, the flagship sailed toward the schooner; but at the same time the Chevalier de Monteil, who understood the schooner's signal, raised the signal of "enemies in view on a northeast course." Instantly the fleet commandant gave to the entire fleet the signal of general pursuit, hauling the wind as closely as possible. The pursuit continued until four o'clock in the afternoon, when the scouting frigates arrived, reporting that they had reconnoitered the entire channel without sighting any vessel whatever in it or in the Northern Keys. The captain of the schooner that had alarmed us was called aboard the flagship, and from his account we learned that on the previous night he had accidentally met our fleet while the fleet was tacking, that the cannon shots of the signals and the lanterns had persuaded him that he was amidst an enemy convoy, and that after wandering about all night, fleeing from one side to another, he had come in the morning in search of the fleet, to give notice of the encounter he had had on the previous evening. At six o'clock in the evening, aware that all had been pure illusion on the part of the captain of the schooner, we tacked to return to Havana, standing on the northeast course.

25 March 1781

At eleven o'clock in the morning that part of the Island of Cuba called Jaruco was sighted, so that according to observation the current had dragged us twenty-five leagues to the northeast during the previous night.

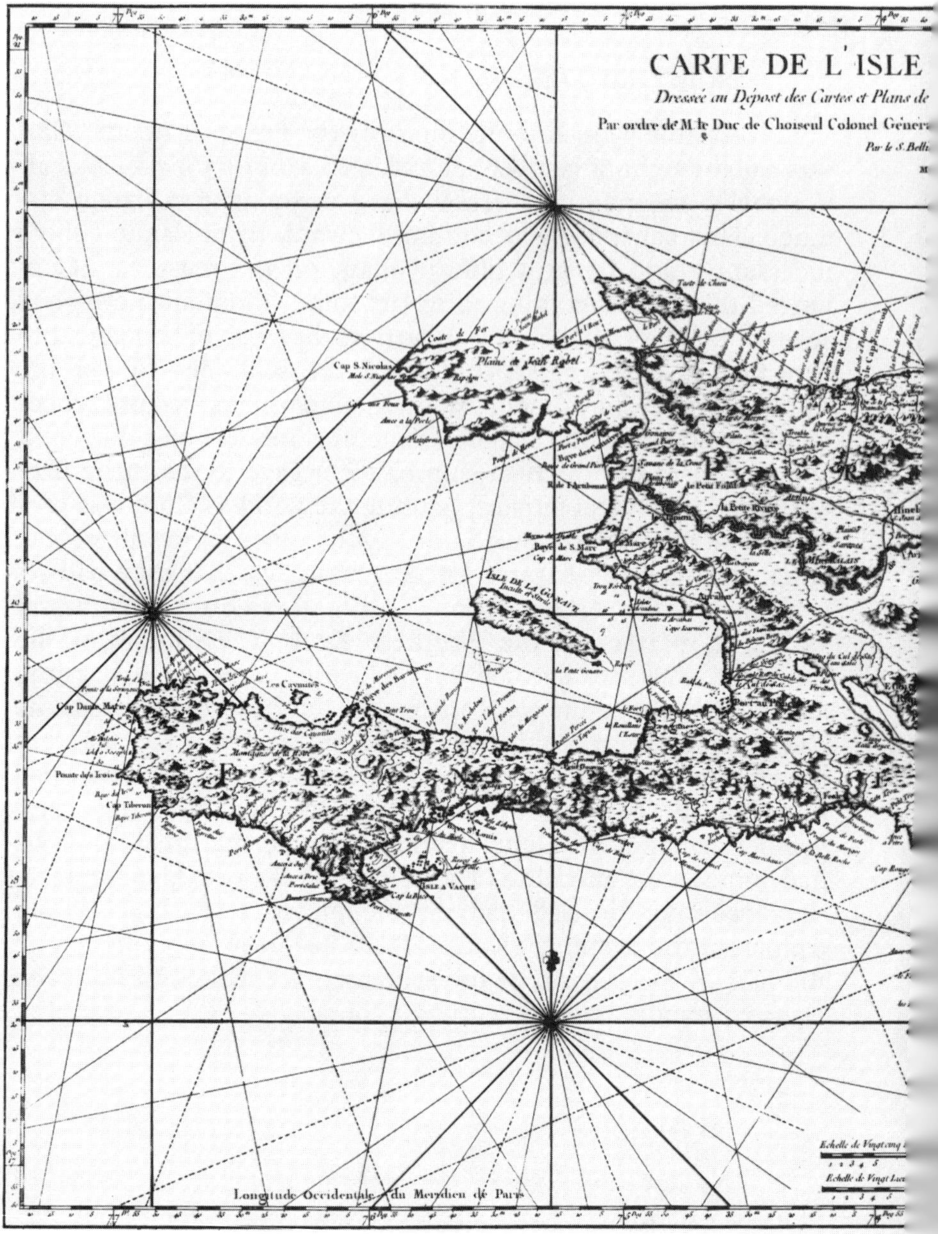
CARTE DE L'ISLE
Dressée au Dépost des Cartes et Plans de
Par ordre de M. le Duc de Choiseul Colonel Généra
Par le S. Belli
Cap S. Nicolas
Plaine de Jean Rabel
Baye de S. Marc
Cap S. Marc
ISLE DE LA GONAVE
Les Cayemites
Cap Dame Marie
Pointe des Irois
Cap Tiberon
ISLE A VACHE
Echelle de Vingt Lieu
Longitude Occidentale du Meridien de Paris

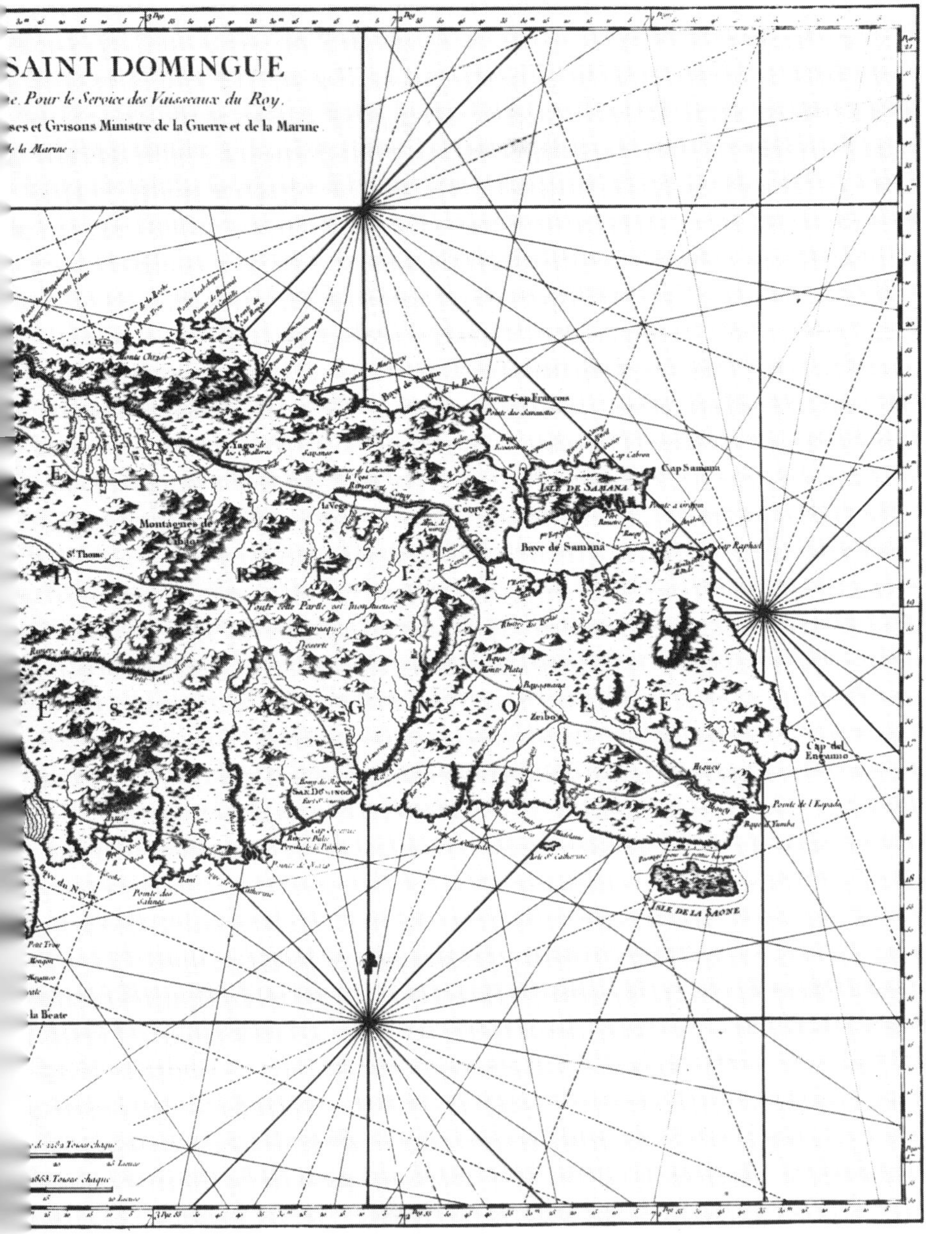
SAINT DOMINGUE
e. Pour le Service des Vaisseaux du Roy.
ses et Grisons Ministre de la Guerre et de la Marine.
le la Marine.
Cap Samana
ISLE DE SAMANA
Baye de Samana
Cap Raphael
Vieux Cap François
Montagnes de Cibao
St. Thome
la Vega
Cotuy
Zeibo
Cap del Engaño
Pointe de l'Espada
ISLE DE LA SAONE
SAN DOMINGO
Pointe des Salines
la Beate

26 March 1781

At two-thirty o'clock in the afternoon the fleet began to put into the port, and at four o'clock the whole fleet was already inside except the four French warships, which remained outside.

This same evening there was a junta to reply to an official paper sent by the Chevalier de Monteil, who requested that he be told definitely whether the fleet and the convoy were to go out soon, for if not he would go with his warships to Guarico, where they were sorely needed. The junta resolved that he be told that he would be given a final answer on this point within four days at most. It was also resolved that the silver should be put back aboard the warships that were prepared to go with the fleet, from which it had been removed.

On the following day the four French warships entered, but they remained at the mouth of the port.

28 March 1781

An American brigantine arrived. Her captain stated that he had seen sailing out of the strait between Caicos and Mayaguana a large English convoy escorted by warships and war frigates and that from all signs it appeared to be bound for Europe from Jamaica. It was learned later that in fact it was the convoy we had been expecting and that the English, fearful of entering the Gulf of Mexico, had, at cost of enormous effort and requiring many days, managed to double Point Morant. They had passed between the islands of Cuba and Santo Domingo and had sailed out of the strait at the place where the American had seen them.

30 March 1781

Several vessels originating in Veracruz put into the harbor, bringing 6,000 quintales of flour, 1,200 *tercios* of dried vegetables, and 180 boxes of gunpowder.

On this day there was a junta to decide about the departure of

30 March 1781

the fleet for Spain and that of the fleet and convoy for Guarico. The voters were perplexed, and really the importance of the matter, and the difficulties that were at the center of it, made the resolution awkward. On the one hand, the orders of the king proscribed that either the fleet or the squadron be moved from Havana until after having had notice that the French fleet was in the Windward Islands; on the other hand, those same orders commanded that the fleet reach Europe by the end of April, or at least when the English fleets had not yet gone out of their ports. If the fleet set sail at once, the first part of those royal orders was not obeyed; if it was detained to await the notice previously mentioned, the second part was disobeyed; and if afterward there occurred one of the many misfortunes to which the fleet and the convoy were exposed, the junta would be blamed for not having obeyed the royal mandates. Moreover, M. de Monteil was clamoring to go out without more delay, and the intendant had demonstrated that there absolutely was not enough money to defray the expenses that the departure of the convoy required. In this troubled situation the voters did not dare to decide upon either course, and they agreed that they would meet again on the first day of April and that each would bring his vote in writing.

1 April 1781

The junta met as announced. Each voter expressed in writing what seemed to him most fitting to the critical situation in which we found ourselves. Governor Navarro was of the opinion that neither the fleet nor the convoy should go out before the arrival of the notice that the French fleet was in the Windward Islands, as much in order not to become responsible to the court for the consequences that could supervene unexpectedly as in order not to leave Havana without forces with which to reinforce the Pensacola expedition, still pending, in case of misadventure. Don Juan de Tomasco thought the same. The other voters desired that the fleet be detained until the arrival of the said notice but that the fleet and convoy of troops leave for Guarico at once.

As the differences could not be reconciled, I then proposed a method I had devised that reconciled as much as possible all the difficulties. The substance of it was that the fleet be detained until July and Madrid be so informed; that two of the four warships destined to accompany the fleet be added; that the fleet with troops of the expeditionary force go out on 8 April for Guarico; that the other two warships of the fleet and their garrisons of troops, which had been destined to be added to the army, remain in Havana in order to reinforce the Pensacola expedition in case of need; that two of the dismasted warships be repaired with the masts that had just arrived at the navy yard and then be dispatched immediately to Veracruz for funds; that as soon as the surrender of Pensacola was reported, the 1,000 men of the garrison who remained in Havana still without assignment be sent to Guarico; and, finally, that there be removed from the fleet the amount of money deemed necessary for the expenses of the dispatch of the convoy and a message be sent to the viceroy of New Spain requesting that he replace those funds immediately. The voters agreed to this proposal unanimously, with only the difference that the warships of the fleet that were to be added to the convoy should be three in number, as the naval commandant demanded, and that only 640 men of the troops already added to the army should remain in Havana to reinforce Pensacola. The junta also resolved to send corresponding official papers to the Chevalier de Monteil and to the intendant of the army, advising them of the said resolution.

At four o'clock in the afternoon of this day, one of the merchant frigates that had remained at Veracruz put in here, bringing correspondence from New Spain and Guatemala. From the latter it was learned that the Castillo de San Juan de Nicaragua had been successfully recovered from the enemy by Spanish arms on 4 January.

2 April 1781

I had a long conversation with the naval commandant about what had been decided in the junta of the previous day.

4 April 1781

A settee arrived from New Orleans with the news that the expedition of Don Bernardo de Gálvez had reached its destination on 8 March, that on the ninth he had taken possession of Santa Rosa Island, situated at the mouth of the port of Pensacola, and had established on it a battery of 24-caliber cannons which drove into the interior of the port two English frigates that had fired broadsides at them at the entrance.[97]

5 April 1781

An express mail-packet was hurriedly made ready to take news to Spain of the junta's latest resolution.

It was learned this evening that the warship *San Román* was in the port of Matanzas, having come from Pensacola. This event caused great surprise, because we were at the same time told that that stronghold, although already under attack by our forces, was not yet in a state to surrender and might not be so for several days. The captain of the *San Román*, Don José Calvo, was a distinguished officer, and we did not know to what cause to attribute his having left the expedition before it was concluded. But some army officers who were in the garrison of the warship cleared up our confusion by telling us all that happened.[98]

The fact was that when the expedition reached the vicinity

---

97. On the same day, 9 March, Ensign Miguel de Herrera brought to Ezpeleta the order from Gálvez written aboard the *San Román* at sea. The general had changed his plans and was sailing toward Santa Rosa Island (Medina Rojas, 691). [Tr.]

98. Gálvez had concealed in the juntas of general officers, where he ought to have declared it, his intention of attacking Pensacola with the convoy that set sail on 28 February rather than of reinforcing Mobile before proceeding to Pensacola. The general officer most injured by this concealment was José Calvo de Irazabal, commandant of the *San Román* and commander-in-chief of all the escorting fleet (ibid., 695). The discord between Gálvez and Calvo is treated by Caughey, 202–4; by Jack D.L. Holmes in in "Bernardo de Gálvez: Spain's 'Man of the Hour' During the American Revolution" (in *Cardinales de Dos Independencias* [see n.79]),

* 141 *

of Pensacola the harbor pilots examined the entrance of the port and found that it had only nineteen to twenty feet of water, so that the *San Román* could not forge over the shoal under a press of sail except after being much lightened; and the English had built a battery of fourteen 36- and 18-caliber cannons on a promontory called the Red Cliffs, or Barrancas Coloradas, whose fire dominated all the entrance of the channel formed by the said cliffs and Santa Rosa Island, apparently about 700 toises distant from each other. It was almost impossible for the warship to destroy this battery because of the altitude at which it was placed, and it seemed very hazardous for the convoy to pass as long as the battery was there. Finally, the warship undertook to force the port, but it ran aground twice, loosening some planks on the bottom, and it had to draw back. The other warships and the rest of the convoy feared to go in under the fire of so formidable a battery as the one on the cliffs. Two or three days were passed in this uncertainty, during which there were bitter disputes between Don José Calvo and Don Bernardo de Gálvez. To take the battery by land was an arduous business because it required a formal siege, and it was likely that the battery would be assisted by all the forces of Pensacola, superior at that time to those of the Spanish army, to which the forces from the Mississippi and Mobile had not yet been added. To destroy the battery from the sea was impossible, and to keep the ships outside the port was dangerous because if a storm came up from the southeast they would all be lost and the army would remain on Santa Rosa Island without food, without ammunition, obliged to surrender to the enemy.

In this agonizing situation, Don Bernardo de Gálvez, without sharing his decision with anyone, embarked on a corsair brigantine from New Orleans named the *Gálveztown*, raised the flag of the commandant, set sail, and entered the port, passing without any damage whatever through the continuous fire that was directed at him by the battery on the Red Cliffs. Immediately the frigates and other war and transport vessels imitated his example; all succeeding in gaining entrance to the harbor, without

---

168–70; and by Eric Beerman in "*Yo Solo* Not '*Solo*'," *Florida Historical Society Quarterly* 58, no. 2, 174–81. [Tr.]

5 April 1781

the more than 400 cannon shots fired by the enemy having caused important damage or any notable misadventure.[99] Then the warship *San Román*, being unable either to enter the harbor or to remain outside it without great risk, considered her mission accomplished and retired to Havana.

On this same night, a sloop arrived from Pensacola. It confirmed what the officers from the *San Román* had told us, adding that at the end of the previous month there had been added to the forces of Don Bernardo de Gálvez the troops from Mobile brought overland by Don José de Ezpeleta, as well as those from New Orleans, with which reinforcement his army was increased to 4,000 men.[100]

6 April 1781

A junta began in the morning and lasted until four o'clock in the afternoon. There was deliberation as to whether three of the warships destined for the fleet should be added to the expeditionary fleet or only two, as I had proposed. Naval Commandant Bonet warned of the lack of crews to man the three ships and the critical scarcity of military stores in the navy yard. In view of everything, it was resolved that only two of the four warships named for the fleet should be added to the squadron and that, in order to remedy in part the want of seamen, fifty soldiers should be put aboard each warship, with the stipulation that whenever the commanding general of the army might need them they would be returned to the army immediately.

---

99. Bernardo de Gálvez forced the bay on the *Galveztown*, accompanied by Naval Lieutenant Juan Antonio de Riaño aboard his own sloop *Valenzuela*, together with two row galleys. [Tr.]

100. After crossing the Perdido River on 21 March, Ezpeleta reached Tartar Point (Punta de Aguëro) the next day. The New Orleans contingent arrived the following day. For the composition of these forces see William S. Coker and Hazel P. Coker, *The Siege of Pensacola 1781 in Maps* (Pensacola: Perdido Bay Press, 1981), 103–10. [Tr.]

7 April 1781

At nightfall the commandant of the stronghold received an express messenger from La Filipina with the report that a fisherman who had come there declared that on the afternoon of 30 March he had seen eight English warships and one frigate in search of Cape San Antonio and that they were firing cannon shots as if signaling each other. A junta was called immediately, and because it seemed to all those present unlikely that those ships had any destination other than to reinforce Pensacola, as the English in Jamaica could have had a prompt report of the attack on the stronghold brought by a swift brigantine that had been cruising near Pensacola and had sped away under a press of sail at sight of our expeditionary force on 7 March, it was decided that our fleet should sail at once, carrying as many men as possible to reinforce that enterprise.[101]

8 April 1781

The staff and detachment of troops to be used in this service were formed by the commander of the army and the commandant of the fort. It was composed of 1,627 men detached from the following regiments: the King's, Soria, Guadalajara, España, Navarra, Hibernia, Aragón, second of Cataluña, Flanders, and the permanent regiment of Havana, and sixty-two artillerymen. Field Marshal Don Juan Manuel de Cagigal commanded this corps, which was divided into two brigades commanded by Don Geronimo Girón and Don Manuel de Pineda.

Already in formation, the troops were reviewed at three o'clock in the afternoon, and at five o'clock they embarked, together with artillery, ammunition, provisions, etc., so that everything was on board by nine o'clock in the evening.

Several messages were sent to M. de Monteil, inviting him to accompany our fleet with his warships, with the intent of leav-

---

101. The British sloop *Childers* arrived at Pensacola from Jamaica in early March. It was at Pensacola on 9 March when the Spanish fleet appeared off the bar, but *Childers* got away safely and sailed for Jamaica (Starr, 189). [Tr.]

ing us later in order to go to Guarico, which, according to reports, was blockaded by a small English squadron at that time. At first he responded negatively, but finally he agreed to do as requested.

At ten o'clock that evening I embarked on the flagship, which was the *San Luis*.

9 April 1781

As day broke the fleet began to weigh anchor and at nine o'clock twelve warships were already outside; but the wind shifted to the northeast and going out became impossible for the *Arrogante*, the *Astuto*, the *San Gabriel*, and the hospital ship *La Mexicana*, the only merchantman that accompanied the fleet of fifteen ships-of-the-line, eleven of them Spanish and four French, three frigates, one brigantine, and two cutters, all commanded by the fleet commandant, Don José Solano.[102]

At noon, seeing that it was impossible for the ships mentioned above to sail until the next day, a signal was given for the fleet to begin to navigate on a NW¼W course in three columns, in which formation it proceeded carrying an easy sail, the frigates constantly scanning the horizon.

10 April 1781

At twelve-thirty o'clock that night a signal was given for the fleet to form the fifth order of navigation in lines of natural convoy, navigating toward the W5°N, and at six-fifteen o'clock in the morning a signal was given for the fleet to reverse and to navigate in lines of convoy, maintaining its same order and formation, and on a NW¼W course. At four o'clock in the afternoon a signal was given to form the line diagonally or obliquely on a larboard tack.[103] A little later the signal of cancellation was given and then a signal to form three columns, with the

---

102. For composition of the reinforcement see Coker and Coker, 111–14. [Tr.]

103. The expression means in check or checkmate. [Ed.]

flagship to the right, the vice-admirals in the vanguard, and the columns ten cables' lengths apart.

There was some hanging back in the execution of these maneuvers because of the bad condition of some of the warships.

11 April 1781

At five-thirty in the morning the warship *Palmier* gave the signal of having sighted sails to the WNW, and at six o'clock vessels were seen from the topmasts to the SE$\frac{1}{4}$W, two of them larger than the others; they were following our course, from which it was inferred that they were the warships that had fallen behind. A signal was given to the frigates *Licorne* and *Nra. Sra. de la O* to go to reconnoiter and to report the number and class of the sighted vessels.

At midday we observed that we were at latitude 23°39' and considered ourselves to be at 292°5' longitude, hindering the angle of the sounding line to the NW for twenty-two leagues.

12 April 1781

During the previous night we had navigated with only the topsails, in order that the warships that had fallen behind could rejoin the fleet, and indeed at dawn they were already reunited with it. At five-thirty o'clock a signal was made to the cutter *Serpent* to reconnoiter to the N without losing sight of the signals of the flagship. The *Andromaque* was signaled to reconnoiter to the NW, the *Nra. Sra. de la O* to the WNW, and the *Licorne* to the ESE, and at six-thirty o'clock a signal was given to the entire fleet to proceed in three columns, hauling the wind to the designated course, the vice-admirals at the vanguard of their divisions. At seven o'clock a signal was given to the entire fleet to increase sail. The wind was blowing from the NNE, and we continued steering toward the NW; the wind was increasing so much that at four o'clock in the afternoon the topgallant sails were furled, and the main-topsails were reefed.

13 April 1781

At six o'clock in the morning the brigantine *Pájaro* reported her mainmast gravely damaged, and she retired to Havana. The wind continued fresh from the NE, with high seas, and the whole fleet proceeded, with the six principals in their ordinary formation of three columns and on a NNW course. At five forty-five in the afternoon the frigate *Andromaque* signaled the sighting of a sail on the same course. She was ordered to give chase with the "O" and the cutter, but by nightfall they had rejoined the fleet. Near midnight a signal to increase sail was given, and we bent the sails of the stay and the main-topgallant sail.

14 April 1781

At daybreak there was a fresh wind from the ESE; the sea was quiet and the horizons calm. A little later, a signal was made to the *Andromaque* to take a sounding, and she did not find bottom. The *Licorne* did the same at eleven o'clock. At midday we made an observation and determined our position at latitude 26°N, longitude 298°24′, with a fresh wind from the SE. At five-thirty o'clock a signal was made to take reefs in the main-topsails, and later the fleet was ordered to steer toward the N½NW, and to form the lines of the course by evolution. At nightfall the horizons were clouded, with a fresh wind from the SE and a heavy sea from the NE, and at ten-thirty in the evening we furled the main-topsails, because the wind had increased. Our speed was in excess of seven knots.

15 April 1781

At dawn we sighted a schooner, and a signal was made to the *Asís*, which had it abeam, to reconnoiter it. At seven o'clock in the morning the cutter *Serpent* came within hailing distance, and her commander reported to the general some damage, not very serious. At eight-thirty o'clock the sighted schooner came, flying a Spanish pennant, and said she was the *Sourris*, which left Havana on the tenth bound for Pensacola with official papers. She was ordered to remain near the flagship and not to leave it for any reason. At nine o'clock in the morning the wind shifted abruptly to the NNW, with a strong squall and the fog that precedes a thunderstorm. The main-topsails were clewed up and furled, and at twelve o'clock we were in a dead calm.

From midday on we proceeded with foresail and mizzensail, hauling the light wind from the N, with considerable rain and fog. At one o'clock the breeze changed to the E, and we steered with the foresail to the N5°E. At two o'clock the *Andromaque* signaled having sounded thirty-nine fathoms, and we ourselves found seventy fathoms over sand. At four o'clock the frigate *Nra. Sra. de la O* came within hailing distance and was ordered to send to the *San Luis* her first pilot, who was a harbor pilot with some experience in those regions. At five-thirty o'clock a signal was made for the fleet to wear around in evolution and to steer to the W¼NW in a formation of three columns. The said evolution was executed promptly, and the fleet was on the other tack with a fresh wind from SSW. At ten o'clock we took a sounding without finding bottom in 110 fathoms. At twelve o'clock the wind veered to the WSW; a signal was made to wear around, and the fleet continued toward the SSW with a fresh wind from the W.

16 April 1781

The day dawned very clear; the sea was heavy and the wind from the WNW. All twenty-three ships of the fleet were in sight. At eleven o'clock the frigates were sent to scout, and the warship *San Nicolás* signaled eighty fathoms over sandy, leaden mud. An observation was worked in latitude N 28°36'; longitude 290°12'. According to these observations, the charts of those coasts made by the pilots of Havana were defective.

The wind continued from the fourth quadrant, its strength diminishing greatly, and we proceeded with the six principal vessels hauling the wind to the N¼NE, the whole fleet united.

At three o'clock in the afternoon the lookout on the topmast reported sighting a vessel to the NNE, and then the warship

16 April 1781

Guerrero, which was to leeward, reported the same. Immediately the brigantine *Levrette* and the cutter *Serpent* were ordered to give chase on the NE course where the sighted ship still lay. We could then see it clearly from the quarterdeck. It appeared to be a 30- to 40-gun frigate. At three-thirty o'clock the frigates "O" and *Licorne*, which were forward, also gave chase, and then the warship *Intrépide*, which was the swiftest vessel of all the fleet. At five o'clock the "O" advised that the sighted ship was fleeing and that she could attack it successfully. One-half an hour later the entire fleet wore around, and we lay to aboard starboard tacks to the N. We took a sounding in thirty fathoms.

At six o'clock we saw that the enemy frigate was proceeding crowding sail in a turn from the SE with wind from the $W\frac{1}{4}NW$, and the five pursuers were behind her. At six-thirty o'clock the "O" signaled that the pursued vessel was an enemy ship, whereupon the packet *Renombrado* was ordered to occupy the space between the *Intrépide* and the flagship in order to relay signals from one ship to the other. At seven-thirty o'clock the signal was made to come around to the starboard tack, and the stern lanterns were lighted. At eleven-thirty we took a sounding over sixty fathoms. At this hour the wind shifted to the NNE, fresh. Immediately we steered toward the $W\frac{1}{4}NW$, firing rockets at intervals so that the pursuers would know our position.

17 April 1781

At five o'clock in the morning the *Levrette* came within hailing distance, and her commander reported that because the frigate they were pursuing had disappeared; the *Intrépide* signaled a return to the fleet, and all took measures so as to draw near to it. The commander said that he had surmised that the frigate was English because he had distinctly seen on the stern the boom or stanchion used only by the English. The *Intrépide* gave the same reason for a similar supposition with which we confirmed as true the notice sent to Havana from Cape Corrientes, and we believed that we were going to attack the enemy very soon.

At six o'clock we trimmed all the sails, and at nine-thirty a signal was made to the fleet asking the general staffs of the troops and crews aboard the ships to form, in case of necessity, a single corps of the whole and to attack the enemy in whatever situation he might be found. The Chevalier de Monteil acquitted himself with great gallantry on this occasion, offering his fleet to the last man.

On this day, as on the three or four previous days, many logs of extraordinary size were sighted, thrown into the sea no doubt by the Mississippi and Apalache rivers with their strong freshets.

At noon we lay to, awaiting the general staffs, who had been summoned. At three o'clock in the afternoon, after all the reports had been received, we made a careful estimate of our position. From the reports it was learned that our fleet could give us 1,500 soldiers and the French fleet 725, who when joined with the detachment of land troops from Havana formed a corps of 3,850 men.

At sunset we counted twenty-two vessels; the French frigate *Licorne* was missing, not having reappeared since she was sent to give chase on the previous day.

18 April 1781

At five-thirty o'clock the *Andromaque* was ordered to take a sounding, and she signaled 128 fathoms. Afterward she was sent to scout to the N, and the *Renombrado* was ordered to follow her so as to relay signals.

The frigate came alongside and reported to us the same thing the *Intrépide* had said concerning the ship pursued the previous day, adding that she had made both Spanish and French signals to that vessel, to neither of which it had responded.

Position observed: 29°13' of latitude; 290°16' longitude.

After noon we navigated steering toward the W$\frac{1}{4}$NW, with the fleet united in a formation of three lines. At six o'clock in the afternoon, considering that we were on the meridian of Pensacola, a signal was made for the fleet to lay to.

19 April 1781

At two-thirty o'clock in the morning a signal was made to trim the sails, firing several rockets so that the distant ships could comprehend it. At dawn each ship had its signal numeral on the highest point of the mast, and the *Andromaque* and *Renombrado* were sent to scout to the N. The brigantine *Levrette* was sent with an order to stand inshore[104] and to investigate whether or not the port of Pensacola was in the hands of the Spaniards and any new circumstances she might observe. A similar order was given to the captain of the *Andromaque*, M. de Ravenel. At seven o'clock the fleet was ordered to assume the formation of pursuit in two lines with bowlines hauled and to crowd sails, making the formation on the flagship.

At nine o'clock the sounding was twenty fathoms. We then steered to the N$\frac{1}{4}$NE, with the wind E$\frac{1}{4}$SE. At ten o'clock the *Andromaque* signaled land to the NNW and that she was in ten fathoms over sand.

At twelve o'clock land was sighted bearing to the N; we proceeded until we were two leagues from land in ten fathoms of water. We saw all the coast distinctly, Santa Rosa Island, and the entrance of the port; also visible were a frigate which appeared to be a 30-gun vessel, at anchor within the port, and other smaller ships. At two o'clock we saw the *Andromaque* and the *Levrette* bearing away, running along the coast of Santa Rosa Island toward the W, and they signaled to us that we were masters of the port, whereupon the ensign was extended and the flag was made fast.

At two-thirty o'clock the *Andromaque* signaled that she was aground; the general immediately ordered that the "O" and the *Renombrado*, as well as the longboats of the warships that were cruising closest, go to help her.

At four o'clock the fleet tacked to the outside with the wind from the E. At five o'clock the *Levrette* came within hailing distance, and her captain reported that he had talked at the entrance of the harbor with the commander of the war sloop *Carmen*, Don N. Sapian, who told him that the army of Señor Gál-

---

104. Saavedra says *aterrase*, which means to approach the earth. [Ed.]

vez was before Pensacola, hurriedly making preparations for the attack, which had not yet begun, and that the general had been slightly wounded on one finger and in the abdomen.

At five-thirty o'clock the majors of the army and the fleet went aboard the said brigantine with letters to Señor Gálvez from the general officers of the land and sea forces, informing him of the purpose and circumstances of their armament.

20 April 1781

The fleet had followed the same course all night. At six o'clock in the morning the cutter *Serpent* came within hailing distance. Her captain gave the general the same information given by the *Levrette*, adding that the *Andromaque*, having lightened her weight by removing water and fourteen guns, had been freed at eight-thirty that night with the aid of the launches and longboats of the fleet, which were sent for that purpose, and that she did not appear to have suffered appreciable damage in the hull as a result of running aground.

At twelve-thirty the whole fleet came about, navigating toward land, with a light wind from the SE. At four o'clock Field Marshal Cagigal with his son and two aides-de-camp transferred to the French cutter in order to enter the port and go to see General Gálvez. I took advantage of the opportunity and went aboard the cutter for the same purpose. We hoped to pick up on the way a harbor pilot for the entrance who was aboard the *Andromaque*, but her captain told us that the *Levrette* had taken him off that morning. The wind slackened greatly, and we could not reach land until nightfall. At about nine o'clock we found ourselves embayed on the lee shore of Santa Rosa Island, and having no knowledge of those places we cast anchor at once. We fired several cannon shots and rockets, so that on perceiving those signals the detachments of troops who were on Santa Rosa Island would send us a bar pilot, but it later became evident that we were too far away.

21 April 1781

At seven o'clock in the morning we weighed anchor, and we sailed in search of Siguenza Point on Santa Rosa Island, with a very light wind from the SE; and at two-thirty o'clock in the afternoon we were off another point, at the very entrance of the port and opposite the Barrancas Coloradas, where the English had their battery called the Red Cliffs battery. Naval Lieutenant Villavivencio came alongside in a boat, and he guided us into the entrance of the port, although he had protested that he did not know it very well.

When we passed in front of the battery, the enemy fired at us eighteen cannon shots of heavy caliber; they fell near us but none struck our vessel, although we ran aground on the bar within their range, but M. Lalone, commandant of the *Serpent*, an officer of much ingenuity and intelligence, ordered all the men and artillery moved to the bow and the vessel floated free without giving the English time to secure their aim. At first glance it seemed strange that this battery had not done notable damage to as many vessels as passed within range of its guns daily, but there were two reasons for this: first, the distance from the battery to the opposite extreme of the channel is greater than it appears, and in my opinion is more than 700 toises; second, because the battery is on an elevated site, the firing was aimed without variation and therefore was very inaccurate.

Once we were within the harbor, the frigate captains Don Miguel Alderete and Don José Serrato came to the *Serpent* to greet General Cagigal. They accompanied us on their longboats, and we went in through a kind of inlet, called there a bayou [*estero*], which penetrates inland more than one league. We landed at a structure somewhat like a redoubt, built provisionally to contain the attacks of the Indians, and from there we proceeded overland to a place where our troops were encamped, about one-quarter of a league distant.

Gálvez received us with a vivid display of joy. That evening, when he and I were alone, he related to me the entire sequence of his operations and described his distress at finding himself obliged to lay formal siege to three forts garrisoned by soldiers almost as numerous as those he had brought. Moreover, the English had on their side many Indian nations, warlike, cruel, excellent marksmen skillful in the handling of muskets, who had harassed his small army sorely in the march it had had to make in a country full of dense forests and with many obstructions, the most appropriate land in the world for ambushes. Seven times he had been obliged to move the encampment before being able to take post in a location advantageous for launching the attack.[105]

He described to me the intense fright caused him by the appearance of our fleet. The English had announced the imminent arrival of reinforcements, whereas he had not the least idea that he would be sent such a powerful assistance from Havana, because its hasty preparation had not given time for sending him any advance notice. Therefore, believing that his expedition was doomed, he learned to his surprise that the warships in sight of the port were Spanish and French. He was slightly wounded on one hand and in the abdomen.[106]

That night I availed myself of a comfortable sort of barrack which belonged to Father Cirilo, vicar of the troops of Louisiana,[107] and the next day I was given a tent with the King's Immemorial Regiment, the regiment in which I had served, where I stayed throughout the siege.[108]

Sunday 22 April 1781

On the previous afternoon the combined fleet had cast anchor half a league from land in seven fathoms of water, in or-

---

105. For location of the successive encampments, see Coker and Coker, 37–56. [Tr.]

106. During Gálvez's brief convalescence Ezpeleta was in command (Medina Rojas, 759–60). [Tr.]

107. Even before the capture of Pensacola, Bishop Echevarría had appointed a Capuchin priest from Louisiana, Father Cyril of Barcelona, to serve as *vicario*, or vicar forane, over West Florida (Gannon, 91). [Tr.]

108. Saavedra was admitted to the Immemorial Regiment of the King as an ensign in 1768 and promoted to lieutenant the following year. [Tr.]

22 April 1781

der to prepare for the landing of the troops, which began that same night.

At six o'clock in the morning Field Marshal Cagigal, Major General Ezpeleta, and the quartermaster went out with a party of chasseurs to reconnoiter Fort Deanes [the Queen's Redoubt], also called the Media Luna [Half Moon] Fort, which was the dominant one of the three. They reached a point 300 toises from it but soon had to retire, having been discovered and fired upon by the enemy.

On the same morning two companies of French chasseurs and the French artillery company came into the camp. During the remainder of the day the rest of the troops who had come from Havana were arriving, without suffering the least damage on passing in front of the battery of Red Cliffs, although the English directed a lively fire on the longboats and launches that conveyed them.

Cagigal's detachment consisted of 1,617 men, the corps contributed by our navy numbered 1,505, and that of the French 725, who, when joined with the army Gálvez already had, brought the entire force to 7,806. For the best order of service the troops were divided into five brigades: the first commanded by Brigadier Gerónimo Girón;[109] the second by Colonel Don Manuel de Pineda, the third by Colonel Don Francisco Longoria, the fourth by Naval Captain Don Felipe Lope López Carrizosa, and the fifth, which was composed solely of French troop, by Naval Captain M. de Boiderant.

The camp was enlarged, doubling its former expanse. The place that each brigade was to occupy was marked out. A strong parapet of logs and earth was raised all around the camp the height of a man and seven feet thick, with its corre-

---

109. Bernardo de Gálvez's general staff for the planned expedition against Pensacola as announced on 1 April 1780 included Gerónimo Girón as major general (Coker and Coker, 8). That expedition did not take place. When on 7 April 1781 the junta of general officers in Havana decided to send reinforcements to Gálvez at Pensacola, Field Marshal Juan Manuel de Cagigal was to command the army troops, which were divided into two brigades commanded by Gerónimo Girón and Manuel de Pineda (ibid., 64). [Tr.]

sponding moat and banquette, to ensure against the sudden violent attacks of the Indians, who, even despite this precaution, used to kill our men inside their own tents at night by climbing into the dense foliage of the trees that overhung the parapet. The camp was well located. On the right it was protected by the inlet or estuary by which supplies were brought in from the port; it faced the forts of the enemy, about 1,500 toises distant; a part of the back was protected by the bayou; and the center was surrounded by the forest, which had been cleared somewhat by the cutting of the trees and branches used in raising the parapet. These trees were rather tall pines, and the forest, although dense, was not as rank and tangled as are those of the tropics, where the vegetation is more luxuriant than in the temperate zones. Redoubts crowned with heavy and small-caliber artillery were constructed in the corners of the camp and in places most exposed to attack. Outside our camps, by the front right-hand corner and a short distance away, was located the camp of the Indians of our alliance, which comprised men of several small nations, to be described later. For their protection they had huts made of tree bark which, although small and uncomfortable, withstood inclement weather very well.

23 April 1781

In the morning the quartermaster[110] went out with a detachment of chasseurs to extend the parallel before the Half Moon, but the enemy, upon perceiving the operation, opened a lively fire against them.

At noon an Irish drummer deserted to our camp. He related that General Campbell[111] was planning to erect a provisional battery near the Half Moon, that the garrisons of all the forts slept on their weapons, fearing a sudden attack, that they were dispirited because of the arrival of the Spanish rein-

---

110. Saavedra says *cuartel maestre*, which means staff. [Ed.]
111. Brigadier General John Campbell had been sent to Pensacola by General Clinton in October 1778 (Starr, 130). [Tr.]

forcements, and that they feared that they would not be able to sustain a long resistance but that, nevertheless, they did not plan to surrender until the very end.

24 April 1781

Brigadier Girón went out at dawn with two engineers and the artillery officers, supported by three companies of chasseurs, to survey the place where the attacks against the Half Moon were to be based; they were discovered by the enemy, who began to direct cannon fire at them. A short time later, a small body of soldiers sallied forth from the fort; together with the Indians they annoyed our men with musketry, and a rather brisk skirmish was begun. The clash lasted for more than one hour, until the enemy retired to the shelter of its artillery, and our companies returned to the camp, having had two officers and fifteen soldiers wounded. Losses of the other side were not learned, but it was known that some Indians were killed.

At eight o'clock General Cagigal and his aides-de-camp with several naval officers embarked on a small brigantine, which had two 24-caliber guns on its bow, to test whether Fort George could be attacked from the sea. I also took part in this test. With the brigantine at anchor in sixteen feet of water, its two cannons were fired, using an elevation that in my opinion probably reached twelve degrees. One of the balls passed over the fort, the other struck with considerable force in its esplanade. While we were conducting this test, the enemies brought two howitzers to the beach and fired them at us, one grenade falling very near the brigantine. This test proved that one or two of the warships that drew less water, by entering the port, could demolish the fort or at least harass it considerably. We returned to the encampment at noon.

In the afternoon our advanced posts warned that some parties of Indians and infantry were advancing, led by some officers on horseback. Our chasseurs went out and, after a skirmish in which we had three men wounded, the enemy retreated. One soldier of the Hibernia Regiment was missing. It was not known whether he had deserted or had been killed. A Spanish Negro who had been taken prisoner a short time earlier got out of the fort.

After nightfall the enemy fired from all sides of Fort George a general salvo of their artillery, which was followed by another volley of musketry. We were unable at that time to learn the motive for the demonstration.

Today the entrenchment of the camp was concluded. The terrain of it was like that of all the area. It is noteworthy that for many leagues around not one stone of any size is to be found. The first conquistadors of Florida had already noted this peculiarity, which our ancient histories of the Indian record.

25 April 1781

At six o'clock in the morning the commanding officers of the artillery and the engineers and some French officers went out guarded by a party of chasseurs to survey the place selected for the attack and to conclude their operations. When they drew near to Fort Half Moon, they met two enemy infantry companies drawn up on the very terrain they had surveyed on previous days and alongside the English companies hordes of savages, who were firing with more order and regularity than usual. A bloody skirmish ensued which lasted until seven-thirty o'clock, when both sides retired. We had five men wounded, and there came over from the enemy a dragoon who said he was a Frenchman and who in reality was a great rogue.

At eleven o'clock in the morning Councillor Stephenson came to the camp, sent by the governor of Pensacola, Peter Chester[112] to parley with us. In order to comprehend the purpose of his coming, one must consider that as soon as General Gálvez disembarked his army, he begged the English commandants not to destroy the town, promising that he would not take advantage of it in any way in order to direct his at-

---

112. Peter Chester held the office of governor of West Florida from 11 August 1770 until the surrender of the province to Spain in 1781 (Starr, 27). As early as March 1777 Chester protested against the transmission of arms and ammunition up the Mississippi River under the protection of the Spanish flag, and "every possible Countenance and Encouragement given to the Rebels in Louisiana" (Caughey, 123–92). [Tr.]

25 April 1781

tacks against the forts, which were located apart, and that neither his troops nor his Indian allies would molest the citizens or cause them the least damage. On this basis a solemn agreement was made between the generals of both nations, and many families who had fled toward Georgia returned to Pensacola. Because an experiment had been conducted on the previous day with a brigantine to see whether Fort George could be attacked from the sea, and because the English foresaw that if this project were put into practice, the town, being in the middle, could not fail to be damaged severely, Stephenson came to demand fulfillment of that agreement. He dined with the general and withdrew in the afternoon well satisfied. He had told us that the salvo heard on the previous evening had been in celebration of a victory won by Lord Cornwallis against the Anglo-Americans, news of which had come to them from Virginia.[113]

26 April 1781

At a little past three o'clock in the afternoon five companies of grenadiers and chasseurs commanded by M. de Bouligni, captain of the fixed regiment of New Orleans, went out in support of the engineers who were going to survey the trench that was to be opened that night. A short while after this operation was begun, they were attacked by more than 200 English soldiers and a large number of Indians, who penetrated the forest to their right, apparently with the object of cutting off one company which was far advanced. Our own men perceived this movement, and several parties were sent to that area with two field guns. They forced the Indians to fall back toward the English soldiers who, losing ground little by little, were pushed back against Fort Half Moon, which opened a lively artillery

---

113. The victory celebrated was that of Lord Cornwallis over General Nathanial Greene at Guilford Courthouse, North Carolina, 15 March 1781. See Mark Mayo Boatner III, *Encyclopedia of the American Revolution* (David McKay Company, Inc., 1966), 460–71. The log of *H.M.S. Mentor* states that the news came with an express from Georgia and North Carolina (Rea and Servies, 183). [Tr.]

fire. Seeing that their task was frustrated and that it was growing dark, our men retired; they had, however, marked the place where the trench must be opened.

At ten o'clock in the evening 700 laborers with fascines [bundles of sticks] went out supported by 800 armed men to begin the work on the site that had been surveyed. The night was dark and stormy. In order to avoid discovery, they took a circuitous route through the forest, where the dense underbrush slowed their progress considerably. Also they were slow in finding the signs that had been left in the afternoon and in posting the troops in the pathways. At two o'clock in the morning, not yet having been able to commence their work and judging that they could not advance the trench enough to be under cover when day came, they suspended the operation for the time being and returned to the camp, leaving two companies of grenadiers posted in that spot.

27 April 1781

At six o'clock in the morning the grenadiers who had remained on watch were relieved by two companies of chasseurs.

At eight o'clock there came to our camp two deserters who asserted that the enemy was making great efforts to augment its defenses. Another deserter from the Waldeck regiment who came over the previous day had said the same.

At nine o'clock a report was brought to the general that the enemy was felling trees in the forest; he assumed that it was for the purpose of advancing a redoubt that could hinder our projected attack, so he sent four companies with two field guns to investigate their activities and to join with the chasseurs posted there to dislodge them from the forest.

Indeed the troop proceeded to the place where the trees were being felled, and the advance parties discovered the beginnings of a parapet that was on a line with the terrain where our parallels had been drawn. Some cannons had already been mounted there, and more than 200 men and some Indians were in position to defend this post. Our chasseurs attacked them vigorously, and although they answered with a lively fire, we should

27 April 1781

have succeeded in dislodging them had the Half Moon Fort not protected them with its artillery, which controlled that place. At two o'clock our troop withdrew, leaving five men dead, and fifteen wounded, among them three officers.

In part because of this event, and in part also because two German soldiers of the regiment of Louisiana had deserted, the order previously issued to go out that night to continue work on the trench was revoked.

After nightfall there came over to the camp a deserter from the enemy who detailed with considerable clarity the defenses that the English had already prepared and the troops, sailors, armed civilians, and Indians (they were counted as troops); and he stated that they were constructing a battery to the right of Fort Half Moon for better defense of that fort. This deserter also related that the English had on that day hanged a sergeant of ours from the regiment of Flanders, who had gone a few days earlier over to Fort George. They sentenced him as a spy, because they had surprised him taking the dimensions of the artillery and having in his possession plans of the certification.

28 April 1781

After daybreak it was clearly seen that the enemy had constructed a redoubt at the edge of the forest where the skirmish of the previous day had taken place. At nine-thirty o'clock the engineers went out with 200 laborers supported by three companies of chasseurs to look for another place from which the attacks against the forts could be directed. In fact they found a sufficiently clear and wide road, made in advance by the dragging of trees or some other means. They carried out their operations without being molested by the enemy who, doubtless believing that our attack would be made by way of the place where we had made repeated inspections, was awaiting us in the forest, toward which, as was seen from the port, they had been having artillery dragged since early morning. This operation was concluded in a little more than an hour.

At six o'clock in the evening two companies of grenadiers went out to occupy the post surveyed in the morning, and at about eight o'clock all the rest of the detachment composed of 700 laborers with 350 fascines went out, supported by 800 soldiers and all the tools necessary for opening the trench through the area. The enemy, who no doubt was awaiting us in the place previously contemplated, more than 600 toises from there, did not perceive anything at all, and thus the work was concluded successfully, all the troop being under cover long before daybreak.

The commanding officer at the trench was Don Gerónimo Girón.

Three deserters came to the camp from the fort, while three grenadiers from New Orleans and three fusiliers of the Hibernia Regiment went over to the enemy from our camp.

29 April 1781

At four o'clock in the morning the sappers were relieved in order to finish the trench and to continue the opening of a covered way, which had also been begun. At a little after six o'clock the enemy observed the work that had been done, and they opened a cannon and mortar fire, firing quite briskly at first, and more slowly later, until eleven o'clock, when the firing ceased altogether. We had only two men killed and one wounded as a result of that firing. Some 4- and 8-caliber cannon shots were fired from our trench to frighten away some parties of soldiers and Indians who were approaching to examine it.

That afternoon I went with several officers to see the work done up to that time. The trench was about 1,000 toises distant from our camp. It must have been about 350 toises in length, and it comprised two galleries. The troop was sheltered perfectly, and the work demonstrated the diligence of those who had done it. It would have been unattainable even with a force of twice as many sappers if sandy soil had not spared them many difficulties. I also inspected with some attention the site where the first battery was to be placed. Some people there said that it was little more than 300 toises distant from Fort Half Moon and 500 toises from Fort George. It appeared to me that the distance from both was much greater and that it was at least

29 April 1781

500 toises from the former and 700 from the latter.

The terrain was deceptive because there was a ravine midway between the trench and the forts, and experience proved later that it had indeed misled the calculations of the experts.

At eight o'clock in the evening all the guard of the trench was relieved by an equal number of sappers and soldiers commanded by Colonel Don Manuel de Pineda. The work continued all night, and a battery of six 24-caliber cannons and four mortars was laid out; also two redoubts were formed to the left and right of the trench for its defense. At nine o'clock the enemy opened fire with cannons, mortars, and howitzers, although somewhat slowly. The firing ceased at a little past one o'clock, and we had three soldiers and one officer wounded.

30 April 1781

At dawn the enemy opened a rather lively fire.

At seven o'clock in the morning an English deserter came over. A short time later the firing from the forts ceased, and our sappers employed the entire day in widening the trench and perfecting the battery of cannons and mortars and finishing the two redoubts.

At ten o'clock in the morning some parties of savages approached within half a musket shot of our camp, and under cover of the thickets of the forest they opened fire on the advanced posts. The latter responded at once with artillery, and the savages retired, after having mortally wounded a soldier inside his own tent. From there the savages, concealed by the forest, went to the banks of the creek by which launches came into the camp. They surprised four sailors who were loitering carelessly and killed and scalped them.

At midday the French frigate *Andromaque* put into the port. She was fired on fiercely as she passed in front of the battery of Red Cliffs, but only two or three shots reached her, causing little damage.

At nightfall an enemy deserter came over.

1 May 1781

The enemy's fire commenced at dawn with more rapidity and better aim than in previous days; from ten o'clock on it became slower. The banquette of the trench was completed, as well as the parapet and esplanades of the battery, in which six bronze 24-caliber cannons and four mortars were placed that night.

Some parties of savages came into view in the forest hard by the camp; the mulattoes and Negroes of Louisiana, who are famous marksmen, went out against them and frightened them away; nonetheless, they killed a sailor who was bathing in the creek.

At three o'clock in the afternoon the general visited the trench; Naval Captain Larizosa was commanding there because of the illness of the colonel from Aragón, Don Francisco Longoria, who had suffered a grave accident a few days earlier.

2 May 1781

At six o'clock in the morning the enemy opened fire with several cannons, three mortars, and four howitzers. At ten o'clock our battery opened its own fire, directing the fire of the cannons against Fort Half Moon and the fire of the mortars against Fort George. The troops of the trench were relieved at the usual hour, the chief officer being the French Naval Captain M. de Boiderant.

Near noon the general went out with an escort of chasseurs to observe, from a copse located to the right and contiguous to the town, the effect of our artillery fire on the enemy forts. I accompanied the general in this inspection, and it confirmed for me the opinion I had formed from the beginning, that the battery was much farther from the forts than had been calculated. Moreover, the battery was built in such a way that at the same time that the fire from Fort Half Moon struck it on the front, that of Fort George harassed it on the opposite side.

That day we had eight men wounded, and a deserter came over to us from the Waldeck Regiment.

2 May 1781

In the afternoon the quartermaster went out with other engineers to trace out the continuation of the trench and to extend it to the Pine Hill, up to a point a little more than 250 toises from the Half Moon, where another stronger battery would be built. Shortly after dark 800 soldiers and an equal number of laborers went out to execute this project. By midnight the troop was already under cover, without having been noticed, and the man who brought the report added that our enemies were laboriously occupied in restoring the parapet that our artillery had partly destroyed.[114]

3 May 1781

Beginning at dawn the enemy directed a heavy fire against our battery and the works on the left, which our men answered with no less vehemence and a sufficiently accurate aim. We had eight wounded and one killed, and the trench was relieved as usual, its commander being Don Pablo Figuerola. All the materials necessary for the construction of the battery planned on the previous day were transported. The general visited the new works at four o'clock in the afternoon. Three Germans and one English deserter came over to us. They described the good effect that our fire, especially that of the mortars, had produced on the enemy forts.[115]

4 May 1781

During the previous night the left gallery of the trench was finished, and a redoubt formed in the end of it was com-

---

114. The trench was 900 paces long, four yards wide, and one and one-half yards high. A redoubt was built in its end, a long musket shot distant from the advanced British fortification (Medina Rojas, 770). [Tr.]

115. During the night of the third, the 8-caliber cannons that had been left in the old trench were brought to the new redoubt. With this protection, a branch sixty paces long was opened, running from the new redoubt toward the left, closing it with another at the end. The two 4-caliber cannons still in the redoubt of the old trench were brought to it. The projected second redoubt had not yet been completed (ibid.). [Tr.]

pleted, so as to protect that part of the trench.

At dawn the enemy opened their usual fire, but it ceased before ten o'clock. They had planned to surprise our trench this day, and in fact they did, in the following way:

From the time dawn began to break, some enemy parties sallied forth and came by a circuitous route to conceal themselves in the dense woods to the left of our latest works and a short distance from them. Frigate Captain Don Andrés Tacón noticed some of these parties with his field glass by the dim light of dawn, and he reported the sighting to Don Pablo Figuerola, the commander of the trench, who attributed no importance whatever to this warning. Thus 200 chosen men were assembled in that spot, where they remained hidden until noon, the hour when the troop was eating, when the sun was very powerful in that climate, the hour they judged most opportune for a surprise attack.

At twelve-thirty the forts commenced heavy firing which forced our troop to remain under cover in their entrenchment, not fearing any other danger than that which could come to them from the artillery barrage. Presumably the two sentinels who were in gallery and the redoubt on the left either hid themselves behind the parapet also or, if they looked out, looked only at Fort Half Moon, which was in front of them. What is certain is that the enemies in ambush in the thickets to the left came out of the woods undetected, and while the fire from the forts continued briskly, without cannonballs so as not to injure their own men, they assaulted the redoubt, surprised three companies that were in it, put to the sword those who tried to resist them, and put the others to rout. All the troops on guard were terror-stricken. The enemy overran the trench up to the redoubt at the angle of the two galleries, where they spiked four cannons and burned the couplings and fascines, then retired, carrying off as prisoners three officers, all gravely wounded.

The news of this disaster reached the camp immediately; and instantly the major general went out with five companies of grenadiers, but he found that the enemy had already withdrawn. The guard of the trench was reinforced at the most exposed part, the fire was extinguished, and the damages caused by the enemy were remedied as speedily as possible. In this action we had twenty killed, included among them four officers, and as many wounded.[116]

In the order of this day Field Marshal Don Juan Manuel de Cagigal was recognized as commanding officer of the flying corps of 1,600 men.

The trench troops were relieved. Its commander was Don José de Pereda. Two Negroes and one Negress came over to us from the city.

5 May 1781

The enemy's fire was lively today, with the result that we had nine killed and eleven wounded. The fire from our battery was brisk also. In the afternoon four deserters came over, but it was impossible to get any news of importance from them.

The trench was relieved, its commander being Naval Captain Zavala. Tonight a barrier of cotton bales and sandbags was constructed on the left side of our parallel to cover the sappers and protect the building of the battery previously planned.

6 May 1781

At one o'clock in the morning a furious storm broke, with wind, rain, and thunder; a tornado uprooted many tents and the camp was flooded. The fleet, which was lying at anchor outside the harbor, had to set sail and abandon its anchors for fear of being dashed to pieces against the shore, and there remained at anchor only three French warships whose cables were new and strong enough to resist the force of the storm and the terrible sea it raised. The gale was blowing from the southeast, and our ships would have perished in the bay formed by the land on that side if by good fortune there had not come a contrasting wind from the north which threw them out to sea. I have never in my life heard

---

116. The British force that carried out the surprise attack was made up of 120 Loyalists led by Major John McDonald and eight Waldecker regiments commanded by Lieutenant Colonel Albrecht von Horn. The major general was Ezpeleta (Coker and Coker, 80n3). [Tr.]

such terrifying claps of thunder. The rain penetrated my tent even though the fabric was double, and all night long I was soaked with water and stiff with cold. The day dawned fair, but the northeast wind that set in at daybreak was imperious and so icy that it was unendurable. The wind, which in winter in those regions freezes the deepest rivers such as the Mississippi, is extremely frigid even in the intense heat of summer.

Despite the bad night, and although the trenches and batteries had been severely damaged by the water and the hurricane, our firing commenced at seven o'clock in the morning, directed against Fort Half Moon; it was seriously impeding our work on the left side, especially with the howitzers, whose shells killed many of our men, including four grenadier officers from Aragón and Navarra.

The trench was relieved at the accustomed hour, its commander being Colonel Pineda. Two howitzers were mounted in the redoubt on the left, and they began to fire that same afternoon with good effect.

A rumor was spread that the enemy had abandoned the battery on the Red Cliffs. In order to make sure of that, the General ordered a party of Tallapoosa Indians, led by a warrior who was famous among them, to go to reconnoiter it and to bring in some prisoners if they could. They executed their commission quickly and returned at nightfall with two soldiers from the Waldeck regiment whom they caught unaccompanied a short distance outside the fort, and from them it was learned that the rumor of the abandonment of the battery was false. The Germans came in trembling, because they believed that the Indians were going to give them a cruel death, according to their customs. Because they had brought the prisoners in alive, the general gave the warrior and his tribesmen three times the reward he had promised them, and that is the only method of assuring that the Indians treat prisoners humanely.

That afternoon the general told me of the great difficulty in which he found himself and the enterprise he had planned. In Havana he had been given a very scant supply of cannonballs, and already there were so few remaining of the 24-caliber balls, which were the ones needed most, that there were not enough

6 May 1781

to supply the batteries for two consecutive days. Almost all the cannonballs fired by the enemy were gathered up; the soldiers were paid two reales for each one brought in, but this did not make up the shortage.

Earlier the general was able to turn for help to the fleet, but that recourse no longer was available because the fleet had been forced to sea by the storm, and it was unlikely that it would reappear for many days. The French warships that had remained at anchor could contribute very few cannonballs. In this situation, he was resolved to assault Fort Half Moon by escalation that very night. Possession of it would oblige the other two forts that were dominated by it to surrender, and thus the siege, which was already greatly prolonged and with its length was causing damage to the earlier projects, would be shortened. I did not think the idea bad after he had explained to me his plan of operation and the precautions he contemplated in order not to endanger its success.

7 May 1781

All preparations for the projected assault having been made as quickly as possible, there went out at one o'clock in the morning 900 chosen men commanded by Brigadier Girón, divided into three groups. They were to attack the fort on the front and the gorge entrance,[117] for which they carried ladders, axes, and various other tools. Serving as guides were a German deserter and an officer from the New World who had come over to our camp. In order to reach the point of attack without being seen, they had to take a long circuitous route which consumed considerable time. The moonlight was bright, and dawn was about to come; for these reasons the operation had to be postponed to a more propitious occasion, so the troops retired to the camp without having been noticed by the enemy.[118]

---

117. Saavedra says *gola*, which means entrance from the bastion plaza. [Ed.]

118. At 12:30 midnight on 8–9 May, the principal officers met in Ezpeleta's tent to complete the details of the attack. It was to be made by 700

At six o'clock in the morning Fort Half Moon commenced firing on our left; as a result we lost five soldiers and one ensign of the Hibernia Regiment and had several wounded.

At eight o'clock some fascines in the enemy fort began to burn, but the fire was extinguished quickly.

The savage Indians attacked our advanced guards and killed one soldier and wounded another. Some troops went out against them, and they killed two more men, scalping them, and even carried off one prisoner, whom General Campbell saved from the cruel death they were preparing for him.

In the afternoon work was begun on the battery on the left side, where the work was continued all night with great courage and perseverance.

8 May 1781

By dawn the battery 250 toises distant from the Half Moon was already completed, and it lacked only the glacis, which was begun without loss of time, the eight 24-caliber cannons that were to be mounted being ready close at hand. The enemy continued its fire against that area. We could respond to it only with the two howitzers that had been placed in the redoubt on previous days.

At nine o'clock Don Benito Pardo and I advanced from the camp to a place from which the three enemy forts could be seen clearly. A short time later we saw Fort Half Moon explode with a terrifying noise. It had been set afire by a shell from our howit-

---

to 800 men, grenadiers of the regiments of the Prince, Soria, Guadalajara, Navarra, España, and the 3d Marine Company, and chasseurs of the regiments of the Prince, Soria, 2d of Navarra, Havana, Aragón, and Hibernia. From this last would be sent 100 additional men, and 100 French chasseurs would be added also. These troops were to be ready at midnight on the ninth. They would be commanded by the brigadier Girón, the lieutenant of Soria Salla, and the lieutenant colonel of Hibernia Arturo O'Neill. They would appear to be going out for the relief of the trench. Ezpeleta would remain in the trench to reinforce Girón if necessary. Moreover, in the trench would be the forces sent there on the sixth, 800 men from various corps, who were guarding the 800 laborers engaged in the construction of the new battery (Medina Rojas, 773–75; Starr, 209). [Tr.]

8 May 1781

zers, which fell into the powder magazine within the fort. We ran back to the camp from which the general and other officers were already emerging because of this remarkable event. They hastily headed for the trench at a quick march, with all the companies of grenadiers and chasseurs. There they ascertained what had happened and learned that the majority of the garrison had perished in the explosion. Without losing a moment, the troop from the trench and the reinforcing companies commanded by Girón and Ezpeleta flung themselves impetuously upon the fort and, climbing upon its ruins, took possession before the enemy could prevent it.(119) Fort George and the fort in between opened a heavy fire of grapeshot and muskets, but our troop, stationing themselves in the Half Moon and placing in it some cannons and howitzers, returned their fire so accurately that the fire of the middle fort fell silent, and at the same time some of our battalions entrenched themselves in a commanding site so near that fort as to leave the enemy no possibility that their artillery would be effective.(120) Seeing that they were inevitably lost, the English quickly sent away the Indians who were assisting them, distributing among them a large quantity of powder and cannonballs; they detached 300 men overland to Georgia, to spare them from becoming prisoners; and at three o'clock in the afternoon Fort George raised a white flag, and an aide sent by Campbell came to where the general was, proposing a cessation of hostilities until the following day, when the capitulation would be made.(121)

---

119. Other columns came out of the camp later to cover all the objectives, while the first group hastened toward the Queen's Redoubt. Captain Johnstone, commanding the British artillery, checked the Spaniards in their first attempt, giving time to Captain Byrd with seventy men of the 60th Regiment to arrive and assist in carrying out the wounded and some artillery pieces. Before retiring to the Prince of Wales Redoubt, the English spiked the guns (Medina Rojas, 775–78; Starr, 210–11). [Tr.]

120. The Prince of Wales Redoubt. [Tr.]

121. Ezpeleta answered for Gálvez, who was not in the camp at that time, giving the English only three hours instead of the nine and one-half hours (until noon of the following day) they requested (Medina Rojas, 780). [Tr.]

The general refused to accede to the truce unless the capitulation was begun. Campbell immediately sent a nephew of his, a sergeant major of the same name, with full powers for this purpose. He proposed several articles, some of which were accepted and others denied, in a long conference that took place at eleven o'clock in the evening, and the articles of capitulation were issued and signed on the following day. The substance of the surrender was that Pensacola and all of West Florida would remain under Spanish domination, that all honors of war would be conceded to the English troop, except that they would be prisoners of war sent under parole to the British dominions.[122]

10 May 1781

In the afternoon six companies of Spanish grenadiers and the French chasseurs drew up in battle formation 200 toises from Fort George, out of which emerged 900 men with General Campbell at their head, and they, also drawn up in battle formation, facing our men, surrendered the banners of the Waldeck Regiment and a banner of the artillery and laid down their weapons. Two of our companies took possession of Fort George, and the French took possession of the circular battery. A detach-

---

122. Rendón reported to Cagigal and Bernardo de Gálvez the storm of protest aroused in the Continental Congress by the terms of the capitulation of Pensacola (Rendón to Cagigal, 12 June, 10 September 1781, AGI:Cuba 1319). On 2 October he reported that in the *New York Gazette* of 15 September there had appeared letters written by members of Congress, found in a pouch intercepted by the enemy. Among the letters Rendón translated was a letter addressed to Thomas Nelson, Esq., governor of Virginia, from the Virginia delegates Joseph Jones, James Madison, Jr., Theodorick Bland, and Edmund Randolph: "No doubt Your Excellency had heard of the extraordinary capitulation to which the Spanish commandant agreed at the time of the reduction of Pensacola, by which the prisoners taken there have been permitted to be transported to any British port save Jamaica and Saint Augustine in Florida, and that General Campbell consequently has chosen the port of New York, to which we have been advised some of them have already arrived, and where they will undoubtedly be employed in the defense of that post" (ibid., Rendón to Cagigal, 2 October 1781). On 7 October, Rendón wrote to Bernardo de Gálvez:

ment was sent to occupy the battery of Red Cliffs, whose garrison numbered 139, including the officers.

The total number of men taken prisoner amounted to 1,110. Adding to them 105 who were killed by the explosion at the Half Moon, 50 who perished in various encounters, 56 deserters, and 300 who set out for Georgia before the surrender, it appears that the total garrison of Pensacola numbered 1,621 men when the attack on it began. The English also had many Negroes who served them well as laborers in the fortifications and a large aggregation of Indian allies. The English and German troops had in their retinue 101 women and 123 children. In the siege we lost 10 officers and 84 soldiers; 5 officers and 180 men were wounded.[123]

11 May 1781

A large warehouse was consecrated to serve as a chapel, and the *Te Deum* was sung in it. An inventory of the provisions, artillery, and military stores that were in the stronghold was begun, and the commander-in-chief advised the major general and the commandants of the corps to begin to embark all that were on shore, so that without any loss of time they should be returned to Havana.

In the forts they found 143 cannons of various calibers, a mortar, 6 howitzers, 40 swivel guns, 2,150 fusils, a large store of cannonballs, sacks of grapeshot, cartridges, and other effects.

"Because the Congress has not concealed from me the great effect caused by the terms of the Capitulation of Pensacola, I desired to dissuade the members from their hasty judgements, but I lacked a perfect knowledge of the matter. With receipt of Your Lordship's esteemed letter, the copy of your letter to Comte de Grasse, and a copy of the Capitulation, I was able to show them to the President of the Congress, so that he could inform the whole body, and explain to the members the just and indisputable motives which obliged you to agree to that pact. The President replied by assuring me that the Congress was perfectly satisfied as to Your Lordship's friendly inclination toward the United States" (ibid., Rendón to Bernardo de Gálvez, 7 October 1781). [Tr.]

123. Reports of the numbers of casualties differ (Coker and Coker, 120–21). [Tr.]

Provisions were found in great abundance, so that there were enough to supply the warships and transport vessels with enough left over to sustain for several months the garrison that was to be left there.

At ten o'clock in the morning I went into the city and lodged with several officers in tents near large quarters in which three battalions were housed comfortably.

The town seemed to me to have a lovely plan, similar to that of Kingston in Jamaica, the wooden houses of delightful appearance arranged on spacious streets and squares but separated one from another so as to prevent the spread of conflagrations. The government house, the quarters, the warehouses, and other public buildings are sufficiently capacious and suitable for their respective purposes. For the convenience of commerce, six wooden wharves on pilings extend out into the sea far enough that not only longboats and lighters but also sloops, schooners, and other vessels of middling size can come alongside.

Facing the countryside there is a stout palisade flanked by wooden towers in the shape of bulwarks, which can hold cannons of small caliber, and a moat or ditch of adequate width and depth for the defense of the town against the attacks of the Indians. The three exterior forts had been built after the declaration of war. They occupy the heights that overlook the city. Two of them are temporary and short lived, but Fort George, although it is built of wood, could be maintained for a long time by keeping it in good repair.

In Pensacola there were many public shops stocked with all kinds of European and Asiatic goods, which gave an idea of the immense trade carried on there by the English, but it appeared to me that the population of the place, which did not exceed 6,000 souls, was incapable of consuming so great a store of goods; therefore I formed the judgment that Pensacola was one of the depots that the English have in America for conducting contraband trade with Spanish possessions.

As soon as the English took possession of Pensacola, ceded by Spain in the year 1763, they established in it the same system of government that rules all their other colonies. At that time there were few [Spanish-speaking] inhabitants there, and those few had moved to Havana over the span of a few years, so that in 1781 none of them remained in Pensacola. Some buildings from the time of the Spaniards remain; however, they are so ruinous and poor that they give a clear idea of the small degree of esteem with which that settlement was regarded.

More than thirty ships from different ports of England used to contribute annually to the commerce of Pensacola. For the most part they bought in Asiatic and European goods, and they took out hides bought from the Indians,[124] tar, and timber for construction and for masts, especially the pines that abound in these forests. At the time of the conquest, a frigate was found loaded with a cargo of masts, and there were many in the warehouses. This settlement will again become as useless and burdensome to the Spaniards as it was before it was ceded to the English if an effort is not made to trade with the Indians as did the English, profiting by their example to this end.[125]

Until now I have refrained from speaking about the Indians, so as not to interrupt the thread of the military operations with a long digression. During the siege I applied myself to getting acquainted with the nations who had gathered to assist us and to examining their character, government, religion, and customs, as much as was permitted by the imperfect kind of communication that could be achieved through some rude interpreters with people whose languages, limited to a few words, are essentially nothing more than an aggregate of arbitrary gestures.

All the Indians of those regions are known there under the general denomination of savages, and in reality they are not undeserving of this appellation, for they are still in the first stages of social life. There were Indians of various nations, the principal ones being the Choctaws, the Creeks or Tallapoosas, and the Alabamas. They inhabit the vast wildernesses that

---

124. Originally in the diary, after *indios* (Indians), he continued, "in exchange for rum, guns of little value and less security, and a sort of half-cloths called Limburg," but all this part was crossed out. [Ed.]

125. For a recent study see J. Leitch Wright, Jr., *The Only Land They Knew: The Tragic Story of the American Indians of the Old South* (New York: Macmillan, 1981). [Tr.]

stretch between Canada, the Mississippi, and Florida. The Choctaw nation formerly was numerous and formidable, but their number has declined notably. At present the Tallapoosas are the strongest and most bellicose nation known in these districts, and Americans, Englishmen, and Spaniards vie for their friendship with equal ardor. The Alabamas are brave and warlike, but their number is small; nonetheless an alliance with them is valuable to those who possess Pensacola and Mobile.

The nations differ from each other not only in language but also in certain exterior signs. For example, the heads of the Choctaws are flattened in an operation practiced on infants from the moment of their birth. The Alabamas lengthen their ears, have them pierced in several places, and wear earrings of strange shapes. But the customs of all are almost identical because they all lead the same kind of life, their needs are the same, and they have the same method of satisfying those needs. Amidst their barbarity they consider themselves to be the most fortunate people in the universe, and they look with horror on every new thing that may alter their system. Therefore, despite the fact that they have known Europeans for more than a hundred years, that they trade with Europeans and permit them to dwell in their towns, the advancements in civilization made up to now by the Indians are so few that the nations present a clear idea of the infancy of the human race.

The least civilized nations of whom ancient scholars acquired knowledge were much more civilized than any of these. Hence it is not to be wondered at that those scholars should have formed erroneous ideas about " natural man" or that the first discoverers of the New World, prejudiced by their opinions and ignorant of philosophical principles, should have attributed to the physical imperfection of its inhabitants what was the precise effect of their political and moral situation.

These nations know no other occupation than hunting and warfare. The first satisfies their needs, the second assures their independence. The only advancement that until now they have obtained from their contact with Europeans is the improvement in their means of destruction, substituting weapons of gunfire and steel for the bow and arrow; but because the Indians are not capable of manufacturing those weapons, far from profiting from them, they have lost much in this exchange, becoming dependent for the acquisition of the tools most necessary for their subsistence and defense on trade with their greatest enemies. They cultivate some produce and raise some cattle, but they do not regard these products as the basis of their livelihood, only as an aid in case of necessity. Therefore they leave agriculture and animal husbandry to the care of the women and the infirm, deeming them occupations unworthy of strong men.

Generally the Indians of these nations, or rather of these barbarous tribes, are vigorous, well formed, tall, and extremely agile. Many of the illnesses that afflict civilized man, the consequences of idleness and comfort, are unknown to them, but in exchange the fatigues and accidents of the nomadic life greatly damage their constitutions, so that their normal life span, if not inferior, is at most the equal of the civilized nations.

They are indubitably of the same race as the rest of the indigenous people of the New World, although they are beyond comparison more active, robust, and valorous than those who live in the subtropics. Generally they lack beards, their eyes are small and lively, their features heavy, their color red with a copper cast, and their hair black and straight; but there are to be seen many exceptions to this general rule, and one cannot fail to perceive that several of them have a mixture of the European, resulting probably from the great ease with which their women are used by the Englishmen and Americans who go to trade with them.

Although we call them barbarous because they do not know the arts and sciences that constitute our culture, they clearly have some natural cultural attainments. They have quick comprehension and abundant cunning, and, within the limited sphere to which their close attention is reduced, no people can boast of surpassing them in intelligence. Their character is energetic and decisive, passions operate in them with all their natural vigor, and they are as capable of a remarkable generosity as of a horrendous act of vengeance.[126]

They have several languages. Each nation, no matter how

---

126. On a separate piece of paper, apparently to be inserted here, Saavedra wrote these lines from Horace's *Art of Poetry:* "Impiger, iracundus,

small, has its own particular language. All consist of very few words. They cannot express any abstract idea, and yet they are eloquent in their discourse, because the ostentation of the words does not weaken the force of the sentiments. One Indian chief who came to our camp from far away with ten individuals of his nation told the general when he presented himself: "Thirty times have we seen this globe of fire be born and die before arriving before thy presence. We come to aid the Spaniards, believing them to be more just than other white men. Although we are a small nation, our assistance is not to be despised, because we know how to shed our blood for our friends, and we are accustomed to drink the blood of our enemies." This harangue depicts the forceful character and manly eloquence of the savages.

Man cannot live except in society because, in whatever situation he may be placed, the sum of his individual needs is greater than that of his physical powers. Therefore the human species has never been found so widely scattered that it is not united at least in families. It is true that among the savages the domestic union is less strong and lasting than among civilized peoples; the father acts as the head and the sons recognize his authority only up to the precise point at which they cease to need his help. The women remain dependent always. They are burdened with all the tasks of domestic servitude, and because the savages regard the amorous instinct as a necessity and not as a passion, their companions are treated without esteem and without jealousy, as if they were animals of a lower class.

Each nation consists of an indeterminate number of families who, having few social relations with one another, have surrendered a small part of their independence in order to form a union of public force, which we call government. Monarchy is

---

inexorabilis, acer jura neget sibi nata, nihil non arrget armis" (vv 121-22); "[If Homer's great Achilles tread the Stage] Intrepid, fierce, of unforgiving Rage, Like Homer's Hero, let him Spurn all Law, And by the Sword alone assert his Cause": The Rev'd Mr. Philip Francis, *A Poetic Translation of the Works of Horace*, 3d ed. (Printed for A. Millar in the Strand, 1749), 2:447. [Tr.]

unknown among them. The fathers of families meet to deliberate concerning the common objectives of the nation, the most prudent and experienced among them having preeminence; according to their judgment, public resolutions are taken, war is declared or peace adjusted, and the few disputes that can arise among persons who hardly recognize the right of ownership are decided.

They do not have written laws. They are guided by customs which are preserved by a sort of tradition from fathers to sons. Among all the nations there is at the center their certain kind of public law composed of the pacts and stipulations made for their mutual security. There is no guaranty except the interests of the contractors; nonetheless, the small nations know how to ally themselves together in order to balance the predominance of the large ones.

Although in time of peace each savage lives for himself and is subject to little domestic or civil subordination, in wartime all are subject to the orders of their chiefs and render unlimited obedience to them. The subordination lasts as long as the danger exists, and afterward each man returns to his habitual independence.

The religion of these nations is far from perfect. It is limited for the most part to certain superstitious practices inspired in them by precognition or fear. Its rite, if it has any, is simple, because among the Indians there are neither temples, priests, nor sacrifice. I could not discover that they recognize or worship any invisible Being; however, the veneration they observe for their deceased elders, the ceremonies with which they bury them, and the zeal with which they aspire to posthumous fame prove that they have some kind of presentiment of the immortality of the soul and of a future life.

They come frequently to the settlements of the Europeans and carry on a continuous trade with them, limited to bartering the objects they do not need for the articles they lack. Usually they bring in hides, feathers, and resin; and in exchange they receive axes, knives, hoes, shears, firelocks, powder, a supply of rum, and cloth with which to cover themselves. Most of this trade is conducted through the agents whom the neighboring European nations have among the Indians, where they are treated very hospitably.

Some tribes of savages have fixed settlements. This is the case with the Choctaws, Tallapoosas, and Alabamas. Others are nomadic and move their dwellings according to the seasons. As they practice hunting from childhood, they carefully cultivate all the qualities necessary for excelling in this kind of occupation, and it can be asserted that they are the most accomplished hunters in the world. Their bodies, hardened by hardship, resist all the vicissitudes of the nomadic life without being affected by the continuous changes of climate and diet. In urgent cases they walk twenty to twenty-five leagues per day without appearing to become tired. They have a marvelous patience for enduring inclement weather and for remaining immobile for days and nights in one spot, lying in wait for some game bird or animal.

Their vision is keen, and they discern at incredible distances objects that other men would not even suspect. They distinguish the different species of animals by their tracks, they calculate how far away the prey is, and they follow it through the densest forests with an astonishing certainty. They also pursue their prey by means of the sense of smell, which is as subtle in them as in hunting dogs, so that they follow animals and men by means of the scent and can even distinguish some nations from others, a thing that would seem to be exaggeration if those who have lived among them did not swear to it unanimously. Their aim with a musket is extremely accurate. Throughout the siege we saw them give amazing proofs of their marksmanship. They acquire this accuracy by dint of practice, for in addition to their continuous performance in the hunt, even when they are idle they usually have a stick in hand, and they aim with the stick at any object that passes before them.

In war they apply the same skills they use in the hunt, because for them war is nothing more than a hunt for men. They go always in small parties. They never meet the enemy face to face, nor do they fight with him strength to strength. They try to catch the enemy unprepared, and their entire military science is limited to the craftiness of the hunter. They are extremely prolific in stratagems, and if they were capable of union and order they would be the best light troops in the world in countries filled with dense forests like those of America. Among them the most acclaimed warrior is he who knows how to prepare his ambush and do great damage to the enemy without exposing himself to danger. The most glorious action is regarded as a calamity when some of them who engage in it lose their lives. A chief who would contend for mastery in hand-to-hand combat would be treated like a rash man unworthy to command them.

These ideas do not proceed from a lack of valor. The Indians regard the proximity of death with the greatest serenity, and their constancy in the tortures in which they generally lose their lives when they fall into the hands of their enemies as prisoners exceeds anything recounted to us by history; but they are frugal with the blood of their compatriots, for the reason that the nations consist of a small number of individuals. When I was talking about this point with a Tallapoosa, an intelligent man and a famous warrior, he told me that in the world there were three races of men, white, black, and red; that the first and the second were innumerable, and therefore the loss of some of them was not a cause for grief; but that there were very few of the third, and therefore it was necessary to preserve them with great care. For this reason, during the siege, they were quick to harass the English every time they were ordered to do so, but never could they be persuaded to attack those Indians who were allies of the English, and when one day our parties brought in one of them who had been killed, our Indians even gave a great funeral and buried him with demonstrations of intense grief.

They use no weapons other than the musket and a short axe, hollow at the handle, which serves them also as a pipe; they call it a tomahawk. With this they cut everything they need, and in war it is used to scalp the enemies either dead or badly wounded, which is in fact to pull out by the roots the hair which covers the cranium, the scalp being a trophy which they keep in their families as the escutcheon and irrefutable testimony of their heroic exploits. They handle the musket with great dexterity; their aim, as has been said, is almost unerring; they load the weapon with extreme rapidity, perhaps while running stooped close to the ground amidst the underbrush of the forest, so that when one goes to search for the savage in the spot from which the musket shot came, he himself is far away from there, and he can fire many shots without being discovered. The Indians approach without being seen because, besides being the color of the earth, they are accustomed to walking leaning forward so that in height they do not exceed the lowest bushes; at other times they carry a large branch in their hands and draw near concealed behind it. In forests without underbrush they dig holes in the ground where they hide themselves up to their necks, and there they lie in wait for the enemy and take unfailing aim without being seen.

In order to undertake any military action they strip themselves almost naked and adorn their heads with a sort of turban formed of the scalps they have taken from their adversaries; they anoint their entire bodies with foul-smelling grease, and they paint their faces with various colors to make them terrifying. This custom of freakish appearance is founded upon two good reasons: the anointing of the body makes it impervious to the bites of mosquitos and frightens away the venomous reptiles which abound in the forests, and when the face is covered with paint, one cannot perceive that the face changes color at the approach of danger, and this prevents fear from becoming contagious. On going forth to war they utter a shout which they call the cry of death, and it is a kind of terrible howl; they utter it also at the moment of attacking the enemy. The rest of the time they maintain a profound silence. They never walk in pairs but go one behind another, and they always go in parties of no more than twenty or thirty.

To direct their military operations they elect chiefs, whom they obey voluntarily but with great punctiliousness. The election of chiefs falls always upon the most valiant and experienced of those who are called warriors, and subordination to them is the more certain the more it is based upon confidence.

For their rations they carry a portion of cornmeal, cassava, or beans enough to sustain them for one week. If the campaign lasts longer, they eat what they hunt, what they steal, or the fruits afforded them by nature in the forests through which they pass. If they can they carry some fermented liquor, especially rum, of which they are fond, so as to become exhilarated and to face danger with a certain exaltation.

In this manner they make marches of two and three hundred leagues in a short time, and they always take unawares the enemy upon whom they seek to avenge themselves. It is impossible to wage a crueler war with fewer means. If they are feared now, if they were more numerous and if they had more ambition, conquerors as famous as the Tartars and the Celts would emerge from them.

I marveled at the fact that they do not use horses, as other barbarous nations of America do, but one of them cleared up the problem for me. He told me with an acuteness more proper to a Spartan than to a savage, "We do not need horses for our marches because our feet are stronger and not less agile than theirs, nor in order to attack the enemy, because in so critical an occasion we cannot trust our existence to the blind ferocity of a brute, nor to carry our baggage, because our simple kind of life frees us from that burden."

Such is the military system of the savages. Their moral character is a monstrous and almost irreconcilable aggregate of good and bad qualities. They are generous, valiant, patriotic, inclined to hospitality with strangers, but irascible, cruel, distrustful, and vengeful in the extreme. They are faithful friends and implacable enemies. A savage will walk two hundred leagues to avenge an insult to anyone of his nation. The cruelties and injustices that the whites have inflicted on them are deeply engraved in their hearts and are perpetuated in their families as the most important part of their history. Hatred, vengeance, and cunning are imbibed with their mothers' milk, and this is the true cause of that profound dissimulation, of that continual distrust, and of that inexhaustible fund of artifices that is regarded as the essence of their character, not being in reality a defect inherent in the savage man but a consequence of the political situation of these nations, surrounded by active, ambitious enemies much stronger than they. The Indians who are to be found remote from the hostilities of the Europeans are frank and simple; so must they all have been before the discovery of those regions. In short, they have by nature all the virtues that are not incompatible with their state of barbarity, and they would be good if their character had not been depraved by the tyrannies and example of Europeans. Even among the most corrupted are found traces of that primitive generosity that man takes from the hand of the Creator, when injustices or the example of his fellow creatures have not perverted it. As the savages come to be persuaded of the rectitude and good faith of a European, they deposit in him a confidence without limits, and they obey him more punctiliously and more gladly than they obey their own chiefs.

These cases are not frequent, because neither are the virtues that produce them. The usual thing is that all these nations regard whites with irreconcilable hatred, especially Anglo-Americans, whose vexatious proximity, usurping their lands every day, is reducing them to deeper poverty. The Anglo-Americans have driven some nations entirely out of their original territories, appropriated the greater part of the territories of many others, exterminated some, and caused others to lose their numerous population, their warlike spirit, and their primitive independence. Against all they are waging a cruel and continual war in order to penetrate the country and advance their settlements. At times the savages succeed in surprising them and sacrifice some families to their hatred, but the Anglo-Americans who inhabit the borderlands of their provinces and call themselves "frontiersmen" are intrepid, great hunters, skillful in ambushes, and as accustomed to the roving life as are the Indians themselves. Although the dwellings of these Anglo-Americans are scattered, they form a kind of chain, so that at the slightest alarm all the settlers join together and go out in search of the enemy, taking to assist them English hunting dogs, from whose scent and agility the Indians cannot hide in their ambushes.

In order to form some judgment of the devastation that the Indians have suffered in the vast regions that stretch between New Spain and the Canadian lakes, an area equal to that of all Europe, suffice it to say that among more than sixty nations that are known there and that used to be numerous, today there cannot be gathered 80,000 warriors; and since among them all who can be are warriors, one infers that their entire population is very little more than 400,000 souls. Among our allies the Choctaws, the Crasches [Cherokees?—Tr.], and the Chickasaws, hardly 1,000 warriors can be mustered; among the Alabamas 600, and among the upper, lower, and middle Creeks who inhabit the borderlands of Georgia and both Floridas, 4,000. War, smallpox, strong liquors, and other evils with which the whites have infected them are rapidly diminishing these numbers. The Indians are incapable of resisting European dominance, of freeing themselves from the influence of European politics, nor can they take on its yoke and live as a dependent and subordinated class. Therefore it can be predicted that in less than a century one of two things will happen: either the savage tribes, dragged by the torrential tide of trade and civilization, will be assimilated into the mass of the Anglo-Americans and the other nations that surround them, or an aggregation of inevitable causes will complete their extermination.

[?] May 1781

Two war vessels, a corvette and a packet boat, had been made ready to carry to Spain the news of the capture of Pensacola. On each of them I sent to the minister of the Indies a full and detailed account of this happy event. I conferred with the general about sending a swift vessel to Havana with the same news, and as soon as the French cutter *Serpent* was selected for this purpose I arranged to embark on it myself. The whereabouts of the fleet had not been known since the storm of the sixth had forced it to go out to sea, and the army was ready to embark as soon as the fleet reappeared. Don Bernardo de Gálvez told me that he intended to go to Louisiana as soon as he could leave everything in order in Pensacola, to await there the court's orders as to his destination.

16 May 1781

At dawn I set sail on the *Serpent*. Her commandant, M. Lalone, lodged me as comfortably as the small size of the vessel permitted. There was little wind, and we spent the entire morning in sailing out of the port. In the afternoon we saw far away our fleet which, now that the weather had moderated, was returning to the roadstead. We went to meet the frigate "O," which was farthest advanced. M. Lalone went aboard the "O" and told her captain about the capture of the stronghold. In turn the captain reported the news to the commodore of the fleet by means of signals agreed upon in advance. We proceeded on our voyage, which was uneventful. The weather was almost calm and the light winds variable; the navigation, which for a vessel as swift as the *Serpent* ought not to exceed five days, required ten, and this despite the fact that we used the oars many times. The inaction of the calm gave us time to observe the power of the currents in the waves of Tortuga. At time we encountered lines of waves that bore the ship away and made it run some leagues on courses different from the one it was following, while the oars and the sails were unable to counteract their strength.

During the voyage I had time to observe at my leisure the way in which the French manage their navy and to compare it with those of the English and Spanish, at least with respect to those most conspicuous subjects that do not require the knowledge of a professional for their discernment. I was greatly aided, however, in forming my opinions by the knowledge and reflections of the Chevalier de Monteil, who was a gallant officer, experienced and well informed; he looked at things with a fine critical sense and made his judgments with uncommon impartiality. The two of us were almost always chatting alone on the poop

16 May 1781

deck, and my inquisitive inclination frequently led me to impose upon his good nature.

The French navy never had a fixed system of regulations. It has followed the continual mobility of the ministers who have been placed in charge of it, and its development has depended always on the reputation, intelligence, and individual character of a single man, perhaps trained in a different profession. Within the same reign this nation has been seen to promote its navy in an extraordinary fashion, making amazing expenditures on it and then, within a short time, to let it fall into a pitiful abandonment, giving to England through those instable policies a superiority that her natural resources could not assure her.

Louis XIV, wishing to humiliate the maritime powers of Europe, as he had humiliated the land powers, created within a short time a military marine, by that sort of magic with which superior beings can make the impossible happen. For a second time Europe saw the phenomenon with which the Romans had astonished it two thousand years before, to wit, a land power suddenly converted into a sea power and disputing with Carthage the trident of Neptune.

In a short time France erected arsenals, built fleets, trained admirals, and won victories. But these successes were fleeting, because they had no other support than the talent of Colbert[127] and the ambition of his sovereign. Louvois managed to persuade the king that the expenses of the navy were useless, that in order to bend Europe to her authority, France needed nothing more than her armies and her forts.[128] He directed

---

127. Jean Baptiste Colbert was Louis XIV's comptroller general. A mercantilist, he believed in a regulated economy, protective tariffs, and the development of trade and colonization. When in 1669 he was made secretary of state for naval affairs, he constructed shipyards, arsenals, and ports and began building a large navy to protect commerce. See André Maurois, *A History of France* (New York: Farrar, Straus and Company, 1956), 209–11. [Tr.]

128. Michel Le Tellier, Marquis de Louvois, created for France the first true standing army of modern times, as well as a "table of command" which put a stop to conflicts of authority in the army. For the management of supplies he inaugurated the system of army intendants (ibid., 211). [Tr.]

the entire attention of the king and the entire resources of the nation toward the land forces, and her maritime power vanished as rapidly as it had arisen.

In the following reign of Louis XV, the French navy experienced similar inconsistency. The regent began to promote its development, but then later it was neglected by Cardinal de Fleury, whose timid policy treated France like a convalescent who needs a long repose in order to recuperate her extenuated forces.[129] The long abandonment of so important a branch converted into a political maxim the pernicious preconception that France could do without navies.[130]

The adversities of the war that ended in 1763 made her abjure this error. Plans were made to form a powerful navy, but adequate measures for the project were not taken. On the very eve of the outbreak of the present war, it was necessary to create almost anew the fleets that are playing so brilliant a role in it. It is certain that today France has many excellent ships, gallant officers, and numerous crews and that with the aid of Spain she has succeeded in counterbalancing the British superiority that has won so many battles. But is this success, purchased at the cost of immense riches, based on solid fundamentals that assure its stability?

The good politicians believe that it is not. They regard it as a momentary strength that manifests the great resources of the French nation and the wisdom of its present ministry, but

---

129. André Fleury, Cardinal de Fleury, had been the tutor of Louis XV, who as king turned everything over to him. The cardinal was a pacifist. Despite the efforts of Rouhier and Machault, two competent naval ministers, to build for France a new fleet, and despite the Family Pact with Spain that united the fleets of the two nations, the Peace of Paris in 1763 at the end of the Seven Years War cost France her empire and created England's (ibid., 235–40). [Tr.]

130. Upon the death of Louis XIV in 1715 and the accession of his young grandson who became Louis XV, the late king's brother Philip, Duke of Orleans, was regent until his death in 1723; he was succeeded as regent by the Duke of Bourbon, Prince of Condé, who later became prime minister. During the regency the government of France lost its feeling for the national interest and gave up the effort of holding its own on the sea (ibid., 235–36). [Tr.]

16 May 1781

they proclaim that unless the essential ills from which the corps is suffering are cured, if it is not based on principles more fundamental than those it has had until now, the era of its decline is not far distant from that of its grandeur. The French navy needs an established constitution, stable and independent of the whims and shortcomings of its ministers. It needs an admiralty like England's, a Board of Commissioners of the Navy, and permanent body placed near the throne as a trustee of intelligence capable of directing the ministry in the employment of the maritime forces, to combine means with needs, regulate operations, obtain what is lacking, examine inventions, and consolidate a wise system. England owes the magnificence of her navy to such a body. I think Spain needs it, too, but the constant and subservient character of the nation has, until now, made the want of it less perceptible than in France.

One of the effects of the continual change and the bad organization of the French navy was that when the present war began it did not have half as many officers as its fleets required. In this predicament it turned to the ministry of the merchant marine, taking out of it the ablest captains and pilots and transferring them to the navy under the title of auxiliary officers. Because it was badly planned, this measure has produced and is producing very bad effects. The old corps of the navy looks on these officers with disdain and calls them intruders. The latter reciprocate with the most unmistakable disdain and call them ignoramuses. These factions have the navy divided into scandalous bands; each ship-of-the-line, each vessel, is a battlefield. This sort of schism has spread to the point of making their successes against the enemy appear less than glorious to the major portion of the population of the nation. The nobility defends the cause of the old navy, the commoners that of the auxiliary officers, and God knows to what point these seeds of discord can ferment. Of course discord has already resulted, and it will not be surprising if it causes some momentous defeat.

Once M. de Monteil complained to me with reason about the custom instituted in the navy whereby the captains provide the mess for their subaltern officers. This system, also adopted by the Spanish navy, produces serious harm. It greatly prejudices subordination; it attracts some officers who possess excellent qualities but lack the wherewithal to accept commands which they would fill very well; and it is the reason that warships always go crammed with the accoutrements of a splendid table. The method observed among the English is preferable; in it each officer is responsible for his own subsistence, or he shares the cost of the mess with others on board ship.

The French are accustomed to giving fresh bread to their crews two days each week. At first glance this practice seems to be beneficial to the health of the crews, but basically it is harmful. They are obliged to have a large oven between decks for this purpose, concentrating there a foul-smelling smoke that pervades the entire ship, infects the air, and causes illnesses. Moreover the practice exposes the ship to the danger of conflagrations, and it makes necessary the loading of a great store of firewood.

Also the French give wine to their crews. This presents some advantages, but they are counterbalanced by its inconveniences. What is by no means advantageous, and for many reasons seems to me prejudicial, is what they do in America when their supply of wine loaded in Europe is exhausted: they give the crews an inferior kind of rum called tafia. It is a fiery drink, unsuited to European constitutions; it irritates the blood, and frequent use of it produces a thousand kinds of ailments. It brings about another vexation greater if possible than those already mentioned. They have to store a large quantity of this highly flammable liquor; they go down twice a day to bring it up from the hold, using artificial light, and no matter how many precautions they take, they do not prevent the risks involved in this operation. It was the cause of the burning of the ship-of-the-line *Intrépide*, of which I shall speak later, and of the frigate *Inconstante*, which occurred off Port-au-Prince at almost the same time, when only one-third of the crewmen could be saved. On the *Palmier*, too, we had a great fright for the same reason, and it would be tedious to enumerate all the accidents I have heard about that have resulted from this custom. The English also are accustomed to give their crews in America a moderate quantity of rum, but only during combat so as to inspire in them an extraordinary kind of courage in an action requiring it.

Commonly in the French navy there is less subordination on the part of the subaltern officers, as well as among the sailors and soldiers, than there ought to be. One does not note on their ships that silence, that prompt obedience, that cleanliness, that good order, that precision in maneuvers, that prevail in the English navy, and in this regard the French navy is even inferior to that of Spain. Many particular cases could be cited in support of this assertion, to which even their generals agree. Weighing all the circumstances, it appears that the French are still far from the maritime perfection that their rivals have attained and that, if they do not improve their system, they will not succeed in taking the control of the seas away from those rivals as speedily as they had confidently hoped to do.

26 May 1781

I arrived at Havana at dawn, disembarked at six o'clock in the morning, and went to call on the governor and gave him the news that Pensacola had been taken, which caused universal joy. I learned that a few days earlier a mail packet had come from Spain with the order that Don Diego Navarro, Don Victor de Navia, and Don Juan Bautista Bonet were to relinquish their respective positions, that of interim governor to Field Marshal Don Juan Manuel de Cagigal, that of general of the Army of Operations to Don Bernardo de Gálvez, and that of commandant of the navy to Don José Solano.[131]

27 May 1781

I had a vessel go out to meet the fleet with letters for Cagigal in which I informed him of his new position. I enclosed a

---

131. AGI:Ind. Gen. 1578. [Tr.]

letter for Don Bernardo de Gálvez, requesting that, if Gálvez was not coming with the fleet, they would send it on to him by an armed vessel to Pensacola or wherever he might be.

28 May 1781

The brigantine *Pájaro* went out in search of the fleet with letters for Solano, to inform him of his new position. Naval Commandant Bonet had relinquished the command of the department to Brigadier Salaverría.

29 May 1781

Nothing worth noting happened.

30 May 1781

We were advised that vessels were in sight to leeward, and it was believed that they were the fleet returning from Pensacola.

31 May 1781

At midday the fleet began to enter, and by nightfall had concluded, the *Magnánimo*, the *Gallardo*, the *O*, and the *Destin* having run aground at the entrance.

Until 18 June the official papers that the frigate *Lucía* had left in Baracoa did not arrive here, and I was undecided as to whether to go to Spain to arrange the plan of the next campaign or to go to Guarico to confer with the French general about the same matter. In the mail I received a letter from Don José de Gálvez which made up my mind for me, for he commanded me positively to go to confer with Comte de Grasse about the operations that must be executed.[132]

---

132. Admiral François Joseph Paul, Comte de Grasse, had served in Haiti in 1775. Back in France the next year he took command of the *Intrépide*, and on 1 June 1778 he became a commodore. He commanded a

18 June 1781

The Chevalier de Monteil's fleet was about to set sail for Guarico. They were shipping the *situado* of Puerto Rico and that of Santo Domingo,[133] and 200,000 pesos for the French Cape. I went to see the chevalier, and he offered me passage on his fleet.

20 June 1781

I embarked on the *Palmier* at five o'clock in the morning. At six o'clock the fleet began to go out. At eight o'clock all were outside: the *Intrépide* the *Triton*, the *Destin*, the frigate *Andromaque*, the cutters *Serpent* and *Levrette*, and a small convoy of twelve merchant ships bound for the same destination.

21 June 1781

At dawn we were off Matanzas, and a northeast course was set so as to enter the mouth of the Bahama Channel.

22 June 1781

We entered the channel, but that day the *Triton* was missing and there were various conjectures as to its whereabouts.

Navigation continued smoothly until the thirtieth. On this day and the previous night there was a severe storm in which the *Intrépide* lost bowsprit and foremast.

---

division at Ushant in July 1778 before returning to the West Indies, where he led a squadron in de Guichen's engagement with Rodney off Martinique. He returned to France with de Guichen. On 22 March 1781 he was promoted to rear admiral, and the same day he sailed from Brest for the West Indies with a fleet of twenty ships-of-the-line, three frigates, and a convoy of 150 ships (Boatner, 444). [Tr.]

133. The income (*situado*) was a quantity of money that a strong royal treasury (Mexico, for example) sent annually as assistance to a poor region, such as Puerto Rico. [Ed.]

9 July 1781

We discovered the Turk Islands on one side and the Caicos on the other, and we endeavored to enter the mouth of the intervening channel.

10 July 1781

We passed through the channel, and we gave chase to some vessels we sighted.

11 July 1781

At dawn we caught sight of Monte Christi, the Granja, and then Guarico. We were drawing near to Guarico, but it was impossible to put into the port because the wind was so light.

12 July 1781

We entered the port at three o'clock in the afternoon. At five o'clock we disembarked and went to see the governor, M. de Reinaud,[134] who gave us a magnificent dinner that evening.

13 July 1781

I called on the intendant,[135] the Marquis of Saint Simon,[136] and other distinguished persons of the colony. This day the frigate *Aigrette* returned from Havana, where she had gone after our departure. The French Cape seemed to me a very

---

134. As Saavedra explained later, Reinaud was the former governor. [Tr.]

135. Le Brasseur was a quartermaster acting as interim intendant. [Tr.]

136. Claude-Anne Maubléru, Marquis de Saint Simon, had commanded the Regiment of Touraine from June 1775 to April 1780, when he was sent to the West Indies. On 15 August 1782, with de Grasse, he brought 3,000 men from the Agénois, Gatinais, and Touraine regiments to reinforce Comte de Rochambeau at Chesapeake Bay. He was commandant of the French army at the French Cape. [Tr.]

13 July 1781

beautiful place. It probably has about six thousand inhabitants. It has a certain order; however, the streets are not laid out in straight lines, the surface is uneven, and the paving is bad so that it is very uncomfortable and almost impassable for carriages. This town has the disadvantage of cleaving closely to a lofty hill called the Monne, which to a great degree cuts off the circulation of the air and from which, in heavy rainfalls, torrents of water plunge, causing devastation. The town was founded by *filibusteros,* who sought the proximity of the hill as apt for defense. It would be much better located in a site called the *petite Anse* [little cove], which is in the center of the port, where it would have all the advantages I saw plus many that it lacks. Of course the French know that, but it is already too late to make the move, as it would be very costly today.

The French Cape has no defense save some unimportant batteries situated on different heights. The best of them, called Picolet, defends the entrance of the port. It has eighteen 24-caliber guns; it is closed at the gorge; and it is located on a site that dominates the channel in such a way that ships have to come in with the prow toward [Saavedra's text unreadable]; but it can be attacked from behind, where there are several easy elevations that can be taken without entering the port. For the defense of the country the French rely upon the numerous veteran and militia troops that they have always had in it.

In the town there are unimposing buildings. For the most part the rows of houses are uniform but humble. In almost all the lower rooms are occupied by shops and warehouses. Government House, formerly a Jesuit school, is in an elevated spot, and it has in front a spacious garden, which serves for public recreation and lends beauty to the place. Near this garden is an Ursuline convent school for girls. Beyond it is a small square where the theater of the *comédie* is located. Its shape is a semi-ellipse with two rows of boxes. Comedies and tragedies are presented there, but usually operas or musical pieces are given.

In a spacious square shaded by trees and with a fountain in its center is the only church there is on the cape. It is large and not badly constructed, but it has little ornamentation and its height is not in proportion to its other dimensions. The original plan envisioned a grandiose dome, but the columns and frontal arches were not strong enough to support it. The builders had to be content with a dome in the shape of half an orange, covered with wood and without windows. The church has only one altar upon which the offices are celebrated. A kind of mission of Capuchins is in charge of it; the superior acts as parish priest, and they are supported at the expense of the king, because neither tithes nor primacies are paid there, but they do pay parish taxes. I was not able to ascertain precisely their quota and distribution.

14 July 1781

On this day I went to dine with Monsieur de Monteil aboard the *Palmier*. There I learned that the frigate *Concorde*, which has been here since a little before our arrival, had earlier gone to conduct Monsieur de Barras[137] to Rhode Island so that he could assume the command of the French fleet there, which had been vacant because of the death of the Chevalier de Ternay;[138] on her return to the French Cape she had

---

137. Jacques Melchior, Comte de Barras Saint Laurent, arrived at Boston on the *Concorde* on 8 May 1781 to take command of the French fleet based at Newport. He transported the Comte de Rochambeau's heavy artillery to Virginia for the Yorktown campaign and entered the port of Yorktown on 10 September 1781 after a battle off the Virginia Capes in which he captured the British frigates *Iris* and *Richmond* on 5 September. Despite his seniority and even though he shared with de Grasse the permanent rank of commodore, Barras placed himself under de Grasse's command at Chesapeake. In 1782 he distinguished himself in the West Indies. See Harold Larrabee, *Decision at Chesapeake*. (New York: Clarkson N. Potter, Inc., 1964), passim. [Tr.]

138. Charles-Louis d'Arnac, Chevalier de Ternay, in 1780 organized the fleet that was to escort the expeditionary force of General Rochambeau to America. With eight ships-of-the-line, two frigates, and two bomb-galliots, he arrived off Newport on 10 July 1780, just three days before a British fleet under Admiral Thomas Graves arrived off Sandy Hook to give the British an advantage of thirteen more powerful ships-of-the-line against Ternay's eight. The French fleet was blockaded in Newport. Ternay died there on 15 December 1780, and the Chevalier Destouches commanded the French fleet until the arrival of Barras in May 1781

brought twelve harbor pilots experienced in those northern seas, about whom there was much secrecy. This indicated that Comte de Grasse must be going to lead an expedition to those parts.

15 July 1781

Monsieur de Monteil attempted to leave the port to free a French convoy that the English had blockaded in the San Luis Keys, but there was no land breeze that morning so he could not sail. Today I dined in the house of Monsieur le Brasseur, the quartermaster, who was acting as interim intendant.

16 July 1781

Monteil went out early with his four warships, but hardly was he outside when he saw Comte de Grasse's fleet approaching the port. I went aboard the flagship and learned that de Grasse had dispatched from Puerto Rico some swift vessels to fetch the convoy Monteil was going to assist and that therefore it was unnecessary for him to go out.

In the afternoon I went to Picolet with Labat and Lentillano, and we watched as all the ships of Comte de Grasse's fleet put in. Together with Monteil's squadron they formed a fleet of 31 ships-of-the-line, 7 frigates, 6 cutters, and a merchant convoy of 160 sails. Besides the 110-gun flagship called *Ville de Paris*, there were five 80-gun, nineteen 74-gun, and six 64-gun ships-of-the-line.

Only fourteen of these ships-of-the-line were sheathed with copper, as were all the frigates and cutters. This mixture of vessels sheathed with copper and those not copper-clad, which was causing a marked inequality in the way of the [unreadable] fleet, had already caused Comte de Grasse to lose a fortuitous opportunity to attack the English, who had only nineteen warships in the Windward Islands under Rodney's command.[139] In fact, af-

---

(Boatner, 1093–94). [Tr.]

139. Admiral Baron George Brydges Rodney sailed from Plymouth in December 1780 with a fleet of twenty-one ships-of-the-line, several frig-

ter de Grasse had pursued them for fourteen hours, when his vanguard was almost within gunshot range of Rodney, finding that the French ships without copper sheathing had fallen so far to leeward and so far behind that they could not be seen from the highest point in the vanguard, de Grasse was unable to proceed without running the risk of having his ships attacked singly.

The Comte de Grasse was carrying dispatches for the interim governor of the colony, Monsieur de Lillancourt, a senior colonel who for a long time had been the King's Deputy there. This man doted on de Grasse, whereas Reinaud, his predecessor, was a partisan and creature of Comte d'Estaing,[140] and between d'Estaing and de Grasse there prevailed an irreconcilable enmity. Consequently, Lillancourt's preferment over Reinaud was celebrated by the supporters of de Grasse as a triumph over d'Estaing, with no concern for the loss to the colony because Reinaud, while he had a violent temper, was upright, active, and enterprising; he had done many beneficial things for the country

---

ates, and a convoy of store ships and transports. On 17 April, three weeks after his arrival in the West Indies, Rodney was engaged in a battle with the Comte de Guichen, who had assumed command of French naval forces there in March. They met twice again, indecisively, in May. In August, when de Guichen sailed for France with fifteen ships, Rodney divided his fleet, leaving half in the islands and taking the remainder to New York. He returned to the West Indies after having escaped by his absence the great hurricane of October 1780. When Holland declared war against England, Rodney seized the Dutch islands of Saint Eustatius and Saint Martins, causing severe losses to the shipping of the United States and the French and Spanish islands. With AdmiralSir Samuel Hood, Rodney defeated the Comte de Grasse in the Battle of the Saintes, 11-12 April 1782. See Alfred Thayer Mahan, *The Influence of Sea Power upon History, 1660-1805* (Englewood Cliffs, N.J.: Prentice-Hall, Inc., 1980), 150-73, 188-97. [Tr.]

140. Charles Hector Théodat, Comte d'Estaing, became a vice-admiral in the French Navy in 1777, and in 1778 he took command of the fleet organized to fight the British in America. He sailed from Toulon in April 1778, spent the summer in New York and Newport, and sailed for the West Indies in November of that year. He captured the islands of Saint Vincent and Grenada. Wounded in the assault on Savannah in October 1779, he returned to France early in 1780 (Boatner, 349-50). [Tr.]

and had contributed to the decoration and comfort of the towns. Lillancourt was known as an urbane man with a placid disposition, but he did not give promise of the strength of character that the command of that colony required.

In the late afternoon I saw Comte de Grasse in Lillancourt's house, but I did not introduce myself to him amidst the large crowd of people who gathered to congratulate him. In the evening there were fireworks in the Theatre Square. Reinaud's admirers cut the cords of the fireworks, so that they were continually going out. This motivated great vexation, and the merriment was on the point of ending in despair. Reinaud and Lillancourt did not have personal motives for enmity, but the former was a partisan and even a creature of Comte d'Estaing, and the latter had been reared in the Royal Navy. These factions, which reached an incredible degree of rancor, produced on that occasion some ridiculous scenes, but the entire colony cherished the memory of Comte d'Estaing, who had been their governor, and this made me form a favorable opinion of his character.

17 July 1781

With Monteil I went to see the Comte de Grasse. He was very cordial to me, and we made an appointment for early the following day.

At four o'clock in the afternoon the 36-gun French frigate *Foi* put into the port, towed by a multitude of launches. She had just fought a tumultuous battle with an English frigate of equal burden off San Nicolás Mole. Both had been dismasted and on the point of sinking. The *Foi* had lost sixty men, among them three officers, and was bringing in more than 100 wounded. Her hull had been riddled, she had not a vestige of a mast, and she was being steered with some jury-masts made from two half-destroyed yards. The captain was slightly wounded, and his disembarkation on the dock amidst the acclamations of an innumerable throng was a gratifying kind of triumph.

Journal of Don Francisco Saavedra de Sangronis

18 July 1781

At six o'clock in the morning I went aboard the *Ville de Paris*. Comte de Grasse showed me the orders that he had from Paris to confer with me, and I showed him those I had from Madrid to confer with him. First we talked about the cordiality and good faith with which the Spaniards and the French must cooperate toward the humiliation of a nation that so openly claimed dominion of the seas.

Next we examined the various operations that could be executed against the English up to the month of July of the following year with the great forces that the two nations were going to unite in those places. And we decided upon the three enterprises that offered the greatest advantages and that could be realized without anxiety, taking advantage of the season most opportune for each of them. These were to aid the Anglo-Americans powerfully, in such a way that the English cabinet would in the end lose the hope of subduing them; to take possession of various points in the Windward Islands, where the English fleets lying in protected ports were threatening French and Spanish possessions; and to conquer Jamaica, the center of the wealth and power of Great Britain in that part of the world.

Then Comte de Grasse made known to me the project already agreed upon, that of taking possession of Chesapeake Bay in North Carolina and penetrating inland by way of the deep rivers that empty into it, in order to cut off the retreat and prevent the reinforcement of the army of Lord Cornwallis,[141] who was in that area. At the same time General Washington,[142] Comte

---

141. British General Charles, Lord Cornwallis, sailed for America in February 1776 as commander of the 2,500 troops convoyed by Admiral Peter Parker's fleet to join Sir Henry Clinton for operations in the South. In August he went to Long Island, then returned to England. He was again in America from April to December 1778. When he returned to America from England almost a year later, he took part in the Charleston expedition of 1780; and after Charleston surrendered, Cornwallis was left to hold the South (ibid., 185–89). [Tr.]

142. The American commander-in-chief, General George Washington, was at White Plains, New York, where he was joined by the French commandant, the Comte de Rochambeau. They had reports that Cornwallis

18 July 1781

de Rochambeau,[143] and the Marquis de Lafayette,[144] who had already agreed to the plan, would encircle him on all sides with their respective troops and totally destroy him or oblige him to surrender.

Monsieur de Grasse was planning to take no more than twenty-four ships-of-the-line for this enterprise because it was necessary to leave five or six to protect the commerce of Guarico. I was of the opinion that he ought to take the thirty he then had at his orders, for besides the fact that according to reports Admiral Graves[145] had twenty with him in New York, they were expecting Admiral Digby[146] there from one

---

had extended himself at Yorktown in Virginia and that Clinton was reinforcing the garrison at New York. Washington was uncertain as to which course to take. De Grasse's message to Rochambeau that he was about to set out for Chesapeake Bay settled the question. The French and American armies proceeded overland toward the south. See Jean-Edmund Whelen, *Rochambeau, Father and Son* (New York: Henry Holt & Co., 1936), 99. [Tr.]

143. At Yorktown, Lieutenant General Jean-Baptiste de Vimeur, the Comte de Rochambeau, commanded the four regiments of 900 men each who came from Newport (Bourbonnnais, Royal Deux-Ponts, Soissonais, and Saintonge) the three regiments of 1,000 men each brought from Saint Domingue by Saint Simon; and 600 artillerymen, 800 marines, and 600 horse and foot of the Duc de Lauzun's Legion (Boatner, 1241). [Tr.]

144. Marie Joseph-Paul du Motier, the Marquis de Lafayette, a French volunteer in the American army, came to America in June 1777. KDAfter taking part in several campaigns, he returned to France, where he laid the groundwork for sending a French expeditionary force to the United States. He returned to Boston on 28 April 1780, and in July a French army of 4,000 men commanded by the Comte de Rochambeau reached Newport. When Rochambeau and Washington moved southward for the Yorktown campaign, Lafayette was given command of the light division for the final action against Cornwallis (ibid., 591–93). [Tr.]

145. Admiral Thomas Graves was sent in 1780 to join Admiral Marriot Arbuthnot, British commandant at New York. In July 1781 he became temporary commander when Arbuthnot returned to England (ibid., 446). [Tr.]

146. Admiral Robert Digby was sent to America as commander-in-chief to succeed Graves, but, arriving just as the latter was about to sail for the Chesapeake, he courteously deferred the assumption of command (ibid., 332). [Tr.]

day to the next with a reinforcement of warships and troops. And never in order to save resources ought one to risk the success of an expedition that was perhaps going to decide the fortune of the entire war.

Then he suggested to me that, in order not to diminish the force of his fleet without leaving the French Cape unprotected, four Spanish ships-of-the-line could accompany him in the said enterprise. I told him that because Spain had not yet formally recognized the independence of the Anglo-Americans, there could perhaps be some political objection to taking a step that appeared to suppose this recognition; but that by an indirect measure it was easy to gain the same end with greater security, for if he took all of his ships-of-the-line, leaving for the present only some frigates, four Spanish ships-of-the-line would go there from Havana to protect the commerce of the colony.

This expedient pleased the comte enormously, and from that moment I noted on his part a great reliance on everything I proposed to him.

Later we talked about the expedition against Jamaica, as we considered a quite exact plan I was carrying and another less exact but much more detailed one that he had. I explained to him minutely the plan of attack that had been formed for taking possession of the capital points of that island. Consequently we agreed that he would come down to the Windward Islands at the beginning of November to await the great reinforcements they were promising him from France for the next campaign year. In the interim before they arrived, he would attack the island of Barbados, Saint Lucia, or Saint Christopher. And at the beginning of March, at the latest, he would dispatch all the forces he could to Guarico, where they would unite with ours to begin the expedition. Besides the 6,000 men he was taking to the north under the command of the Marquis de Saint Simon, who would already have returned by that time, he committed himself to send at least eight ships-of-the-line and 3,000 soldiers, nonetheless still keeping forces sufficient to contain the enemies in the Windwards and prevent their reinforcing Jamaica in the interval before it was attacked.

18 July 1781

After we had agreed upon the operations, and talked over all the circumstances that occurred to us, he asked me to record in writing the plan we had agreed upon, reducing it to precise propositions and leaving the details to the judgment and prudence of those who were going to execute it.

At ten o'clock I retired, despite the comte's insistence that I remain for supper on his ship, and by midnight I had already written the plan. I was tempted to return at that hour to show it to the general, but because no time would be lost in leaving that until the next day, it seemed to me that such haste would have a certain air of juvenile presumption.

19 July 1781

At ten o'clock in the morning the felucca of the *Ville de Paris* was already waiting for me at the dock. I carried the plan of campaign to the comte, who liked it very much, and between the two of us we translated it into French. It was summarized in four simple propositions: (1) the Comte de Grasse would go to North America with thirty ships-of-the-line, and, in addition to the 3,000 men detached from the garrison of the French Cape, he would take two regiments that the French court had placed there to garrison the Spanish part of the island of Santo Domingo; (2) the naval commandant of Havana would send four ships-of-the-line, as soon as he could, to protect the commerce of Guarico; (3) Comte de Grasse would place at the French Cape on the first of March, at the disposition of the Spanish generals who were in charge of the Jamaica expedition, at least 3,000 soldiers and eight 74-gun ships-of-the-line, and he would remain with the rest of his land and sea forces in Martinique, threatening the English so as to keep their attention divided; (4) if the Spaniards wished to join the comte for the operations that he was to execute in November in the Windward Islands, he would gladly relinquish the command to any one of their generals, and he would be delighted by the cooperation of the two nations, especially because in this way they could more quickly be made ready to launch the principal enterprise.

I dined on the *Ville de Paris*, where there was a brilliant company of ladies and officials; and in the afternoon I went to see several warships of the fleet, among others the *Saint Esprit*, the *Auguste*, and the *Languedoc*, to which the Chevalier de Monteil had moved his ensign as chief of squadron.

20 July 1781

I spent the greater part of the day in making six copies of the plan, two of them in French and Spanish.

21 July 1781

The Comte de Grasse came to my house to see me. He and I signed the six copies of the plan, I gave him three, and we agreed that as soon as possible he would dispatch a cutter to take it to France.

That afternoon Labat and I climbed a rather lofty hill where signals are placed to advise vessels that come to the port. The ascent is rugged, but from the summit one enjoys a delightful view. On one side a limitless sea and the coasts of the island bordered by capes, promontories, and reefs, which seem to jut out to defy the daring of navigators. On the other side the city, well-built and almost entirely new, overlooking a spacious port where there were in addition to forty warships some 600 merchantmen and transports. Farther away the great plain of the cape which in many places frames the horizon, abounding with evergreen foliage, and scattered over it innumerable *haciendas* of every kind, separated one from the other by dividing hedgerows like an immense garden.

22 July 1781

Governor Lillancourt and Intendant Le Brasseur sent a message that they had something urgent to communicate to me and that they would meet me at the Government House at the hour I indicated. In fact I went there at nine o'clock in the morning, and together the two, who were waiting for me, after some preambles, described to me the total lack of money that existed in the colony, earnestly entreating that I give them at least 100,000 pesos from the 500,000 destined for Puerto Rico and Santo Domingo, which the Court of France would repay to that of Spain. Comte de Grasse also spoke to me urgently that day about the same thing. I took some time before responding to them.

Indeed on Monteil's squadron had come the aforementioned 500,000 pesos, of which one-half must be remitted to the two places mentioned. In the interim before this was done, the funds were deposited for safekeeping in the Royal Treasury of the French Cape itself; and I had written to the president of Santo Domingo so that he would send a trustworthy person to carry the part which corresponded to him, while I had already made an agreement with the Comte de Grasse that a frigate of his fleet that soon would sail for Martinique would put in at Puerto Rico to leave there its *situado*.

23 July 1781

At eight o'clock in the morning it was reported that the 74-gun warship *Intrépide* had caught fire, and at ten o'clock the ship exploded. This calamity resulted from imprudence with rum. The general and officers of the fleet made the greatest efforts to extinguish the fire but, seeing that it was irremediable, they managed to bring the ship aground on the reefs at the entrance of the port. They took off the ship forty barrels of gunpowder, saved the mainmast and many effects, and did not abandon the vessel until the fire was inside the powder magazine. The damage caused by the explosion was not great.

24 July 1781

I went to see the Comte de Grasse and gave him two copies of the agreement, which we both signed.

25 July 1781

By dint of the urgings of the intendant, the governor, and the Comte de Grasse, and seeing that de Grasse absolutely was not finding any money for his expedition to the north, I gave him 100,000 pesos from the income of Santo Domingo, with the proviso that they were to be discounted from the 1 million which, according to orders from the French court, were to be delivered to the French generals in Havana for the months of July and August.

26 July 1781

A cutter was dispatched for France with news of the expedition that the Comte de Grasse was going to execute and of our convention. I gave him a letter for the Conde de Aranda[147] and another enclosed for Señor Gálvez, including a copy of our covenant. This was reduced to four simple propositions: (1) that the Comte de Grasse will go to the north with thirty warships, and will carry the 2,000 French troops which Paris had placed at our disposition; (2) that the Spaniards will send from Havana to the French Cape, as soon as they can, four warships to safeguard its commerce; (3) that at the beginning of March, the Comte de Grasse will give to the Spaniards 3,000 men and eight 40-gun warships; (4) that if the Spaniards wish to join with the French for the operations which the Comte de Grasse will execute in the Windwards in November, they can do so, and he will gladly relinquish to them the command of the operations.[148]

---

147. Pedro Abarca y Bolea, the Conde de Aranda, had been prime minister of Spain before becoming ambassador to France. In Paris he dealt with the envoys sent there by the United States. He was convinced that the independence of the United States would be prejudicial to the Spanish Empire in America, but he saw the inevitability of its independence and sought to combine Spanish interests with those of the emerging new nation. See Miguel Gómez del Campillo, *Relaciones Diplomáticas entre España y los Estados Unidos* (Madrid: Consejo Superior de Investigaciones Científicas, Instituto Gonzalo Fernández de Oviedo, 1944), 1:vii. [Tr.]

148. De Grasse and Saavedra drew up the plan of operations to be followed in the next nine months. It had three goals: to aid the Americans and to defeat Admiral Arbuthnot (temporarily commanding the British

27 July 1781

I went to dine with the governor.

28 July 1781

There came a report that near the San Luis Keys the frigate *Inconstante* had burned, for the same accidental reason as had the *Intrépide,* and that four officers and more than 100 crewmen had perished in it.

29 July 1781

I dined with the Comte de Grasse, and we talked at length about the operations of the campaign; he confided to me several good ideas about it. After having held a meeting with the planters and merchants of the French Cape to the end that they should lend him the money he needed for the expedition to the north, and having sent official papers concerning the same matter, the Comte de Grasse today put printed notices on the street corners, inviting all who were willing to supply their money to him in exchange for bills redeemable at the Treasury of Paris at a profitable rate of interest. All these expedients produced absolutely no effect; the total sum that could be collected

---

naval force at New York), to capture the British Windward Islands, and to take Jamaica. Spain would send four warships to Guarico. De Grasse would take his fleet to the North American continent in July and operate there until October. He would return to the Windwards in November for three months of operations. At the beginning of March 1782, de Grasse would send to the French Cape or to the San Nicolás Mole at least eight 74-gun ships-of-the-line and 7,000 men, where they would rendezvous with the Spanish for the attack on Jamaica. Final planning for the Jamaica campaign began after the Spanish Court's acceptance of the de Grasse–Saavedra Convention. The Spanish force would be 10,000 to 11,000 troops and fifteen ships-of-the-line. The combined force would be 15,000 to 20,000 troops and forty to forty-five ships-of-the-line. Bernardo de Gálvez would command, seconded by Bouillé and Bellecombe. See Johnathan R. Dull, *The French Navy and American Independence* (Princeton, NJ: Princeton University Press, 1975), 249– 52. [Tr.]

was 50,000 *livres*. It was said that this reluctance of the French to serve their king in so urgent a juncture originated in the fact that, having on another occasion lent money against bills of exchange drawn on the Royal Treasury, the people lost confidence when the redemption of the bills was delayed for a much longer period than was stipulated in them, and so they refused to give their money even for a premium of 25 percent.[149]

31 July 1781

The Comte de Grasse sent for me and described the stringent circumstances he was in, telling me that the lack of money was making it impossible for him to launch the expedition to the north and that consequently his fleet would remain idle in port, thus losing the opportune juncture for executing an operation apt to hasten an advantageous peace. I told him that I had absolutely no authority to give him more money but that, as he was under orders from Paris to have recourse to the Spaniards in case of finding himself in need of funds, he should send a frigate to Havana to solicit what money they could give him and that he should indicate the rendezvous to which the frigate should go to meet him. He replied that he would think it over.

---

149. On 6 June 1781 Rochambeau wrote to de Grasse that his funds on hand were insufficient to maintain his army after 20 August, that it was impossible in that area to raise at any price money enough to meet the army's needs, and that it would be advantageous to the royal service for de Grasse to borrow in the islands 1,200,000 *livres* in gold, by means of bills of exchange drawn on M. de Serilly, treasurer general of the army. Both de Grasse and his wife owned rich sugar plantations in Haiti. De Grasse tried to use his plantations as collateral in order to raise the money but failed. He tried to obtain the money through Governor Lillancourt but failed again. Then he turned to Saavedra, as recounted in this journal. De Grasse reported to Rochambeau on 26 July that he could depend upon receiving the requisite funds. See Henri Doniol, *Histoire de la participation de la France a l'établissement des Etats-Unis d'Amérique* (Paris, 1884–92), 4:649; Eduardo J. Tejera, *La Ayuda Cubana en la Lucha por la Independencia Norteamericana* (Miami: Ediciones Universal, 1972), 24– 67. [Tr.]

1 August 1781

The Comte de Grasse came to find me, to say that the exigency in which he found himself and the confidence he had in the Spanish nation and in my good faith were causing him to venture a risky operation. He had decided to go with all his fleet by way of the Old Channel, even though the season was already dangerous; he would send ahead a swift frigate, on which I could go if I wished; the frigate would bring from Havana the money Spaniards there could contribute to him and would then go to await his fleet off Matanzas, whence all would set a course for the Bahama Channel. His plan seemed good to me; we agreed that the fleet would go out at dawn on the fourth and that the frigate on which I should go ahead of him would be the *Aigrette*, commanded by an excellent youth named M. Traversai.

2 August 1781

I began to prepare my things, and I advised the fiscal of Mexico named Alva [Lorenzo Hernández de Alva Alonso, *fiscal del crimon* for the Mexican audiencia until 1784], who for five months had been detained on the French Cape, with Bonavía, Bertucar, and other Spaniards who were awaiting an opportunity to go to Havana, to get ready to depart.

3 August 1781

I said farewell to the governor, the intendant, etc., and at ten o'clock in the evening we all embarked.

4 August 1781

The fleet began to weigh anchor at daybreak, but there was no land wind that morning and it was necessary to drop anchor again.

5 August 1781

The fleet weighed anchor at daybreak, and at ten o'clock

was already outside, with the exception of the warship *Bourgogne*. At noon a sail was sighted, and we gave chase, finding that it was the warship *Accionario*, which was coming from the San Luis Keys.

6 August 1781

We stood on the course from early morning, and the *Aigrette* with the cutter *Alerte* drew ahead of the fleet. At ten o'clock in the evening four large ships were sighted to windward. We hauled the wind and began to make signals; they made signals also. We identified them as warships, but we could not understand each other.

9 August 1781

In the morning we saw that in fact the two warships were following us, and it was perceived that they were French. We came within hailing distance and found that they were the 70-gun warships *Souverain* and *Citoyen*, coming from the San Luis Keys to join the fleet, and they announced that the other three warships were coming behind them, as was the convoy. We told them that the Comte de Grasse was coming behind with all his fleet, and that he was going to wait for them at San Nicolás Mole. At ten o'clock we chased a frigate of about twenty-four guns, which fled. At five o'clock in the afternoon we caught sight of Baracoa. The *Alerte* headed for the port to pick up twelve harbor pilots for the fleet, and we proceeded without a harbor pilot but with one who knew the Old Channel. In the rest of the navigation nothing notable occurred.

15 August 1781

We reached Havana, I disembarked, and I went to see the generals, then the intendant and the treasurer. I told them that the Comte de Grasse was coming behind the *Aigrette* with thirty ships-of-the-line, and that his only reason for coming through the Old Channel was to take out of Havana 500,000 pesos in order to carry out his expedition to the north. They informed me that there was no money in the treasury because the ships that had gone out for Veracruz on 26 June had not returned, although they were expected from one day to the next; they said that private citizens, both merchants and landowners, had lent much money to the king and that what had remained in the treasury had been sent to Spain with the fleet that went out on 24 July. Amidst all this difficulty a decision urgently had to be made, because without money the Comte de Grasse could do nothing, and to allow him to wait off Matanzas for a long time was to expose his fleet to great danger. It seemed that the best thing to do was to turn once again to the citizenry, making known the urgency of the case, so that each man would give what he could.

16 August 1781

In fact the announcement was promulgated among the citizens, and it was proclaimed that anyone who wished to contribute toward aiding the French fleet with his money should send it immediately to the treasury. Two French officers went to collect the funds, and in six hours the requisite amount was gathered. The money was put aboard the frigate, and at six o'clock in the evening the frigate set sail. Don Bernardo de Gálvez had arrived at one o'clock in the afternoon. His arrival caused joyous celebration.[150] He was told of what had happened and of the promptitude with which the 500,000 pesos needed by the Comte de Grasse had been collected, and he was delighted.

---

150. At the beginning of the siege of Pensacola, General Campbell appealed for the support of the settlers at Natchez, which had come under Spanish authority when captured by Gálvez in the fall of 1779. An uprising was instigated which led to the capture of Fort Panmure, but the rebellion ended when news was received that Gálvez had taken Pensacola. Gálvez felt that in order to maintain control of the Natchez area he must go in person to New Orleans rather than return to Havana with the army of operations (Caughey, 215–42). [Tr.]

17 August 1781

The frigate set sail at midnight. In the morning I went to see Solano. I showed him the agreement I had made with the Comte de Grasse, and he found it satisfactory. I urged him to send the promised warships to the French Cape with all possible speed, and he replied that it was necessary to wait until the weather became calm, as we were at the equinox, and if we were hit by one of the storms which in this season are so frequent in these climes, or our ships dismasted or some of their rigging and tackle lost, there was absolutely no way to replace them. But nonetheless he would send the four ships as soon as possible.

18 August 1781

As soon as Don Bernardo de Gálvez had rested from his voyage I went to see him, and we talked at length about my voyage to the French Cape. I told him what I had discussed with the Comte de Grasse and showed him the agreement I had made with him, and he was well satisfied. A mail-packet went out for Spain. I reported my arrival and the pact I had made with the Frenchman.

19 August 1781

The cutter *Alerte* of the Comte de Grasse's fleet put into the port leaking badly; her commander reported that on the eighteenth the frigate *Aigrette* had rejoined the fleet, that on the same day the money had been transferred to the warships, and that the fleet was sailing toward the Bahama Channel.[151]

---

151. On 15 August de Grasse wrote to Rochambeau that he was sailing toward Chesapeake Bay and would bring the 1,200,000 livres in gold furnished by the citizens of Havana for the campaign (Doniol, 4:649). Reassured by Saavedra's promise of four Spanish warships to guard the French islands, de Grasse took virtually his entire fleet, as Saavedra advised, leaving only the 64-gun *Sagittaire*. Saavedra released to de Grasse the French corps at Santo Domingo that had been placed at the Spanish service. De Grasse later attributed his success at Chesapeake in part to Saavedra: "The million that was supplied by 'las damas de la Havana' may

20 August 1781

I conferred at length with Gálvez about the preparations for the contemplated enterprises, and we discussed many things pertaining to the matter.

21 August 1781

Nothing notable happened.

22 August 1781

Because the governor had shown me letters he had had from Cartagena, in which the viceroy of Santa Fe described to him the uprising that was occurring in the interior provinces of that realm and begged for reinforcements, I conferred about the matter with Don Bernardo de Gálvez at length, pondering the expedient that would be most adaptable to the circumstances.[152]

---

in truth be regarded as the bottom dollars upon which the edifice of American independence was raised": Stephen Bonsal, *When the French Were Here* (Garden City, NY: Doubleday, Doran and Co., 1945), 119–20. The ladies of Havana are said to have contributed their jewels to make up the sum needed. The money was a donation, not a loan (Tejera, 65). [Tr.] [That the ladies contributed their jewels is disputed by James A. Lewis, "Las Damas de la Havana, El Precursor, and Francisco de Saavedra," *The Americas* 37 (July 1980): 83–99.]

152. Rather than an early movement toward independence, the revolt of the Comuneros del Socorro of Colombia and Paraguay in the vice-royalty of New Granada (now Colombia) was a protest against taxes imposed by the inspector general, Juan Francisco Gutiérrez de Piñeres, who was attempting to tax tobacco and liquor and put in a sales tax.[Tr.] The taxes caused an uprising of the colored masses led by Berbeo y Galán. The rebellion extended all the way to Maracaibo and Mérida. The viceroy was Manuel Antonio Flories; his successor, Archbishop Antonio Caballero Góngora, quieted the uprising. Juan Francisco Gutiérrez de Piñeros had arrived in Santa Fe in 1778 with the purpose of imposing new taxes that would increase the price of products, and this intent caused the uprising of

23 August 1781

The mail-packet went out for Spain, and I was busy writing to the minister about the state of affairs.

24 August 1781

I conferred at length with Solano about the affairs of Santa Fe, and I urged him anew to despatch to the French Cape the four warships agreed upon.

25 August 1781

Nothing worth noting occurred.

26 August 1781

From Trinidad came a report that corsairs of that port had captured a vessel that was coming from Jamaica loaded with various goods. This vessel was carrying a passport from the captain general of this island to prevent any Spanish ship from molesting it. It was one of the vessels belonging to Don Pedro Ruiz, which was bringing news from Jamaica. The captain general complained to the naval commandant about the offense committed by the corsairs authorized by the commissioner of registry of Trinidad, who gave them leave to go out at a time when the port was closed.

27 August 1781

The *Batabanó*, the mail-packet from the coast of Honduras, came into port bringing me letters from the governor of Guatemala in which he outlined the plan he had formed for evicting the English from the coasts of that realm, and he requested that he be reinforced by the month of January with some armed vessels and munitions for its execution.

---

the Comuneros del Socorro. [Ed.]

28 August 1781

I conferred about the reinforcements to be sent to Cartagena and the coast of Honduras, first with Don Bernardo de Gálvez, and then with Solano, and I made an agreement with the latter that when the fleet should go out from here in November for the French Cays, there should also go out one warship, one frigate, and other small vessels, to take on in Puerto Rico the regiment that would be sent there by Royal Orders, to transport that regiment to Cartagena, and then to go to assist the operations of the governor of Guatemala on the coast of Honduras.

29 August 1781

It was announced that on the following day another mail-packet would sail for Spain, and I was writing all day.

30 August 1781

I continued writing; however, the mail-packet did not sail.

31 August 1781

The flag-of-truce ships, which were returning from New York after transporting the English garrison of Pensacola, began to put into this port.

1 September 1781

The flag-of-truce ships from New York reported that there were few English troops in that stronghold because the majority of them had been detached for Charlestown, that the combined French and American troops were encamped three leagues from New York, and that a heavy cannon fire could be heard.

2 September 1781

This day the warship *San Román* and the frigates *Clara* and *Gil*, which had been cruising off Cape San Antonio, came into view. The naval commandant sent them an order to resume their cruising. Because a cartel ship had reported that on the day it arrived at New York the English fleet of seven warships stationed there went out to sea, and that on the same day a rumor was spread that our fleet was going to sail from Havana before the end of July, commercial interests were beginning to fear that the English had gone out in order to intercept our fleet.

3 September 1781

Nothing new happened. I continued my conferences with Gálvez concerning the operations of the next campaign.

4 September 1781

Ruiz came to talk to me and made known to me the grave losses he had sustained, both because one of his ships had been captured in Trinidad, even though it had been authorized by the government, and also because he had not been sent to Jamaica to establish the prisoner exchange by the flag-of-truce ships as I had agreed he would be. During my absence the governor had sent to Guarico the captain of the Princess Regiment, Don Francisco Miranda.[153]

---

153. Francisco de Miranda, a native of Venezuela and a lieutenant general and colonel of the Infantry Regiment of Aragon, was adjutant to Cagigal, who commissioned him to effect an exchange of prisoners in Jamaica and to obtain any information he could about the island's defenses. Upon his return to Havana, Miranda was accused by Intendant Urriza of having brought contraband goods from Jamaica. An order for his arrest and imprisonment sent from Spain to Bernardo de Gálvez arrived at Guarico while Miranda was with Cagigal in the expedition against Providence. Later, to avoid imprisonment, Miranda went to the United States, first to the southern states and then to Philadelphia. Francisco Rendon, after

5 September 1781

I again talked with Solano about the plan of campaign and of how urgent it was to send the four warships to the French. He protested the haste with which he was working to fit out the ships, amass provisions, and seek seamen, and he said it was to be lamented that the fleet was not to go out all together because, if the four ships went out alone and the English learned of it in advance, as was probable, they would sail out from Jamaica to intercept them, as it seems the English have six warships there.

6 September 1781

A very swift vessel, coming from the French Cape and belonging to a merchant of Havana named Bolois, put into port. It brought the news that in Jamaica on 4 August they had experienced a great hurricane which had destroyed an entire English convoy and that the English had ten warships there, four of them small.

7 September 1781

I thought that a vessel should be sent to the Cape to explain that the promised warships had not set out for that port

---

having entertained him in his house for more than a month and having introduced him to the most important members of Congress and the American army, learned about the charges brought against Miranda in Havana and asked him to leave the city. Miranda went to Boston and thence to Europe, where he began the activities that earned him the name "precursor of Spanish American independence." After protracted hearings of the case in Spain, Miranda was declared innocent in 1799. See Herminio Portell Vila, *Vidas de la Unidad Americana* (Havana: Editorial Obispo, 1944), 21–34; William Spence Robertson, ed., *The Diary of Francisco de Miranda, Tour of the United States, 1783–1784* (New York, 1928), passim; Bernardo de Gálvez to José de Gálvez, 18 May 1782, AGI:Ind. Gen. 1578; Cagigal to José de Gálvez, undated, no. 57, AGI:SD 1232; Intendant of the Army to José de Gálvez, 3 December 1784, AGI:SD 1663; Rendon to Luis Unzaga y Amezaga, no. 38, 4 January 1784, AGI:Cuba 1354. [Tr.]

Journal of Don Francisco Saavedra de Sangronis

because funds that were expected momentarily had not yet come from Veracruz.

8 September 1781

A skiff was found that accepted the commission, provided that it was allowed to carry foodstuffs and other permitted goods to the Cape.

9 September 1781

Until this day the sloop that was ready to go to Spain did not sail because of foul weather and because of rumors that English vessels had gone to Cape San Antonio.

10 September 1781

Nothing notable happened.

11 September 1781

The skiff went out bound for the French Cape, and on it I sent letters to M. de Lillencourt, to the intendant, and to Labat, in which was enclosed a letter for the governor of Santo Domingo, advising him that by the month of November our fleet and army would be at the Cape and that therefore he should have meats provided in advance on the frontier.

12 September 1781

I continued conferring with Señor Gálvez about the operations of the campaign; I proposed to him that I was ready to go anywhere and that it seemed to me of primary importance that a reliable person go to Cartagena to obtain a comprehensive knowledge of conditions in Santa Fe and to bring back detailed reports about them, and that another such person ought to go to Mexico to solicit the money necessary for the campaign because the funds on the warships we were waiting for were not sufficient to cover the debts already contracted. I volunteered to do either of the two things, and even to do both if it were not necessary to perform them at the same time. It appeared to Gálvez that it was not wise for me to go to Cartagena, for I should have to embark in Batabanó on a very small vessel and pass through the enemy's cruising station, and if the English managed to catch me they would not release me, as undoubtedly they were by now cognizant of my commission. So we agreed that I should go to Veracruz and that an able and mature officer should go to Cartagena.

13 September 1781

From Cape Corrientes came a warning that a small English frigate had passed there, and the *Matilde* went out in search of it. I began to inquire about officers suitable for the commission mentioned above, and I learned that none was more competent than Don Juan Tufiño, a brevet colonel and captain of grenadiers of the Regiment of Guadalajara; I suggested him to Gálvez, and he liked the idea.

14 September 1781

I summoned Tufiño and told him about the commission for which we wished to make him responsible, so that after considering seriously whether he was in a position to perform it he could give me his answer. He replied that he was, and I made an appointment for him to go with me to see Señor Gálvez on the following day.

15 September 1781

In the morning I talked with the intendant about a vessel to be sent from Batabanó to Cartagena, and he told me that there was a very swift xebec ready at Batabanó. In the afternoon I went with Tufiño to Gálvez's house and presented him to the general, who thought him quite suitable for the task assigned him.

16 September 1781

At midday the warship *Dragón*, one of those which were coming from Veracruz, entered the port; on passing through the narrow strait near the morillo, she ran aground and could not be freed until the next day; a signal was given to the warship *Paula* following her not to come in because the channel was obstructed.

17 September 1781

Six merchant vessels that had come from Veracruz under escort of the warships put into the port.

Note [written on the margin]: According to witnesses the *Paula*, having become separated from the *Dragón*, found herself amidst an English convoy of at least twenty sails escorted by a warship. One of the merchantmen, thinking the *Paula* an English warship, came alongside, and upon recognizing that the *Paula* was Spanish, surrendered. They say that the weather was very rough and that no officer dared to go in the longboat to man the prize, and therefore the frigate was ordered to follow in their wake, but that night it escaped.

18 September 1781

The warship *San Francisco de Paula* entered the port. The two warships were bringing from Veracruz 4,700,000 pesos for army, navy, *situados*, etc. On the merchantmen came 2,400 tercios of flour to be distributed among the army and the fleet, and much merchandise from China and even from Europe. It was surprising that the ships of at least 8,000 tercios had brought only 2,000, when at the same time the viceroy advised that he had 15,000 tercios ready in Veracruz and that ships must be sent for them.

19 September 1781

The money was brought ashore, and a beginning was

19 September 1781

made at once to defray the debts previously contracted with the citizens, so as to preserve public credit and confidence.

20 September 1781

A French frigate named *Amazona* entered the port, saying that she came from Martinique, to which port she had escorted a convoy from Provence that had been joined by nine Spanish merchantmen that were going to Guarico in company with other French vessels escorted by a war frigate.

21 September 1781

The frigate *Clara* and the corvette *San Gil* put into the port returning from their cruising station, where they had become separated from the *San Román* and the brigantine *Pájaro* in a storm.

22 September 1781

The intendant sent for me. I went to his house, where I found the captain of the frigate *Amazona*, M. de Villages, who was carrying a duplicate of our king's orders that 1 million pesos be delivered to the French, the French sovereign's commission authorizing him to receive that sum, and a letter from the Marquis de Bouillé,[154] commanding general of Martinique, imploring that the money be delivered to him as soon as possible. By virtue of this, de Villages requested the entire 1 million. In response he was informed that the Comte de Grasse had taken one-half of the million for his operations in the

---

154. General François-Claude Amour, Marquis de Bouillé, had fought in the Seven Years War, after which he was made commandant of all French forces in the West Indies and governor of Martinique. In 1778 he waged a campaign against the British in Dominica, Saint Martins, Saint Eustatius, Tobago, Saint Christopher, Nevis, and Saba. He supplied 3,500 soldiers for de Grasse's expedition to Chesapeake Bay. After the defeat of de Grasse in the battle of the Saintes, Bouillé went to France to carry descriptions of the situation. [Tr.]

north and that therefore he could not be given more than the other half, but he was not satisfied. Finally we agreed that he would write an official paper setting forth his reason for demanding that he be given the entire 1 million, the intendant would pass the paper on to me, requesting information; I should tell him what I understood about the matter, and at all times everything would be done in order that he be given the greatest possible amount.

23 September 1781

I wrote the instruction for what Don Juan Tufiño must do to accomplish what was required by his commission and the letter of the viceroy of Santa Fe about the matter. Today the intendant invited the French officer to dine. As they were rising from the table, Solano received a letter from Morales, the commandant of the fleet, who sent word by a flag-of-truce ship from New York that he had met: on 12 August, when he wrote the letter, he was on a [unreadable] parallel with Bermuda, sixty leagues from that island, and was proceeding safely.

24 September 1781

The intendant sent me the official paper of which he had spoken. In it he told me that as I was aware 500,000 pesos had been delivered to M. de Traversai, captain of the frigate *Aigrette*, to be delivered to M. de Grasse, who had requested the funds by virtue of orders from Paris, and that now M. de Villages, captain of the frigate *Amazona*, had arrived, and was asking for the entire million. At the same time, he enclosed for me a paper that that same captain had sent him, in which he stated (1) that the aforesaid 1 million pesos were needed for the operations contemplated in the Windward Islands; (2) that without the money, those operations would not be executed; (3) that the Most Christian King had commissioned him to collect it; (4) that the 500,000 pesos given to M. de Grasse was a new favor which had been granted to France; and (5) that it had no connection with the aforesaid 1 million pesos. Today the French officers dined at my house.

25 September 1781

I replied to the official letter of the intendant that in my opinion he should give the entire 1 million to the Chevalier de Villages if it were possible for the reasons he had set forth in the letters to which I was responding. Today one-half of the million pesos were shipped. We dined aboard the French ship.

In the afternoon of this same day the thought occurred to me that it would be prudent to send on the frigate *Amazona* a trustworthy officer to be on the lookout in Martinique for news from our province of Caracas so that in case of an uprising he could send a warning and urge that the prompt necessary assistance be sent; that at the same time he should manage to prevail upon M. de Bouillé to assist us with all the forces he could contribute for the conquest of Jamaica. No one seemed to me more suitable for this undertaking than Lieutenant Colonel Don Bernardo Bonavía. I proposed this to Gálvez, who thought it a good idea. I talked with Bonavía, who greatly appreciated being selected for the commission, and I spoke to the captain of the frigate, who very gladly offered to take him.

26 September 1781

Bonavía was given instructions about what he was to do and a letter for M. de Bouillé.

27 September 1781

The frigate *Amazona* sailed at seven o'clock in the morning. On the previous afternoon a vessel that looked suspicious had been sighted; the *Amazona* gave chase and captured it. Our frigate *Matilde* had gone out at ten o'clock that morning, but she arrived when the vessel was already surrendered and manned. It was an English ship that had gone out from Jamaica bound for Europe loaded with sugar and rum.

28 September 1781

In the afternoon Gálvez, Solano, the intendant, and I held a long conference. In it we decided that the expeditionary force of warships and troops that must go to Guarico would depart from here before the end of October, that 1,500 men would go on the warships, that ships would be made ready soon afterward to transport the rest of the men, that foodstuffs would be prepared, that a warship and other vessels would go to Puerto Rico for the regiment that the court had designated and would transport it to Cartagena, and that a warship should go out immediately for Veracruz and I should embark on it.

29 September 1781

I attended a large gathering in the house of the bishop in honor of Don Miguel de Gálvez.[155] The warship *San Román*, which had been cruising, put into the port.

30 September 1781

On the previous afternoon a cartel ship arrived from Pensacola carrying four howitzers. An English frigate intercepted the ship and removed the howitzers, but it did not capture the cartel ship because of the repeated supplications of the Neile family, who were coming on it.[156]

I talked with Solano about the warship that was to go to Veracruz for the funds, and he told me that he had already assigned the *Asís*, which only needed the galleys repaired.

---

155. The infant son of Bernardo de Gálvez and his wife, Félice de Saint Maxent. [Tr.]

156. Caughey (p. 252) quotes a letter from one Arthur Neile to Bernardo de Gálvez dated 6 October 1783 (AGI:Cuba 1377) in which the Pensacola merchant thanked Gálvez for the courtesy and good treatment accorded him, his wife, and their daughters while they were prisoners and asked the general to take measures to have his lands and possessions returned to him. [Tr.]

1 October 1781

News was circulated that the minister of the navy [The Marqués González de Castejón] had written a letter to Don José Calvo in the name of the king, thanking him and approving his conduct at Pensacola. They say that Don Miguel de Alderete received a similar letter for having forced that port.[157]

2 October 1781

In the morning a brigantine came into view three leagues from the port. Its manuevers looked suspicious. At ten o'clock the frigate *Matilde* and an American brigantine went out, and they recognized it as [unreadable].

At four o'clock in the afternoon I had a long conversation with Solano, who charged me to tell Gálvez to send him for his guidance an official paper about what was discussed and decided in the session of 28 September. At the same time he handed me the convention I had made with the Comte de Grasse, so that I could send him a copy of it as an official paper; it was the original, which he had had in his possession since 24 August. Later I went for a walk with Gálvez. I gave him Solano's message as requested, and we talked at length about the operations of the campaign. In the evening I had a long conversation with the intendant on the same subject.

3 October 1781

Several American vessels entered the port, among them one that brought a letter from the Spanish agent in Philadelphia,[158] with the report that the Comte de Grasse had arrived

---

157. Navy Captain Miguel de Alderete commanded the frigate *Santa Clara* in the expedition against Pensacola which left Havana on 28 February 1781. The port was forced by Bernardo de Gálvez aboard the *Galveztown* accompanied by Lieutenant Juan Antonio de Riaño, commanding the frigate *Valenzuela* and two armed launches. With the exception of Calvo's flagship *San Román* the rest of the fleet put into the port the next day (Beerman, 179–81; Holmes 169–70). [Tr.]

158. The agent at Philadelphia was the Spaniard Francisco Rendón, former secretary of Juan de Miralles; he succeeded his superior after the

at Chesapeake Bay on 26 August; that he had disembarked 3,000 regulars there; that he had closed the mouth of the James River with three warships; that Cornwallis, whose retreat was cut off by this expedient, was blockaded by the Marquis de la Fayette; that Washington and the Comte de Rochambeau with a considerable body of troops were marching many miles a day toward the same destination; and that it was believed that Cornwallis would find himself compelled to surrender. The letter also reported that Admiral Hood, with fourteen warships, had joined Graves, who had nine in New York, that they had set sail with this entire fleet, and that the French fleet of M. de Barras had gone out from Rhode Island.(159)

I spoke with the intendant about whether it was advisable to permit some Dutch sloops that were in the harbor to bring in tackle, canvas, and warlike stores. There was a large reception in my house because it was the day of San Francisco. The general officers dined with me, etc.

5 October 1781

Targets, gazebos, and tents, ordered by the general to be erected for the conduct of drills with cannons and muskets, were by now almost finished, and the general announced that the drills would commence soon.

While walking with me this afternoon he spoke about a great number of petitions that had come to him from Louisiana, motivated by the Intendant [Martin] Navarro's order that a tax of 21 percent be paid on all foreign goods brought in by a French ship that had put into the Mississippi. The general pointed out that

---

death of Miralles in April 1780. The intelligence reported here is contained in a letter from Rendón to Cagigal, 6 September 1781 (AGI:Cuba 1281). See also Bonsal, *When the French Were Here*. [Tr.]

159. Hood and Graves reached Virginia waters after de Grasse's arrival there. For comprehensive accounts of the Yorktown campaign, see Boatner, 1230–49, and Thomas Balch, *The French in America during the War of Independence of the United States, 1777–81* (Philadelphia: Porter & Coates, 1891), passim. [Tr.]

that province must be governed by regulations different from those enforced in the others; in the first place, it must be permitted to trade with the French, both because the inhabitants do not like other goods and wines than French ones and because the Spaniards cannot take out of the province the timbers and hides that constitute its only products. Moreover, it is a province that absolutely must be treated with continued thoughtful attention, because it is contiguous to the Americans and has continuous contact with them. It is the forward wall of our realm of Mexico, and if an uprising were to occur there, it would be uncontrollable, both because of the location and because of the valor of the inhabitants.

6 October 1781

At seven o'clock in the morning the French frigate *Courageuse*, Captain M. de Saint Dominque, entered the port bringing eighty men of those our army had left ill in the Windward Islands. The officers of this frigate said that an American had arrived at the cape with the news that the Comte de Grasse with all his fleet had anchored in Chesapeake Bay on 26 August, that the English fleet of twenty-three warships appeared off that bay, and that the Comte de Grasse immediately set sail; a battle was joined between the two fleets in which the English were defeated and the French took some warships and frigates, and afterward Lord Cornwallis, blockaded on all sides in Virginia, was forced to surrender his arms.

The captain of this frigate brought letters from M. de Lillancourt and M. Le Brasseur in which they clamored for the four warships which I had promised the Comte de Grasse would be sent from this port to the French Cape. They also begged that they be given some money if it was possible.

7 October 1781

I talked frankly with Gálvez about the extreme importance of my advice to the Comte de Grasse that he take his entire fleet to the north and about my promise that we Spaniards would send battleships for the protection of the French Cape, a promise that unfortunately had not been fulfilled as yet. To tell the truth, if the Comte de Grasse had gone out with only twenty ships-of-the-line as he was planning to do, the English with the twenty-three they had brought together at New York probably would have attacked him on 26 August before his rendezvous with the fleet from Rhode Island.

8 October 1781

I dined in the home of the governor with the captain of the *Courageuese,* who gave me a letter from Messrs Lillancourt and Le Brasseur, governor and intendant of the French Cape, in which they remind me of the contract I had made with M. de Grasse, that four of the warships that are in this port would be sent to him there and that they would bring money. I spoke with Solano about our operations, and he said that the warship *Asís* was ready to go to Veracruz but that he thought it should not go out until the end of the month, as the weather still looked bad.

9 October 1781

Gálvez described to me his plan to drill the troop in target practice, the artillery in the use of the cannon, and the engineers and officers in the method of opening trenches, planning attacks, etc., which he was going to carry out soon.

10 October 1781

Don Pedro Brizzio arrived with the mail which he brought from Baracoa, after an extremely difficult voyage of thirty-two days. News of Gálvez's promotion to lieutenant general[160] caused joyful celebration. We talked at length about the operations of the campaign, and I made an appointment with him for the next day.

I went to see Gálvez in the morning. We conferred at length

---

160. By a Royal Order of 9 August 1781, AGI:Cuba 2359. [Tr.]

10 October 1781

about the plan of operation. We then went to Solano's house and the three of us, having reflected upon the state of the preparations, agreed upon the following:

(1) That it not being possible for the fleet to be ready until the middle of December, nor the army either, the four battleships I had promised the Comte de Grasse must go to the French Cape now and that an effort must be made to have everything ready by the aforesaid mid-December.

(2) That in the meantime an expedition will be launched against Providence, which can be started at the end of this month, sending there some launches with embrasures for cannons, some brigantines, and other small vessels.

(3) That at the same time another group of small armed ships will be sent to the governor of Guatemala, so that he can totally expel the English from those coasts.

(4) That on the eighteenth of this month I shall go to Veracruz on the warship *Asís,* in order to expedite the arrival here of the necessary funds and provisions of foodstuffs for the operations contemplated.

In the afternoon Gálvez and I talked about the same matters, and when he consulted me as to whether it would be fitting for him to go in person in command of the Providence expedition, I expressed the opinion that it would not, as much for the reason that only 1,000 men would go, and therefore it was more suitable for a colonel, as because in his absence all the preparations for the other objectives that were incomparably more important would be delayed.

At nightfall a brigantine and an American frigate went out bound for Philadelphia, as well as the brigantine of Bolois and Balaguer and one sloop, all bound for the French Cays.

12 October 1781

I talked with the intendant about the plan of operations that had been agreed upon, to the end that he not waste a minute in the preparations.

13 October 1781

Gálvez went to live outside the town so as to be close at hand to attend the drills which he told me are to begin on the fifteenth. The drills will begin with the troop and the artillery firing bullets, so as to be drilled in marksmanship; then the army will be encamped near the Castillo del Príncipe, a trench will be opened there, and attacks against the fort will be devised.

14 October 1781

They told me that Mr. Smith[161] had had news from an American that twelve English warships were cruising off the French Cape. For this reason I went to see Solano, who told me that even without this report he had decided after mature deliberation not to send the four warships alone to the aforesaid port but to go with the entire fleet and the part of the convoy that would be ready in mid-November, because with the English having ten warships in Jamaica, as they do, we were in danger of their catching a part of the fleet or blockading us on the French Cape or preventing the reunion of the whole fleet.

At the same time I communicated to Solano an idea I had, to wit, that the French frigate *Courageuse*, which is here, go to Veracruz with the *Asís*, obtain there the situado for Puerto Rico and some other funds which the Comte de Grasse will need in order to leave Martinique after his operations in the Windwards are concluded and come to assist us at Guarico. I also said that as soon as I left the money that the *Asís*, ready to be embarked, is to bring, I would return from Veracruz on the frigate, which would stop here only a few days for watering. I should then

---

161. In August 1780 Francisco Rendón sent to Governor Navarro from Philadelphia a letter of introduction for Robert Smith "who goes to Havana commissioned by the Honourable Robert Morris for the direction and custody of the monies acquired there by the sale of cargoes of the ships he has sent and those he intends to send" (Rendón to Navarro, 19 August 1780, AGI:Cuba 1282). [Tr.]

depart on the frigate, leave the situado in Puerto Rico, and go on to the Windwards to solicit the Comte de Grasse's vigorous assistance in our enterprise.

The idea seemed good to Solano except for the part about sending the situado of Puerto Rico on the *Courageuse,* because if possibly, or impossibly, the English captured the frigate, he would be blamed for not having sent it on a warship. My way of thinking seemed very good to Gálvez and the intendant, as by this method I should save much time and hasten the operations, and we agreed that at ten o'clock on the following day the captain of the *Courageuse* would be summoned to Gálvez's house and the idea would be proposed to him to see if he liked it.

15 October 1781

The captain of the *Courageuse* was summoned to the house of Señor Gálvez; the plan was proposed to him, and he agreed to it, but he asked that Señor Gálvez give him an official paper to the effect that the frigate was at his orders, to serve as a pretext for his protection, and we agreed that that would be done.

16 October 1781

Monsieur Saint Dominque came to my house and requested that I give him a good harbor pilot who knew the port and coast of Veracruz, in case the ships were separated. Also he said that it would be useful for the captain of the warship *Asís* to give him some signals for whatever might happen during the navigation. I asked the intendant for a pilot, and he promised to find one. I promised to speak to Domás about the signals.

I was in Gálvez's house, and we discussed the operations of the campaign. Later I went to see Solano, and we had a long conversation about the same matters.

17 October 1781

I went to see Don José Domás, captain of the warship

Asís, to speak to him about my voyage to Veracruz. He told me that the ship was ready, that he was about to bend the sails, and that we should go out very soon. M. de Saint Dominque came to dine at my house, and we talked at length about the voyage.

18 October 1781

On the previous night two Americans came into the port bringing letters from the Spanish commissioner in Philadelphia[162] who confirmed the report of the defeat of the English fleet by the Comte de Grasse. They refer to other letters written from New York that state that there had been a battle between the two fleets, that in view of the superiority of M. de Grasse, who had thirty warships while their fleet consisted of only twenty, the English took flight, but that nonetheless the French sank their 74-gun warship *Terrible* and captured the 64-gun *Ruby* and the 50-gun *Roebuck*, that four warships that put in at New York foundered, among them the three-decker *London*, and that the rest of the fleet was in bad condition. They add that Lord Cornwallis had cut up the 44-gun warship *Charon* and had used its artillery, decks, and sheathing in building a fort but that he was hard pressed and would surrender with all his army.

I went to Gálvez's house; we talked about the consequences of this news, and it caused us the greatest regret not to be able to be at the French Cape with our army and fleet by the time the Comte de Grasse would go to the Windwards, because if the En-

---

162. Rendón reported throughout August and September of 1781 from Philadelphia the movements of the forces that were converging in Virginia, enclosing copies of letters received from French officers and others. On 21 September he sent to Cagigal a detailed report containing a copy of a letter he had received from Theodorick Bland, a delegate to the Continental Congress from Virginia: "I have the pleasure of informing you that I have reliable intelligence that M. de Barras with his squadron has arrived to join the fleet of Comte de Grasse, and that they are now in Chesapeake Bay.... Cornwallis is blockaded in York Town, Virginia, and has rendered useless the warship *Charon* and mounted her artillery for defense. On the 16th of this month all our troops left Annapolis, Maryland, bound for Virginia" (Rendón to Cagigal, 21 September 1781. AGI:Cuba 1319). [Tr.]

glish were sending reinforcements of troops and warships from Jamaica to Saint Lucia, Jamaica was left deprived of a garrison, and we could descend upon it; and if they did not reinforce it, the Comte de Grasse with a victorious fleet and M. de Bouillé's army could throw them out of the Windward Islands. Then I importuned Gálvez concerning the expedition against Providence, and we agreed that it would be made immediately, although Solano wanted it to be postponed until we should leave for Guarico.

19 October 1781

I went to see the drill camp. I talked at length with Solano, and he agreed that the *Asís* would go out on Monday if the weather was good. I was with Gálvez; he showed me the letter he was writing to his uncle [Minister of the Indies José de Gálvez] about the plan of campaign in which he was going to tell him that if the necessary funds and provisions came from Mexico, and if the French gave us 10,000 men, twelve ships, artillery, weapons, etc., the expedition against Jamaica would be made this year; if not, it would be postponed until next year.

20 October 1781

The governor summoned me in order to read me a letter from Cartagena in which Casamayor writes that the turbulence in that realm had already grown much calmer but that nonetheless there are still many disorders and that the fire of sedition is spreading to Quito and Maracaibo.[163]

I went with Gálvez to see the trench they had begun to open in the simulated attack against the Castillo del Príncipe.

21 October 1781

I went to see Gálvez and read him the letter I had written to the minister about the operations of the coming cam-

---

163. See note 152. [Ed.]

paign, which pleased him very much; for this reason we talked for a long time about the matter, and we decided that the expedition against Providence was going to be undertaken without any delay whatsoever.

I advised him to give the command of it to Don Luis Huet, the officer who had devised the plan of attack, who was well acquainted with those places and was a brigadier.[164]

Domás was in my house, and I spoke to him urgently about the sailing of the warship. He told me that it was ready, that I should send my luggage aboard, and that we should sail on the following day if the weather was fine.

At noon there was a strong thunderstorm with considerable wind; naturally we were convinced that the departure would not take place the next day.

22 October 1781

The day dawned fair. At ten o'clock there arose an excellent northeast wind which blew all day, and at nightfall the land breeze sprang up. In the morning the harbor pilot acquainted with the coasts of Veracruz, who was to go on the French frigate, came to see me. I told him to go aboard, and he did. Later an officer of the *Courageuse* came with a message from the captain complaining because we were losing so fine a day and saying that he was unwilling to remain in the port any longer because the provisions were being consumed and the men were falling ill, and even if the warship did not go out on the following day, he was going to set sail.

After dinner I went to see Solano to set forth the urgency of the accomplishment of my commission and therefore of the sailing of the warship. He told me that the weather indeed was

---

164. Bernardo de Gálvez chose instead Juan Manuel de Cagigal to lead the expedition against Providence in the Bahamas. The governor of the Bahama Islands, John Maxwell, surrendered to Cagigal on 8 May 1782; the Articles of Capitulation were drawn up by Francisco de Miranda, Cagigal's aide-de-camp. Juan Daban was acting governor of Havana during the absence of Cagigal (Bernardo de Gálvez to Cagigal, 20 January 1782, AGI:SD 2085; Rendón to Cagigal, 25 June 1782, AGI:Cuba 1319). [Tr.]

22 October 1781

fine, that the warship was ready, and that he would immediately order its captain to put the gunpowder on board and prepare to go out the next morning.

Next we talked at length about the plan of the campaign, and he assured me that he was determined to follow the first plan—that is, to send the four warships to the French Cape and to follow later with the rest of the expeditionary force—first executing the attack against Providence and then sending the requested reinforcements to the governor of Guatemala. This was the decision that ought to have been made ever since August, when I returned from Guarico, because in truth the French probably take us for deceitful people who do not keep our promises, the more so because they had to dispatch a convoy to Europe before the end of this month, and now either they have detained it with great loss to their commerce or they have sent it out at great risk.

In the evening I went to the house of the intendant, where I found the French captain, who was grievously vexed by the delay. I tried to placate him, and I promised him that if the warship did not set sail on the twenty-fourth, I myself would go on his frigate.

At six o'clock in the evening six American ships went out.

23 October 1781

I went to see Solano, who promised that the warship would depart on the following day without fail. I informed the Frenchman of this, said farewell to Don Bernardo de Gálvez, and sent my luggage aboard the ship.

24 October 1781

At seven o'clock in the morning I embarked in company with Don Josef María Peñalver, son of the treasurer of Havana, who wished to take advantage of this opportunity to see the realm of Mexico. At eight o'clock we set sail, and at nine o'clock the whole convoy composed of one warship, the French frigate, and eight cargo vessels was outside the port. The northeast wind was light, so that we made little headway.

KARTE VON
MEXICO
Zur allgemeinen Historie
der Reisen 1754.
von M. B. Ing. de la Marine
Gemeine Franzæsische See-meilen

T. 13

25 October 1781

The land wind lasted until twelve o'clock, then there came a northeast breeze so light that it seemed calm. At nightfall we were hardly sixty miles from Havana.

26 October 1781

The wind was contrary; we ran only nineteen miles on a direct course.

27 October 1781

Calm until three o'clock in the afternoon; we ran fourteen miles and then faced the Pan de Daijabon.

28 October 1781

The winds were variable; sixty-four miles were run. The current carried us five leagues to the west. At nightfall we were north-south with Cape Antonio.

29 October 1781

On the previous afternoon a fresh north wind had begun to blow. We ran 105 miles on a direct course, and at night a bottom was found, for we had entered the zone of Campeche.

30 October 1781

The north wind continued somewhat stronger; 115 miles were run. At nine o'clock in the morning a swift vessel named *Angel de la Guardia* was dispatched to give advance notice of our arrival in Veracruz.

31 October 1781

The north wind slackened and changed to the northwest.

At eight o'clock in the morning the French frigate requested permission to go ahead to Veracruz, and it was granted; the frigate crowded sail and by afternoon was already out of sight.

1 November 1781

The wind veered to the northeast with a slight inclination to the southeast; we ran forty-seven miles.

Both from conversation with the officers and from what I could comprehend I recognized that the warship *Asís* has excellent qualities. It is easy to steer, it carries the canvas well, it easily tacks ahead, it falls very gently, and it sails admirably with the bowline hauled. Moreover it is one of the swiftest we have; it is true that it is not sailing at full speed in this voyage, but in addition to the fact that it is badly loaded, the flats have not been exposed for six years and they must necessarily be dirty. This ship is of the first construction of Gotier, as are the *San Agustín* and the *San Juan*, and as these three warships are the best of the fleet in Havana, according to the same naval officers, I realized that many of the bad things said about their construction were dictated by a partisan spirit. For the most part, our warships are ill provided with ammunition and military stores; they have much unnecessary timber and the tackle and canvas are coarse, thus increasing the weight.

2 November 1781

The currents pushed us toward the west; we ran fifty-six miles; at night we paid out the lead.

3 November 1781

Forty-eight miles were run. The wind was light and almost from the west.

4 November 1781

The wind freshened from the northeast; 126 miles were

run. At two o'clock in the afternoon land was sighted, and with sails reefed we tried all night to approach it.

5 November 1781

At dawn we could clearly discern the coasts of Veracruz, especially the peak of Orizaba, covered with snow to the middle of its slope. The wind was from the land and very light. To leeward we saw the French frigate, which as we learned later had put in at Punta Delgada and, having the wind from the south, had for three days been unable to reach the port. At one o'clock in the afternoon the wind changed to the northeast; the frigate overtook us and even entered the port about half an hour before we did. As night fell we cast anchor about 600 toises from the Castillo de San Juan de Ulúa, and we spent the entire night in warping the ship, so that at dawn we were near the landing rings.[165]

6 November 1781

I disembarked at ten o'clock in the morning and went to lodge in the house of the governor [José Carrión y Andrade], who had sent his son to fetch us. I soon made known to the governor the importance of my prompt departure for Mexico, and immediately he summoned a man who rented litters and horses, to have him furnish those I needed for the journey, but the man replied that he could not serve me before ten o'clock at the earliest, as he kept his animals twelve leagues distant from there.

7 November 1781

I wrote to Mexico to the viceroy and to Cossío, telling them that I had arrived and that within a short time I should begin my journey to that city.[166]

I set about looking at Veracruz, which is well designed; its

---

165. Rings of metal or iron collars used for tying up ships. [Ed.]
166. The viceroy was General Martín de Mayorga, governor of Guate-

7 November 1781

streets are straight and wide, and its houses not unattractive. But its location is unhealthful, in a kind of hollow surrounded by sand dunes. The insalubrity of the town is contributed to greatly by the filth in the streets and the fact that the whole district, exterior and interior, is full of mounds of rubbish; also the slaughterhouse lies to the south, so that the prevailing wind of summer blows in infested with corrupt matter; and finally the majority of its inhabitants drink water obtained from a kind of swamp, even though it is easy to bring good running water into the city, and, moreover, the city has funds earmarked for that purpose.

---

mala from 1773 to 1779, when he became viceroy of New Spain after the death of the Marqués de Bucareli. He was succeeded as viceroy in 1782 by Matías de Gálvez, brother of José de Gálvez. From the beginning of the North American Revolution, Mexico caused Spain increasing anxiety. "The viceroy, Martín de Mayorga, was faithful in giving whatever aid in men and money he could, receiving in return little consideration from the home government. His position was made insecure because several of his associates tried to act independently of his authority": John Rydjord, *Foreign Interest in the Independence of New Spain* (New York: Octagon Books, 1972), 100, quoting Carlos María Bustamente, *Suplemento,* in Andrés Cavo, *Tres Siglos de Mexico* (Mexico, 1836–38), 3:42, 43. Orozco Y Berra attributes Mayorga's difficulties in part to the fact that José de Gálvez had desired that his brother Matías succeed Bucareli: "In November 1781 Don Francisco Saavedra arrived at Veracruz, sent by Gálvez to *fiscalizar* [criticize and report the performance of] the viceroy.... The public took Saavedra for a prince incognito because of the secretive way in which he came, and because he seemed mysterious and did not disdain the obeisances accorded him." See Manuel Orozco y Berra, *Historia de la Dominación Española en Mexico,* vol. 4, *El Poder Real* (Mexico, 1938), 167–68. Pedro Antonio Cossío was called secretary to the viceroy, Mayorga, but was actually the first intendant in New Spain. [Tr.]

8 November 1781

The governor took me to see the Castillo de San Juan de Ulúa.[167] We examined it thoroughly and saw that it has as much fortification as is needed for making a vigorous defense. Therefore it was wise to eliminate the two immense hornebeques of the former plan which was approved by the court in the year '71 and reapproved in '78. The engineer, Corral, who holds the office of Teniente del Rey of the fortress, and has built the new works, is an intelligent, impartial man who has very fine ideas.[168]

The port, however, which by its nature is very bad, has been improved somewhat by the latest works on the fort because advancing the San Pedro bulwark more than twenty varas into the sea has protected ships at anchor in its vicinity on the north side. Likewise, the number of lashing hooks for mooring has been increased.

The port would benefit from other improvements for which several projects have been planned. However, it is still almost in the condition in which nature left it, and indeed it is a pity that the rest of the plans have not been carried out so as to provide easy access to the only port that the richest realm in the world possesses.

9 November 1781

I examined the perimeter of the city in order to see its present defensive capabilities. It seemed to me that 1,000 men can capture and sack the city with the greatest of ease. It is true that the Castillo of San Juan makes the port matchless, but by disembarking to windward or to leeward of the city, capturing the city, as an enemy could do without major hindrance, and

---

167. The fortress of Ulúa, built in the seventeenth century, was much improved and reinforced about 1768. New artillery was sent from Spain, and several field pieces were manufactured in Tacubaya under the direction of the engineer Diego García Panes (Orozco y Berra, 143). [Tr.]

168. Miguel de Corral, number 380 on the promotion list of military engineers, was named governor of Veracruz in 1789. [Ed.]

placing a formidable battery in the lower part of [unreadable], the port would be made as inaccessible to us as it now is to the enemy.

10 November 1781

I went to observe a test of gunpowder that was conducted at ten o'clock in the morning in the Escuela Prática de Artillería [Artillery Drill School]. It was learned from the test that a great portion of the powder recently arrived from Mexico did not reach even as far as forty toises when fired from the mortar and that consequently it is useless for anything except salvos.

At three o'clock in the afternoon Peñalver, the captain of the French frigate, M. de Saint Dominque, and I set out in two litters; the servants went on horseback.[169] We traveled five leagues along the seashore on a sandy plain interrupted by three streams. At eight o'clock in the evening we crossed the river they call the Antigua and entered old Veracruz, where a man named Burgos waited on us very well. We saw the first church founded by Cortez, which is almost in ruins. The population is made up wholly of Negroes and mulattoes, the climate is unhealthful, and there are many poisonous reptiles and insects in the environs.

11 November 1781

We went eleven leagues. We spent the night at Plan del Río, which is a poor inn built of reeds; in its vicinity there is a shallow but clear stream whose banks are delightful.

---

169. Litters carried by mules took nine or ten days, so, fifty-eight years later, Madame Calderón de la Barca chose the stagecoach. She followed the same route as Saavedra and it is interesting to compare their notes. See Madame Calderón de la Barca, *La Vida en México* (Mexico: Editorial Porrúa, S.A., 1967). [Ed.]

12 November 1781

We went seven leagues. At two o'clock in the afternoon we entered Jalapa; it is a pleasant town, healthful and with a cool climate. I have never in my life seen locations more suitable for building beautiful country houses than those offered by the surroundings of this little city, but there is not one.

13 November 1781

The entire road from Jalapa to Perote, which are eight leagues apart, is a steep ascent, which after four leagues begins to moderate somewhat. The slopes are not dangerous, because there are no precipices near them, but their abrupt declivity makes them impracticable for wheeled vehicles, a hindrance that can be remedied with little difficulty. At this time active work is being done to improve this road, and they even say that they intend to take it through an area that avoids the slope of the Soldado, which has more than one league of sharp declivity.

The whole interval from Jalapa to Las Vigas is populated with Indian huts; scattered at random through a craggy terrain full of flowers, they make a picturesque landscape.

From Veracruz to Plan del Río one is conscious constantly of an insufferable heat with all the discomforts of the torrid zone. For four leagues round about Jalapa, a perpetual springtime reigns. Later, as soon as one reaches Las Vigas, one feels all the rigors of winter, which increase as one goes up to Perote. There the landscape is bare of foliage, in several directions there are mountain peaks covered with snow, the forests have no trees other than pines, live oaks, and oaks, and at dawn every morning the ground is covered with frost. This phenomenon of finding at 19°20′ of latitude all the signs of winter at 40° arises from the location of this land. From Veracruz to Perote, a distance of thirty-two leagues, the road is a constant rising slope, so that Perote is at an altitude above sea level which is little different from that of the entire realm of Mexico, which is more than 600 toises, according to the calculations of some experts. Consequently, the air is necessarily excessively rarefied at so high an

13 November 1781

altitude, and it causes a strongly perceptible impression.

Artillery Captain Don Diego Panes came out to receive us at Las Vigas and took us to his house at Perote, where he attended us very graciously.

In the afternoon we examined the fort in a leisurely fashion; its works conform to standard regulations for fortifications and even have a certain air of magnificence. In it are good field equipment and an excellent armory containing more than 3,000 swords and about 6,000 fusils, well arranged and guarded. Regarded as a stronghold designated to check the progress of an invasion, the fort of Perote is totally useless, for the reason that an enemy can penetrate to the realm of Mexico by way of several other areas without touching the vicinity of Perote. If it is regarded as a fortified depot in which can be kept and preserved weapons sufficient to arm the realm against a sudden invasion, and even a regular train of artillery with which to protect the most important posts, it is a very appropriate work, and considering all this I think Madrid would approve of its execution.[170]

14 November 1781

We departed in the morning in a carriage. We drove fourteen leagues, mostly over sandy ground, and reached a hacienda called San Francisco, where we slept.

15 November 1781

We drove twelve leagues. We slept at a hacienda of tolerably good appearance belonging to the Padres Belemitas de Puebla.[171]

---

170. The fortress of Perote was built in 1770–78. [Tr.]

171. The Order of Bethlehem (1667–1820) was founded in the New World by the Canarian Pedro de Betancurt in the seventeenth century. Eventually it had hospitals almost all over the Indies. See A. M. Ruiz de Villarías, *El venerable Pedro de Betancurt* (Madrid, 1981). [Ed.]

16 November 1781

We traveled eleven leagues and slept at the town of Apa, which probably has a population of 1,000 citizens. Four leagues before arriving there, we were overtaken by a servant sent by the Padres Belemitas of Mexico, who offered us lodging in their convent, which I accepted, so as not to be of any trouble to private citizens who I foresaw would invite us into their homes.

17 November 1781

We drove ten leagues. At ten o'clock in the morning we reached a small elevation from which one can see the plain of Otumba, where Cortez won the famous battle that made him master of the Mexican Empire.[172] There is not in all those surroundings any monument whatever to preserve the memory of so significant an action.

After midday we arrived at a town called San Juan de Teotihuacán, where the priest gave us lodging and treated us very well, as did the *alcalde mayor* [chief magistrate]. The population probably exceeds 600; the town is situated in a spacious and pleasant valley, and it has running water in abundance. There the Indians used to have the temples of their gods and the tombs of their ancestors, which are still there in pyramidal mounds. There are vestiges of the ancient town, which surely must have been large, but the buildings, whose foundations can be easily distinguished, were small.

18 November 1781

At seven o'clock in the morning we arrived at the roadside inn of Totolingo. From there one sees the immense plain upon which Mexico is situated. The two great lakes of Chalco and Texoco, the many groves and gardens that surround the city, its sumptuous buildings, and the snow-covered volcanoes

---

172. Hernán Cortés won this battle on 7 October 1520, after abandoning Mexico on 30 June, harassed by the natives who had revolted because of the stupid conduct of Pedro de Alvarado. [Ed.]

that rim the horizons form a magnificent perspective.

At ten o'clock we reached the Sanctuary of Guadalupe, where several people awaited us. We entered the sanctuary to pray. The temple seemed to us to have much treasure, but there is little taste in its decoration. The building is tolerably good, although it is a mixture of Gothic and Roman. At twelve o'clock we arrived at Mexico City. I went directly to see the viceroy, who received us with extreme urbanity. In the afternoon I went to see Cossío, with whom I talked for a long time.

19 November 1781

I had a long session with the viceroy. I informed him about the object of my commission; I told him that in Havana there was great need of money and provisions for the immense operations of this campaign; I also gave him to understand that there was a scarcity of men and that the Regiment of the Crown, which, under the leadership of Don Benito Pardo [a confidant of Bernardo de Gálvez, sent to Mexico on a mission similar to Saavedra's; see Extracto de la comisioón reservada, 23 November 1781, AGI:Ind. Gen. 1580], was being made ready to embark, would be very welcome. But I said that I carried a particular order from Don Bernardo de Gálvez charging me to tell him that if the viceroy had the slightest suspicion or presumption that there could be any rebellion in the realm, he should by no means send troops whom he might urgently need in that event, because sound policy dictated that before one attacks the house of another, one should make his own house secure.

The viceroy answered that although the people of the realm were somewhat displeased because of various dispositions taken recently in the matter of taxes, he had not the slightest fear of rebellion, both because of the timid character of the inhabitants and because of the restraint imposed upon them by the fleet and army of Havana. And even if some disturbance might occur, the troops of the Regiment of the Crown, all being native, were the least fit to contain it, and it was even debatable whether in such a case the use of that troop might cause more resentment than benefit. As for the rest, he promised me that he would get ready as much money as possible, that there were in Veracruz more than enough provisions, and that he desired above everything to contribute to the success of the operations of the war.

In the afternoon I went driving outside Mexico, whose outskirts are extremely beautiful, with two pleasant groves of poplar trees, one for pedestrians and one for carriages; but their fountains and decorations are in bad taste.

20 November 1781

Early in the morning I went out walking to see the city, which surely must be one of the best planned in the entire world. The streets are wide and straight, the houses and churches seen as a whole have a good appearance; there are some public works of considerable magnificence; but unfortunately in so beautiful a city, there is not the slightest trace of orderliness. The city lacks cleanliness, apportionment into districts or *barrios*, lighting, and other requisites of the greatest importance for public order and comfort. The city has great properties, but they are mortgaged.

I saw the viceroy again, and we continued the conversation of the previous day. I dined with Don Guillermo Wanghan. I talked with several individuals who described to me sadly the state of things in the realm. They said that there was prevalent a general discontent, as much because of the increase in taxes on *pulques* which had been initiated and extension of the excise tax to include corn, as because of the vexations, violations, and rudeness of some employees of the *Royal Hacienda*. It was generally thought that the thing that had most disquieted the public was that free trade in grains in Veracruz for supplying the islands had been prohibited and the conduct of shipping restricted to some degree; the fact that the king had become the only purchaser as well as the only shipper of grains had given rise to a monopoly no less prejudicial to hauling than to agriculture.

21 November 1781

I had a conference of more than two hours with Cossío. I portrayed to him forcefully the great urgency of the vast projects for which he must send assistance to Havana, the importance of waging the war vigorously, especially in this truly decisive campaign, and the accuracy of the estimates made by the intendant of the army and the commandant of the navy as to the expenditures of this year.

He replied that I must not doubt that he and the viceroy had made every possible effort to ensure that Havana was well provisioned and that now they were exhausting their resources to that same end. He affirmed that the treasury was depleted, after the large and repeated remittances of money that had been made to various places; that at the present time they were sending 800,000 pesos to Manila and that all the income of the province of Oaxaca, which is one of the richest, had been assigned for the expenditures of Guatemala; that the delay of [the ships that carry] quicksilver was threatening the realm with calamity, by curtailing the working of the mines; that to take out money by extraordinary measures was no longer practicable, after the donation of funds and the increase in various taxes; and finally that to try to borrow would fail because, considering the current mood of the people, hardly 1 million could be collected. At the same time he showed me a letter from the Conde de Regla in which, after relating the great expenditures he had had to make on his mines and how far from what the public imagined was the true status of his fortune, he concluded by saying that far from being able to pay in advance to the king the amounts he would loyally be pleased to pay, he could not without great difficulty pay more than the 800,000 pesos which was the value of the haciendas of the Jesuits which he had bought recently.[173] From all this Cossío concluded that in the present circum-

---

173. Pedro Romero de Terreros, the Conde de Regla, had purchased from the Crown lands confiscated from the Company of Jesus (Jesuits) who, suspected of disloyalty, were expelled from Spanish dominions in 1767. The expulsion from New Spain was carried out by José de Gálvez, who was visitador-general there from 1765 to 1771. See Luis Navarro

stances the sum of 2.5 million pesos was the most that could
From all this Cossío concluded that in the present circumstances the sum of 2.5 million pesos was the most that could be sent to Havana, unless the convoy were detained in Veracruz for three or four months in the expectation that the proceeds from sales should supply larger amounts.

I had already surmised that it was extremely unlikely that the Treasury of Mexico would hastily get ready at once the 9.5 millions they were requesting in Havana, and which constituted more than three-fourths of the income of the realm of New Spain. From the complaints I had heard and the reports I had been given, I was aware of the general discontent of the populace, and I already knew that the rich, disgusted at not having had, on the various occasions when they made loans to the king, more satisfaction than to be treated with despotism, harshness, and deceit, were far from willing to advance large amounts.

In this situation there remained only three methods from which to choose: (1) to promote by means of some extraordinary contribution or donation the collection of all or part of the amounts requested, (2) to have the warship wait the necessary months until the income of the realm should produce the 9 million pesos in question, or (3) to take the 3 million now, which could be supplied, and to arrange for warships to come for the remaining money within a few months. The first method, besides not being reasonable, was risky in the present circumstances; the second exposed us to the danger that, for want of the funds required to leave, the land and sea forces would remain idle in Havana during the entire campaign season; the last method was the only one possible, and if well planned it could be useful.

So I made an agreement with Cossío that the convoy that was at Veracruz would now carry to Havana all or part of the Regiment of the Crown, 3 million pesos, with 2 million for the navy and 1 million for the army, and 9,000–10,000 tercios of flour, meats, and dried vegetables; that another convoy would

---

García, *Don José de Gálvez y la Comandancia General* (Sevilla, 1964), passim; Orozco y Berra, 101–31; Rydjord, 72. [Tr.]

come from Havana within two months to obtain 4 or 5 million pesos and the provisions available; and that at the end of the campaign, if it was necessary, a third convoy would be sent for the same purpose; that in the intervals between the arrivals of these convoys, the requisite sums and provisions would be collected unhurriedly and deposited in appropriate places, so that the ships could be dispatched in a brief time.

After the settlement of this point, which constituted the essential purpose of my coming to New Spain, I adroitly but openly spoke to Cossío about the universal discontent of the entire realm, so incompatible with the beneficent intentions of the king and the ministry and with the prudence, courtesy, and suavity with which the minister of the Royal Hacienda ought to behave in the present critical situation in which the New World found itself, in view of the examples of the English colonists and those of Peru and Santa Fe. Cossío said that the discontent arose in great part from the fact that each of the various agents in the several branches of the Royal Hacienda is dictator in his own department and that this caused a thousand vexations which the viceroy could not remedy; nevertheless, he did not fear the slightest disturbance in the realm and believed that even if a disturbance occurred, he would calm it down very easily alone, because everyone liked him—the people because he dispatched all business quickly and impartially and the merchants because they regarded him as one of their own.

In the afternoon I went to see an extensive suburb of Mexico, where I found dire poverty. I entered some houses, inquired into the cause of the wretchedness of some persons who looked discerning, and learned that their indigence results from lack of employment rather than from the innate laziness that is attributed to those people.

22 November 1781

We saw the mint and the functions of all its divisions, shown to us in great detail by Mangino.[174] It is a vast, well-

---

174. The Casa de la Moneda (mint) was constructed in 1731–34 and expanded in 1772–82. Don Fernando José Mangino, superintendent of the

equipped structure in which a high degree of order prevails, and it gives a lofty idea of the magnificence of our monarchy. The rude aspect of the building does not correspond with its interior richness. The first building, constructed forty years ago for the coining of 7 million pesos, was small and in bad taste. Since then the coining of silver has increased, especially since the decrease in the price of mercury, so that today 20–23 million are minted each year. For this reason, it has been necessary to enlarge all the shops and to build an addition as large as the original structure and of incomparably better appearance. However, since it is attached to the older building with the principal facade, it is poorly lighted, and on the whole it looks more like the house of a rich man of bad taste rather than the sanctuary of the wealth of the world. It would be a fitting act of generosity for the ministry to use the present building for some other public purpose and to build from the ground up, in an unencumbered area, a new mint that would give at first sight an idea of the magnificence of its owner.

From some employees of the plant, and much better from a written report they gave me, I learned about the successive increases experienced in the minting of silver during the past forty years, climbing from 7 to 23 million pesos from silver extracted from the mines annually. This is without doubt the cause in the rise of the prices of everything that has occurred during the same period in Europe, Asia, and America. Indeed it is debatable whether this increase in money has been beneficial or prejudicial to the common good of the human race, because as the value of gold and silver fell in relation to the things they represent, there has not really been an increase in wealth but only in the mass of metal.

The king of Spain could hold in his hand the balance of trade in the world and impose upon it whatever law he desired, for in supplying precisely the amount of mercury necessary to mine a determined quantity of silver, he was arbiter

---

mint, also promoted the creation of the Academia de San Carlos. [Ed.] Mangino was later appointed to the offices of subdelegate of the treasury, intendant of the army, and corregidor of Mexico (Orozco y Berra 179). [Tr.]

22 November 1781

for maintaining the proportion between money and things that he judged to be most profitable to his monarchy.[175]

The Spanish government probably had another, simpler method of performing this operation, without limiting the work of the mines, and that was to permit a greater or lesser exportation of silver to China, in proportion to the quantity that had been determined for circulation in Europe. These speculations would have been a worthy occupation for certain persons of talent and experience able to make political calculations of such magnitude with integrity and whose patriotism was above personal consideration.

After the examination of the mint, we went on to see the Academy of Fine Arts, which is attached to it at present. The academy is directed by Don Gerónimo Gil, an excellent engraver who is in charge of making the dies for coins. Although this project is still embryonic, as funds are now being collected for its support, the beginnings promise happy success. Indeed it is an establishment indispensable in Mexico, whose natives are born with a decided inclination for the arts and where an infinite amount of money is spent on buildings and decorations, which for lack of good design discredit the taste of their builders. I marveled at seeing in Gil's academy youths who, after six months of study, draw from the model and from life as well as do draftsmen in Europe with two or three years of study.[176]

In the afternoon I went to see another suburb of Mexico, and drove to Jitacalco, where the *chinampas,* or floating gardens, are to be seen.

---

175. The supply of mercury was controlled by the government and, at an agreed price, was apportioned among the miners in proportion to the amount of this ingredient they used. It came to America from Spanish and German mines, brought only on the fleets from Cádiz (ibid., 159). [Tr.]

176. In 1784 Viceroy Matías de Gálvez gave great impetus to the Academy of Fine Arts by obtaining for it an annual income of 9,000 pesos from public funds and 4,000 from the secular funds of the clergy (ibid., 173). [Tr.]

23 November 1781

We went to see the House for the Smelting of Gold and Silver, where delicate operations worthy of observation are performed. Next, we went to Monte Pío,[177] a useful establishment but subject to difficulties, especially in Mexico, where the lowest of the common people are very much inclined to petty thievery.

24 November 1781

At eight o'clock in the morning we went to see the gunpowder factory of Santa Fe, which is under construction three leagues from Mexico. We arrived at ten o'clock and examined everything with minute attention to details. It is a simple structure suited to the purpose. The director is the Engineer Constanzó, an intelligent and candid young man, the one who built the enlargements of the mint.[178] In the afternoon we went on to the old gunpowder factory of Chapultepec, where Valera and Dampierre showed us all the workshops. The saltpeter of this factory, of which there is a great abundance there, seemed excellent to us. However, I was told that it is the object of strong controversy and that all this derives from the kind of disorder to which the production of gunpowder in Mexico is liable [see James A. Lewis, "The Royal Gunpowder Monopoly in New Spain, 1766–1783 ...," *Ibero-Amerikanisches Archiv* 6 (1980): 355–72].

25 November 1781

I responded to two questions put to me by the viceroy about the objects of my commission. I visited the *fiscal*, Posada,

---

177. The public pawnshop was founded in 1775 by the Don Pedro Romero de Terreros, the Conde de Regla, "for the relief of the needy" (ibid., 148). [Tr.]

178. The military engineer Miguel Costanzó, author of the main plans of Mexico City, the mint of Zacatecas, and the governor's palace in San Luis Potosí, was sent in 1769 to California to plan and supervise the construction of presidios and Franciscan missions (ibid., 137). [Ed.]

and talked with him for a long time, and he seemed to me to be a youth of excellent ideas and much altruism.[179] In the afternoon I went for a walk with Corres, who talked with intelligence and moderation about the conditions of the realm, the reasons for its discontent, and the means for remedying its abuses. A firm, affable, and impartial viceroy, a secretary with the same qualities, and a commissioner of the Royal Hacienda who is intelligent, humane, and persuaded that the essential element of his job is not to fill the treasury momentarily without promoting the prosperity of the common people, would remedy everything within a few months. The present viceroy is upright and exceedingly humane, but he would be a better viceroy if he were not so kind. The secretary seems zealous, but he is acrimonious, as everyone testifies. The branches of the Royal Hacienda are divided among three or four individuals. Each is despotic in his own department, which he regards as isolated and tries to augment exclusively, and there is no plan that coordinates the interests of the king with public prosperity.

26 November 1781

In the morning I went to the house of an individual who is unbiased and experienced in the affairs of the country. He informed me minutely about the state of the realm and the causes of the general discontent, agreeing in substance with what I had already heard from other sources.

Near midday I went to see the viceroy, who complained to me bitterly about the limited nature of his authority, of how vexing it was to see a multitude of abuses he could not remedy, and of his fervent desires to go to Spain. He assured me that the whole realm was one great outcry against the harshness with which it was treated by the ministers of the Royal Hacienda. I told him that it was not the intention of the king or of the minister that

---

179. Ramón Posada y Soto was the Crown-appointed fiscal, or prosecuting attorney, whose duty it was to defend the Crown and to prosecute civil and criminal charges in cases that affected it. Corres was his associate. [Tr.]

His Majesty's subjects be harassed, but rather that they should be treated with forbearance and liberality, in proof of which I cited various royal orders that express no other sentiment.

In the evening an official of the customhouse gave me detailed information about various matters pertaining to this department.

27 November 1781

I went to see the Convent of San Francisco, an immense edifice which lacks design and is properly no more than an aggregate of fragments. The church is in as bad taste in its construction and adornments as are the rest of the churches of Mexico.[180] In it can be seen the tomb of Hernán Cortez, which inspired in me a feeling akin to veneration. The Guardian of the House, called Father Morfí,[181] told me a lot about the *Provincias Internas*[182] and the advances that the savage Indians are making in them daily, being provided with muskets by way of Texas and Louisiana. Intolerable disorders and abuses prevail in the governments of the *Presidios Internos*,[183] and

---

180. I am surprised by these negative opinions of Saavedra's about the Baroque style that dominates and characterizes his native city of Seville. [Ed.]

181. The Franciscan Father Juan Agustín Morfí, a native of Galicia, was professor of theology in the Colegio de Tlaltecolo. He was born in Galicia and died in Mexico in 1783. He visited New Mexico with Teodoro de Croix, first commandant of the interior provinces, and he wrote a journal, "Noticias históricas de Nuevo México, Diario del viaje a la provincia de Texas," Memorias para la historia de la provincia de Texas (unpublished). [Ed.]

182. The Provincias Internas comprised the northern provinces of Sonora, Nuevo Leon, Chihuahua, Coahuila, Texas (the present-day southwestern United States), and Alta and Baja California. In 1777 the Provincias Internas were set apart with their own governor, Felipe Neve, at Monterey, and commandant, the Marquis de Croix, at Sonora (Orozco y Berra, 69, 157, 265). [Tr.]

183. The Presidios Internos were military posts placed in the Provincias Internas to protect missions and towns. Each was garrisoned by a company of soldiers with its officers who were encouraged to take their families with them to populate the frontier regions (ibid., 155). [Tr.]

27 November 1781

as long as the Indians are not restrained they will advance farther every day; they will convert some of the richest provinces of the realm into wilderness and in time will come even to threaten the capital. A well-established trade with the Indians, and a consistent system of not failing to keep faith with them, nor tolerating any abuse from them, would be the most opportune method of pacifying them. In this regard, the system that the English followed in dealing with the Indians of West Florida is wise. By means of trade the English supplied to the Indians all the goods they needed, but for each Englishman assassinated by Indians two individuals of the nation that had committed the assault had to be surrendered.

At eleven o'clock in the morning I went to see the viceroy. I repeated the urgent requests that I had made several times, that he send ammunition to Bernardo de Gálvez and as many men as he could for the squadron of Havana, which is in urgent need of them. He replied that he had issued effective orders on both counts.

In the afternoon I went with Rivadeneira to see the *Acordada*,[184] a tribunal suitable for public security because of the speed and impartiality with which it punishes criminals. The jails are secure and are as comfortable as is feasible.

28 November 1781

In the morning I saw the treasures of the Cathedral, which are truly magnificent. The oldest especially are in good taste.

I dined in the house of Mangino, the superintendent of the

---

184. Antonio Joaquín Rivadeneira y Barrientos was a noted Mexican poet and jurisconsult. He had been oidor of the Audiencia of Guadalajara and fiscal and oidor of that of Mexico. The Acordada was a lay brotherhood founded in Mexico in 1710 to apprehend footpads, and the name was given also to the prison in which the robbers were incarcerated. Created by the Duque de Albuquerque, this lay tribunal was subject only to the viceroy, who supervised its actions. Its chief officer, known as the captain, named its lieutenants, planned its expeditions, and ranged the entire country unmolested by any other judges or tribunals. Its justice was

mint. I withdrew to a separate room with Velázquez and Lasaga, the two directors of mining, where we talked at length about the important department for that they are responsible. They made known to me the abuses that existed in it, the efforts they were making to remedy them, and the careful attention with which this matter ought to be regarded; they gave me some papers which deal with it.

As the afternoon drew to a close there came news that the Conde de Regla had died that very morning at his estate of San Miguel, twenty leagues distant from Mexico. He was undoubtedly one of the richest private citizens of Europe. The public said he had left 15 million pesos fuertes. He was survived by two sons and two unmarried daughters.

In the evening I was in the house of the viceroy. It was said there that letters dated 1 October had come from Peru confirming that things there were in a worse state than ever: seventeen provinces in revolt, troops without money or food, the Indians given over to fury and cruelty,[185] and the visitador, the viceroy, and the inspector at odds.

29 November 1781

Conjecturing that the 1 million pesos that had gone down from Mexico the day after our arrival were probably already near Veracruz and that the remaining 2 millions had been en route to Veracruz for several days, I decided to sacrifice my curiosity and personal taste to public considerations and planned to depart on the following day.

I was in the house of the fiscal, who as always talked wisely and rationally about the affairs of the realm and even gave me a copy of some papers written by himself.

I bade farewell to the viceroy and Cossío. In the afternoon I went to see the cigar factory, located in one of the suburbs. It is a kind of large compound divided by boards and rush mats into

---

prompt and summary and its punishment swift, and in this way bandits, common earlier in the colony, almost completely disappeared (ibid., 19–20). [Tr.]

185. This refers to the uprising of Tupac Amaru and Tupac Catari. [Ed.]

29 November 1781

workshops for the various tasks. The divisions are compact but small. Five thousand men and 2,000 women work in this factory daily; in it 60 million small boxes containing forty-two cigars each are made per year; 70,000 reams of paper are used. It has a gross income of approximately 5.5 million pesos, the total expenses amount to 2.5 millions, the net profit is 3 millions. According to the administrator, however, twice and even four times as many people are incessantly soliciting employment there, but as they are not needed they are not hired. This is a proof that the idleness of Mexico does not proceed from laziness but rather from a lack of employment.

In general I have observed that Europeans, either because of prejudice or ignorance, are mistaken about the true character of New World criollos. They believe them to be lazy, but to what are the criollos to apply themselves if arts do not exist and industry is prohibited? They say the criollos are wicked, but the Europeans have made them so by treating them with absolute despotism, giving them an example of frequent, repeated, and continued theft, and by sending to the Indies all those individuals for whom, because of their vices and offenses, there was no place in Europe. What right then have Spaniards to complain about the corruption of which they are the cause?

The face of the Indies has been altered greatly with the rebellion of the Anglo-Americans and the independence that they probably are securing; consequently it is necessary that Spain make many changes in the system that, up to this point, she has observed in her colonies. These colonies are different from those of other nations, which are only trading posts or depots for transient traders; by contrast, Spanish colonies are an essential part of the nation but separated from the other part. Thus there are between these two portions of the Spanish Empire sacred ties which the government of the mother country ought to endeavor to tighten by all imaginable means: by attracting the sons of the wealthy of the New World with position and distinction they may enjoy in Spain, by promoting marriages and close ties between the two worlds, by permitting development of their trade and agriculture, by sending to their governments and intendancies men of probity, impartiality, prudence, and talent.

By these means the disdain with which Europeans regard the New World natives will be erased, as will the antipathy and resentment with which the latter, as is natural, reciprocate.

Above all, there ought to be devised equitable trade and tax regulations, which, because they have to do with matters peculiar to sovereignty, no viceroy, governor, intendant, etc., ought to have the authority to change by so much as a comma. As long as this maxim is not established as fundamental and invariable, and as long as an employee of the Royal Hacienda has the authority to impose and increase taxes and to alter the laws of trade, the Americans will not prosper and the mother country will run the risk of losing the colonies when least expected. The rebellion of the English colonies had its origin in taxes, that of Lima had the same beginning, and that of Santa Fe also.

(Note: From records given to me and from investigations I made, I learned that in the year 1781 Mexico's income amounted to 15 million, but her expenditures were 16.)

30 November 1781

I left Mexico at eight o'clock in the morning. Cobarrubias, Rivadeneira, and the Padres de Belém accompanied me. We stopped for an hour at Guadalupe, where they showed me all the jewels of the sanctuary. We dined at Totolingo and arrived at San Juan de Teotihuacán at sunset.

1 December 1781

We traveled thirteen leagues. We slept in a poor inn called the Pozuelo. On the plain of Otumba the road to Apa branches off from the road to Puebla, and we took the latter.

2 December 1781

The road is very rough. At dawn we climed a rather high hill, then got out of the carriage there in order to walk down a

2 December 1781

steep slope. Although difficult, the descent is enjoyable because from it you can see the beautiful plain in which is situated Puebla de los Angeles surrounded by a number of villages.

Six leagues before we reached the city, at the crossing of a beautiful stream, Don Francisco Condé, the prebendary of the Holy Church there, was awaiting us. He took us to a small town nearby, where he had had prepared for us a good dinner, with a variety of iced fruits, among them a black zapodilla plum, and the best fruit sherbet (or ice cream) I have tasted in my life.

At two o'clock in the afternoon we departed and began to drive through those immense flat tracts of arable lands, perhaps the best cultivated lands in the New World. As we went along, Condé informed me about the condition of Puebla and the characteristics of its principal citizens.

That night we arrived at his house, where several people were awaiting us. Dr. Condé is a man of good taste; he has excellent paintings and books, he thinks philosophically, and he has a winning personality. One who is a connoisseur and amateur of the arts must be apropos in Mexico now, as one thinks of plans for its reform and advancement.

3 December 1781

In the morning we went to the house of the bishop, who invited us to dine. Afterward we saw the cathedral, a very good building although with a mixture of bad taste. The facade is magnificent, but attached to it is a very humble chapel of the Indians, which disfigures it. We were in several churches and convents, in particular one collegiate church that used to belong to the Jesuits. The design of the city of Puebla is almost as beautiful as that of Mexico; the streets are wide and straight, and there are goodly houses and other buildings. It contains a population of about 120,000 souls, but there are not so many poor people or so much misery as in Mexico. I believe that this difference stems from the fact that the principal wealth of the capital is derived from the mines, whereas that of Puebla comes from the produce of agriculture, and although this latter branch of industry does not create so opulent a prosperity, it does, for this very reason, distribute the profits more widely and produces fewer inequities.

In Puebla there are many convents of friars and sixteen of nuns, none of which has fewer than eighty sisters. In addition to the many maidens, there are many spinsters in the convents, due, in my opinion, to the fact that in the tropics more women than men are born. In the islands, where a continual commerce is carried on by Europeans, many of whom marry local women, this difference does not become apparent, but in the inland towns one sees unmistakably an inequality that makes many women unfortunate.

At noon we dined in the house of the bishop; he seemed to us a man simple in manner, ingenuous in his way of thinking, and on the whole a good priest. He showed us a library created in his house by Señor Tuero, a magnificent room with an abundance of books.[186]

In the afternoon the bishop took us to see the hospice he is building at his own expense. It can accommodate 400 men and an equal number of women, with the requisite separation. It is a well-designed and well-arranged building in which they have made use of a house of the Jesuits.

After seeing the hospice I went for a drive with the bishop in his carriage, and he talked to me frankly about various abuses, particularly the decree prohibiting free trade in wheat, which has been a calamity for that region, inhabited for the most part by planters. He cited the endless complaints he had heard from his diocesans about the matter and the pacific means with which he had tried to quiet their complaints, which in reality were justified.

Many other persons of the country talked to me about the matter, with such information as the fact that Cossío's brother Don Joaquin is there now to purchase the grain that is to be sent to Veracruz. They assured me that this trade in grain has already been worth more that half a million pesos to the Cossío Company.

I noted in Puebla that all the works built in the time of and

---

186. Bishop Fabian y Tuero was the predecessor of the Bishop López González, whom Saavedra visited. [Tr.]

at the orders of the Venerable Don Juan de Palafox have an air of magnificence and taste, although he exercised power at a time when bad taste was at its height, which proves that he was a man of superior cultural attainments.[187]

4 December 1781

We left Puebla at eight o'clock in the morning. We drove ten leagues and slept at Pinar; the road has bad sections, which could be repaired easily.

5 December 1781

At seven o'clock in the morning we arrived at a kind of sanctuary, where they say that Señor Palafox was hidden when the Jesuits were pursuing him. At noon we dined at an inn near the source of a crystalline stream. That night we slept in another inn named Noria Hedionda [Stinking Waterwheel].

6 December 1781

Don Diego Panes had gone as far as Puebla to fetch us; he took us to dine in his house in Perote, where we stayed until the next day. He talked to me about the disorder that prevailed in the gunpowder factory in Mexico and of how much that disorder had been worsened by dissociating the subordinate employees of the factory from the method and regulations of Don Nicosás Devis. He proposed to me that if the ministry wanted an examination to be made of copper mines in that realm, whether for the artillery or to make copper plates with which to sheathe vessels, he would gladly undertake this investigation, for which he had expert knowledge because of having under-

---

187. Juan de Palafox y Mendoza was obispo-visitador in Puebla de los Angeles and Oaxaca from 1600 to 1649. He became viceroy of New Spain upon the removal of Diego Pacheco y Bobadillo, the Duque de Escalona, whom Palafox had accused of planning a coup d'état and the establishment of a separate kingdom in Mexico in alliance with Portugal, which had just gained independence from Spain. [Tr.]

taken it at another time, when an effort was made to establish an artillery factory in the vicinity of Veracruz.

7 December 1781

We left Perote at daybreak and reached Jalapa a little after noon. En route I reflected on the small cost of constructing an excellent road for wheeled vehicles from Veracruz to Mexico. Work is being done in Mexico to this end, and a good engineer is in charge of it, but it seems to me that what is being done is only mending the road that exists at present, rather than making a well-engineered carriage road. It seemed to me also that after a good road is built it ought to be the only one and that all others ought to be cut off so as to make them inaccessible. This road could be fortified in whatever manner might be desired, so that it would be free of all danger of invasion.

8 December 1781

We spent the night in the Arrinconada. In passing, I considered the site of a place called Lencero the most suitable for building a fortification to defend the ascent to the realm of Mexico.

9 December 1781

We dined in Antigua. We left there at two o'clock in the afternoon; so strong a north wind was blowing that it shook the carriage throughout the three leagues where one travels along the seashore; we saw sand dunes moved from one place to another. At nightfall we entered Veracruz, and went to Carrión's house. As the viceroy had left to my disposition the embarkation of troops, money, provisions, etc., I began this same evening to obtain reports and to give orders concerning the matter. I learned that 2 million pesos had already arrived and that the third million is expected from one day to the next.

10 December 1781

I went to see the captain of the *San Francisco de Asís*, who was ill. He agreed with me that three infantry companies would go on his ship and that, in addition to the 1,200 tercios of foodstuffs that he had on board his ship already, he would carry 800 more on behalf of the king. He requested that in consideration of the service he was rendering, and of how much in debt he was, he be granted a license to carry for his own account twelve bags of cochineal.

I was with the Royal Officers in the afternoon. We agreed that Domás would be given the license he sought; that a junta would be called for the following morning in the house of the governor, to be composed of the governor, Royal Officials, and the naval officer who was second in command of the *San Francisco*; and that the shipmasters ought to be summoned to the meeting, in order to plan definitively the matter of embarkation.

11 December 1781

Indeed the announced junta met, those who were to compose it were called, the shipmasters were summoned, and, with agreement among all, the plan of embarkation was formed. The substance of it was that in the convoy would go 920 men of the Regiment of the Crown, 250 convict laborers for the navy, 9,000 tercios of flour, meats, and dried vegetables, 500 barrels of gunpowder, and 200 quintales of lead, match-cords, etc.

It was decided that the Royal Ministers should hastily prepare as many as 400 pipes, which were needed for the water on board the ships, and that all good springs and cisterns in the vicinity of the wharf should be made available so as to hasten the watering. Also each person agreed to dispatch with alacrity everything pertaining to his department, to the end that the convoy be made ready in the shortest time possible.

12 December 1781

I wrote to the viceroy about the present state of the convoy and how much had been accomplished in its preparation.

Officers of the Regiment of the Crown were empowered so that each would attend to the preparations of one of the merchant vessels of the convoy.

In the afternoon I took a walk with some residents of Veracruz who talked to me about the regulations relating to flour that had been issued by the viceroy at the insistence of Cossío, the losses they caused, and the profits that are being divided among those who are engaged in the business.

I repeatedly recommended to the ministers of the Royal Hacienda to take care that the flour they shipped not be stale, as I was told that there was much spoiled flour in the warehouses. The intendant in Havana had already warned me to be on my guard about that, as it had been necessary to throw overboard large quantities of the flour carried by the *Paula* and the *Dragón*.

13 December 1781

One million pesos were counted; they were packed in the presence of a French captain and were taken to the frigate *Courageuse* on the launches of the fort. Also put on board were provisions for the subsistence of the troop, calculated for two months of navigation.

In the afternoon I went with Governor Carrión to the Castillo de San Juan de Ulúa. There in sight of the port the engineer Don Antonio de Corral showed us the design he had made for a good and secure wharf, which Veracruz needs badly. This plan consists of two wings advanced seventy varas farther than the present wharf, the said wings leaving an intervening space of 300 varas, at the front of which the customhouse and other countinghouses can be placed. The execution of this project will cost little more the 100,000 pesos, a small sum compared with the utility of the present wharf.

At the same time we talked about means of bringing running water to Veracruz, which is easy and would contribute greatly to the public health. It appears that certain monies contributed by the citizenry are now deposited for this purpose.

Corral showed us another vast project that he said he had at one time connected to Señor Don José de Gálvez. This plan is the relocation of the city of Veracruz twelve miles inland on the Xamapa River, in a place called Temascal, which affords an easy channel as far as a point near the sea in front of the Castillo de San Juan de Ulúa, fortification of the new town so that it would not be subject to violent attack, and construction on the present site of Veracruz of a fort that, by crossing its fire with that of San Juan, would make the port matchless. In the fortress located on the mainland there would be built its own capacious wharves and warehouses in which to deposit articles of commerce. Also all of the roads that lead to Mexico would be made inaccessible, except the road that would pass through the new town. The advantages that would accrue from the execution of this project are many, but it is by its nature so enormous that many years would be required for work on it. What is certain is that at present Veracruz is unhealthful, and therefore it does not have the population befitting the port of so great a realm; it is defenseless, so that it can be sacked by a small expeditionary force; and it does not accommodate a numerous garrison, because every garrison must be moved.

In the evening the Frenchmen were in the house of the governor, and we agreed to wait for the north wind that was threatening to set in at any moment; while it was blowing, the final preparations would be made so that when it slackened we could set sail without losing an instant.

14 December 1781

Several orders were issued to hasten the embarkation. In the afternoon, while I was conversing about the matter with Monsieur de Saint Dominque, the north wind set in but with little force. He went aboard his ship at once, leaving an urgent order that we must be ready to go out the moment the north wind stopped.

15 December 1781

I advised Don Juan Cambiaso, colonel of the Regiment of the Crown, to have the companies of grenadiers ready, so as to send them on board the frigate as soon as the weather permitted it. Several steps were taken for promptitude in effecting the watering and the loading of the provisions.

The governor and I passed by the treasury, where we saw that the 2 million pesos that were to be embarked on the *San Francisco de Asís* were being counted and packed in the presence of the auditor of that ship.

Next the governor took me to see two of the gunboats that had been built for the defense of that coast and were beached on the shore near the Artillery Drill School. I examined them carefully and found them to be excellent, and perhaps the best of their kind. I asked the engineer Fersain,[188] who was their designer, to give me the plan and an exposition of their use and advantages, in case they might be useful to Don Bernardo de Gálvez for his operations.

16 December 1781

I made all my preparations so as to depart instantly as soon as the weather permitted. I said farewell to the people of Veracruz, and I wrote a report to the viceroy about the state in which I was leaving the business of the embarkation.

17 December 1781

The north wind continued strong but with signs of stopping soon. I made every request of the governor and Royal Ministers that I thought might contribute to the prevention of delay in the departure of the convoy.

I urged the captain and second officer of the *Asís* to set sail with all possible alacrity, and the captain promised that he would do so not more than six days after our departure.

18 December 1781

The day dawned fair. The wind blew from the northeast with all the signs of affording us good sailing. The two grenadier

---

188. Perhaps a reference to F. de Fersán, military engineer (number 458 on the promotion scale). [Ed.]

companies and the baggage were embarked immediately. At eleven o'clock we went on board, and at noon the frigate sailed. The mail-packet for Havana had gone out a few hours earlier, but at two o'clock we were already ahead of it.

19 December 1781

We were about forty leagues from Veracruz when at two o'clock in the afternoon a furious north wind set in.

20 December 1781

The north wind blew strongly until nightfall, when it changed to the northeast.

21 December 1781

The day was very fine; we crowded sail so as to gain latitude. At nightfall the wind returned to the north with ominous signs.

22 December 1781

At noon the north wind ceased, then it returned to the northeast. We considered ourselves to be already eight leagues from Veracruz, but we still had not rounded the Negrillo.

23 December 1781

The wind was light, and the northeast swells, which were heavy, prevented us from making much headway.

24 December 1781

The wind continued from northeast to east, and we thought that it would veer through the south to the north.

25 December 1781

There were signs that the wind would blow strong from the south, but later it disappeared.

26 December 1781

At daybreak the western horizon looked bad. At midday the wind changed to the northeast and blew violently with rain squalls. We considered ourselves to be at 27° and some minutes.

28 December 1781

We tried to reach Tortuga Sound but made little headway.

29 December 1781

We followed the same course as on the previous day, but the wind was contrary.

30 December 1781

The contrary wind continued, and, seeing that we were losing some latitude, we turned northward again.

31 December 1781

There were moments of a north-northeast wind of which we took advantage.

1 January 1782

We tried to reach the sound. We thought we were very near it.

2 January 1782

We sounded ground at forty fathoms, and we set our course for the south.

3 January 1782

The bottom was diminishing by degrees, and at noon we lost the sounding lead. At three o'clock in the afternoon some twelve sails were sighted to windward, among them some of considerable size. Opinions varied, but most thought that it was an English convoy. In the evening we made efforts to avoid the convoy, but at twelve o'clock, without knowing how, we found ourselves in the midst of it. As we did not know what forces it carried, we fled, crowding sail, and the frigate succeeded in running the gauntlet at a speed of thirteen knots.

4 January 1782

At dawn we saw one vessel of the convoy near us to windward; the others could hardly be seen. We advanced upon the ship and overtook it, and at the first cannon shot it hoisted and struck the English flag. After completing the manning of this ship, which was a merchantman loaded with rum, we discovered on our bow another vessel which was coming to meet us. After a short time it tacked and crowded sail. We gave chase, and at four o'clock in the afternoon we captured it within sight of the Island of Cuba, three leagues from the plateaus of Mariel. It was a 16-gun brigantine loaded with sugar and rum, and it carried considerable sail.

One incident that occurred during this capture must not be omitted. The captain of the frigate already captured was a brother of the master and owner of the brigantine we were pursuing. In the beginning he believed that the brigantine would escape because of its speed, but seeing that we were gaining on it, he dove into the water, so that while our frigate was detained in order to rescue him, his brother would be given time to escape. The moment the cry "man overboard" was heard, the frigate struck sails and lay to, and it must be said in praise of the compassion of her officers that they made every effort to rescue him, without giving heed to the prize that was escaping them. Finally, seeing that their efforts were in vain, despite the fact that the man was a good swimmer, they resumed the chase, and they succeeded in capturing the brigantine after night had already fallen.

At dawn we sighted to windward a frigate which we found to be from Boston. We were off the port two leagues from the entrance, and we put into the harbor at eight o'clock in the morning. Then we heard that the coming of the convoy had been learned about in Havana by means of a warning from Cape Corrientes and that consequently one 70-gun warship and nine other vessels, frigates and cutters, had gone out to intercept it. They did not encounter the convoy because they remained too near the port. If our frigate had had another frigate as a companion, she would have intercepted all that convoy.

As soon as I arrived I went to present myself to the governor and the naval commandant, and in the afternoon I went to see Don Bernardo de Gálvez, at the Quemado, where he was with his wife. I recounted to them what I had done in Mexico, and all were well pleased.

6 January 1782

I went back to see Solano, and I questioned him about the state of things. He told me that in the month of November he had sent to Guarico the four ships-of-the-line I had promised to Comte de Grasse, that in fact they had reached that port, after having left the situado in Puerto Rico, but that after their commandant Don Juan de Tomasco had been at the French Cape hardly six days, he returned to this port, on the pretext of escorting eight or ten Spanish merchantmen that were there, leaving that colony abandoned to enemy pirates.

About the affairs of Santa Fe, he informed me that in view of a letter from the viceroy, which painted in very dark colors the conditions there, the warship *Dragón* and the frigate *Clara* had been sent to take on a regiment in Puerto Rico and to transport it to Cartagena.

He also assured me that the affairs of Guatemala were being taken care of effectively and that he was going to dispatch immediately the frigates *Matilde* and *Cecilia* with the corsairs from Cádiz and other ships to go to support the operations of the governor on the coasts of that realm.

Finally he told me that by the end of this month the fleet would be ready to go out with the four ships that had been promised and had then been returned from Guarico and that on one of them would go Don Bernardo de Gálvez, who had already talked to me about it in the same terms.

7 January 1782

Nothing notable occurred. In the evening I went to the house of the intendant, who informed me in detail about the disagreement he had had with the governor, motivated by the fact that Don Francisco Miranda had brought from Jamaica five flag-of-truce ships loaded with merchandise said to be worth more than 90,000 pesos.[189]

8 January 1782

Gálvez and I went to Solano's house and talked to him about the departure of the four warships, on one of which Gálvez himself was to go, and about other things pertaining to the expedition. We agreed that the warships would go out at once, also that two frigates would set sail for the coasts of Guatemala, and that the rest of the expedition would go out at the end of the month.

9 January 1782

I busily set about writing the correspondence for Spain, as well as that for Mexico and Guarico.

10 January 1782

I got all my things ready so as to go aboard the ship the moment embarkation was ordered.

11 January 1782

In order to hasten the departure of the expeditionary force I returned to Solano's house; he told me that the command of the frigates destined for Guatemala had been given to Naval

---

189. See note 153. [Tr.]

Captain Don Miguel de Sousa. Gálvez showed me the maps of Jamaica brought by Miranda. They seemed to me absolutely correct and very detailed. Also he told me that Miranda had brought one harbor pilot from Kingston and two from the island.

12 January 1782

The French sold their prizes at auction for 73,000 pesos. At midday an American frigate commanded by a brigadier put into the port with five English prizes captured from the same convoy we had encountered. This frigate has the keel of a ship-of-the-line and mounts twenty-eight 36-caliber guns and twelve of 12-caliber. She came by way of the channel of Providence and part of the Bahama Channel.[190]

13 January 1782

I saw Solano again about the departure of the warships and that of the expedition, and he said that everything was being made ready expeditiously.

---

190. The frigate was the *South Carolina*. The brigadier was Alexander Gillon, a merchant of Charleston and commodore of the Navy of South Carolina. Gillon had put into the port of Havana in August 1778, bearing a letter of introduction from Juan de Miralles, the first Spanish agent to the Continental Congress, and a request for assistance from the governor of South Carolina, Rawlins Lowndes. Gillon asked permission to ship the indigo he carried on two of his three vessels to some port of Spain, hoping that with sale of the indigo he could obtain enough money to have three frigates built in France. He also wanted passage to Spain for himself and his officers and repair of his ships to fit them to protect the coast of South Carolina and its shipping. The ships were refitted in Havana, the indigo and the officers were sent to France on French vessels, the freight and passage expenses supplied by the government of Havana. In France, finding it impossible to have three frigates built, Gillon hired from the Chevalier de Luxembourg for a period of three years the beautiful ship seen by Saavedra. See D.E. Huger Smith, "The Luxembourg Claims," in *South Carolina Historical Magazine* 10 (1909):92–115, and Aileen Moore Topping, "Alexander Gillon in Havana," ibid. 83 (1982):34–49. [Tr.]

14 January 1782

I dined in Gálvez's house with the American brigadier, who seemed to be a very sociable man.

15 January 1782

The American brigadier thanked me in the name of his nation for the assistance I had solicited for the Comte de Grasse, who had declared publicly that he was indebted to me in part for his success at Chesapeake. I dined with him in the house of the intendant, and we talked a great deal about the constitution of the colonies.

16 January 1782

Gálvez and I began to try to reconcile the intendant and Cagigal, who were quarreling about the affair of the flag-of-truce ships from Jamaica.

That same afternoon Cagigal talked to me about the expedition against Providence, saying that he would launch that enterprise after the army had gone to the Windwards and that he would induce Commodore Gillon to go with his frigate in support of it. I proposed that to Gálvez, who agreed to it at once.[191]

17 January 1782

Gálvez and Cagigal conferred about the Providence expedition and came to an agreement.

---

191. After the capture of Providence a disagreement arose between Cagigal and Gillon. Cagigal wanted the American to remain with the expeditionary force to safeguard it, but Gillon wanted to resume privateering and did so. See Gardner W. Allen, *Naval History of the Revolution* (New York: Russel and Russel, Inc., 1962). Cagigal was reprimanded by the Crown for having made use of American ships (Marqués González de Castejón, 15 October 1782. AGI:Santo Domingo 2085). [Tr.]

18 January 1782

Cagigal, Solano, and Gálvez with his wife went to see the warship *San Luis* and then to see Gillon's frigate, which is beautiful; it has twenty-eight 36-caliber guns and twelve of 12 caliber.

19 January 1782

I spoke to the intendant and to Cagigal, urging them to meet and to reconcile their differences, and it seemed to me fitting that the two should meet in Gálvez's house to effect their reconciliation.

20 January 1782

The order had been given for the baggage to be loaded on the four warships so that the troops should go aboard in the afternoon and the ship set sail the next day, but because of the probability of foul weather a counterorder was given.

21 January 1782

At daybreak the sky was covered with clouds and the wind was from the north, as it had already begun to blow the previous night. At dawn a courier came in from Cape Corrientes warning that two English warships, two frigates, and two brigantines were heading for Cape San Antonio. Immediately Solano ordered the brigantine *Renombrado* to go out to warn the warship *San Genaro*; he ordered two other warships to go out at once, but the weather prevented it.

Gálvez invited the governor and the intendant to his house, and the reconciliation of the two was effected.

22 January 1782

All morning the wind was from the south and the southeast so that the warships could have sailed, but they did not.

An order was given for the troop to embark at two o'clock in the afternoon, but at that hour the north wind set in with strong rain squalls.

At noon Gálvez and I were in the house of Solano who, as was his custom, told us that everything was ready, that the four warships could set sail on the following day, and that at the beginning of February he would sail with the rest of the fleet. But after Gálvez had departed, Solano asked me whether, in case the *Asís* did not arrive before the aforesaid date, he ought to set out for Guarico or await the arrival of that warship. I replied that it seemed to me that without the money the *Asís* was bringing we could do nothing, especially inasmuch as the treasury was exhausted, but that according to the condition in which I left the warship it could not be delayed more than a few more days unless some misfortune had befallen it.

23 January 1782

Solano put to Gálvez in writing the same question he had put to me orally. Gálvez conferred with me about the matter and, reflecting that such a question was concealing some intention, we pondered in what manner to respond. In order to shed some light on the business, I went to see the intendant and asked him confidentially whether, in case the warship *Asís* did not arrive in time with the 2 million pesos it was carrying, he could hastily provide the necessary money so that the entire expedition could go out for Guarico. He told me that by availing himself of extraordinary means he could supply the amount that would be needed temporarily. With this information, Gálvez decided to respond that the fleet and the convoy should not wait later than the sixth or eighth of February; if the *Asís* did not come by then, the whole expeditionary force should go to Guarico and all means should be exhausted in order to maintain it there, but another warship should be dispatched to Veracruz immediately to fetch the second installment of funds.

24 January 1782

At dawn the north wind was even fresher than on the

previous day, and therefore it was impossible to go out. Gálvez, Monsieur Saint Dominque, and I conferred as to whether, since the season was already so far advanced, it would be wise for the frigate to go to Martinique, where it would arrive at the end of February at the earliest, at a time when Monsieur de Grasse would perhaps have already set out for Guarico, or whether it should go to Guarico as we had planned. After the matter had been examined at some length, we decided that the frigate should go to Guarico, and if perhaps there was no notice there of the imminent arrival of the Comte de Grasse, it should proceed to Martinique. The principal reason that prompted Gálvez and me to take this decision was that, finding ourselves with very little money, and having reason to fear that the warship *Asís* might be delayed even longer, we were in dire need of the 100,000 pesos the frigate was carrying.

25 January 1782

The weather looked somewhat better, but the wind was still from the north.

26 January 1782

The day dawned fair, and at ten o'clock the wind became northeasterly. However, the sailors said that it was necessary to wait another day to see if the weather held.

At eleven o'clock in the morning came news that a sloop had put into Batabanó from Cartagena, with Don Juan Tufiño aboard. In fact he entered this stronghold at nightfall, went to Gálvez's house, where I went also, and reported to us that all the troubles of Santa Fe were absolutely pacified, that the towns in which the rebellion had originated had been the first to beg pardon for their errors, and that, recognizing and acknowledging the integrity of the Regente Visitador, all were urging him to resume the duties of his position.

At the same time, Tufiño told us that things were still very much inflamed in Peru, especially in the province of Charcas, and that in Quito more than 6,000 or 8,000 persons had

26 January 1782

gathered, demanding with loud outcries the extinction of monopolies and of the new taxes; he said that in order to quell these beginnings of disorder, the regent of Quito had asked for 500 men but that it had not been possible to send them to him.

Gálvez immediately began to write to the court, communicating the intelligence from Santa Fe and commending Tufiño for his good performance.

27 January 1782

The day dawned fair. The vessels destined for Guatemala began to sail out, but at ten o'clock the land breeze died and the wind turned to the south, so that the ships that were still inside the port postponed their sailing, and those that had gone out returned. However the corvette *Rey* set sail at nine o'clock and proceeded on its way, and at noon she was lost to view. On the mail-packet went Deans, the English frigate captain, who had been a hostage since the capitulation of Pensacola and had urgently begged to go to Spain. At the same time, Major Campbell, the other hostage, was made to embark for New Orleans, because it appeared that his presence in Havana was prejudicial, and there was even an idea that he was sketching maps, etc.[192]

At two o'clock in the afternoon the troop that was to go with the warships to Guarico was embarked.

28 January 1782

The day dawned fair and the wind from the land, rather light. The pilots met in a junta in which they said that it was necessary to wait until the following day to fix the time of departure.

At eight o'clock the expedition for Omoa went out, composed of two frigates, two gunboats, some brigantines, with various warlike stores, and one artillery company, all of the expedition

---

192. Captain Robert Deans, ranking British naval officer at Pensacola, and Captain James Campbell, nephew and secretary of General John Campbell. Apparently Deans was exchanged, but Campbell remained a prisoner until the fall of 1783 (Starr, 213). [Tr.]

directed to support the operations of the governor of Guatemala on those coasts, and commanded by Don Miguel de Sousa.

In the afternoon the wind changed to the northeast. There was a second junta of pilots and captains in which it was decided that the expedition could not go out the next day. At nine o'clock in the evening the wind began to veer to the north.

The captains of the merchantmen from Veracruz complained that the naval commandant had taken for the fleet so many men from their crews that they absolutely could not go to their destination and that consequently they were being ruined.

29 January 1782

At midnight the wind changed to the north with force. The sky was clouded at dawn, and the north wind was violent.

At two o'clock in the afternoon two large sails came into view to leeward. Everyone believed that they were the *Asís*, which was coming from Veracruz and the *San Genaro*, which was escorting her, but it was seen later that they were the two frigates that had sailed for Guatemala and were returning to the port in distress because of the weather. The *Matilde* came in at nightfall and the *Cecilia* a little later.

30 January 1782

At dawn the wind was from the bay, but the day was cloudy and looked bad.

In the morning Solano sent an official paper to Gálvez telling him that because the time was already so far advanced, one must feel that the four warships should not go out alone but rather that the entire fleet and the army should sail and that the departure could not be delayed more than two weeks at most. Gálvez responded that that was satisfactory but that he himself would go alone on the *San Juan* because he regarded his arrival at Guarico at the earliest possible time absolutely imperative. Later Gálvez went to talk with him in person, after Solano had tried in a thousand ways to dissuade him from going to Guarico, and the admiral consented to his going on the *San Juan*.

30 January 1782

Gálvez informed me that he would like to have one battalion composed of grenadiers from the garrison to go with him. He spoke to Monsieur Saint Dominque about this, to learn whether he was willing to transport them on his frigate. Saint Dominque objected, but in the end he agreed to carry 100 men and four officers. Later I went to talk with the intendant for the purpose of finding out whether there was in the convoy a pair of swift vessels that could transport three or four companies. In fact one swift-sailing vessel was found, but it seemed more opportune not to use it.

31 January 1782

The troop was embarked on the warship, the frigate *Galveztown*, and a brigantine of the navy named *Cazador*. I said farewell to everyone, especially to Solano, from whose remarks I inferred that he was doubtful both about the prompt arrival of the *Asís* and about the departure of the fleet and the army at the appointed time.

1 February 1782

I embarked at daybreak. At seven o'clock the warship *San Juan* went out with Don Bernardo de Gálvez aboard, next went the *Galveztown*, and finally the *Cazador* and two American schooners. There was no wind from the northeast, but there was a wind from the west. We noted the slow movement of the *Galveztown*, which was drifting to leeward.

2 February 1782

It was seen that the *Galveztown* could not continue; when we were off the Pan de Matanzas the troop she was carrying and part of the crew were taken off the frigate, and she was dispatched to Havana.

3 February 1782

The *Cazador* drew away from us and was not seen again. At three o'clock in the afternoon seven sails were sighted to windward and about four leagues distant. The American schooner, which was extremely swift, reconnoitered near them and reported in the evening that they were an English convoy and that the largest vessel, which was escorting it, appeared to be a 20-gun frigate. As night was beginning to fall they changed course. At the same hour the northern keys were sighted, and we came about.

The night was stormy, with thunder, lightning, squalls, and variable winds.

4 February 1782

At daybreak the weather was fine and the wind from the east. We tacked with the bow on the northeast course. At two o'clock we sighted the keys at the mouth of the Bahama Channel. We were not sure that we could round the last one by tacking, and at four-thirty o'clock we went about and held a southeast course all night.

5 February 1782

At five o'clock in the morning we tacked again and took a north-northwest course. The meridian latitude was computed at 24°58′. At that time we bore away toward the north.

6 February 1782

The meridian latitude observed 27°30′. At four o'clock in the afternoon three sails were sighted to windward, and we gave chase. At six o'clock we stopped the pursuit. At eight o'clock a brigantine approached us and told us that the American schooner, which had gone away from us, had captured two prizes and that she was one of them.

7 February 1782

At first light we sighted five vessels to windward. The warship and the frigate began to pursue them. By ten o'clock in the morning the frigate had overtaken and manned a merchant ship loaded with 300 *bucois* [sic] of rum. Immediately we began to pursue another vessel, which the prisoners said was a merchantman armed with twenty-eight guns, on which were carried many of the effects of Mr. Dalling, governor of Jamaica. At three o'clock the wind fell so calm that it seemed impossible to overtake that vessel before dark, and moreover the warship was out of sight, so we abandoned the chase and set our course to follow the warship. The wind fell even more, so that at nightfall only the masts of the warship could be seen. The other vessel that we had captured remained behind the frigate.

8 February 1782

We could not see the warship in any direction whatever, and the captain decided to proceed on our course alone. Also the prize had separated itself from us, so that we were left with only two small schooners.

9 February 1782

There was a fresh wind, especially at night, with squalls. We no longer saw the two schooners.

10 February 1782

It was calm during almost the entire twenty-four hours, with loud thunder and heavy rain showers.

11 February 1782

In the afternoon there came a heavy swell from the northeast, which indicated that there had been some fearful storm in that area. Because of the swells the vessel pitched and rolled insufferably all night, but the wind was good and fresh. As on the three previous days, it was impossible to compute the meridian latitude.

12 February 1782

The wind changed to the northeast; meridian latitude observed 26°10'; we ran thirty-two leagues.

13 February 1782

There was a strong wind from the northeast; we ran forty-three leagues; meridian latitude observed 21°32'.

14 February 1782

Meridian latitude observed 24°. In the afternoon there was a furious thunderstorm with heavy rain. The winds continued ESE; therefore the captain decided to pass between the Caicos and the Turks Islands.

15 February 1782

Meridian latitude observed 23°42'.

16 February 1782

Meridian latitude observed at 23°20'. In the morning a vessel that looked like an enemy frigate was sighted to leeward. We stood on the windward course, but by two o'clock it was already out of sight.

17 February 1782

Latitude observed 22°. The captain decided to pass by way of the headland of the island of Santo Domingo. At three o'clock we sighted to windward two vessels which were tacking. In the evening we were cautious because of the Mouchoir Bank.

18 February 1782

Latitude observed 20°24′, which is the latitude of the Silver Keys. We went forty leagues. In the evening we believed ourselves to be twelve leagues from the Island of Santo Domingo.

19 February 1782

At nine o'clock we sighted the land of the island about six leagues off Old French Cape. At three o'clock in the afternoon three vessels came into view on the port side; they appeared to be trying to intercept us. At four o'clock, having comprehended that they were three frigates and that it was impossible to round the point of Cape Isabela without encountering them, we took refuge in Puerto Plata, which was on our beam, relying on two persons on the frigate who assured us that they had been in that port several times. However, the entrance is so difficult and narrow that it was only by a miracle that we were not wrecked on the rocky reefs which are there on all sides.

We cast anchor then in Puerto Plata at five-thirty o'clock in the afternoon. It is a fine roadstead about twenty feet deep. There is a small brick fort with four 8-caliber cannons and a battery on the point, which dominates the entrance within pistol range, where there is only one 3-caliber cannon fit for use.

As soon as the frigate cast anchor, the longboat was sent to shore with Brigadier Baron de Kessel, who talked with the commandant of the port, a militia captain from Santo Domingo. The captain told him that it was necessary for the frigate to bring the broadside to bear, and even to send some 12-caliber cannons to be placed in the battery on the point, because the three frigates in sight were English and because other English vessels had already tried to force the port. Consequently we brought the broadside to bear, four cannons were sent to shore on a platform made for the purpose, and fifty of the one hundred grenadiers whom we were transporting were disembarked.

As soon as they saw the frigate at anchor under the shelter of the fort, the enemy tacked and went away to windward.

20 February 1782

By daybreak one cannon had already been mounted on the point and another was on its way there. At first light there came into view a packet boat, which was passing off the port and appeared to be French. A signal was made for it to come in, but it went on notwithstanding. The signal was repeated, and a longboat was sent out to the packet, whereupon it lay to, but it fell to leeward so much that, despite the risk it was running, it could not put into the port however much it tried. It was a Spanish packet coming from Saint Christopher, and it was carrying letters for the Comte de Grasse, who was supposed to be in Guarico.

While we were wondering what news the packet was bringing, we saw at ten o'clock in the morning a vessel flying the Spanish flag which was coming from windward straight for the port. It arrived quickly; its master, a graduated mail-packet captain named Domenec, came aboard the frigate and told us that his vessel was an express packet coming from Cádiz and that he supposed that probably there was at the French Cape already a Spanish convoy of four warships, three regiments, and many merchantmen, which had gone out from Cádiz on 3 December bound for that destination. At the same time he gave us the news that the English Windward fleet had captured a French convoy but that, because the French fleet unexpectedly appeared too, at the very moment of manning the convoy, the English had had to abandon it, and that they had also lost more than fifty launches and 300 men. Finally, on the night of 16 February, when he was north of Martinique, he had encountered after dark a convoy of twenty-two sails. He did not know to what nation that convoy belonged.

This small vessel set sail for the cape at five o'clock in the afternoon, after having been given a harbor pilot for the coast and letters for the French Cape describing our situation.

In the afternoon I went ashore to see the town. Near the quay itself, which is bad, there is a place suitable for constructing a battery of twelve 24-caliber cannons to protect the entrance to the port, which in time of war is a refuge for many vessels that are pursued by corsairs. At present there are only five cannons, which are useless and have actually fallen on the ground; higher up there is a badly located fort with four 4-caliber guns.

The town has 1,200 inhabitants, counting black and white, most of them poor. The houses are made of the bark of palm trees; the people cultivate a little corn and fruit and a small amount of sugar; the climate is unhealthful because of the dense forest that surrounds the town.

21 February 1782

Nothing whatever was seen, and we conjectured that the packet, which had made every effort to enter the port on the previous day, seeing that its efforts were useless, had fallen off to leeward for Guarico.

In the afternoon we went walking on the shore of a river that flows into the bay; the soil looks good, as if it is only awaiting cultivation in order to be fruitful.

22 February 1782

By some storeships that were passing, en route from Samaná to the French Cape with salted meat and turtles, I wrote in duplicate to the commissioner of the Spanish nation in that port so that he would urge the officials of the colony to send forces to escort us.

In the afternoon we went walking on a hill that overlooks the town. We saw great ruins of ancient buildings, and I learned that this port formerly was populous and, according to the signs, rich. It was abandoned in the time of the *filibusteros*, and in the year '18 it was populated anew with families from the Canary Islands.[193] In truth, it merited some consideration, because in time of war it is an excellent refuge; two years ago a French

---

193. For information on the importance of Canary Islands emigration to the Antilles, see Francisco Morales Padrón, *Colonos canarios en Indias*, Anuario de Estudios Americanos, vol. 8 (Seville, 1951), and "Las Canarias y la política emigratoria a Indias," *I Coloquio de Historia canario-americana* (Las Palmas de Gran Canaria, 1976). [Ed.]

Journal of Don Francisco Saavedra de Sangronis

fleet of one hundred sails escorted by the frigate *Tourterelle* found refuge in it, and if that fleet had not found this port, it would have fallen helplessly into the power of three English warships and two English frigates that were pursuing it.

23 February 1782

In the afternoon we took a long walk on the shore of a river that empties into the bay, whose banks are beautiful.

24 February 1782

I remained on board all day reading.

25 February 1782

Again I remained on aboard. At four o'clock in the afternoon we saw from the frigate a kind of affray on the shore; the launch was sent with officers to the place, and we learned that after a Spanish soldier had struck a French sailor, the sailors of the longboat, who were six, attacked and maltreated him. Two more Spaniards ran to his aid, and a fight with cudgels broke out; it ended with the arrival of the launch and of some sergeants and soldiers who ran there by land. Later a group of Spanish soldiers fell upon six Frenchmen who were gathering hay and cudgeled them lustily. The Baron de Kessel had gone ashore and had had three soldiers put into prison so as to cut short the consequences of these events.

26 February 1782

At three o'clock in the afternoon two vessels were sighted that appeared to be frigates and seemed to be sailing with the wind right aft; at nightfall it was seen that they had shortened sail.

At four o'clock there were shouts from the shore; the longboat was sent, and they brought a letter for the captain of the frigate from the governor of the French Cape, which had just been brought in by stagecoach by way of Montechristi. In the letter the governor told him that General Gálvez with the *San Juan* had arrived on the twentieth, that there were no French war vessels there save one frigate that had its mainmast on shore, but that two Spanish ships-of-the-line, the *San Felipe* and the *San Pedro*, with one frigate, were going out immediately to escort us; at the same time he sent the signals of recognition.

27 February 1782

Early in the morning a large vessel that appeared to be a warship was sighted. At four o'clock another was seen; some said it was sailing without its foremast. At five o'clock we went ashore; we took a long walk along the riverbank, where we found six or seven very poor dwellings.

28 February 1782

At nine o'clock they went to take a sounding at the entrance to the port and to place a buoy on a rock the size of a launch, eight feet below the waterline which is at the left of the entrance. Miraculously we were not wrecked on it the day we came in.

In the afternoon we went ashore, where we met a man who had just come on a launch from Montechristi; he stated that the prize that the frigate had captured upon sailing out of the Bahama Channel was there and that he had seen two frigates, apparently English, which were cruising toward Point Isabel.

1 March 1782

In the afternoon I went to see a dwelling situated on the riverbank about half a league from the bay. The house is modest, but the terrain, divided into avenues bordered by luxuriant trees, forms a beautiful perspective. The owner is a Canary Islander who settled in this country about twenty years ago after many years at sea. His place maintains fifty head of cattle and forty horses. He plants sugar for his expenses and has six adult Negroes and two boys. He could produce much more, considering the fertility of the land, but crops do not have an outlet in a port where there is absolutely no trade. On our return we were rained upon interminably, and we were drenched to our shirts.

2 March 1782

I did not go ashore, but they sent news from the town that at dawn on the first day of the month they had heard faint sounds of many cannon shots.

3 March 1782

I went ashore, and we walked to the dwelling I mentioned earlier.

4 March 1782

At daybreak three vessels were sighted, one of which looked large. We thought they were the Spanish ships we were expecting, but they proceeded on their course, sailing before the wind. There were several opinions about those ships, but almost all agreed that they were English frigates with some prizes, because five sails were seen in all. Our detention began to become vexatious, the more so because we were beginning to need provision, and it was impossible to buy bread in the port town, as only by a rare chance can flour be found there.

5 March 1782

We went ashore, and we stopped in a dwelling at the foot of the mountain situated in the most delightful landscape imaginable. When we returned to the ship in the evening, we learned that three vessels had been sighted and that they look like the two warships and one frigate we were expecting from the French Cape.

6 March 1782

At daybreak we saw clearly the vessels that had been sighted the previous evening, and by the signals of recognition we knew that they were the two Spanish warships and the frigate that were coming from the French Cape to fetch us. They had hardly been informed that we understood the signals when they crowded sail, apparently giving chase to a schooner that was in sight. In the afternoon the warships were seen again.

7 March 1782

The troops having been embarked on the previous evening, we set sail at seven o'clock in the morning. While going out we were unmistakably made aware of the risk we had run in entering that port. The passage of Puerto Plata is narrow; on each side there are rocky reefs, and in between them there is a raging tide. At ten o'clock we talked with the warship *San Pedro* and a little later with the *San Felipe*, which was the flagship commanded by my friend Don Lucas de Gálvez. At six o'clock in the evening we were off Montechristi, which the French call La Granja [the Grange], not without reason, for indeed it has the shape of a haystack; at ten o'clock, seeing that the northeast wind was strong, the flagship made the signal for lying to.

8 March 1782

At daybreak we were north-south with the French Cape at a distance of six leagues. We entered at ten-thirty o'clock in the morning. I disembarked at eleven o'clock; I went to see General Gálvez, who recounted to me the separation from us of the warship *San Juan*, how they had captured a merchant frigate that was bound from Charlestown to Jamaica, and how that had delighted the captain of the warship.

In the afternoon I went to see the governor, Monsieur de Bellecombe.

9 March 1782

In the morning I went to see the intendant. At midday I dined with the governor. During the meal an officer named Preci put into the port bringing official papers from Spain. After dinner the governor, the intendant, and I withdrew, so that they could describe to me the absolute lack of money that existed in the colony and the hopes they had that the Spaniards would furnish them some assistance, without which it was impossible for them to make the indispensable preparations for quartering the troops expected from Brest who were to assist the Spaniards in their operations. I responded that we should discuss the matter with Señor Don Bernardo de Gálvez and that of course they could be sure that we would furnish them as much assistance as was in our power.

10 March 1782

The general came at eight o'clock in the morning. I told him what I had discussed with the governor and the intendant on the previous day. We dined with the governor, and after dinner we withdrew in order to talk privately. We conferred about the encampment of the Spanish troops, and the general proposed that in order to have the troops nearer at hand, and so as to avoid a delay of several days after the union with the troops and fleet expected from Brest and from Havana, it would be wise to quarter 2,000 men on the San Nicolás Mole; if all were quartered in Dejabon, which is to leeward, many days would be required to bring them here, whereas they could be got quickly if quartered on the mole.

At two o'clock in the afternoon Don Carlos O'Neill entered the port; he brought official papers from Spain and had made the crossing from Bilbao in twenty-eight days on a swift American brigantine. He reported orally that the Spaniards had taken Castle Marlborough in Porto Mahon by assault and that it was said that several well-known officers had died in the assault, among them Brigadier Don Luis de las Casas; that the French convoy that had gone out from Brest at the beginning of January had experienced a severe squall, which had damaged it badly; that although the convoy was escorted by twenty-two French warships, those ships having fallen to leeward, the English fleet had had time to attack the convoy and capture eighteen transport vessels; that the French ships had put into Brest badly damaged; and that on 5 Februray they had not as yet gone out again.

11 March 1782

In the morning I went to visit the commandant of the Spanish fleet. Later I went on to see the captain of the French frigate, and I told him that if he had no objection the money would be taken ashore on the following day. At noon I dined with General Gálvez. I proposed to him that without loss of time a small vessel be sent to Cuba,[194] so that the governor of Cuba would purchase as many mules as seemed appropriate for the hauling of the artillery, provide a supply of meats, and prepare some hospitals. Also I proposed to him that in case the troops had to spend the summer here, it would, for many reasons, be prudent for 4,000 or 5,000 men to go to Cuba to be quartered there.

12 March 1782

I wrote the correspondence for Havana. At midday Señor de Gálvez's secretary consulted me as to what ought to be done about the American brigantine that the officer O'Neill had brought from Spain, since on the one hand the general wanted it to remain here because so swift a vessel might be needed in an emergency, and on the other hand it was carrying a large store of muskets and blankets for the Indians of Mobile and Pensacola, which ought to be taken forthwith to that destination. I responded that it seemed to me that the most reasonable solution was to transship the blankets and muskets to other ships of the

---

194. "Cuba" refers to Santiago de Cuba, a port city on the southern coast and the first capital of the island, founded in 1514. [Tr.]

convoy and send them to the intendant of Havana and that if the transshipment could not be made the brigantine ought to be let go, because the blankets could not be replaced, whereas it was not likely that swift vessels would be lacking.

The silver was brought ashore and deposited in the house of the Intendant Barrutia.

The artilleryman Rey gave me information about the condition of the artillery and the measures he was taking to make up what was lacking in it.

13 March 1782

I went to the house of Estrada and talked with him at length about Cuba's ability to provide meats and quarters for the troops, establish hospitals, and furnish mules for the use of the army. I had already obtained this particular report from the Intendant of the Army Don Juan Antonio Barrutia and from the naval officer Estrada. We agreed that the greatest possible use should be made of Cuba, and therefore we told the secretary of the captaincy general that it was imperative that an order be sent to the governor of the stronghold commanding him to purchase 200 mules for hauling, to collect a large number of beef cattle for the provisions of the army, to make ready a hospital for about 400 patients, and to begin taking steps so as to be prepared, if necessary at the beginning of summer, to quarter in that town and in neighboring villages 4,000 to 5,000 men, who will be supplied flour, vegetables, etc., from here.

For want of a favoring wind the convoy could not go out in the morning. The blankets and muskets for the Indians that the American brigantine had brought were transshipped to other vessels.

14 March 1782

Señor Gálvez came down from his country house, and we dined together in the home of the governor.

The general showed me the letters he had received most recently from Martinique, from Monsieur de Grasse and Monsieur de Bouillé, in which both left indefinite the time of their departure from there. They reported the damaged condition of the convoy that sailed from Brest in mid-December and announced as true that Rodney had arrived earlier from Europe and that consequently the English retain superiority in those waters.[195] The letter from Bouillé makes some suggestions about how far advanced the season is now and speaks of how scant is his supply of weapons and ammunition as a result of the loss of one of his ships that was loaded with those items.

The general made known to Ezpeleta and me that he was thinking of forming a secret junta of the most highly regarded officers of the army, so that by conferring about the enterprise they could assist him with their knowledge, both for the preparation and for the execution of the expedition.

The general pointed out the inconveniences resulting from detaining here the American who had arrived recently with the mail-packet: it was absolutely necessary to give him, from this treasury deficient in funds, the 8,000 pesos stipulated by his contract; the detention was causing him to lose money; it was impossible to force him to go to Spain, and he had already indicated that he was unwilling to go; it was depriving our colony of the shipment of sugar that he wished to carry to Boston; and, finally, it would be possible to obtain a swift American vessel, or one from some other nation, in case of having to send mail from here to Spain. By dint of these reasons, the general ordered him to go to Havana.

The Spanish convoy started to sail, and some vessels even left the port, but the land breeze failed and they could not proceed.

15 March 1782

The convoy went out at daybreak, and at noon it was already lost to sight.

I went to the general's house and showed him the notation of what I thought ought to be said to the governor of Cuba. Briefly

---

195. See note 139. [Tr.]

it was that he must buy 200 mules for the army, collect meats in that stronghold so that they would be available when needed, prepare a hospital for 400 to 500 wounded, and take measures to prepare quarters in that town and its vicinity for eight battalions, in case the projected expedition could not be executed now.

The general and I talked at length about the present conditions and about the dilemma in which he finds himself. On the one hand, Madrid positively commands that Jamaica be attacked; on the other hand, Solano's fleet, which is bringing troops, provisions, money, military stores, etc., is not here yet, and the French, who constitute one-half of the army and the major part of the fleet, have not yet arrived. Finally, the spring season is beginning, and by the first of April the season for operations will already have been lost. Moreover, Rodney's arrival is expected momentarily, and with it the English will unite thirty-three warships and will reinforce Jamaica with 6,000 men. In this exigency I advised Gálvez to dispatch a mail-packet to the Spanish Court describing his situation, the measures that he took from the beginning, and the efforts he has made, so that it will be understood that on his part he has in no way failed but that a bad combination of circumstances has ruined everything. He accepted this idea of mine, so I told the minister of the hacienda, Barrutia, to seek secretly a swift vessel to send to Spain as a mail-packet.

16 March 1782

A swift brigantine was sought to go to Spain as a mail-packet. There was uncertainty as to whether it was wiser to purchase the vessel, as they were asking for it no more than 8,000 pesos, or to charter it to the account of the Royal Treasury. The decision was postponed until the next day.

Three vessels put in; one ship from Bordeaux said that on 10 February twelve vessels had left that port under the escort of a frigate, bound for Brest, to join the convoy that was to go out from there. The second one was Danish, and the third was a flag-of-truce ship from Saint Cristopher, which asserted that the English fleet had been reinforced with seven warships. Because of the arrival of these ships many false rumors were spread among the public.

17 March 1782

In the morning an English corsair appeared off the port, and in sight of all it captured a French vessel which was about to put into the port.

Señor Don Bernardo de Gálvez communicated to me several useful schemes which had come to his mind, and we discussed them.

We dined in the house of the governor, who showed us several maps of Jamaica, in my opinion not very accurate.

The efforts to charter a swift vessel to go to Spain as a mail-packet were renewed; the charter, which had been half completed, could not be concluded.

In the afternoon a Spanish soldier was maltreated by the owner of a tippling-house. According to the statements of witnesses the incident was unprovoked.

18 March 1782

In the morning they reported to the general that on the previous evening the Spanish guard of the Regiment of Zamora had been insulted by a French patrol and even that a soldier of the patrol had aimed a gun at the sergeant of the guard. The Zamora officer, seeing that as a result of this insult his men were causing a disturbance, closed the Caurtel and placed the guard inside. The French fired two musket shots, and one bullet passed above the head of the sentinel. This incident and some other events that occurred on the same night were misrepresented in such a way that it appeared that only the Spaniards were to blame for the disorders, a bias about which the general complained bitterly to Monsieur de Bellecombe.

At ten o'clock in the morning the governor, the intendant, and I met by chance in the house of the general. The question of money was touched upon, and the general and I told them that we should give them as much as we could but that, as we did not know whether there had yet arrived from Veracruz a ship that was expected in Havana at the time of our departure, we could not liberally supply the amount we should like to give them. After they had departed, Don Bernardo and I conferred, and we decided that in view of their great need we should give them 50,000 pesos, which was all that could be done.

A swift vessel for Spain was found and an effort made to charter it, but they could not tell me the final price.

19 March 1782

At noon Don Bernardo and I were in the house of the governor, and so was the intendant. Again they spoke of the absolute necessity they felt that we lend them at least 100,000 pesos, without which it was impossible for them to make the necessary preparations to receive the troops who were expected from Brest. At last Don Bernardo and I agreed to give that amount to them, but with the condition that everything we might need for our troops that was here in the warehouses of the king would be supplied to us as a loan.

The governor showed us the strict orders he had issued for the maintenance of good order between Spanish and French troops.

In the afternoon there was a drill of the Zamora Battalion so that the French might see the quality of our discipline, and they enjoyed it very much.

20 March 1782

The owner of the galley that was wanted as a mail-packet for Spain answered that he would charter it for 20,000 livres per month; the general said to wait for Domenec, who had gone to Tortuga Sound with the three vessels of the Port of Santa María to fetch planks for esplanades.

I was in the intendant's house to find out whether one could safely send correspondence on the flag-of-truce ships that were to convey to Europe the prisoners from Saint Christopher;[196] he told me that a French commissioner was going on the ship

---

196. Saint Christopher was captured by de Grasse on 12 February 1782. He seized there many richly stocked warehouses and 100 ships. [Tr.]

but that he was of the opinion that one should not write except in general terms.

21 March 1782

Señor Don Bernardo communicated to me a plan he had in mind in case the projected expedition does not take place this year, which seemed good to me, and consequently I began to seek some means to facilitate it for him.

I copied some letters of the Comte de Grasse and Monsieur de Bouillé; the handwriting was very difficult.

There was great celebration because of the birth of the dauphin.[197] All the Spanish and French troops were in battle array, the former comprising only three battalions, the latter six. There was a *Te Deum*, salvos of artillery and musketry. In the evening a comedy *gratis*, fireworks, a magnificent supper in the government house with more than 400 covers, and later a public ball in the theater. The governor gave one bottle of wine per head to each soldier, and General Gálvez gave double their daily pay to all the French and Spanish troops.

22 March 1782

I was told of several acts of piracy committed by the corsairs of Cuba, including their having captured a Portuguese ship which, under the flag and passport of its nation, was going from here to Jamaica carrying on trade in lawful goods, and likewise their having captured a French vessel which took refuge in a small port of the island, fleeing from the enemy corsairs. In spite of the reasons given by their owners, these two ships were sold and the money received distributed. The governor of Guarico complained to the governor of Cuba, who replied that he had no control over this particular branch of the navy. The fact that there exists in America any authority independent of the Ministry of the Indies causes grave difficulties. Jurisdiction by

---

197. The dauphin whose birth was celebrated lived only until 1789. His younger brother then became dauphin and later the titular king as Louis XVII; he died in prison in 1795. [Tr.]

the navy is a scourge that is destroying the Island of Cuba, and until it is reformed or contained the island will never have prosperity or an increase in population.

23 March 1782

The general and I conferred about fixing the ultimate date beyond which the projected expedition could not be undertaken until next winter. We decided that if the Spanish and French forces were not united by the first of April, nothing whatever could be done because more than a fortnight would be required to arrive at the point of attack, and more than twenty days would be necessary for disembarkation, conveyance of the artillery, ammunition, etc., so that the high point of the attack and of the arduous work would catch us in the worst part of the summer and heat, rains, and illnesses would not leave one man alive. We agreed, therefore, that in case the enterprise were postponed until November, Gálvez would employ the time of inaction in making an attack on Providence, if that had not already been done, and in the other operations that seemed advisable, and that I should go to Spain during the summer to confer with the ministry about the affairs of this area.

At four o'clock in the afternoon there came in view to windward a 40-gun frigate, apparently Spanish, but it did not put into the port, perhaps because the hour seemed late. At six o'clock it executed certain manuevers that made one suspect that it was an enemy vessel; in fact it was an English frigate named *Fox*, which doubtless had come to investigate what forces there were in the port.

24 March 1782

The frigate of the previous afternoon disappeared, but the English corsair *Porkin* was sighted off the port.

In the morning I went to see the intendant, so that he could show me some intelligence he had received from France. He told me that by a vessel that left Nantes on 20 February and put into a port of this island named Jacmel on the seventeenth of

24 March 1782

this month they learned (1) that Comte de Guichen had gone out from Brest on 15 February with eighteen ships-of-the-line and the convoy bound for these islands and that therefore he could not have failed to arrive at Martinique by now; (2) that Admiral Rodney, upon going out from Plimow [Plymouth] with his fleet and convoy, had experienced a violent windstorm which obliged him to return to the same port with his damaged warships, after the convoy had been scattered; (3) that according to letters from Marseilles, news of the capture of Mahon was expected there from one day to the next.

At two o'clock in the afternoon a schooner from Havana put into the port; its captain reported that on the fifth of this month Solano had sailed from Havana with seven warships and a convoy transporting 5,000 men. This schooner had sailed in company with the convoy as far as the latitude of Matanzas and had then proceeded by way of the Old Channel.

25 March 1782

I conferred with the general about the reports of the previous day; it seemed to us that if the union of forces was effected before the end of April, it was absolutely imperative to execute the projected attack, because if our troops suffered from the heat, those of the enemies would suffer even more. From the moment we landed measures would be taken to quarter the army in the towns that would be captured, whereas the opposing forces would have to remain inside the forts and encampments, where the illnesses would be more frequent and more acute.

I dined in the house of the commandant of engineers, Monsieur Rabie, who showed us maps, drawings, and very pretty paintings done by himself. I was amazed that this officer, an amateur of the fine arts, had not heard of any Spaniard distinguished in any of them. Such is the obscurity with which the things of Spain are veiled by our national character, which is not at all fond of aggrandizing them. I spoke of Berruguete, Herrerra, Velázquez, Rivera, Murillo, Cano, etc., and he heard the names as if he had not the slightest knowledge of them. I have had the same experience in conversation with Englishmen and Dutchmen. For the majority of the nations the things of Spain are buried in an abyss; nonetheless they are itching to criticize them. Nothing is as prejudicial to our renown as the discomfort of the roads and inns of Spain, for they pose an insurmountable barrier to the curiosity and enlightenment of foreigners.

26 March 1782

Barrera, a captain of the Regiment of Aragón, having left Havana on 12 March, arrived with the news that Solano was coming. A French vessel that was going to Cádiz was furnished to the general, and he decided to place aboard it a Spanish officer to carry official papers to the court.

27 March 1782

I dispatched my correspondence and delivered it to the officer commissioned to carry it.

I dined in the house of the governor, M. de Bellecombe, who charged me to tell General Gálvez, if I went to see him, that he had received a report that two English frigates were cruising to windward, with the intent of intercepting the flag-of-truce ships from Saint Christopher and taking them off to Jamaica, thereby increasing the defenses of that island by 1,000 men. He begged the general to write to Monsieur Borja [Barras?], to the end that Barras might give him a warship which, with the frigate *Railleuse*, could escort the said flag-of-truce ships as far as the exit from the Caicos passage.

At twilight I went to see the general at his house, which is reached by a rugged climb of three-quarters of a league. The residence is cool, healthful, and beautiful.

I told the general of M. de Bellecombe's request, and he immediately wrote the official paper requested and sent it to the governor, to be transmitted in whatever way he deemed opportune.

28 March 1782

Because the flag-of-truce ships and the mail-packet that was going with them were detained, the general continued writing to Madrid.

In the afternoon the ship of Barras himself came in sight to leeward and other vessels to windward. At nightfall the corvette *Santa Catalina* came in, having sustained damages. In the evening the general and I spent two hours strolling in a beautiful garden, talking about the operations of the campaign. I expressed to him my thought that if the French came the attack ought to be made, even though the spring season had begun, so as not to disappoint the hopes of the king and not to waste the immense expenditures that had been made. He had thought the same, and he communicated to me his plan of operations, which seemed to me well done.

29 March 1782

During the morning a corvette and a brigantine flying the Spanish flag entered the port, which aroused curiosity.

Later an officer who had come with them came up to the residence and told us that they were the corvette *Liebre* and the brigantine *Galgo*, that they had sailed from Havana with Solano on 5 February, had been forced to return to that port on the seventh because of difficulties; then they had gone out again on the ninth, and had come by way of the Old Channel, taking twenty days for the trip. He said that he had met the convoy of quicksilver in the Old Channel forty-five leagues from Baracoa.

I had a long conference with the general about the same matters we had discussed on the previous evening, and among other things we agreed that as soon as he came down into the town he would have me informed by Colonel Heredia as to how best and most quickly the twelve cannons *de releje*[198] that are in Santo Domingo could be brought here.

I went down into the town at dusk; Heredia was asked the

---

198. *Releje* is raised work in the chamber of a piece of ordnance where the powder is placed in order to economize on it. [Tr.]

question suggested by the general, and he said that the cannons could be brought here overland within twenty-five days, provided that a letter went to the governor at once.

This afternoon there was a dispute between French and Spanish soldiers which almost reached the point of causing unfortunate consequences. Some French grenadiers were fighting with sabres near the *toseta*;[199] several Spanish soldiers who were walking nearby tried to stop the fight but were unable to do so; not daring to separate the fighting men hand to hand, because they themselves had no weapons, they began to throw stones at the combatants. The Frenchmen turned on the Spaniards yelling; people from both sides came running, and in a short time a general rock throwing began. A party came out from the quartel of the Regiment of Zamora in order to contain the disorder, but it was impossible. Some French soldiers came there and even some officers, one of whom was wounded by a Spaniard with a blow from a cudgel, while another stabbed a Zamora soldier. Finally, the Spaniards, who saw that armed Frenchmen were coming firing musket shots, ran to their quarters for weapons. There, the officers, who had been attracted by the noise, succeeded in subduing and confining them, although they were in a state of fury which almost knew no respect for orders. Besides the officer mentioned above, several Frenchmen and five Zamora soldiers were wounded.

There was widespread consternation in the town. The French regiments sounded the drumbeat that calls to arms and got ready for action, the citizens locked the doors of their houses, and the women ran screaming. After things calmed down, when it was already dark, four French grenadiers insulted three officers; indeed one grenadier drew his saber and stabbed an officer of the Regiment of Soria, who defended himself with his umbrella; the officers drew their swords, and the grenadiers fled.

---

199. *Toseta* indicates an area of fields in which wheat has been harvested, i.e., stubble-fields. [Tr.]

30 March 1782

The general came down from his residence; he held a long conference with the French commandants to consider the way to contain disorders that had such bad results. They all decided to issue a proclamation: life imprisonment for any French or Spanish soldier who used musket, bayonet, saber, knife, cudgel, stone, or any other weapon in self-defense or to injure anyone of his own nation or of any other. Moreover, it was ordered that there be placed in the principal guard post every day a guard of twenty-five Frenchmen and an equal number of Spaniards, commanded one day by a French captain and a Spanish subaltern, and the next day by a Spanish captain and a French subaltern. Their commanding officer would report any disorder that might occur, and credence would be given solely to his report. Also it was decided to mark a terminal limit, at one-quarter of a league from the town, beyond which the Spanish troops could not pass, as had been done with the French troop, so that they could not go into neighboring residences to commit disturbances, about which there had been complaints.

In the afternoon I went to Colonel Heredia's house to discuss the method of bringing the cannons and mortars from Santo Domingo, and as I passed by the quartel of the Regiment of Extremadura, I saw a French soldier being brought in by two corporals; he had just struck a Spanish soldier a few minutes after the proclamation was made public.

31 March 1782

At daybreak the flag-of-truce ships from Saint Christopher went out escorted by the frigate *Railleuse;* with them went the French merchant frigate that was to leave in Cádiz the officer in charge of the official papers for Madrid.

I dined in the home of the governor.

1 April 1782

In the morning the French frigate *Néréide* arrived from

Havana (where it had been sent to obtain money for this government). It had gone out from Havana in company with the fleet and convoy of Señor Solano. Bertucar, who came as a passenger on this frigate, informed us that they had left the convoy after having sailed out of the Bahama Channel, that they had encountered eight English merchantmen of which they had captured two interesting ones, and that before entering the Bahama Channel twelve transports had disappeared from the convoy and it was not known what had become of them. Solano in a letter to the general confirmed this, adding that the warship *Asís* had been obliged to make a forced arrival at Havana because it was leaking badly.

Bertucar added that a Venetian ship and one of the feluccas it was conducting had informed him that the French convoy from Brest had already put into Martinique.

Near noon they took to the general an excerpt from a gazette brought by a flag-of-truce ship that arrived from Jamaica the previous day. In the gazette it was said that news had been received of the arrival of Don Gálvez [sic] at the French Cape and of the convention signed at the courts of Versailles and Madrid to attack that island, and it told of the preparations they were making in order to repulse any invasion: augmenting batteries, blocking roads, enlisting men, etc. It also gave as certain the arrival of Rodney at Antigua with twelve warships, two of them three-deckers, and 8,000 soldiers, and it added that eight more warships were following him and that General Clinton was sending 2,000 of his best troops from New York to Kingston.[200]

In view of these reports, Don Bernardo and I withdrew to confer secretly. We began to consider the present circumstances, which in reality are not favorable to the designs of our government; even supposing that these reports from Jamaica are exaggerated, we ought always to reckon that the English would reinforce to the extent possible a position that

---

200. After having served under Generals Thomas Gage and William Howe since May 1779, Sir Henry Clinton became commander-in-chief in America in 1780 and served until 1781. He led the Charleston expedition of 1780, and after capture of the city he retired to New York, leaving Lord Cornwallis in command in the South. [Tr.]

is so valuable to them, and, being already acquainted with our plans, they would have built all imaginable works in order to repel an attack. Moreover, the season is already inappropriate for executing expeditions in the Indies, and it must always be calculated that even if the fleets of Solano and the Comte de Grasse arrive within three or four days, the operations absolutely cannot be commenced before the first days of May. If Rodney assembles a fleet equal or superior to that of Monsieur de Grasse, it is unlikely that the latter can leave the Windward Islands, unless there has occurred previously a decisive battle in which he has been victorious. And even when he might be able to come here, and both nations could combine fifty warships and 20,000 men, it would never be a prudent thing to attack Jamaica while they have forty English warships there.

Also one must reflect that our fleet, which we had thought would comprise sixteen warships, consists of no more than eleven, of which the *San Felipe* and the *Santo Domingo* cannot take the line because of the small caliber of their artillery, and those from Havana are coming without enough men. The troops from Havana, who we believed would number more than 6,000 men, have turned out to be 5,200, because Cagigal kept more than 1,000 for the Providence expedition, and even that number will have been diminished considerably if many transports have been separated from Solano.

On the other hand, we reflected on the nature of the urgency with which Madrid is commanding us to attack Jamaica, the necessity of making peace quickly, the expenditures that have been made up to now in order to execute this operation which perhaps cannot be repeated in the coming campaign.

Amidst this confusion of ideas and thoughts we agreed that what could be done would be done and that no advantageous opportunity that presented itself would be squandered but that it is impossible to make a positive decision until we know the true state of the English and French forces in the Windward Islands. In truth it is exceedingly strange that they do not write from Martinique with any continuity about what is happening there. This negligence, and that of not advising this government about the preparations they must make, inclines me to suspect that the French generals are not sure of executing the Jamaica expedition this year.

2 April 1782

There was a *Te Deum* of thanksgiving for the victory at Chesapeake and the conquest of Saint Christopher.

I dined in the governor's house. I went to supper in the house of the mayor of the fort. It was a rainy day, and at night there was a high wind.

3 April 1782

The rainy weather continued. In the morning the three flag-of-truce ships that had gone out three days earlier made a forced return to this port.

4 April 1782

In the morning I was in a long conference with the general and dined in his house.

In the afternoon three Danish vessels arrived. A rumor was spread that with them came a French prisoner who had been turned over to them by an English corsair. This Frenchman, who was supposed to have gone out from Guadeloupe twelve days ago, declares that the convoy from Brest is already at Martinique; he does not state the number of ships and troops it has brought but does say that eight transport vessels came with it. He also affirms that Admiral Rodney had arrived at Barbados with only eight warships.

A merchant, a reliable man, assured us by way of Saint Thomas that the Comte de Grasse had thirty-six warships and Rodney thirty-five and that from one moment to the next a fierce battle was expected.

We went to see a field tent invented by the artillery officer Rey. It can hold thirty-five men comfortably, it can be raised on all sides so that the air penetrates it, and it saves much canvas and wood. This officer, who is the one now in charge of the artillery here, works with incomparable energy, and in a few days he has made forty-five esplanades and a large number of tents, cartridges, etc.

To meet the extremely high cost of subsistence, they began to give to the officers a ration of one and one-half pounds of bread, eighteen ounces of meat, and some vegetables.

5 April 1782

I added a few things to the letters I had written to be sent on the French vessel that went out with the flag-of-truce ships and was obliged to return to this port. I made known to the minister how little hope remained to us of accomplishing anything at all in this campaign.

In the afternoon I was in the house of the general, and we talked for a while about our affairs.

One of the Danish vessels that had arrived the previous afternoon was a slaver carrying 380 Negroes who were to be sold. Several persons who had commissions from Havana were planning to buy them. I tried to persuade the owner of the cargo to send the ship to the Island of Cuba, but it was impossible to get him to accept that idea. If in Havana they had adopted the system of availing themselves of the services of neutral nations to transport Negroes for them, that island would not have suffered such a great lack of Negroes, and it would have flourished extraordinarily.

If the king desires that the Island of Cuba be one of the most profitable possessions in the Indies, it is essential that he promote the trade in Negroes by allowing free trade, by removing from it all duties, both import and excise, as well as taxes on second sales, and by abolishing the inhumane and odious custom of branding the slaves. The Negroes ought to be regarded as necessary tools of agriculture, and importation of them, far from being taxed, ought to be rewarded. Moreover, it is essential that the king treat the Island of Cuba in such a way as to enable it to attain the level of prosperity that its location and fertility can support, both because that island is a possession easier to preserve than is the continent and because it serves as a brake on the realm of Mexico.

6 April 1782

At midday the French war frigate *Vestal* put into the port. She had gone to Caracas by order of the Comte de Grasse to escort eleven vessels from La Guaira, some of which remained in Puerto Rico, and only three of which entered this port.

From letters from Martinique that were received by this route, it is known that Rodney arrived at the Windward Islands with twelve warships and troops, that the French convoy was not expected to sail from Brest until the end of February, and that as a consequence the French and English fleets were almost equal but that the French were badly damaged.

A Provençal vessel that arrived this same day gave the report that Mahon had already been taken, but all those who are acquainted with that stronghold say that this required confirmation.

7 April 1782

The general had a long conference with M. de Bellecombe and Lillancourt about the contemplated operations. They told him frankly that they already reckoned it impossible for the operations to be executed in this campaign year. In truth, in view of the tardiness of the two convoys and the lateness of the season, the enterprise does not appear to be feasible this year.

Later I was in the general's house to dine. He related to me his conversation with the two Frenchmen, and we talked about a highly secret project about which we had conferred earlier.[201]

Several Spaniards went aboard the Danish slaver to pur-

---

201. It may be that the "highly secret project" was an attack on Saint Augustine and an invasion of East Florida. In December 1781, while still in Havana, Bernardo de Gálvez sent to the minister of the Indies copies of letters written to him by Rendón, Solano, Bouillé, and Bonavía, and of his replies to them. Rendón stated that the time was propitious for the con-

7 April 1782

chase Negroes; they were expensive; no fewer than 300 pesos

quest of East Florida because of the defeat of Cornwallis and sent a translation of a letter written to him by General George Washington from Virginia: "You can assure General Gálvez that nothing would be more advantageous to the northern states than an operation in which his forces were employed against East Florida." Solano, in reply to Gálvez's question as to whether an expedition to take East Florida would be more prudent than an expedition against Jamaica in the current campaign year, suggested, "It appears to me that it is imperative, and more fitting, to predetermine the rendezvous of our land and maritime forces and those of the French for the Jamaica expedition for the last days of February in Guarico, whence, if the accomplishment of that enterprise is not found to be prudently certain, our troops can proceed to accomplish the conquest of East Florida, and the French that of Charlestown, with the combined fleet covering both operations." Gálvez asked, "Would it not be better to avoid the inevitable expense and waste of time, and to take better advantage of the campaign year, to embrace the plan he had explained earlier ... which was to leave the French to operate this year in the Windward Islands, to urge the Americans, particularly General Greene, to attack Charlestown or Savannah, and for us to undertake in February the Conquest of Florida, and to proceed from there to Santo Domingo, so as to prepare the Jamaica enterprise more safely, less hastily, and with more assistance the following year?" Solano replied that because of the assistance promised by Bouillé, as reported by Bonavía, he thought it wise to go to Guarico, that March or April would not be bad, and that "if the expedition is not attainable, we shall be able with fewer forces and even later to make a descent from there for the conquest of East Florida, and the French for that of Charlestown, and the two will result in that of Georgia, the two fleets protecting the operations." Gálvez answered that he was wiling to accept Solano's judgment, even though launching the Saint Augustine expedition from Guarico would involve more costs and more dangers, "provided that it does not lead to the loss of the time and the opportunity."

Bernardo de Gálvez sent copies of the letters mentioned above to the minister of the Indies, saying that he had almost decided to undertake the Florida expedition "because it would remove dangers and would safeguard His Majesty's dominions, and make it possible to negotiate with the Colonists the cession of their new settlements on the Ohio and Mississippi Rivers, in compensation for their offer to turn over to Spain the Plaza of Saint Augustine." But because the king preferred the Jamaica expedition, because of the de Grasse–Saavedra agreement, and because of Solano's assurances that the attack on East Florida could be launched from Guarico, he had decided to set out at once for the French Cape, despite his each were demanded. The owner again was told by several persons that he ought to go to Havana, where he would find quick sales, but he again declined, citing among other reasons that a countryman of his who went to Havana a few months ago with a cargo of canvas and rigging was subjected to a thousand extortions by the navy, which tried to force him to sell the canvas at a price arbitrarily set by it and that, because he refused, the navy detained him in that port for three months and allowed him to depart only because of the intercession of Señor Gálvez, after he had been ruined by expenses. This and other acts of a similar nature are the source of the reputation Spaniards have among other nations as tyrants and men of bad faith.

8 April 1782

At daybreak Solano's convoy was sighted. At ten o'clock in the morning one of the feluccas from Cádiz went out loaded with harbor pilots for the fleet and convoy. At three o'clock in the afternoon the convoy began to enter, and it was all at anchor by nightfall.

Six warships, some smaller war vessels, and forty-five transports with 4,500 men arrived. Of the rest, one went to Veracruz, another to Cartagena, another went out with the convoy and had to return to Havana because of a leak; of the other three, one is useless and two remained undergoing repairs. The troop was supposed to number 6,500 men, but Cagigal kept 1,000 for the Providence expedition, and 800 were separated on nineteen vessels which are missing from the convoy, having been obliged to return to Havana because the separation occurred before they had entered the Bahama Channel.

---

feeling that they were sacrificing a sure victory for an uncertain hope (Bernardo de Gálvez to José de Gálvez, 24 December 1781. AGI:Ind. Gen. 1578). [Tr.]

9 April 1782

There was a reception in the house of the governor; the general officers of the land and sea forces were present.

I talked with some of our naval officers about the condition of the fleet, and they declared that the *Dichoso*, the *Magnánimo*, the *Asís*, and the *San Gabriel* are absolutely useless, that if they are sent to Spain immediately and put into dry dock they can be like new again, but that if they remain in America, either they will sink when least expected or they will have to be abandoned or used as pontoons.

General Solano and Governor Bellecombe conferred at length about the operations, and it seems that they agreed that it was already impossible to perform them. Later I talked with the general privately, and I agreed to go to his house the next day to discuss the same matters with Solano and him.

10 April 1782

The general, Solano, and I met, and, after having conferred for a long time about the operations, we agreed that even if the French were not delayed much longer it was already impossible to execute the contemplated enterprise in this campaign. However, it seemed to us that it would be prudent to wait until the first of May. Then, if the French came, we would execute whatever the circumstances dictated, and if the French did not come before that time we would distribute our troops in places where they would be free from the illnesses of summer—that is, on San Nicolás Mole, in Port-au-Prince, in Cuba, etc., and that the fleet should go to the Mole if that port is secure and is large enough to accommodate it.

We were still in this conference when we were told that a mail-packet had just arrived from Spain with good news. We went out and learned that the official papers and the gazettes from Madrid were announcing the capture of Port Mahon on 5 March.[202] The packet brought official papers for Don José So-

---

202. Mahon, the chief port of the Balearic island of Minorca, had been held by the British since 1708. [Tr.]

lano but not for Don Bernardo de Gálvez, because when the order came for the packet to sail, only the correspondence from the Ministry of Marine had arrived and not that of the Indies.

11 April 1782

At ten o'clock in the morning I went to the general's house. I found that reports had just arrived from Martinique brought by way of Puerto Plata, where a mail-packet dispatched by the Comte de Grasse had put in when pursued by enemies. Briefly, the news was that the English had united a fleet of thirty-three warships and that they had received a convoy of 120 sails, which were believed to be transporting troops; also the convoy from Brest had arrived, although it had by a kind of miracle escaped falling into the power of the English fleet, which was waiting for it. It brought only three warships and many fewer troops than had been expected, so that the Marquis de Bouillé, who announced that he will come to this island within a few days on a frigate, will bring only 2,500 men. The train that the convoy has brought from Brest consists of only forty siege guns, twelve howitzers, and other munitions.

The Comte de Grasse writes that he will be coming here with his fleet about a fortnight after the date of his letter. His fleet consisted of only thirty-six warships, many of them crippled, while the English had thirty-nine, seventeen of which had come from Europe recently and five of which were three-deckers; at the same time he requested the governor of this colony to have ready [unreadable] quintales of gunpowder, as he has absolutely none and none has come to him from Europe, as well as provisions of victuals for three months, 300 quintales of matchcords, and other articles that it is absolutely impossible to find in this colony. Bonavía wrote from Martinique making known the superiority of the English fleet, the great risk run by the convoy from Brest, the imminent arrival here of Monsieur de Bouillé and the Comte de Grasse, and also that Jamaica had already been reinforced with the Fourteenth Regiment.

12 April 1782

I dined with the general, who had invited the governor and several other distinguished persons. The governor told me that he was expecting Monsieur de Bouillé from one day to the next and that the Comte de Grasse was urgently begging that he be given 4,000 quintales of gunpowder, as his fleet had only an estimated supply of fourteen shots per cannon.

They gave the general a report of the troops, provisions, and warlike stores that were on the vessels that had been separated from the convoy, and it was found that there were missing many cannons, two mortars, two howitzers, more than 10,000 cartridges made for cannons, 400 quintales of gunpowder, 150,000 bullets for fusils, 890 men, and one large vessel loaded entirely with victuals.

13 April 1782

At three o'clock in the afternoon the French frigate *Iris* came in, and on it were the major, several officers, and 300 men of the Regiment of Dillon.[203]

Monsieur de Traversai, the captain of the *Iris*, told us he had gone out from Saint Christopher with the frigate *Medea*, on which Monsieur de Bouillé was coming and that the marquis had remained in Guadeloupe because his wife had fallen ill, but he would arrive here within a few days.

Also he and the Dillon major told us how Admiral Rodney was cruising to windward of Martinique with forty-four warships, all copper-clad, of which thirty-nine were ships-of-the-line and five were 50-gun warships, and that there were five three-deckers among them; that the Comte de Grasse had thirty-six warships, some of them crippled, of which eighteen to twenty were sheathed with copper, but the others were sluggish and inclined to drift heavily to windward, which gave a great superiority to the English whose warships all had a uniform way.

---

203. The *Iris* and the *Richmond* were captured from the British by de Barras off the Virginia Capes, on 11 September. The *Iris* was the former Continental frigate *Hancock*. [Tr.]

Monsieur de Traversai called me aside and told me that the object of his mission was to go to Havana to obtain 1 million pesos which our court ordered to be delivered to the French. I told him how little money there was in Havana and that, although the 1 million pesos for which there was an advance order there had been solicited from Veracruz, I doubted that the funds had arrived yet, as the return voyage from that port always required at least one month and a half.

14 April 1782

Monsieur Traversai came to see me, and I repeated the same thing I had told him on the previous evening. I gave him a letter for the intendant, in which I indicated the destination of the two frigates. He assured me that he must set sail on the following day without fail.

The French completed mounting the field artillery they had, which included twelve 24-caliber cannons, six of bronze and six of iron, and eight 4-caliber cannons. In a few days they had made the great number of gun-carriages they needed.

15 April 1782

The *Iris* and the *Vestal* went out at dawn bound for Havana.

I spent the entire day in the general's house, conferring about what course it was prudent to take in the present circumstances. For one thing it is certain that the season is already spent, and for another that the English have a superiority of naval forces. With respect to the French, even when their forces are joined with ours, there will be equality at least, but the English will have the advantage of speed and of more powerful ships. In the presence of a fleet as powerful as Rodney's, to venture to take out convoy as numerous as that which must be assembled in order to attack Jamaica seems contrary to all reason. For the fleet to go out alone, to undertake a decisive battle against the enemy, and then to come back later to fetch the convoy, besides being an operation of doubtful outcome, would employ much time, and the winter season would be already upon us. In these circumstances, only one course is left us to take, which in truth is daring enough, but for its execution there is required a combination of things that there is little likelihood of bringing together.

In the afternoon we learned that the warships *San Juan* and *San Pedro* had been ordered to go out the next day to fetch several Spanish ships that had taken refuge in Puerto Plata.

16 April 1782

The warships *San Juan* and *San Pedro* went out at dawn.

I went to the house of the intendant Barrutia. I asked him questions about the quality of the provisions, and I learned that the major part of those foodstuffs that had come from Havana were spoilt, especially the meats, and that much flour and vegetables were missing because several vessels loaded with them had been returned to Havana. I also found out from him that we should never lack food in case we undertake the execution of some project because, in addition to his having always ready for use enough biscuits, vegetables, and salted meats for two and one-half months, the Americans had made a contract with the general to supply as much flour as might be needed.

The expenditures that are being made for the preparation of this expedition are indeed immense, but many of them are useless. For example, two hospitals have come from Havana, each provided with sixty-one attendants, whose wages amount to 7,000 pesos per month, and an additional hospital has come from Spain. If each hospital were provided with twelve attendants, their needs would be met very well, whereas they are not met now with so great a number, for they encumber the ships and occupy space that properly belongs to the patients.

The chaplains constitute another branch that is large and difficult to manage. One chaplain has come on each ship, whereas those of the regiments were sufficient, for although each corps may be distributed on many ships, a longboat can be put into the water to fetch the chaplain in case of need.

In the matter of the troop, the method used by the French ought to be followed. They never send new regiments to their colonies but send instead disengaged troops to complete or augment those regiments already stationed there, thereby sparing the treasury the great expense of the bodies of officers of the regiment. In the Spanish army that is here such an operation could be practiced in the following manner: by integrating some regiments with others, the staffs and bodies of officers of four regiments could be sent to Spain, and, in addition to reducing expenses here, this nucleus of the regiments would go over there to commence to recruit men and to restore their complements.

17 April 1782

The brigantine from Martinique that had been blockaded in Puerto Plata put into the port. Its news was already old, the most recent being that received on the *Iris*.

I dined in the general's house, and we conferred for a long time about the present conditions. The odd combination of circumstances that had occurred gave us abundant food for thought.

Preparation of the train of artillery continued but, according to what I could ascertain, not with the efficiency and economy with which Rey used to manage it.

18 April 1782

It rained heavily all day. The repeated rains of recent days proved how correct had been the idea of not placing the encampment of the troop in the *foseta*, as had been planned, but instead leaving the men aboard the ships, making them go ashore each afternoon, and giving them as much exercise as possible.

19 April 1782

I went to the general's house and conferred with him for a long time. At midday the lookout signaled that a large convoy had been sighted. Suddenly the wind changed, veering from east to northeast, and the convoy could not approach the port. There were many varied opinions as to what vessels these were; some said that they were the fleet and convoy of La Motte Piquet;[204] others, that it was the fleet of de Grasse; and others, that it was an enemy convoy. The certainty was that according to the signal from the lookout they numbered more than sixty-nine. In the afternoon I was in Picolet, and I could not sight anything.

20 April 1782

At first light the convoy could be seen clearly. At noon vessels began to put into the port, and until well into the night not all were inside. It was the convoy from Martinique, which came escorted by two 50-gun warships, the *Sagittaire* and the *Expérimenté*, and two frigates, the *Engageante* and the *Richmond*.

As soon as the people began to disembark the word was spread that the French and English fleets had fought two battles, the first one slight, the second bloody and not advantageous to the French. I asked some French naval officers if they knew anything about the matter, and they answered me in terms that revealed despair. Later, listening now to some of them and now to others, especially to the colonel of the Dillon Regiment, I was able to ascertain that on 8 April the Comte de Grasse dispatched his convoy from Martinique for this port; that the English, who were to windward with forty-four warships, immediately set sail toward him; that the Comte de Grasse went to meet them with thirty-two warships and, placing himself between the English fleet and the convoy, made a signal to the convoy ordering it to put into Guadeloupe; and that he did battle with the English fleet for a space of five hours during which, having had the good luck that twelve English warships fell to leeward, he had some advantage over the enemy that forced the

---

204. Admiral Guillaume, Comte de La Motte Piquet, was coming from Europe. A few months earlier he had captured many ships of a convoy in which Rodney was transporting the rich booty he had taken in the capture of the Dutch island Saint Eustatius. [Tr.]

latter to retire. On the twelfth, with the convoy still in sight, the battle was renewed; it went on for fifteen hours, and the English, having succeeded in getting all their warships into action, profited by their superiority, although the French fought heroically, captured three of their warships, and sank one, both sides having suffered terrible carnage and loss.

They asserted that the warship *Glorieux* had surrendered when there remained alive on it only one marine guard and thirty-five men and that according to the signals the two Admirals, de Grasse and Rodney, had either been killed or gravely wounded in action. At the beginning of the engagement, the Comte de Grasse made a signal to the convoy to go away crowding sail but for the frigates to remain there until after the action was concluded, when they would come to rejoin the convoy. They said that after the affair ended the Marquis de Vaudreuil[205] had gathered twenty-two warships which were still in moderately fit condition and had set out in pursuit of the English, to see if he could recapture from them the prizes they were taking away. These reports ran through the town, now augmented, now diminished, but I postponed my judgement until confirmation.

21 April 1782

In the morning I went to the general's house. He had heard the same account as I, but he had heard it from the captain of the *Engageante* and therefore with indications of more authenticity. We talked for a long time about this calamity, which appeared to cut short all our plans, and we decided that it was imperative that without a moment's delay our fleet go out to protect the French warships that were coming here badly damaged and join the Comte de Grasse's fleet so as to reinforce

---

205. Louis Phillipe de Rigaud, Marquis de Vaudreuil, had taken part in the battle of Ushant in 1778 and in 1779 had been sent to capture Senegal. After having taken many prizes from the English in those campaigns, he distinguished himself in America under the command of d'Estaing. Vaudreuil replaced de Grasse as commandant after the latter's capture in the Battle of the Saintes. [Tr.]

21 April 1782

it, if perhaps it was fleeing from the English. The general went aboard ship to discuss this and other matters with Solano.

I went to verify the news of the previous day, and all I could learn was that in fact there had been two battles, the second one bloody, but that no one could give an accurate account of it; that it is certain that the warships *Glorieux, Ardent, César,* and *Hector* were in combat with ten English warships and that they were in bad condition, but no one could declare for certain whether they had been surrendered or sunk.

At midday the picket ship raised the signal of the sighting of a squadron. In the afternoon it was seen that they were the warships *San Juan* and *San Pedro,* with the vessels from Caracas that had been blockaded in Puerto Plata. Another vessel of the same burden as the warships was coming with them; it appeared to be French. Solano made a signal to the warships to remain outside, and, in fact, as dusk fell they began tacking back and forth. At nightfall eight infantry companies were ordered to garrison the warships that were to sail the next day. At eleven o'clock a shot was fired to signal weighing anchor, and at dawn the ships began to go out.

22 April 1782

Five Spanish warships went out and four remained in port at the [unreadable] picket ship.

At noon the picket ship signaled that it had sighted many French warships. Three came in at two o'clock, the 80-gun *Coronne,* the 74-gun *Magnifique,* and the 80-gun *Duc de Bourgogne.* Their hulls were all riddled with cannon shots, as were their sails; their masts were in bad condition; the ship that had fewest casualties had had 127 killed or wounded. Other warships and some frigates were sighted far away.

All that could be ascertained was that after the first battle, in which the French had had some advantage, on 12 April the two fleets found themselves in sight of each other off Guadeloupe, but the French were en route to come here. One warship of the French fleet, the *Zélé,* which is sluggish and difficult to steer, had fallen to leeward, and the English began to pursue it. The

Comte de Grasse made a signal for all the warships to come toward the *Zélé*, and indeed they did so, but as among them some were sheathed with copper and some not so they were unequal in speed, the French ships became separated from each other. The English were coming in a well-formed line. The Comte de Grasse ordered his line to be formed, but already there was scant space between the two fleets, and the French fleet was almost becalmed, so that the English succeeded in attacking them while the French warships were still in disarray. Once the line was broken, ships of the two fleets were intermingled, and an extremely bloody battle began at pistol range. The Comte de Grasse thrust his flagship into the thick of the fight, and it is thought that it may have been blown up or captured. The same is thought about the *Glorieux*, the *César*, the *Ardent*, and the *Hector*. The English also had many ships dismasted. It is believed that some French ships may have put into Grenada in distress, but, according to the seamen, at least five or six probably have been captured, blown up, or sunk.

23 April 1782

The wounded from the warships, who were going to hospital, passed by my house in the early morning.

I went to the house of Señor Don Bernardo de Gálvez, with whom I had a brief conference; then we went to dine with the governor. There we learned that Monsieur de Vaudreuil was in sight with fifteen warships and that it was known for certain that the *Ville de Paris*, after having been under attack on the twelfth from eight o'clock in the morning until five o'clock in the afternoon, seeing that the French line was broken and that several warships were about to be captured, thrust herself into the most violent area of the battle and was once surrounded by fifteen enemy warships, three of them three-deckers, which attacked her from all sides. She maintained a lively fire from port, starboard, stern, and prow, until ten o'clock in the evening, when the firing stopped, presumably because her ammuntion was exhausted, and she surrendered.

Marquis de Vaudreuil went with his warship to see if he could

23 April 1782

extricate the *Ville de Paris*, directing incessant fire on the enemies who were attacking her, but they were so inflamed that they paid no attention to him. The *Hector*, the *César*, the *Glorieux*, and the *Ardent* also surrendered. It is said that Bougainville's division, composed of seven warships, took refuge in Grenada, but there are rumors in the town that the division abandoned the battle from the beginning of the action.

So the destiny of the thirty-six warships of Monsieur de Grasse's fleet is as follows: four are in this port, fifteen are in sight of it, and the two 50-gun warships accompanied the convoy; seven are believed to be in Grenada; the *Saint Esprit* remained in Martinique in careening; the *César* and the *Zélé*, which were dismasted, took refuge in Guadeloupe from the beginning of the battle; and the English captured five. Don Bernardo Bonavía is said to have been aboard the *Ville de Paris*.[206]

The governor called me aside to talk about the disaster. He said that it seemed to him that it had cut short all our plans. I replied that I felt it had only interrupted them for some time, that this was the moment to display more vigor and steadfastness; that two nations as powerful as France and Spain ought not to be overwhelmed by a single blow; that more than anything else, it was a lesson warning us that we ought not to keep our forces divided as we had done heretofore; that I felt that the warships that needed to go into dry dock ought to be sent to France; that those needing only to be fitted with masts ought to be sent to Havana; and that with the remaining French warships and all of the Spanish there must be formed a

---

206. On 12 April 1782, in the second Battle of the Saintes, de Grasse's flagship, *Ville de Paris*, was captured. The French admiral was taken to Jamaica as a prisoner, then placed aboard the *Sandwich*, commanded by Admiral Parker, who was to take a convoy to Europe. The *Sandwich* sailed on 25 May, and de Grasse was in London by 5 August. The British king ordered Admiral Keppel to convey de Grasse and his officers to France, and de Grasse reached Paris on 16 August. See John Gilmary Shea, *Journal of an Officer in the Naval Army in America in 1781 and 1782* (New York: Bramford Club, 1864), 178. After the full import of the defeat of de Grasse was comprehended in France, the French government decided that with the French West Indies fleet so sadly depleted, no effort against Charlestown or other Continental port could be made (Dull, 369). [Tr.]

fleet that would command the respect of the enemy, to prevent him from blockading us in this port or investing any of our possessions; and finally that at the same time they should give me a swift frigate on which I should go to France and Spain to obtain reinforcements sufficient to maintain superiority over the enemy.

I also talked about this with Don Bernardo de Gálvez, and the idea seemed good to him. At the same time I mentioned to him another thought having to do with his secret projects, which he also applauded, and we agreed that on the following day I should go to his house early so that we could talk about it.

24 April 1782

I went to the general's house early, and we conferred until noon about the steps that must be taken in the present circumstances. We propounded to each other the pride and enthusiasm that the English must have acquired with this blow, the superiority of forces they had obtained, and the discouragement felt by the French. Nonetheless, it seemed to us that as we were able to put together a fleet of some thirty warships, including our own, and those French ships that required few repairs, it would be wise to go to sea with them and to serve notice on the enemy, at least, so that they would not make any attempt against our possessions. I said further that a frigate should be dispatched for France, where I should go to give intelligence of this fatal event to both governments, so that they could either make some vigorous effort to reestablish the superiority of our armed forces or take the course most adapted to their purposes.

In the afternoon we walked alone, reflecting on these things. We went to see the warships come in, and only the frigate *Astre* entered; the other ships, apparently about twenty-four, went about toward the open sea.

It was said that the frigate had brought the news that off the head of the island toward Samaná the English had captured the warship *Jason* and the frigate *Cérés*, which were coming to this port; and that the English were proceeding in this direction with twelve warships, detached no doubt to pursue the scattered warships. If this report is true, it seems probable that the fleet that is still outside will make an effort to encounter them.

25 April 1782

It was confirmed as true that off Puerto Rico the English had captured the warships *Jason* and the 64-gun *Caton*, as well as the frigates *Cérés* and *Aimable*.

There was talk of sending a French frigate to Europe with news of the disastrous fate of the fleet, and I requested to go there in order to inform both courts about the situation in which we found ourselves.

A junta was called for the following day, to be composed of General Solano, Monsieur de Bellecombe, and Monsieur de Vaudreuil, at which I also must be present.

26 April 1782

The junta took place. It was agreed that it was impossible to attack Jamaica as long as the English had superior maritime forces. The French tried to persuade us to go to the north, but we rebuffed the proposition for the same reason that was causing us to abandon the plan to go to Jamaica. We agreed, then, that we should continue to observe the enemy and be in readiness to go wherever defense might be required, until we received the decision of our governments. I was in the general's house until eleven o'clock, when he handed me the letters. At twelve o'clock I went aboard the *San Luis* and talked with Solano there until three o'clock, when I embarked on the frigate *Richmond*.

27 April 1782

We sailed at daybreak in company with the frigate *Astre*, which Monsieur Poirouse commanded; she was to escort us until we sailed out [of the Caicos Passage]. At midday we saw three vessels that were flying the Spanish flag. They were sailing toward the port; one appeared to be a frigate.

Journal of Don Francisco Saavedra de Sangronis

28 April 1782

We had a wind from the north. Meridian latitude observed 20°5'. In the afternoon we saw Great Inagua and Little Inagua.

29 April 1782

Latitude observed 22°. From noon on we could see Mayaguana, but we could not proceed because the wind was northeasterly.

30 April 1782

At daybreak we sailed out of the channel between Caicos and Mayaguana. The *Astre* bade us farewell at six-thirty in the evening. Meridian latitude observed 22°12'.

1 May 1782

We had a wind from the SE which fell calm at midday. Latitude observed 23°24'; twenty-six leagues were run.

2 May 1782

Wind from the SE; it fell calm at midday. Latitude observed 24°32'; twenty and one-half leagues were run.

3 May 1782

Calm weather all night. Twenty-eight leagues were run; an observation was worked at 25°45' latitude, 73° longitude.

4 May 1782

Fresh wind from the SE and the S. At two o'clock in the morning the frigate prepared for action because of a vessel sighted to windward; at first the vessel looked large, then it was seen to be a small [north?] American vessel. Fifty leagues were run. An observation was worked at 27°22' latitude, 71° longitude.

5 May 1782

Fresh wind from the SE; during the night we reached a speed of ten and one-half knots. Fifty-four leagues were run; an observation was worked at 29°52′ latitude, 67°13′ longitude.

6 May 1782

Strong wind from the SW; we sailed before it all night at eleven knots. In the morning there was rain, then calm. Nevertheless, the day's run was sixty-two leagues. No observation was worked because of cloudy weather.

7 May 1782

Calm with variable breezes. Nineteen leagues were run. An observation was worked at 31° latitude, 64°13′ longitude. I wound the clock, which had stopped because of neglect.

8 May 1782

The calm persisted. Thirteen and one-half leagues were run. An observation was worked at 31°44′ latitude, 63°53′ longitude.

9 May 1782

In the early hours of the night the wind set in from the E. Thirty-six leagues were run. An observation was worked at 33°12′ latitude, 62°42′ longitude; this [unreadable] Bermuda to the west-southwest of us.

10 May 1782

Calm weather. Wind from the SE. We ran thirty-three and one-half leagues. An observation was worked at 33°58′ latitude, 60°14′ longitude.

11 May 1782

Calm until midnight, when the wind rose from the SW. We ran forty leagues. An observation was worked at 34°52' latitude, 58°12' longitude. We reckoned ourselves to be 145 leagues from the Banks of Newfoundland.

12 May 1782

At night a fresh wind rose from the west. We ran forty-six leagues; an observation was worked at 35°58' latitude, 56°33' longitude. At nightfall we reckoned ourselves to be NS with the western tip of the Banks of Newfoundland.

13 May 1782

Very fresh wind from the west. Eleven knots were made almost all night and twelve in the morning. Seventy-two leagues were run. An observation was worked at 37°43' latitude, 53°27' longitude.

14 May 1782

Fair light wind from the SW; forty-five leagues were run. An observation was worked at 38°40' latitude, 50°10' longitude.

15 May 1782

Very strong wind from the SW. Seventy-four leagues were run. An observation was worked at 40°25' latitude, 45° longitude. We reckoned ourselves to be 570 leagues from Brest.

16 May 1782

Until midnight an extremely strong wind from the west with a terrifying sea; then the wind changed to the west-northwest. We ran sixty-six leagues. An observation was worked at 11°30' latitude, 41°25' longitude; we reckoned ourselves to be 500 leagues from Brest.

17 May 1782

At daybreak the northeast wind fell calm; it had been light all night. We ran thirty-four leagues. An observation was worked at 42°10' latitude, 33°53' longitude.

18 May 1782

Calm until midnight, when the wind began to blow from the south. We ran twenty-eight leagues. An observation was worked at 42°54' latitude, 38°20' longitude. We set a course E by NE.

19 May 1782

Fresh wind from the SW and the W; we ran sixty-one leagues. An observation was worked at 43°30' latitude, 34°42' longitude.

20 May 1782

Calm all night with thick fog. We ran thirty-eight leagues. An observation was worked at 42°42' latitude, 32° longitude.

21 May 1782

Fresh winds with rain squalls until eight-thirty o'clock in the evening, when suddenly there came a violent contrasting wind from the northeast. As it caught us unawares and under much sail, we were on the point of capsizing. The water entered through all the starboard portholes; the wind carried off the brigantine sail. Finally we succeeded in lying to, and so we endured the entire night, while the wind blew furiously. At daybreak it changed to a fresh north wind, and we set out on our course once more but with high seas and frightful swells. We ran thirty-eight leagues. An observation was worked at 43°51' latitude, 29°20' longitude.

22 May 1782

The weather was violent with horrible swells. The battering waves of the sea entered everywhere. We ran sixty-six leagues. An observation was worked at 44½° latitude, 23° longitude.

23 May 1782

The foul weather continued with even greater fury. We ran seventy-five leagues. An observation was worked at 45½° latitude, 19° longitude.

24 May 1782

The stormy weather continued, diminishing somewhat until nightfall, when a hailstorm calmed the sea, and the wind leapt to the north. We ran fifty-six leagues. An observation was worked at 46°12′ latitude, 15° longitude.

25 May 1782

At twilight we saw two vessels which [unreadable] effort for us. At three o'clock on the following morning there arose a very strong wind from the south, which obliged us to lie to; the wind continued from the southwest and the west with equal force. No observation was possible. We ran forty-three leagues.

26 May 1782

At ten o'clock in the morning the lead was heaved, and a bottom was found at seventy fathoms. We recognized that we were already near Brest. At eleven o'clock we gave chase to a vessel which was found to be Portuguese. From it we learned that there was an English fleet cruising off [unreadable] that had tried to intercept it. At three o'clock land was sighted. It was thought to be the Pointe du Raz. At five o'clock we passed through the Angostura de Paz [Etroit de la Paix], a dangerous passage because of the rapidity of its currents. At nine o'clock the Strait of Tulinger was passed, and at eleven-thirty we cast anchor in the Bay of Brest.

27 May 1782

In the morning the Vicomte de Montmart presented me to Monsieur Hector, commandant of the department, with whom I talked at length about the state of things in the Indies. Although the morning was rainy, I visited all the navy yard, docks, arsenals, etc., which are really magnificent. I dined with Monsieur Hector. At five o'clock in the afternoon I departed in a post chaise with the Vicomte de Montmart. We spent the night five leagues from Brest.

28 May 1782

We drove twenty-five leagues, traveling day and night.

29 May 1782

We drove twenty-four leagues, idem.

30 May, Corpus Christi, 1782

We traveled forty-six leagues and arrived in the morning at Nantes, a large and rather beautiful town.

31 May 1782

We traveled forty leagues, and we passed Angers and through Le Mans.

1 June 1782

We traveled twenty leagues. We rested in Pontchartrain, and at eleven o'clock in the morning we entered Versailles.[207] About one-quarter of a league before reaching Versailles, we

---

207. Louis XIV had moved the royal court to Versailles. It was returned to Paris in 1790. [Tr.]

met the king of France, who recognized Vicomte de Montmart who was with me. The king stopped his carriage, summoned the vicomte, commanded him to enter his carriage, and interrogated him about the Comte de Grasse's battle. As soon as I arrived at Versailles I inquired for the Conde de Aranda,[208] and they told me that he was in Paris. Immediately I had a post chaise brought, and as I was about to enter it a message came for me from the minister of the navy, Monsieur de Castries[209] summoning me; I went to see him; he received me very graciously; I excused myself from dining with him and then set out for Paris, where I arrived at three o'clock in the afternoon. I went to call on the Señor Conde de Aranda, who was delighted at my arrival. We talked at length about the affairs of America, and he told me to return on the following day so that we should go to Versailles to see the Comte de Vergennes[210] and the Marquis de Castries, to learn from them what decisions the French Court was thinking of making in regard to the problems of America.

The Conde de Aranda told me that he was going to dispatch an express post for Spain immediately, and I, without losing a

---

208. Pedro Pablo Abarca y Bolea, Conde de Aranda, a former prime minister of Spain, had become ambassador to France in 1773. In Paris he dealt with the envoys sent there by the United States. He prepared a memorial to the king of Spain in which he warned that the independence of the United States would be prejudicial to the Spanish Empire in America. [Tr.]

209. Charles Eugene-Gabriel de la Croix, Duc de Castries, a marshal of France, was minister of marine. His predecessors Choiseul and Sartine had rebuilt the French navy after the disasters of the Seven Years War. When war broke out in 1778, France had eighty ships-of-the-line in good condition and 67,000 seamen on the maritime conscription rolls (Mahan, 253). [Tr.]

210. Charles Gravier, Comte de Vergennes, became foreign minister when Louis XVI succeeded to the throne in 1774. With his Spanish counterparts Grimaldi and Floridablanca, Vergennes gave secret assistance to the North American colonists, but he was unwilling to recognize the independence of the United States or to enter into a formal alliance with them until their victory at Saratoga convinced him and his sovereign of their probable success. Thereafter, Vergennes made a persistent effort to persuade Spain to enter the war. [Tr.]

1 June 1782

moment, wrote to Don José de Gálvez of my arrival at this court. The Conde also told me to be at his house at eight o'clock on the following morning in order to go to Versailles to be presented to the French ministers.

2 June 1782

I went to Versailles with the Conde de Aranda, who presented me first to the Comte de Vergennes, with whom I spoke frankly about the battle fought by Monsieur de Grasse and the state of things in America, and second, to Monsieur de Castries, who made an appointment with me for Tuesday morning. Later we went to the palace; I saw a part of it, and while the Conde de Aranda went to see the king, who was kind enough to speak to him about me, I amused myself by seeing the famous gallery. The Palace of Versailles is immense, but it is made up of detached parts and so is wanting in plan and taste. The interior adornments are magnificent. At noon we started back to Paris, and en route the Conde de Aranda told me that the king had deigned to inquire about me.

I dined in the house of the conde. In the afternoon I went to see the opera. The theater is beautiful; there are more than 200 actors and more than 100 dancers, and the ballets are in excellent taste.[211] The piece was *Iphigénie en Tauride*, divine music by Gluck sung in the French style, which foreigners do not like. In the evening I went to see the masked ball, which the dukes of Russia were to attend.[212] It was held in the Theater of the Opera; it is a crowd where one does not dance, and the whole affair is no more than noise and jostling. The masquerades were neither rich nor splendid, and most people go in ordinary dress.

---

211. At that time the Opéra was located at no. 75 Rue Richelieu. See Howard P. Clunn, *The Face of Paris* (London, 1960), 171. [Tr.]

212. The Grand Dukes of Russia, the Czarevitch Paul, future Paul I, emperor and czar of Russia, and the Czarina Fredericka. In Paris they preferred to be called the Counts of the North. [Tr.]

3 June 1782

In the morning I went to the house of Lecoutraix to cash a bill of exchange. I returned to the house, where I found Monsieur Maxent, General Gálvez's father-in-law.[213] I dined in the conde's house; and from there I went to see the Comédie Française; the theater is new and magnificent.[214] Racine's *Mithridate* was presented with superlative realism. I was profoundly moved. Later they performed a scene from Rousseau's *Pygmalion*, a piece with only one character, in exquisite taste.

4 June 1782

I wrote to Madrid to the Conde de Floridablanca and Don José de Gálvez. I was summoned to the house of the Conde de Aranda, and we had a conference of one hour with the Marquis de Castries. In it each of us set forth in detail what seemed to him most prudent for the sake of the common cause. In substance we all were in agreement; the Marquis de Castries promised to speak to the king on Saturday about the matter and said that on the same day we should go to Versailles to dine with him. I dined with the Marquis de Lupac and Monsieur Monteil, and afterward we went to see the Tuileries and walked through the Louvre.[215]

5 June 1782

I went to call on the Conde Castrillo. I dined with the Conde de Aranda. I went to the Italian Theater,[216] where *Les Mariages des Samnites* was being presented.

---

213. Gilbert Antoine de Saint Maxent was a French merchant and planter of Louisiana. His daughter Félice was the wife of Bernardo de Gálvez. [Tr.]

214. The Comédie Française attended by Saavedra was built by Louis XVI. The present Comédie Française was built in 1786–90. [Tr.]

215. The Tuileries Palace was sacked and plundered in the Revolution of 1848 and was destroyed by the Commune in 1871. The old Louvre had been superseded as a royal palace by the Tuileries. The Champs Elysées was called the Avenue des Tuileries (ibid., 40). [Tr.]

216. The former name of the Opéra Comique. [Tr.]

6 June 1782

I strolled in the Tuileries and dined with the Conde de Aranda. I went to the Italian Theater, where they played *Zamire et Azor* and another superb piece by Marmontel.

7 June 1782

I went to see some excellent engravings and bought some of them. I dined in the house of an uncle of Monsieur de Bougainville.[217] I attended the opera of Teseo. The Dukes of Russia were there.

8 June 1782

The Conde de Aranda took me to Versailles. He presented me to the king, the queen, the Comte d'Artois, Madame Elizabeth, Victoire, etc.[218] I dined with Monsieur de Castries, who told me his plan of operations in America and asked me several questions. At eight o'clock in the evening I briefly attended the ball given in honor of the Comtes du Nord. The hall, the illumination, the dress of those present were all magnificent. We returned at eleven o'clock in the evening.

9 June 1782

I dined with the famous banker Monsieur La Borda. We talked about several matters having to do with Negroes in our colonies. I went to the Opéra.

10 June 1782

I dined with the Chevalier de Monteil; we strolled along

---

217. The famous explorer Louis Antoine de Bougainville commanded a French division of seven warships in the Battle of the Saintes. [Tr.]

218. The members of the French royal family were King Louis XVI, Queen Marie Antoinette, the king's brothers, Louis Stanislaus Xavier, Comte de Provence, and Charles Phillipe, Comte d'Artois, the king's sister, Elizabeth, and his aunt Victoire. [Tr.]

the bank of the river. We saw the Hôtel de Ville, which is not particularly interesting.[219] I spoke for a long time with a field marshal who informed me in great detail about the affairs of the court.

11 June 1782

I dined in the home of Lecoutraix; I went to the Opéra, where the *Iphigénie en Tauride* was repeated. I talked with Izquierdo for a long time.[220]

12 June 1782

I dined with the Conde de Aranda. In the afternoon Izquierdo took me to see several things: the Hôtel des Invalides,[221] an enormous structure with a superb dome and a capacity of 4,000 persons; the Ecole Militaire, a rather beautiful and well-planned work; the Champs de Mars in front of it, being very spacious, gives it a very elegant aspect;[222] the garden of the Duc de Biron, which is enchanting; the Luxembourg Garden, a public park in front of a royal palace;[223] the Eglise de Sainte Geneviève, which is being rebuilt and will be a grandiose edifice;[224] the Sorbonne, a large building in whose

---

219. At the beginning of the Hundred Years War in the fourteenth century the citizens of Paris took over a large house in the Place de Grève as the seat of their government, and called it the Hôtel de Ville (ibid., 65).

220. Izquierdo was at the Spanish Embassy in Paris. [Tr.]

221. The Hôtel des Invalides was built for Louis XIV between 1670 and 1674 as an asylum for wounded and aged soldiers (ibid., 196). [Tr.]

222. The Ecole Militaire was completed in 1757, to accommodate 500 gentlemen preparing for a military career. It is now called the Ecole Supérieure de Guerre. The Champs de Mars, originally reserved for the school, was from 1770 to 1900 the great center for military reviews and exhibitions (ibid., 199–200). [Tr.]

223. Begun in 1613, the Luxembourg was in 1782 the most frequented promenade area in Paris (ibid., 104–5). [Tr.]

224. The church, begun in 1764, was built to the glory of Ste. Geneviève, patron saint of Paris, by Louis XV. In 1791 it became the Panthéon and was dedicated to the memory of the great men of France (ibid., 115). [Tr.]

12 June 1782

church, which also is rather large, is the mausoleum of Cardinal de Richelieu, a sculpture by Girardon worthy of ancient Rome;[225] and the Académie de la Chirurgie, a beautiful and well-proportioned work.[226]

13 June 1782

I was with the Conde de Aranda, examining several maps of America in order to send to Don José de Gálvez some that he had requested. At midday the conde and I went to Versailles, having been summoned by the Comte de Vergennes. In the house of the latter there was a junta composed of the ministers of state, marine, and treasury, the ambassador, and me, in which we discussed the logical steps to take in the present circumstances. The minister of marine read a memorial concerning this question which he had prepared in consultation with the king. Everyone thought it was well done, and we agreed that I should go to Madrid to carry it and to explain to the Spanish ministers the circumstances that were making the execution of it almost imperative.[227]

The conde and I were in the famous factory at Sèvres, where

---

225. The present seat of the University of Paris, the Sorbonne was begun in 1253 by Robert Sorbon as a college of theology. The church, all that remains of the original, was built between 1635 and 1653 (ibid., 114–15). [Tr.]

226. The Académie de la Chirurgie (Surgery) was the former name of the Ecole de Médecine, begun in 1769 and completed in 1786 (ibid., 111). [Tr.]

227. The plan to be explained by Saavedra was imposing: a force of 7,000 men and 40 warships was to sail from Brest to Cádiz, where about 13,000 men and 40 warships were to be gathered, creating a force of about 20,000 men and 50 ships-of-the-line. This force was to sail to the West Indies to merge with the troops and vessels already operating there. Eventually the armada would number at least 66 ships-of-the-line and 24,000 men. See Louis Gottschalk, *Lafayette and the Close of the American Revolution* (Chicago: University of Chicago Press, 1942), 379–88. There were estimates that made it even larger. Once Jamaica was captured, all the Allied naval forces would be returned to Europe to crush the British, if that were still necessary, Spain's response was to invite d'Estaing to San Ildefonso for consultations. When d'Estaing began his

we saw marvelous things, especially the dressing case that the king has given to the Duchesse du Nord.

14 June 1782

The Conde de Aranda summoned me in the morning so that I could respond to several questions put by the Marquis de Castries concerning the condition of the artillery of the army at the French Cape. I answered them insofar as I could. The conde gave me a collection of maps of the Indies as requested by Señor Gálvez, and I paid 136 livres tournois for them. I dined in the conde's house where all the Russians of the entourage were invited also. I went to the Opéra with the conde for a performance of the magnificent opera *Castor and Pollux*. The queen was there in her box with the dukes of Russia.

15 June 1782

The conde summoned me, to tell me that my journey to Madrid was arranged, and I assured him that I should get ready immediately. Indeed, I made my preparations and sent to the post to order horses, but I was waiting for them all afternoon and all evening, because most of them were being used by the Comtes du Nord.

16 June 1782

The horses did not come until three o'clock in the morning. I departed at once, and in twenty-four hours we traveled forty-two leagues.

17 June 1782

We passed through Tours, a beautiful and rather large city. We supped at Chatellerault and departed at midnight.

---

journey to Spain on 13 October, he went with the intention of convincing Spain that the military situation demanded negotiations for peace, but he was prepared, if peace failed, to command the most massive military operation ever undertaken (Dull, 287–317). [Tr.]

18 June 1782

Three leagues from Poitiers the English post chaise broke down, and it was repaired as well as could be done on the road. We reached Poitiers, and there a new grommet was made to replace one that had broken. We departed at three o'clock in the afternoon, and at the second post the ring broke again. We came to a neighboring village, and again a new one was made.

19 June 1782

The repair of the post chaise was completed at two o'clock in the morning. We departed, and in the subsequent twenty-four hours we traveled fifty leagues.

20 June 1782

We arrived at Bordeaux at noon. We spent an entire day in Bordeaux. The post chaise was securely repaired. I saw the port, the jardin, and the theater, which is magnificent.

21 June 1782

I left Bordeaux at three o'clock in the afternoon, and we entered the Landes, where it was necessary to proceed step by step.

22 June 1782

There were no horses at the post houses, because they had been ordered sent elsewhere by the Comte d'Arron, so that in the whole day we made little progress.

23 June 1782

Again there were no horses; so seeing that we absolutely must press on, we took the road to Aux, on which there are five posts, and we stopped beyond Horder at the house of the Chevalier de Sainte [unreadable].

24 June 1782

I departed for Bayonne. I traveled all day and all night and reached Bayonne at six o'clock in the morning.

25 June 1782

I hired four mules, set out at two o'clock in the afternoon, and that night slept at Saint-Jean-de-Luz.

26 June 1782

At eight o'clock in the morning I reached the river that divides Spain from France. I presented my passport to the French commissaries; I went to dine at Hernani and to sleep at [unreadable].

27 June 1782

I traveled fourteen leagues. I slept at Victoria; midway the carriage struck a check stone and was badly damaged. Viscaya is exceedingly monotonous but well cultivated. The towns are small but numerous. The roads, built with great solidity through mountains and precipices, are worthy of the Romans.

28 June 1782

In Victoria I engaged a carriage to serve me as a stagecoach from there to San Ildefonso.[228] In fact, I departed at daybreak, and that day I traveled fourteen leagues. The good road ends two leagues from Victoria. Near the rocks of Pancorbo, which form one of the most difficult canyons in the world, one finds a road built by the commercial interests of Bilbao.

---

228. The site of a royal palace, referred to elsewhere by Saavedra as "el Sitio" from the name "Sitio Real de San Ildefonso" (royal country residence of San Ildefonso), situated in the province of Segovia, seventy-seven kilometers north of Madrid. See also note 234. [Tr.]

29 June 1782

At mid-afternoon we arrived at Burgos, an ancient town, irregular, in which one sees reminders of its having been a court at one time, but it has fallen into decadence.

30 June 1782

I dined in Lerma. There is a magnificent palace there built by the duke, the favorite of Philip III, who at the same time founded three convents of monks and three of nuns, with a beautful collegiate church. The town has 260 citizens. We slept at Aranda de Duero. A great part of the road goes through uncultivated and uninhabited lands.

1 July 1782

I traveled thirteen leagues and came to a small village, where I slept with extreme discomfort.

2 July 1782

I spent the night at San Ildefonso. As soon as I arrived there I presented myself to Señor de Gálvez and the Conde de Floridablanca and delivered to them the official papers I was bringing for them.

3 July 1782

I was talking with the French ambassador,[229] to whom I delivered the letter from the Comte de Vergennes; he made an appointment with me for the following day so that we could talk at length.

---

229. Armand Marc, Comte de Montmorin de Saint Herem. On 14 June 1782 Vergennes wrote to Montmorin recommending Saavedra as a man of true merit and advising that he would be as sensible of Montmorin's friendship with Saavedra as if it were direct and personal for himself (Dull, 287). [Tr.]

4 July 1782

I had a long conference with the minister about New World affairs, and I told him how I felt about many things. I called upon the Marqués Gonzáles de Castejón [minister of marine] with whom I spoke about some things concerning the navy. In the evening I had a long conversation with the ambassador of France, to whom I described the condition of the Spanish and French forces in the Indies and explained what seemed to me most prudent to be done in the present circumstances.

5 July 1782

I talked with the minister about various important matters. In the evening I met with Señor Floridablanca in the minister's house and had a good session with them both. I kissed the hand of the king.

6 July 1782

I called on Don Miguel de Muzquiz [minister of finance]. I reported several things to my minister. I kissed the hand of the princes and infantes.[230]

7 July 1782

I continued my sessions with the minister, and I spoke about various things that his nephew had charged me to tell him. Fearful that there might be an insufficiency of gunpowder for our enterprises, I ascertained by inquiry that for Gibraltar there were no more than 32,000 quintales of gunpowder, 200,000 cannonballs, and 30,000 bombs, and I made a calculation for the minister, indicating that all these articles were in too scant a supply for the siege of that stronghold.

---

230. The príncipes were the Prince of Asturias, the future Charles IV, king of Spain, and his wife, María Luisa, daughter of the Duke of Parma. The infantes were the other children of the king. [Tr.]

8 July 1782

I dined with the French ambassador, with whom I spoke about our contemplated operations, and I suggested that he urge his court to issue orders for powder and a supply of cannonballs to be sent to Cádiz if possible.

9 July 1782

I wrote to the Conde de Aranda to inquire if there were gunpowder and cannonballs in that kingdom, and I entrusted the letter to the French ambassador. I spoke to the minister about the route that I thought the mail-packet about to be sent to the Indies ought to take.

10 July 1782

I wrote to Don Bernardo de Gálvez; I made an appointment with Campo,[231] so that we could talk at length. I learned that there were twenty to thirty howitzers in Gibraltar.

11 July 1782

I made a copy of the plan of campaign devised by France and Spain, and I delivered it to my minister. The mail-packet for the Indies was dispatched, and I informed Don Bernardo de Gálvez enigmatically about all that had happened.

12 July 1782

By appointment with Don Bernardo del Campo I strolled with him through the gardens for a long time, and we talked about several important matters. I learned that the camp at Gibraltar had requested that those authorities in charge of the siege send 75,000 quintales of powder.

---

231. Bernardo del Campo was secretary to the minister of state. [Tr.]

13 July 1782

I spoke with the minister about various matters having to do with the Indies, and I made known to him many abuses which I felt must be remedied and several provisions it would be wise to make.

14 July 1782

I took to the Conde de Floridablanca the representation sent by the Province of Louisiana in favor of Don Bernardo de Gálvez,[232] and he told me that on Wednesday evening we should talk about the matter. I had a long conference with the minister of the Indies. He asked me what were my intentions as to my employment, once the war was concluded, and I replied that my intention was to go wherever the public cause required, even if it were to the ends of the earth.

15 July 1782

I had a long conversation with my minister's wife, and I spoke to her about diverse things concerning my future employment and plans.

16 July 1782

I was with the French ambassador, and we talked about what length of time might logically be estimated for concluding the siege of Gibraltar. I mentioned to him the promise made to me by the Marquis de Castries, that a swift French vessel would be at my disposition to take me to Santo Domingo.

---

232. On 12 October 1781 leading French citizens of Louisiana signed a petition to Charles III requesting special honors for their wartime governor, Bernardo de Gálvez. He was honored with the Cross of Charles III, the titles of Conde de Gálvez and Vizconde de Galveztown, and the rank of lieutenant general of the royal armies and inspector general of all the troops in America, and he became captain general of the Province of Louisiana and of the two Floridas and viceroy of New Spain (Holmes, 161; Caughey, 252–57). [Tr.]

18 July 1782

I talked with Señor Gálvez about many observations I had made in the Indies and about abuses I had noted. In the evening I went to talk with Señor Floridablanca, but he was busy.

19 July 1782

I had a long conference with Señor Gálvez. I told him about various individuals who I thought were prejudicial in the Indies, about the freedom to trade in Negroes which I thought ought to be permitted in the islands, about different abuses I had noted in Havana, particularly in the administration of the supply of meats, the monopoly of bread, the registers, the fortifications, etc. He told me that as soon as peace was made all that would be remedied.

20 July 1782

Nothing notable occurred except the arrival of Don Martín Huarte, the aide-de-camp of Don Bernardo de Gálvez, with letters from this general, which were duplicates of those sent from France by the Marquis de Bouillé.

21 July 1782

I again talked with the minister about diverse topics concerning the Indies—among other things, the necessity of having a port in the Windwards.

22 July 1782

I spoke again with the Conde de Floridablanca but very briefly.

23 July 1782

At nightfall the Comte d'Artois arrived.

24 July 1782

I departed for Madrid, to complete various necessary tasks. I left at four o'clock in the afternoon and arrived at one o'clock in the morning.

25 July 1782

I was in the house of Don Miguel de Gálvez,[233] with whom I talked at length about New World affairs, especially about the same things I had already discussed with Señor Don José.

26 July 1782

While I was in Barea's house a severe hailstorm began; it broke all the windows in Madrid on the west and south sides. In the afternoon I took a walk with Don Miguel and communicated to him everything I deemed useful.

27 July 1782

I made a multitude of visits. At eleven o'clock in the evening I took the road for the Sitio.[234]

28 July 1782

I arrived at eight o'clock in the morning and went to the minister's house. In the evening I was with the Conde de Floridablanca.

29 July 1782

I was with the French ambassador to request that he present me to the Comte d'Artois. In the afternoon I went to Segovia where the comte was, and the cadets and artillerymen pre-

---

233. The king's counselor of war and a brother of José de Gálvez. [Tr.]
234. The Reales Sitios or Sitios Reales were residential palaces constructed by Philip II, Philip V, Ferdinand VI, and Charles III. [Ed.]

sented very good drills with fusil and cannon.

30 July 1782

I went to the palace to be presented to the Comte d'Artois, but I did not find the ambassador there.

31 July 1782

I talked at length with my minister about affairs in the Indies.

1 August 1782

I was with the Conde de Floridablanca who, although he was busy, talked with me for a while about political matters.

2 August 1782

The Comte d'Artois departed for Madrid.

3 August 1782

In the afternoon the Duc de Bourbon, son of the Prince de Condé, arrived; his personality and gentility impressed everyone favorably.[235]

4 August 1782

I talked at length with Campo about various matters.

5 August 1782

Nothing notable happened.

---

235. Louis-Joseph, Duc de Bourbon, and his father, the Prince de Condé, belonged to an influential cadet branch of the royal Bourbon family. [Tr.]

6 August 1782

I talked with Don José de Gálvez about matters concerning New Spain.

7 August 1782

I talked with him again about the same things, especially about the Academy of Fine Arts which Mangino and Gil are thinking of establishing in New Spain.

8 August 1782

Nothing worthy of consideration occurred except the arrival of the news that the Comte d'Artois and the Duc de Bourbon had departed for Gibraltar on the sixth, having been well pleased by the treatment and courtesies they had experienced.

9 August 1782

I was with the minister of state, who was very busy. Castejón was attacked by a kind of cholera morbus, which caused anxiety to everyone. I spent a long time with Alvarez.[236]

10 August 1782

Nothing worthy of note happened.

11 August 1782

I talked with the minister about the same things we always discussed.

12 August 1782

Señor Roda[237] was afflicted by a serious stroke; they

---

236. In 1776 Saavedra had served as an aide in the secretariat of inspection, headed by Martín Alvarez, inspector of militias. [Tr.]

237. A former minister of state, Manuel, Marqués de Roda. [Tr.]

sent for a priest to administer the last rites. However, he was able to get out of bed, and he himself went to meet with the confessor.

13 August 1782

Roda was still gravely ill, and Holy Oil was administered.

14 August 1782

Señor Roda awoke feeling better. The minister gave me the Plan for Intendants to read.[238]

15 August 1782

In the evening a report was received that the two express mail-packets that had been dispatched from Cádiz to advise Don Bernardo de Gálvez about the decision of both courts had been captured and that the two officers [Antonio?] Wall and Crespo, who were carrying the official papers, had been put ashore in Faro and were already back in Cádiz.

16 August 1782

A post arrived from France with letters that had come

---

238. One of the chief political reforms of Charles III divided Spanish America into intendencias under officers known as intendentes. This system, a French device, had been installed in Spain in the early eighteenth century, and it was now extended to America. The advance agent of this reorganization, José de Gálvez, was sent as visitador general to Mexico in 1765. Returning to Spain as minister of colonies, he reorganized the colonial government. By 1790 all Spanish America was thus apportioned. The intendentes were charged with the administration of justice, the collection of taxes, the promotion of business and trade, and the organization of the provincial militia. Governors, corregidores, and alcaldes mayores were displaced and their tasks were allotted to the intendentes. The new system provoked angry criticism. See Hubert Herring, *A History of Latin America* (New York: Alfred A. Knopf, 1961), 167–68. [Tr.]

from the French Cape; I was unable to ascertain their content with certitude.

17 August 1782

Roda continued to improve, jesting a little about the prognostications of the physicians. I had a letter from Paris in which they told me that, from letters that had come from the French Cape, it had been learned that Monsieur de Vaudreuil had gone to the American colonies with fifteen warships, and that Solano had retired to Havana with his fleet, making use of the pretext that most of the ships in it were in bad condition.(239)

18 August 1782

I dined with the French ambassador, and from him I had confirmation of the report of Solano's return to Havana. [19 and 20 August omitted because of no importance.]

21 August 1782

Prince Masserano arrived in the post stage from Gibraltar. At first various rumors were spread concerning the news he was bringing. Later it was learned that he was coming to report that, from the most advanced battery constructed by Alvarez before his departure, an entrenchment had been opened toward the

---

239. Rendón reported from Philadelphia on 30 July, "Reliable intelligence from Chesapeake Bay informs us that the French squadron commanded by Monsieur de Vaudreuil had been sighted off the Capes. It comprised thirteen ships-of-the-line and two frigates and came from Guarico, whence it had sailed with fourteen Spanish ships under the command of His Excellency Señor Solano, which were bound for Havana. A frigate was detached from the French fleet to take letters to the Comte de Rochambeau, commanding general of the French Army, who is at Baltimore, Maryland. Subsequently, two general officers from that army arrived here today accompanied by engineers, en route to Boston to build the fortifications at the entrance of that harbour, necessary for the defense of the ships which will spend the winter there" (Rendón to José de Gálvez, 30 July 1782, AGI:Cuba 1319). [Tr.]

left, 250 toises long, with more than 600 toises of connecting passages. This work was executed on the night of the fifteenth to the sixteenth by 10,000 men, without their having been perceived by the enemy. It is 450 toises from the battery of the mountain.

22 August 1782

I talked for a long time with the minister about the operations of the next campaign.[240]

23 August 1782

I went twice to talk with the Conde de Floridablanca, but he was busy.

24 August 1782

There were rumors of the coming of Admiral Howe with thirty-seven warships to reinforce Gibraltar, and it was even said that a post had arrived from Galicia with the report that the English fleet had been sighted from its coasts.

25 August 1782

It was a day of fiesta for the princess. Roda's condition became worse, and everyone believed that he could not last much longer.

26 August 1782

I went to talk to the Conde de Floridablanca, but he was busy.

---

240. Saavedra was to be sent to the West Indies in late August or early September, in advance of the armada, to carry instructions to the officials and commanding officers there (Dull, 291). [Tr.]

27 August 1782

It was said that a powder magazine had exploded in the camp at Gibraltar and that fifteen men had perished in it. Roda was attacked by gangrene.

28 August 1782

Again there was talk of the appearance of the English fleet off the coasts of Portugal.

29 August 1782

It was learned from the post that the construction of the works at Gibraltar was continuing and that there had been some misadventures, although few. Also it was learned that an incendiary bomb had burned out part of a trench but that they had succeeded in extinguishing the fire.

30 August 1782

Señor Roda grew worse, and at a quarter to nine o'clock in the evening he died. An express post went out, bound for the French Cape. I talked with the minister about my voyage and told him I was ready to depart the moment it was advisable.

31 August 1782

There was a report that the combined fleet had arrived at the vicinity of Cádiz and was cruising in front of the strait.[241]

1 September 1782

Nothing notable happened.

---

241. The total strength of the Franco-Spanish fleet assembled at Gibraltar would be nearly fifty ships-of-the-line. It would support a grand combined attack by land and sea (Mahan, 176). [Tr.]

2 September 1782

It was reported that the English had detached part of their fleet in order to protect the convoy from the Baltic, and it was even rumored that they would not come so soon to reinforce Gibraltar.

3 September 1782

It was said that the king had told the ambassador of Holland that the fleet of his nation had captured thirteen English vessels of the convoy from the Baltic.

4 September 1782

I wrote to the cape to Señor Don Bernardo to tell him about the determinations made by the courts. This letter was sent in duplicate.

5 September 1782

I made arrangements to go to Madrid to complete some necessary tasks, departing in a carriage at nine o'clock in the evening.

6 September 1782

I was en route all day and reached Madrid at eight o'clock in the evening. Almost the entire city was ill of a respiratory infection called influenza.

7 September 1782

I was with Don Miguel de Gálvez, and we talked at length.

8 September 1782

Nothing notable happened.

9 September 1782

I dined with Don Miguel de Gálvez, and I informed him about some things pertaining to good government of the Indies, so that at an opportune moment he could remind his brother of them.

10 September 1782

I became ill the previous day with a chill, or influenza, and it afflicted me seriously. In the afternoon I again went driving with Don Miguel de Gálvez, in order to talk with him at leisure.

11 September 1782

I was in bed with fever.

12 September 1782

At noon I arose for a short while.

13 September 1782

I wanted to return to the Sitio, but I was persuaded not to undertake the journey until I was completely recovered.

14 September 1782

I came to the Sitio, arriving there at eight o'clock in the evening. I found that mail had come from the French Cape. I talked with His Excellency for a long time and proposed to him that it would be wise for me to set out for Algeciras, where I could await the outcome of the siege of Gibraltar and be ready to embark immediately once that was decided.

15 September 1782

I was with the minister. He told me that he had talked with the king and the prince about my going to the Indies, which His Majesty approved, but that the Conde de Floridablanca had persuaded him that I should wait here a little longer, because it would be necessary for us to confer about certain points of which I probably had knowledge.

16 September 1782

Nothing notable occurred.

17 September 1782

An officer arrived from the camp at Gibraltar with a report that on the thirteenth they had put into place three floating batteries, which were successfully striking the stronghold between the two jetties, and that the other seven floating batteries would be placed very soon.[242]

18 September 1782

A post from the Indies arrived, bringing correspondence from everywhere except Buenos Aires and Caracas. It was said that two posts had come from the camp at Gibraltar, with reports that were not made public. In the morning I was with Campo, talking about affairs of state. In the evening I went to see the Conde de Floridablanca, but I did not find him in his rooms. In the evening I was in the house of the minister, who was in bed, ill with the influenza.

19 September 1782

The reports that arrived on the previous day from the camp at Gibraltar were that the floating batteries designed to strike the wall on the side that faces the sea had been destroyed by fire, that 74 Frenchmen and about 100 Spaniards had perished in them, and that 308 men had been taken prisoner. It was

---

242. The ten praams, flat-bottomed lighters of a type used in Dutch and German ports, were floating batteries, contrived to be shot- and fire-proof, carrying 154 heavy guns. They were anchored in a line along the west front of the works, at a distance of about 900 yards. They were supported by forty gunboats and an equal number of bomb vessels (Mahan, 176–79). [Tr.]

also said that an express messenger had arrived from France advising that the English fleet had gone out of its ports with forty-two warships and that it was coming determined to take reinforcements into Gibraltar.

20 September 1782

When the first agitation caused by the report about the floating batteries had passed, it was told about that the Duc de Crillon[243] had written that the burning of them was deferring the surrender of the stronghold but had not made it impossible; that the fire on land had destroyed the battery of Ulysses; and that the merlons of the Puerta de Tierra were ruined.

21 September 1782

It was said that more mail had come from the camp, but its contents were not divulged.

22 September 1782

Quesada arrived.[244] He had brought official papers from Guarico, and he informed me about the condition of things there, the many deaths and illnesses that our troops were suffering, and their quarrels with the French.

23 September 1782

The Marqués de Cruillas arrived; he also brought official papers, and he confirmed Quesada's report of events over there.[245] It seems that up to the end of June there had been more than 400 deaths, and 2,500 men were ill.

---

243. The Duc de Crillon had come to Gibraltar from Minorca, where he commanded the combined army during the final phase of the siege of Mahon (Hargreaves-Mawdsley, 160– 62). [Tr.]

244. Juan Nepumuceno de Quesada would be governor of East Florida from 1790 to 1795. [Tr.]

245. Joaquin Montserrat, Marques de Cruillas, was a former viceroy of New Spain (1760–66). [Tr.]

24 September 1782

The post for the Indies was dispatched and was to leave the next day.

25 September 1782

The mail-packet for the Indies departed. On it I wrote to Don Bernardo de Gálvez the true state of our affairs here. I was talking with the French ambassador, who declared that it was almost impossible for the aid promised by both governments to be sent to America in the present circumstances.[246]

26 September 1782

It was said that an officer from the camp at Gibraltar had arrived and that they had locked him up so that his arrival would not be suspected.

27 September 1782

The captain of the Mallorca Regiment, Don Nicolás Mazé, arrived with the news that eight English warships had passed off El Ferrol in pursuit of a French frigate.

28 September 1782

There was much talk of peace, and the word was spread about that we were returning to the English everything that had been taken away from them in the New World, that they were being given a port on the Mediterranean, and that they were giving up Gibraltar to us and leaving Mahon in our possession.

---

246. One of the effects of the catastrophe at Gibraltar was that French Ambassador Montmorin felt that he had to use the Jamaican expedition to persuade Spain to abandon hopes of taking Gibraltar directly. He reported this to Vergennes, who had informed him that Vaudreuil and Solano had selected Puerto Cabello as the rendezvous, on the northern coast of Venezuela. There was some fear that the Spaniards' desire to conquer Gibraltar would prove to be a deterrent to an early peace. See Gottschalk, 360. [Tr.]

29 September 1782

A rumor was circulated that the English fleet had gone out of its ports with thirty-four warships.

30 September 1782

I talked with the minister about various important matters.

1 October 1782

Nothing notable happened.

2 October 1782

I was with the Conde de Floridablanca, to consult him about my departure for the Indies, and he told me to await the outcome of the siege of Gibraltar, which probably would not be long delayed.

3 October 1782

The king made Don Francisco [José?] de Viaña [1744–1826] official of the secretariat of the Indies. I set out for Madrid to complete the preparations for my departure.

4 October 1782

I arrived in Madrid at noon.

5 October 1782

During most of the day I was talking with Don Miguel, to whom I expressed my way of thinking about several matters.

6 October 1782

I went to see Lieutenant General Don Diego Navarro, with whom I reminisced about events in Havana.

7 October 1782

Nothing notable happened.

8 October 1782

I went to see several pieces worked in silver and gold by Martínez, in the most exceptional taste. In the afternoon I went to the house of a Malagueño who makes special clay figures.

9 October 1782

Vague rumors about Gibraltar ran through Madrid.

10 October 1782

I returned to the Sitio with the new official and presented him to the minister.

11 October 1782

An express messenger arrived from the camp, with the report that they had advanced a passage of the entrenchment as much as 250 toises.

12 October 1782

Another express messenger arrived from Lisbon to advise that on the sixth the English fleet came into view off that port.

13 October 1782

There was no news.

14 October 1782

Unfounded rumors were spread that the two fleets had been sighted.

15 October 1782

In the night an express messenger arrived with news that the English fleet had entered the Mediterranean and that ours had followed it.

16 October 1782

The report of the previous night was released, with the added news that four English transport vessels and two frigates had entered Gibraltar and that our warship *San Miguel* had been dashed to pieces against Europa Point.

17 October 1782

It was said that another report had come that the English fleet was entering the Mediterranean and that our fleet was following it closely.

18 October 1782

By the post from Andalucía it was learned that the English vessels that had entered Gibraltar numbered more than twelve, among them two frigates and one 50-gun warship.

19 October 1782

By letters from the camp at San Roque it was learned that the warship *San Miguel* had run aground on a sandbar, which is near the new mole, and that the English had immediately sent launches to take possession of the ship and to take its crew prisoner; also that the English would have found provisions on the ship for 700 men for a period of four months.

20 October 1782

At midday a post arrived from Algeciras with news that the warship *San Dámaso*, which had remained in that roadstead for repair of some damage it had sustained in the storm of the thirteenth, was indeed undergoing repair. It was said that another post had arrived in the night, but it was not known exactly what news it was bringing.

21 October 1782

It was said that two posts had arrived, but the news they brought was not made public.

22 October 1782

It appears that the report that came on the previous night and was not made public was that the major part of the English fleet and convoy had entered Gibraltar and that the combined [French and Spanish] fleet had fallen to leeward in the Mediterranean.

23 October 1782

Two more posts arrived, and it was said that they were bringing the news that the English fleet had passed out to the ocean.

24 October 1782

Despite the fact that the matter was kept secret, it did not fail to come to light that the English fleet really had returned to the ocean, after having reinforced Gibraltar.[247]

25 October 1782

It was said that the French troop that was in Gibraltar

---

247. Lord Howe's fleet and supply vessels were sighted off Gibraltar on 11 October. Four of the transports entered the port, the other ships drove eastward into the Mediterranean. The combined allied fleet followed on the thirteenth, but although the allies were thus placed between the port and the British forces and were not encumbered, as was the relieving force, with supply ships, they permitted most of the latter to slip in and anchor safely. Provisions, ammunition, and troops were landed. On the nineteenth the English repassed the straits with an easterly wind, having within a week's time fulfilled their mission (Mahan, 179). [Tr.]

had gone to Cádiz to be embarked, that some Spanish regiments had gone to the same port, that the Duc de Crillon would continue the siege of the stronghold with 12,000 men, and that he was declaring that it could be taken, in spite of what had happened.

26 October 1782

I endeavored to investigate what course our cabinet would take after the events at Gibraltar, but it appeared that nothing has been decided. At midday there was a long conference of ministers.

27 October 1782

I talked with Señor Gálvez to see if he would tell me something about the date of my departure. He responded that as soon as the fleet returned to Gibraltar, it would be seen which ships were in condition to go to America, so as to send them without delay, and that then I should be told exactly when I could go.

28 October 1782

It was said that news had come that the two fleets had had an encounter in which they exchanged fire for a period of three hours, but night came and next morning the English fleet had gone.

29 October 1782

Don José informed me that it was imperative that I depart for Cádiz instantly and that I must meet with the Conde de Floridablanca before going, to receive his instructions.

30 October 1782

I arranged for my departure, and Don José told the Conde de Floridablanca in advance that I must meet with him on the following day.

31 October 1782

Early in the evening I talked with the conde for more than an hour and a half, in which time he described to me the state of the negotiations. He told me that the Comte d'Estaing would arrive in Madrid within a few days, and that they would inform me in Cádiz whatever might result from the conferences with him.

1 November 1782

I began my journey to Madrid at nightfall and arrived there at ten o'clock.

2 November 1782

I concluded some necessary tasks and got ready to take the road the next day.

3 November 1782

I left Madrid at noon, bound for Cádiz but passing through Granada.

12 November 1782

The journey was uneventful. I reached Granada at eleven o'clock in the morning today and remained there through the thirteenth.

14 November 1782

I set out again at daybreak.

19 November 1782

I arrived at Puerto Real at midday and went to see Don Antonio de Gálvez,[248] who took me to his house with many kind expressions and attentions.

---

248. Commandant of the port, a brother of José de Gálvez. [Tr.]

20 November 1782

I talked at length with Don Antonio about the preparations made for the fleet and the army, and he gave me detailed intelligence about many things.

21 November 1782

I went to see Don Juan Bonet and found him sick and troubled because of having lost his reputation in the business of Havana. He complained to me bitterly of having been undeservedly ill treated. I told him that I had informed the minister of the Indies that, at least while I was there, he discharged his duties well, as was shown by the results.

22 November 1782

I dispatched the correspondence for Madrid. I found out that the Spanish fleet was in need of timber to replace some topmasts and yards that were lacking and also that the French had to careen and sheathe with copper three three-decker warships, which would require some time.

23 November 1782

They told me that there was widespread discontent in the French fleet owing to the circulation of a rumor that the Comte d'Estaing was coming to take the command of the entire combined fleet.[249]

24 November 1782

I was in the Caño del Trocadero, where they are planning to build good docks. There is one good dock there which has been rented by the king from the private merchant who owns it so that the royal frigates can be repaired there. In the Caño del Trocadero they confirmed to me that the preparations of the

---

249. D'Estaing was considered to have little skill in seamanship. His promotion to vice-admiral had caused considerable jealousy among his fellow flag officers (ibid., 162). [Tr.]

French were going slowly, and they were displeased because the Comte d'Estaing was coming to command them.

25 November 1782

I was in Don Juan Bonet's house, and we talked about various particulars relating to the navy.

26 November 1782

I dispatched the general mail, and in the afternoon I was by the sea at the Caño del Trocadero.

27 November 1782

I learned that the French general officers and even the Spanish were querulous because, in the entire campaign in the English Channel and in Gibraltar, their advice had not been taken even once for anything whatever. Also they assured me that the combined fleet had not maneuvered even one single time in the entire campaign.

28 November 1782

Nothing notable happened.

29 November 1782

There were rumors of the imminent arrival of the Comte d'Estaing.

30 November 1782

Nothing worthy of mention occurred.

1 December 1782

Chacón, the naval officer, came to see me, and we talked at length.[250]

---

250. José María Chacón commanded the packet-boat *San Pío* in the expedition against Pensacola which left Havana on 28 February 1781 (Medina Rojas, 667–68). [Tr.]

2 December 1782

The order came for me to embark on the brigantine *El Cubano*, which was ready to sail as a mail-packet.

3 December 1782

I took several measures in preparation for my voyage.

4 December 1782

I talked with the captain of *El Cubano*, who aquainted me with the ship's characteristics.

5 December 1782

Quesada, the governor of Camayagua, came to see me. He had come in charge of the official papers that *El Cubano* had brought and those to be returned on it.

6 December 1782

I dispatched the mail for Madrid.

7 December 1782

Nothing worth mentioning occurred.

8 December 1782

I talked with a rather well-informed merchant of Cádiz about the present miserable condition of commerce there, cut off at every turn, short of money, and near bankruptcy. Also he told me how much it had been damaged by the contraband trade that the French had carried on in our possessions during this war. He himself had a shipment of Catalonian wine in Havana which was selling at 160 pesos per cask, but there was so great an importation of Bordeaux wine there that no one was willing to pay any money at all for the Catalonian.

9 December 1782

The general post arrived, and it was said that the Comte d'Estaing would arrive at the Puerto de Santa María between the thirteenth and the fourteenth of this month.

10 December 1782

I dispatched the mail for Madrid. The news of the comte's arrival was confirmed. Another merchant told me the same things I had been told on the eighth and added some complaints about how onerous the proceedings and procrastinations of the customhouses were to trade.

11 December 1782

Nothing notable occurred.

12 December 1782

They came to tell me that the Comte d'Estaing was arriving at the port on the fifteenth.

13 December 1782

I received mail from Madrid.

14 December 1782

I dispatched the mail.

15 December 1782

I went to the Puerto de Santa María to confer with the Comte d'Estaing, who was not to arrive until the following day.

16 December 1782

The Comte d'Estaing did not arrive.

17 December 1782

I was in long conferences with some French officers with whom I had become acquainted earlier at the French Cape. The Comte d'Estaing did not arrive.

18 December 1782

The comte arrived at four o'clock in the afternoon. He called on the governor, visited the hospitals, and embarked for Cádiz. When on the dock he asked about me; I presented myself to him. He was very civil and said that we must confer at length. I departed for Puerto Real immediately.

19 December 1782

As it seemed to me that the Comte d'Estaing probably would be busy, I postponed going to Cádiz until the next day.

20 December 1782

I went to Cádiz, and that evening the Comte d'Estaing promised to go to the house of Don Antonio de Gálvez so that we could talk, but he could not go because he felt indisposed.

21 December 1782

I called on the Conde O'Reilly, governor of the stronghold.[251] The Comte d'Estaing was in Don Antonio's house in the evening, and the three of us had a long conversation. I told the comte that I was at his orders and that I would gladly do whatever might be useful to the common cause, as I had done before. I mentioned my sailing, and he answered that he would place at my disposition any French or Spanish frigate I chose for my voyage to the Indies but that he thought I ought

---

251. Major General Alejandro O'Reilly was Saavedra's former commanding officer and the former inspector general of Spanish armed forces in America. In 1769 he served as governor of Louisiana, having been sent there to put down a rebellion. See M. Serrano y Sanz, *Documentos de la Florida y la Luisiana* (Madrid, 1912), 295–312. [Tr.]

not to undertake my voyage until there was news or until the convoy from Brest arrived.

22 December 1782

I returned to Puerto Real to finish some necessary business more at my leisure.

23 December 1782

I was in the Puerto de Santa María to talk with Chacón of the Navy.

24 December 1782

I returned to Puerto Real in the morning. In the afternoon I went to Cádiz, taking all my luggage.

25 December 1782

In the evening I had a long conversation with the Comte d'Estaing in which he asked me questions about several things pertaining to the Indies. We talked about my departure, and he said it did not seem wise to him for me to go on an unaccompanied frigate, liable to be captured by other frigates which the English inevitably would have cruising off the French Cape to observe our movements; a better plan would be for me to embark with the expedition, on one of its swiftest warships, which with two or three other ships-of-the-line would go ahead, so as to arrive eight or ten days in advance and advise Señor Gálvez so that he would be prepared. I did not want to disagree with his opinion, although it seemed urgent to me that I go to those dominions quickly.

26 December 1782

I dined in the house of the Conde de O'Reilly.

27 December 1782

I dined in the house of the president of the Casa de la Contratación.[252]

28 December 1782

I continued copying the journal of my previous voyage.

29 December 1782

The convoy from Brest arrived, but it could not put into the port because a strong east wind was blowing. I went to see the Comte d'Estaing but could not see him because he was busy.

30 December 1782

He summoned me at midday, and I went to his house at three o'clock in the afternoon. We talked for a long time about the present state of affairs. He told me he was expecting from one day to the next an express post with news of the decision for peace or war and that he would like to have a vessel ready to carry intelligence to Don Bernardo de Gálvez at the French Cape. Immediately I communicated this to Don Antonio de Gálvez, who said to assure the Comte d'Estaing that a vessel was ready for whenever he might want it.

31 December 1782

The official paper came in which I was informed that an order was being sent to Don Luis de Córdova to present to me the Cross of Charles III.

---

252. The House of Trade was the institution through which the Crown insured safe passage of its Indies revenues, including those taxes levied on the commerce itself. See Eugene Lyon, *The Enterprise of Florida* (Gainesville: University Presses of Florida, 1976), 8. [Tr.]

1 January 1783

Early in the morning Don Antonio de Gálvez and I went to see the Comte d'Estaing; he was told that the report was ready and that there was a completely trustworthy officer who would go with it. I went to see Señor Córdova, who had not yet received the order to put a ship at my disposal.

2 January 1783

An express messenger arrived with letters for the general officers, but apparently it did not bring definitive information concerning peace or war. I went to see the Comte d'Estaing, but I could not talk with him because he was dispatching an express post.

3 January 1783

Señor Córdova sent me an official paper telling me that he had the order to present the cross to me, and I answered that I should go to see him the next day. I went to the house of the Comte d'Estaing, who had summoned me, and we talked about how uncertain people were about peace or war.

4 January 1783

I went to the island. Señor Códova pinned on me the Cross of Charles III. The witnesses were the Marqués de Castillas, chief of Squadron Osorno, and two naval captains.

5 January 1783

The public was talking about peace treaties, saying that the governments were already in agreement, that the English were not ceding Gibraltar, that the French were giving Guadeloupe to the English, and that we were giving Santo Domingo to the French.

6 January 1783

News came of the army and navy promotions motivated by the siege of Gibraltar, the number of them having come to four hundred. An express messenger arrived bringing official papers for the Indies, and from all indications it was inferred that the expedition would be carried out.

7 January 1783

The brigantine *El Cubano*, which was prepared to go as a mail-packet to America, could not sail today because of a fresh northeast wind which had set in.

I presented to the Comte d'Estaing, Quesada, the governor of Camayagua, who was to carry the official papers for Don Bernardo de Gálvez. The comte gave him a letter in code, to the end that the governor of the French Cape would give credence to what he said, and he explained to me the proposals I must communicate to Quesada so that he could explain them to Señor Gálvez.

8 January 1783

The brigantine *Cubano* sailed at nine o'clock in the morning. Quesada was with me earlier, and I gave him a paper reduced to simple propositions of what he should say to the Señores Gálvez and Bellecombe, ordering him to commit them to memory and then to destroy the paper. The paper was sealed with the order that he was not to open it until he was at sea.

9 January 1783

I was with the Comte d'Estaing. I read to him the paper I had given to Quesada, and he liked it very much. We talked at length about what had been prepared for the expedition, and he expressed his satisfaction with the speed of Don Antonio de Gálvez's performance.

10 January 1783

I dispatched the general mail.

12 January 1783

A special post arrived with official papers for the Indies. With it came an order that in case I did not carry the papers, they must be carried by an officer named by me. I named the regimental captain Don Fernando de la Concha. In a confidential letter Don José de Gálvez commanded that I read those official papers to the Comte d'Estaing, and I did so.

13 January 1783

I wrote letters for the Indies and picked up the Comte d'Estaing's code so that Monsieur Bellecombe would give credence to the words of the officer commissioned to carry the official papers.

14 January 1783

I accompanied Concha to Puerto Real, returned in the afternoon, and dispatched the general mail.

15 January 1783

I told the Comte d'Estaing how Don Antonio de Gálvez was seeking transport vessels on which to send the artillery for which there was no space on the French warships and that I was working diligently to have the ships watered as quickly as possible.

16 January 1783

The weather continued foul, with signs of worsening. I dined with the Comte d'Estaing.

17 January 1783

The Comte d'Estaing summoned me and asked me to

Journal of Don Francisco Saavedra de Sangronis

find for him a harbor pilot for the coast of Caracas.[253] I dined with the president.

18 January 1783

I went to see the Prince of Nassau[254] and Don Juan de Lángara.[255] Concha's brigantine sailed. Another special delivery arrived with duplicates of the official papers for the Indies. I went to introduce to the Comte d'Estaing a harbor pilot acquainted with Caracas.

19 January 1783

It was arranged that the Lieutenant Ayala of [the Regiment of] Spain should go on Benítez's brigantine; indeed the vessel set sail at nightfall and by eight o'clock was already outside.

20 January 1783

Don Antonio de Gálvez wrote to me. In order to hasten the watering of the French fleet he had contrived to take out of his own hacienda to the seashore four conduits of good water, but he said that it was necessary for the Comte d'Estaing to order that tubes and funnels be provided and to commission Rengel, the aide-de-camp of the Prince of Nassau and a diligent officer, to be sure that the watering was done promptly and in an orderly fashion. I saw the Comte d'Estaing, who expressed his extreme gratitude for the zeal with which Don Antonio de Gálvez was taking care of the prompt dispatch of the expedition, and he ordered his secretary to go to see the Prince of Nassau, request of him his aide-de-camp, and ask that the tubes and funnels be sent by the town mayor's office.

At two o'clock I went with Rengel to Puerto Real, and from there I went on to the Puerto de Santa María.

---

253. See note 246. [Tr.]
254. The Prince of Nassau, in the French service, commanded the floating batteries at Gibraltar. See note 242. [Tr.]
255. See note 8. [Tr.]

21 January 1783

In the Puerto de Santa María I dispatched the mail for Madrid.

22 January 1783

I returned from the Puerto de Santa María to Puerto Real but was unable to go on to Cádiz because there was a strong south-by-west wind.

23 January 1783

I went to Cádiz early in the morning. I was with the Comte d'Estaing, and I suggested that he order the French ships in need of watering to use the new fresh water supply on Don Antonio de Gálvez's estate.

24 January 1783

I dispatched the post for Madrid. The Comte d'Estaing went to Puerto Real and later to the Puerto de Santa María to review the French troops.[256]

25 January 1783

I went to speak to the Comte d'Estaing about my embarkation, and we agreed that it would be on the French warship *Royal Louis*, commanded by my friend Monsieur Duplessis Parscau.[257]

I noted that the French universally expected peace and that

---

256. Over 12,000 French troops were collected at Cádiz. The Marquis de Lafayette had arrived there on 23 December 1782 to accompany the fleet as the future governor of Jamaica. Twenty-four Spanish ships-of-the-line were ready to embark Spanish troops (Dull, 319). Lafayette had been selected by d'Estaing to command the land forces that were to go with him. In Cádiz, d'Estaing named the marquis maréchal général des logis (quartermaster-general) (Gottschalk, 388). [Tr.]

257. Duplessis Parscau commanded the warship *Intrépide* in the Chevalier de Monteil's squadron which accompanied Solano to Pensacola in April 1781 (Coker and Coker, 113). [Tr.]

as a consequence they were unconcerned about the departure of the expedition.[258]

26 January 1783

A warship and an English frigate were sighted; they seemed to be observing the movements of our fleet. I was in the house of the Prince of Nassau.

27 January 1783

I dined with the Comte d'Estaing. He talked about the near certainty of peace that existed and stated that if it were necessary for the expedition to go out, it was already in such a condition that it could do so within a few days.

In the morning one of Izquierdo's frigates went out and another of Rábago's, the first with a Portuguese flag, the second with an imperial. By way of La Coruña a post from the Indies was received; from it was learned that at the end of November a convoy of thirty sails was to have gone out from Havana escorted only by corsairs, because Solano had not been able to give it warships. Recognizing the risk this convoy would run at its landfall, the consulate sent an official paper to Señor Córdova so that he could send warships to protect its arrival.

28 January 1783

Because on the previous evening I had received a letter from the minister in which he pressed for the prompt departure of the expedition, I went early to see the Comte d'Estaing, who reiterated his hope of peace and said that he expected to know the final decision by early February. I inferred from this that the governments of France and Spain were thinking differently

---

258. Rendón reported from Philadelphia on 31 December 1782 the departure from Boston on 24 December of the French fleet commanded by Vaudreuil. Aboard the fleet was the French army commanded by Vioménil (Rendón to José de Gálvez, 31 December 1782, AGI:Cuba 1354). The French forces arrived at Puerto Cabello on 10 February 1783, expecting to join Solano and d'Estaing there. See Balch, passim. [Tr.]

about the expedition.

In the afternoon word was spread that the English warship and the frigate that were cruising in sight of the port had captured Izquierdo's frigate.

Ayala arrived in the evening, having had to make a forced landing at Málaga with a brigantine as a result of a severe storm that caught him twenty leagues from Cádiz.

It was learned that Señor Córdova had answered the official papers of the consulate by saying that he had no forces in condition to go out to protect the convoy from Havana but that the Comte d'Estaing, who had all his warships ready, could decide what to do about it.

29 January 1783

The Comedia was closed because of the many disorders and disturbances committed in it by the French.

I talked at length about the political situation with the Comte d'Estaing. He assured me that on the next day eight French warships, one of them a three-decker, would go out to pursue the English warship and frigate that were cruising off the port.

Córdova also ordered two warships and one frigate to go to find and escort the convoy expected from Havana. Don Antonio de Gálvez arranged for an Indies schooner that was matchless for its speed to serve them as a fly-boat.

30 January 1783

The eight French warships and four frigates set sail.

31 January 1783

The two Spanish warships prepared to sail but could not because the wind had changed.

A post for the Comte d'Estaing arrived. I went to see him, and he told me that things were still uncertain, that he had been ordered to be ready for the first notice but that he was not to depart until ordered to do it.

I asked him if it was true that two frigates were being made ready to go to the Indies, as had been rumored. He replied that it was true that two frigates were to sail the next day but that they were going in search of the eight warships, with an order for them to anchor in the Placer of Rota, where they would be able to embark the troop instantly.

1 February 1783

Zarate went out on a xebec with the official papers for the Indies, and I wrote to Don Bernardo de Gálvez, describing to him the present state of things.

2 February 1783

At seven o'clock in the morning a post arrived bringing an order for the governor dated 29 January, in which Muzquiz informed him that peace had been made. This prompted general rejoicing in the town. Don Antonio de Gálvez and I immediately arranged for the revenue cutter to be made ready, and he sent Ayala on it to take this important news to Guarico. Ayala left at nightfall.

3 February 1783

A post from Madrid arrived, but since it was dated 28 January and the news of the peace had come in the mail of the twenty-ninth, the letters said nothing at all about peace. I was in the house of the Comte d'Estaing and talked with him at length about various matters.

4 February 1783

An express messenger from the minister of the Indies arrived; it included an extract of the preliminary articles insofar as they pertained to Spain. Briefly stated, we were keeping Mahon and West Florida, they were ceding East Florida with San Agustín to us, and a certain district was being designated in which the English might cut logwood of Campeche.

The minister wrote to me that I should do whatever I wished but that he thought it would be best for me to go to Guarico with the preliminary articles of the peace treaty, and he would recommend me for the post of Intendant of Caracas, as we had planned in San Ildefonso. I replied to his letter saying that of course I should do so at once and that as soon as I received the preliminaries I should embark on the ship *San Miguel*, of the house of Ustariz, which was ready.

5 February 1783

The Conde de Reparaz informed me that his ship could not call at Guarico because it was insured for Havana and Veracruz. Then we thought of a good brigantine that had been captured recently. A mail-packet went out for Guarico.

6 February 1783

An express messenger went out for Buenos Aires.

7 February 1783

I wrote to Madrid. The mail-packet that had gone out bound for Guarico was forced to return.

8 February 1783

There were rumors that the mail-packet for Buenos Aires had been lost. A special courier came with duplicates of the official papers for Guarico.

9 February 1783

Nothing notable happened.

10 February 1783

There was a severe storm from the southwest.

11 February 1783

The weather moderated.

12 February 1783

The wind began again to blow fiercely from the west. I was in the house of the Comte d'Estaing but was unable to see him.

13 January 1783

I did not have a letter from Madrid. I devoted the day to making some preparations for the voyage to the Indies.

14 February 1783

I dined with the Comte d'Estaing; we talked about the Peace Treaty for a long time.[259]

15 February 1783

I continued my preparations for the voyage to the Indies. A post arrived from Guarico. The officer who carried it described to us the miserable condition in which our troops were found there, in need of flour, because the port was blockaded by the English; and the troops were being killed by illnesses, which had caused almost 2,000 men to perish. Don Bernardo de Gálvez was ill, too.

---

259. On 9 and 12 April 1783 Rendón reported to Luis Unzaga y Amezaga, who on 31 December 1782 had succeeded Cagigal as governor of Havana, the arrival at Philadelphia of the French cutter *Triomphe*, commanded by the Chevalier de Duquesne; it had been sent out from Cádiz on 14 February by d'Estaing and Lafayette with the news that the Preliminary Articles had been signed and with orders to all French privateers on the American coasts to end their cruises (Rendón to Luis Unzaga y Amezaga, 9, 12 April 1783, AGI:Cuba 1354). [Tr.]

Glossary

Acordada. An association formed in Mexico in 1710 to apprehend footpads; the jail in which these criminals were incarcerated.

Aguada. Water on board a ship.

Aguadero. Watering-port for ships.

Aguardiente. Brandy.

Alcalde mayor. The presiding officer of a governing council of a community; a magistrate.

Aliseos. Trade winds.

Arabia Felix. An ancient division of Arabia in the southern part, sometimes restricted to Yemen.

Armada. An organized squadron or fleet.

Arroba. (1) A Spanish weight of 11.5 kilos. (2) A Spanish measure containing 33 pints.

Asiento. An agreement of contract. The Asiento Company held the contract for introducing African slaves into Spanish-American ports.

Bagasse (French), *bagazo* (Spanish). The residue of sugarcane after it has been pressed.

Bajareque (Central America). Latticed with woven sticks.

Barrio. One of the districts or wards into which a large city is divided; a suburb.

Battery. Fortified works on which artillery is mounted.

Battleship. See *Ship-of-the-line.*

Belén, Belém, Bethlehem. Padres Belemitas, a religious order.

Bicho (Colombia). A general name for small grubs or insects; an illness, proctitis.

Brig. A two-masted armed vessel with brigantine rig.

Brigantine. A two-masted vessel with square sail.

Brisa (northeast coast of South America and in the Caribbean). An easterly or northeasterly trade wind.

Cable. A heavy rope used in anchoring or mooring. Also a measure of length: one cable's length is 100 fathoms, or 600 feet.

Cartel vessel. Also called flag-of-truce ship. A vessel that had an agreement for the exchange of prisoners. It carried a white flag identifying it as in communication with the enemy but not subject to capture.

Casa de Contratación. A Crown-appointed body that controlled the trade and commerce of the Indies, enforced regulations on navigation, and assessed duties.

Cassava. Any of several tropical plants of the genus manihot, cultivated for their tuberous roots, the source of tapioca.

Castillo. A castle or fort.

Chinampas (Mexico). A small plot where flowers and greenery are cultivated, a floating seedbed.

Close-hauled. Sailing close into the wind.

Cobre. Copper

Cochineal. A red dye prepared from the dried bodies of the females of a scale insect *Dactylopius coccus*, which lives on the cactuses of Mexico and Central America.

Corvette. French Navy ship of fewer than twenty-eight guns.

Criollo. One born in America or the West Indies of European parents.

Cruise. An expedition in quest of enemy vessels.

Corregidor. A Spanish magistrate, the mayor of a city.

Degredo (Venezuela). A pesthouse, a hospital for those who suffer from smallpox or other contagious diseases.

Ducado. Ducat, an ancient gold and silver coin.

Doctrinas. The Spanish colonial religious enterprise that involved the close relationship of a missionary or mission-

Glossary

aries, a native settlement, and training in doctrine, often aided by Spanish or native youth.

Draft. The depth of water drawn by a ship when laden.

Embrasure. Opening in an earthwork through which a cannon may be fired.

Fanega. A measure of grain and seed of about a hundred weight, or an English bushel.

Fascines. Long bundles of sticks of wood bound together, used in raising batteries.

Fathom. Six feet.

Filibusteros. Name given to freebooters or buccaneers who plundered America in the seventeenth century.

Fiscal. Attorney-general, a ministerial officer, who acts for the government by which he is appointed, and who ex officio represents the king or the people, a public prosecutor.

Flag-of-truce. A plain white flag identifying vessels in communication with the enemy but not subject to capture. Such ships were called cartel ships because of the customary cartels or agreements.

Flota. A fleet of merchant ships.

Foremast. The mast nearest the bow.

Frigate. A small warship next in size to a fourth-rate ship-of-the-line and usually carrying between twenty and forty guns on a single flush gundeck, and on both forecastle and quarterdeck, which were connected by gangways along the side.

Galera, galley. A vessel with oars, rigged as two-masted lateener, sloop, or schooner, and carrying one to twelve guns.

Guairo (Cuba and Venezuela). A small two-masted craft with triangular sails called guairas, used for coastal traffic. Guarito, a small guairo.

Gunboat. Small craft of one to four guns.

Gun-port. Opening on the side of a ship through which guns are directed.

Hacienda. Landed property, estate. Real Hacienda, exchequer, Royal Treasury, in Spanish America.

Jardin. Garden. Los Jardines, the Gardens.

Junta. A congress, an assembly, a council, or tribunal.

Launch, longboat. One of the largest of a ship's boats, used for transporting water and supplies.

Livre (French). Monetary unit of one pound, an old French unit divided into twenty sols (sous), about equal to the franc.

Logwood. The heartwood of an American tree, so-called because imported in logs; the dye or drug extracted from it.

Machete. Cutlass, cane knife, chopping knife.

Mainmast. The middle mast of a three-masted vessel.

Malagueta. Tabasco pepper.

Mizzenmast. The third or rear mast of a vessel.

Observant. A monk of certain branches of the order of St. Francis.

Oidor. One of the members or judges of a Spanish or Spanish-American audiencia.

Old Channel. Between the Archipelago of Camaguey, off the northern coast of Cuba, and the Great Bahama Bank.

Peso fuerte. The international weight, the Mexican silver peso of eight reales value.

Picarón. Great rogue, villain.

Placer. Sandbank.

Plaza. Used here to mean a fortified town, a stronghold.

Presidio. A garrison of soldiers, a fortress garrisoned by soldiers.

Pulque. Liquor prepared in America from the maguey or agave plant.

Quarterdeck. That part of the upper deck abaft the mainmast, reserved for the captain and other officers.

Quintal. A weight of 100 kilograms.

Glossary

Real. One silver real was worth two reales vellon.

Real vellon. A copper coin.

Redoubt. A small enclosed fieldwork used in fortifying tops of hills or the approaches to larger fortifications.

Regente Visitador. Regent, one invested with vicarious royalty. Visitador, one who makes a special ad hoc investigation into the governmental or ecclesiastical affairs of a Spanish or Spanish colonial jurisdiction, appointed by and reporting to a superior official.

Releje. Raised work in the chamber of a piece of ordnance where the powder is placed in order to use less of it.

Ría. The mouth of a river or stream.

Rigging. The shrouds, stays, braces, and other ropes supporting the masts of a ship.

Río. A river.

San Jaime, San Tiago. Two forms of the name Saint James.

Schooner. A small two-masted vessel.

Settee (English), *saetía* (Spanish). A decked vessel with a long, sharp prow, carrying two or three masts with lateen sails, i.e., triangular sails suspended by a long yard at an angle of about forty-five degrees to the mast.

Ship-of-the-line, battleship. Carried 60 to 140 guns on two or more completely armed decks, with armed forecastle and quarterdeck in the smaller and earlier ships.

Situado. An allowance or stipend for expenses of government.

Tack. To change the direction of a vessel in a contrary wind; to progress to windward in a zigzag direction.

Tafia (Venezuela). Inferior rum.

Te Deum. From the first words of the Latin "Te Deum laudamus," "Thee, God, we praise." An ancient Latin hymn sung as a Thanksgiving on special occasions.

Tercio (Cuba). A measure, approximately one quintal.

Tierra Firme. The northern coastal region of the continent of South America.

Toise (French). A unit of measure, approximately 1,949 metres.
Toseta. A field or fields where wheat has been reaped.
Trenching. Extending.
Triste. Sad.
Vara. A unit of measure, approximately one yard.
Vellon. See ***Real vellon.***
Wear ship. Change the course of a ship with the wind astern.
Weigh anchor. Hoist the ship's anchor.
Xebec (English), ***jabeque*** (Spanish). A small three-masted vessel in the Mediterranean and on the coasts of Portugal and Spain.
Yards. The horizontal spars on which the sails are hung.

Index

Abarca y Bolea, Pedro Pablo. *See* Aranda, Conde de
Academia de la Historia, xxi
Academia de San Carlos, 252n174
Académie de la Chirurgie, 337, 337n226
Academy of Ávila: inauguration of, xvii
Academy of Buenas Letras: and Saavedra, xii
Academy of Fine Arts (of Mexico), 253, 348
Academy of Marine Guards: and Saavedra, xiii
Accionario, 210
Acordada (of Mexico), 257, 257n184
Acosta, Don Ignacio, 121–22, 128, 130
Africa: and rum trade, 80; and slave trade, 38n42
Agriculture: and British methods, 66, 77, 71, 90–91; and cacao, 73; and climate, 88–89; and coffee, 75; and corn, 89; and cotton, 74, 89; of Cumaná, 25–26; and exhausted land, 73; and France, 90–91; and ginger, 74–75; and indigo, 73–74; in Jamaica, 59, 64, 68, 68n58, 69, 71–78, 87–88; methods of, 73; of Mexico, 261; and missions, 25; in the New World, 71–72; of Puerto Plata, 287, 289–90; and slaves, 68, 76, 309; and Spain, 90; in Spanish colonies, 259; and steam engines, 90; and sugar, 76, 78, 89–90; and Tabasco pepper, 75; and trade, 75; and water power, 89; and windmills, 90
Aguila, Conde de: friend of Saavedra, xv
Aguirre Aristegui Company of Cádiz: and slave trade, 38n42

Aigrette, 194, 209, 210, 212
Aimable, 325
Alabamas: Saavedra describes, 175, 176, 180, 185
Albuquerque, Duque de: and the *Acordada*, 257n184
Alcazaba: excavations of, xxi
Alderete, Don Miguel de: at Pensacola, 153, 225, 225n157
Alerte, 210, 212
Alexandre, 42n47
Algeciras, 354, 360
Algiers expedition: and Gálvez, Bernardo de, 98n68; and Saavedra, xvi–xxi
Alicante: and Saavedra, xv, xviii
Allspice. *See* Tabasco pepper
Allwood, Mr. (of Kingston): and contraband trade, 38, 38n42
Almodóvar (Spanish ambassador), 4n4
Alva Alonso, Lorenzo Hernández, 209
Alvarado, Pedro de: in Mexico, 246n172
Álvarez, Don Martín: inspector of militias, xxii; and Saavedra, 348, 348n236
Amazona, 221, 222
America, United States of: agriculture of, 72; climate of, 88; constitution of, 275; and Cuba, 107n80; and England, 51, 54, 54n52, 80–81; and English taxes, 92–93; and food exports, 106n80; forests of, 181; and the Navigation Act, 79
American Revolution: allied aid to, xxv, xxvii, xxviii, 3, 3n3, 5n7, 6n10, 7n11, 8n14, 9n16, 54n52, 98n68, 100n73, 101n76, 106, 194n136, 196, 196n137, 196n138, 198n140, 200–203, 206n147, 206n148, 212n151, 226n159, 323n206,

* xlv *

Index

332n210, 380n259; and Annapolis, 232n162; causes of, 50–51, 54, 54n52, 260; and Charlestown, 311n201; and Clinton, Sir Henry, 200n141, 306n200; and Cornwallis, 159, 159n113, 200, 200n141; and England, 3, 92–93, 159, 159n113; and Mexico, 241n166; and New York, 8n14, 172n122, 198n139, 198n140, 200n142, 201n145, 207n148, 215, 222, 226, 228, 232, 232n132, 306, 306n200; and Parker, Peter (admiral), 200n141; and repercussions of, 9n16, 54, 54n52, 259; and slave trade, 38n42

Americans: and the allies, 295, 317; on British ships, 132; in Havana, 106, 138, 225, 235, 274, 274n190; and Indians, 177, 184, 185; and Louisiana, 227; and St. Augustine 311n201; settlements of, 311n201

Amherst, Sir Jeffrey, 6n9

Andalucía, 360

Andalusia: Saavedra retires to, xxxii

Andaluz: and Pensacola expedition, 128

Andromaque, 101, 127, 134, 146, 147, 148, 150, 151, 152, 163, 193

Angel de la Guardia, 238

Angers, 331

Anglo-Spanish Struggle for Mosquitia, The. See Floyd, Troy S.

Angostura de Paz (Étroit de la Paix), 330

Angulo Iniguez, Diego: *Bautista Antonelli: Las Fortificaciones Americanas del Siglo XVI,* 131n96

Annapolis: and American forces, 232n162

Antigua, 30, 44, 264, 306

Antigua River, 243

Antilles, 75

Antonelli, Bautista: and the Morro, 131, 131n96

Antonioti, Don Antonio: and Guatemala, 121; in Jamaica, 39

Apa, 246, 260

Apaches: and Gálvez, Bernardo de, 98n68

Apalache River, 150

Aranda, Conde de, Pedro Pablo Abarca y Bolea (Spanish ambassador to France): and allied operations, 332, 334, 338, 343; and the American Revolution, xxvii, 54n52, 206, 206n147, 332n208; masquerades of, xiv; police force of, xiv; and Saavedra, 333, 335, 338; and Versailles junta, 337

Aranda de Duero, 341

Aranjuez, xxix, 11

Araya, 24

Arbuthnot, Marriot (admiral), 201n145, 205n148

Architecture: in Mexico, 262–63

Archivo de Indias de Seville, xxxiv

Archivo General de Indias, xxviii, xxviiin12, 4n5

Ardent, 19n26, 321, 322, 323

Areo River, 25

Army of Operations (Havana): and Navia, Victor de, 99, 99n70

Arriaga, Don Julín de, xxi

Arrinconada, 264

Arrogante: and Pensacola expedition, 145

Arron, Comte d', 339

Articles of Capitulation: and Providence expedition, 234n164

Artillery: condition of the allies', 294, 316, 318

Artillery Drill School. *See* Escuela Práctica de Artillería

Artois, Comte d', Charles Philippe (later Charles X), 345, 346, 347, 348

Asia: and Spanish silver, 252

Asiatic goods: and contraband trade, 85

Asiento de Negros, 84

Asís, 147, 224, 228, 229, 230, 232, 233, 239, 277, 278, 280, 281, 306, 313. *See also* San Francisco de Asís

Astre, 324, 325, 326

Astuto: and Pensacola expedition, 145

Atlantic Ocean: and canal to the Pacific, 39, 39n45, 43,

Auguste, 204

Aux, 377

Index

Ayala (lieutenant of the Regiment of Spain), 374, 377, 378
La Ayuda Cubana en la Lucha por la Independencia Norteamericana. See Tejera, Eduardo J.
Ayusa, Don Juan de, 39
Azores, 19, 48, 112

Bahama Channel: and shipping routes, 37, 129, 130, 193, 209, 212, 274, 282, 289, 306, 312
Bahamas: and Cagigal, Juan Manuel de, 100n72; and Providence expedition, 234n164
Bajareque: and construction in Cumaná, 28, 28n37
Balboa, Vasco Núñez de: and lawyers in the New World, 27n34
Balch, Thomas: *The French in America during the War of Independence of the United States, 1777–1781,* 226n159
Balmis, Francisco Javier: and smallpox vaccination, 19n27
Baltic, 119n88
Baltic Sea: and the British fleet, 353
Baltimore: and Rochambeau, Comte de, 350n239
Banks of Amortization (of Spain): created by Saavedra, xxxii
Banks of Newfoundland, 328
Baracoa, 31, 192, 210, 228, 303
Barbados: and agriculture, 75; and allied plans, 202; and hurricanes, 30; and Rodney's fleet, 308
Barcelona: district of Cumaná, 25, 26; and Saavedra's regiment, xvi
Barcelona Company: in Cumaná, 26, 26n33
Barea, 346
Barnett: and Jamaican agriculture, 59
Barrancas Coloradas. See Red Cliffs
Barras, M. de, Jacques Melchior, Comte de Barras Saint Laurent: and flag-of-truce ships, 302; French fleet of, 226; joins de Grasse, 232n162; mentioned, 303
Barrera (captain of the Regiment of Aragón), 302

Barrutia, Don Juan Antonio, 294, 296, 317
Batabanó, 95, 97–98, 214, 219, 278
Baton Rouge: captured by Bernardo de Gálvez, xxviii, 98n68
Battery of the Apostles, 60, 61, 63
Battle of Pensacola: agreement to spare the city, 158–59; and British hostages from, 279, 279n192; British surrender in, 171–73, 191; maneuvers of, 156–71; spoils from, 173–74. See also Pensacola expedition
Battle of Pensacola, The. See Rush, N. Orwin
Battle of the Saintes: and allied defeat, 319–24, 325, 335; and de Grasse, 198n139, 319–23; and Rodney, 198n139
Battle of Ushant: and the American Revolution, 3n3, 193n132; and de Vaudreuil, 320n205
Battery of Ulysses: destruction of, 356
Bautista Antonelli: Las Fortificaciones Americanas del Siglo XVI. See Angulo Iniguez, Diego
Bay of Brest, 331
Bay of Cienfuegos, 96n66. See also Bay of Jagua
Bay of Jagua, 22, 95, 96. See also Bay of Cienfuegos
Bayonne, 340
Belamites: in Havana, 104. See also Padres Belemitas
Bellecombe (governor of French Cape): and allied strategy, 323; and conduct of the French forces, 297; and Jamaica expedition, 207n148, 302, 310, 313, 325, 372, 373; and Spanish aid, 291, 292
Berbeo y Galán (leader of rebellion in New Granada), 213n152
Bermuda, 125, 132, 222
Bernardo de Gálvez in Louisianna, 1776–1783. See Caughey, John Walton
Bernal, Jacob, 45
Berry, Edward: and an Atlantic-Pacific canal, 43; role in Jamaica, xxx, 42, 42n47

* xlvii *

Index

Bertucar, 209, 306
Betancurt, Pedro de: and Padres Belemitas, 245n171
Bilbao: and roads, 340
Biron, Duc de, 336
Black River Bay, 58
Blackstone, Sir William: *Commentaries on the Laws of England*, 50
Blackwater River, 120n88
Bland, Theodorick: and capitulation of Pensacola, 172n122; and the Chesapeake Bay expedition, 232n162
Bluefields Bay, 61
Boatner, Mark Mayo, III: *Encyclopedia of the American Revolution*, 159n113
Bocas de los Dragos, 23
Boiderant, M. de (naval captain): and Pensacola expedition, 155, 164
Bolois, 217
Bonavía, Don Bernardo: and Battle of the Saintes, 323; and East Florida expedition, 310–11n201; in French Cape, 209; and Martinique, 223; mentioned, 314
Bonet, Don Juan Bautista: commodore of combined fleet, 134; condition of, 364; naval commandant at Havana, 99, 99n71, 112, 113–14, 117, 121–22, 133, 143; reassignment of, 191, 192; Saavedra visits, 365
Bonsal, Stephen: *When the French Were Here*, 213n151, 225n158
Bordeaux, 296, 339
Bordeaux wine: and contraband trade, 366
Borja Medina, Francisco de: *José de Ezpeleta, Gobernador de la Movila, 1780–1781*, 7n13
Boston, 196n137, 216n153, 271, 295, 350n239, 376n258
Bougainville, Louis Antoine de: and Battle of the Saintes, 323, 335n217
Bouillé, Marquis de, François-Claude Amour: and East Florida expedition, 310–11n210; French forces of, 314, 315; and Jamaica expedition, 207n148, 223, 233, 294–95; role in West Indies, 221n154; mentioned, 299, 345
Bouligni, M. de: and Battle of Pensacola, 159
Bourbon, Duc de, Louis-Joseph, 347, 347n235, 348
Bourbon, Duc de, prince of Condé, 188n130
Bourbon, House of, xxvi, 5n7, 6n10, 347
Bourbon reforms (in Spain), 9n15
Bourgogne, 210
Brazil, 6n8
Bread: monopoly of, 345
Brest: and West Indies shipping, xxvii, 5, 13, 100n75, 123, 126, 132, 193n132, 292–93, 295, 296, 298, 301, 306, 308, 310, 314, 328, 330, 331, 337n227, 369, 370
Brigantium, 16. See also La Coruña
Britain. See England
British. See English
Brizzio, Don Pedro, 39, 42, 228
Bucareli, Marqués de, Antonio María: and New Spain, 241n166
Bucareli y Ursúa, Francisco de Paula (governor of Buenos Aires), xiii, xiiin5
Buccaneers: and Jamaica, 67, 76. See also Corsairs; Pirates; Privateers
Buenos Aires, 17, 18, 355, 379
Burgos, 341
Burke, Barry (of Kingston), 49, 94
Byrd, Captain: and Battle of Pensacola, 171n119

Cacao, 25, 64, 73. See also Cocoa
Cádiz, xii–xiii, xxiii, xxvi, 17, 18, 286, 100n72, 101n75, 104, 108, 112, 243n175, 272, 302, 305, 337n227, 349, 352, 352n241, 362, 366, 367, 368, 369, 375, 377, 380n259
Cagigal, Don Juan Manuel de: and West Indies campaigns, xxxi, 100, 100n72, 144, 153, 155, 155n109, 157, 167, 172n122, 191, 215n153, 232n162, 234n164, 273, 275, 275n191, 276, 307, 312, 380n259
Caicos, 31, 33, 129, 138, 194, 284, 302, 325, 326
Calderón de la Barca, Madame: and

Index

Mexico, 243n169
California, 8n14, 256n182
Calvo de Irazabal, Don José : and Pensacola expedition, 141-43, 225, 225n157
Camayagua: and Juan Nepumuceno de Quesada, 366, 372
Cambiaso, Don Juan (colonel of the Regiment of the Crown), 267-68
Campbell, James (English captain): and Battle of Pensacola, 279, 279n192
Campbell, John (English general): and Battle of Pensacola, xxxii, xxxv, xxxvi, 156, 156n11, 170, 171-73, 211n150, 279n192
Campeche, 76, 84, 107, 238, 378
Campo, Bernardo del, 343, 343n231, 347, 355
Campomanes, Conde de, Pedro Rodriguez, xxii
Camus, M. (captain of the *Alexandre*), 42n47
Canada: and Indian territory, 176
Canaries-Indies route, 22n28
Canarros, 95
Canary Islands, xxix, 17, 18, 19, 19n27, 90, 287, 287n193
Cándido, Pepe, xii, xiin4
Caño de Trocadero, 364-65
Cantofer (Madrid businessman): and Company of the Philippines, xxv
Cape Antonio, xxxi, 128, 129, 238
Cape Corrientes, 129, 133, 149, 219, 272, 276
Cape Finisterre, 12, 13, 17, 79
Cape Isabela, 285
Cape of Santa Maria, xxvii
Cape San Antonio, 6, 19n26, 101, 117, 129, 130, 133, 144, 216, 218, 276
Cape Vincent, 6n9
Cap Haitien. See French Cape; Guarico
Capuchins, 31, 196
Caracas, 19n27, 25, 26, 26n33, 27, 28, 30, 223, 310, 321, 355, 374, 374n253, 379
Caracas Company, The. See Hussey, R.
Cárdenas, Don Alfonso de, 121-22

Cardinales de Dos Independencias. See Solano, Francisco de
Caribbean Islands, 76
Caribs: in Cumaná, 29
Carmen, 151
Caro García, Don Bernardo: and Spain's maritime mail service, 12
Carrión y Andrade, José (governor of Mexico), 240, 264, 266
Cartagena, xv, 213, 215, 218, 219, 224, 233, 272, 278, 312
Cartas, Don José de: prisoner of the English, 31, 38, 42, 94
Carupano, port of, 23
Casa de la Contratación (House of Trade), 370, 370n252
Casa de la Moneda (Mexican mint), 251-52
Casamayor (official of Cartagena): and rebellion in Cartagena, 233
Casas, Don Luis de las, 292
Casa Tócame-Roque, xiii, xiiin6
Cassava, 76-77, 95
Castejón, Don Pedro. See González de Castejón, Don Pedro
Castillas, Marqués de, 371
Castillo de Araya, 29
Castillo del Príncipe, 230
Castillo de Rockfort, 61
Castillo de San Juan de Nicaragua, 39, 40-41, 101, 121, 140
Castillo de San Juan de Ulúa, 240, 242, 242n167, 266, 267
Castillo Viejo, 39n44
Castle Marlborough, 292
Castor and Pollux, 338
Castries, Duc de, Charles Eugene-Gabriel de la Croix (French minister of marine), 332, 332n209, 333, 334, 335, 338, 344
Castrillo, Conde, 334
Castro, Don Ramón de (lieutenant of the Regiment of the Prince), 120
Catalonia, xvi, xxiv
Catalonian Company. See Barcelona Company
Catalonian wine: and contraband trade, 366
Caton, 325

Index

Caughey, John Walton: *Bernardo de Gálvez in Louisiana, 1776–1783,* xxxiv–xxxvi, 32n40
Caulican, 134
Caura River: and Gualiquirie Indians, 27n35
Cavallos, Don Pedro de, xxiii
Cavo, Andrés: *Tres Siglos de Mexico,* 241n166
Cazador, 281, 282
Cecilia, 113, 127, 272, 280
Central Junta: and French invasion of Seville, xxxii
Cérès, 18, 324, 325
Cerf, 135
César, 321, 322, 323
Ceuta, xxxii
Chacón, José María, 365, 365n250, 369
Chambequín, 119
Champs de Mars (of Paris), 336, 336n222
Chapultepec: gunpowder factory of, 254
Charcas (province of Peru): rebellion in, 278
Charles, prince of Asturias (son of Charles III), 342, 342n230
Charles I (king of Spain and Emperor Charles V of the Holy Roman Empire): and Atlantic-Pacific canal, 29, 39, 39n45
Charles Phillipe, Comte d'Artois (Louis XVI's brother), 335, 335n218
Charles III (king of Spain): and Spain's joining France against England, xvii, xxiv, xxv, xxvi, 4n4, 6n10, 9n17, 311n201, 342, 344n232, 346n234, 349n238, 353, 354
Charlestown, 200n141, 215, 274n190, 291, 306n200, 311n201, 323n206
Charon, 232
Chatellerault, 338
Chesapeake expedition, 194n136, 200, 201, 201n142, 201n146, 212n151, 221n154, 226, 227, 232n162, 275, 308, 350n239
Chester, Peter (governor of West Florida): and English surrender of Pensacola, xxxi, 158–59

Chickasaws, 185
Chihuahua, 256n182
Childers, 119n88, 144n101
China: and trade, 220, 253
Choctaws, 175, 176, 180, 185
Cholera, 348
Cigars, factory for, 258–59
Cimarrones. *See* Maroons
Cirilo, Father (vicar of troops of Louisiana), 154
Citoyen, 210
Clara, 113, 127, 216, 221, 272
Climate, West Indian: and agriculture, 88–89; effect of, 47, 62, 63, 104, 177, 180, 300, 301, 307, 313, 318, 380; of Jamaica, 54, 56, 66; and shipping, 193, 283–84, 377, 379; mentioned, 166, 243, 244, 276, 277, 278, 279–81, 287
Clinton, Sir Henry (English general): in America, xxxvi, 45n50, 156n111, 200n141, 201n142, 306, 306n200
Coahuila, 256n182
Cobarrubias: accompanies Saavedra in Mexico, 260–64
Coche, 27
Cochineal: trade of, 265
Cocoa: and trade, 79. *See also* Cacao
Coffee: in Jamaica, 25, 54, 75, 77, 79, 89
Cognai, port of, 64, 65, 69
Coker, William S. and Hazel P.: *The Siege of Pensacola 1781 in Maps,* 143n100, 154n105
Colbert, Jean Baptiste: and French navy, 187, 187n127
Colegio de Sacromonte, x
Colegio de Santo Tomás, xi
Colegio de Tlaltecolo, 256n181
Colombia, 22n29, 213n152. *See also* New Granada
Colón, 19n26
Colonia del Sacramento, xxiii
Columbus, Christopher, 23n31, 24–25, 25n32, 59, 64, 64n55, 97n67
Columbus, Don Diego (admiral): and settlement of Jamaica, 64
Comédie Française: Saavedra visits, 334, 334n214

* 1 *

Index

Commentaries on the Laws of England. See Blackstone, Sir William
Commerce, 72, 78–86, 203, 366, 370n252. *See also* Trade
Compañía de la Mar del Sur: and the slave trade, 68n57
Compañía de Negros de la Havana, 38
Company of the Philippines, xxv
Comuneros del Socorro, 213n152
Concha, Don Fernando de la, 373
Concorde, 196, 196n137
Condé, Don Francisco, 261
Condé, prince de, 347, 347n235
Conquistadors: of Florida, 158
Constanzó, Miguel, 254, 254n178
Continental Congress: and the allies, 3n2, 4n5, 5n6, 105n80, 172n122, 217n153, 232n162, 274n190
Contraband trade: in Cumaná, 25; and England, 92; and the French, 366, 367; and Havana, 115; and Jamaica, 38n42, 83–86, 92; and Jews, 45; and Miranda, Francisco de, 216n153; and Pensacola, 174; of Spain, 83–86; mentioned, 23, 68. *See also* Trade
Convention of Aranjuez: Spain and France become allied against England, 5n6
Convent of San Francisco, 256
Convict labor, 265
Copper: mines, 263–64; on ships, 197–98, 322, 364
Córdova, Don Luis de, 19, 19n26, 48, 370, 371, 376, 377
Corn: in Jamaica, 76–77, 89; taxes on, 248
Cornwall (county in Jamaica), 71
Cornwallis, Charles, 1st Marquis Cornwallis: in America, 45n50, 159, 159n113, 200, 200n141, 200n142, 226, 227, 232, 232n162, 306n200, 311n201
Coronne, 321
Corral, Don Antonio de (of Veracruz), 266–67
Corral, Miguel de, 242, 242n168
Corres (of Mexico): and the state of New Spain, 255
Corsairs, 46–47, 94, 299, 308. *See also* Buccaneers; Pirates

Cortez, Hernán, 243, 246n172, 256
Cossío, Don Joaquin: and grain trade, 262
Cossío, Pedro Antonio (intendant of New Spain), 240, 241n166, 247, 249–50, 258, 262, 266
Cossío Company: and grain trade, 262
Cotton: in Jamaica, 25, 54, 64, 74, 77, 89
Council of General Officers. *See* Junta de Generales
Courageuse, 227, 228, 230, 231, 234, 266
Crame, Don Augustín, xxviii
Crasches. *See* Creeks
Creeks: Saavedra describes, 168, 175, 176, 180, 181, 185
Crespo (Spanish officer), 349
Crillon, Louis des Balbes de Berton de, Duc de Mahon: and Gibraltar, 356, 356n243, 362
Criollos: character of, 259; of Cumaná, 25
Crocodiles, 97
Croix, Marqués Carlos Francisco de, xiii, xiiin5, 256n182
Croix, Teodoro de: in New Mexico, 256n181
Cross in the Sand, The. See Gannon, Michael V.
Cruillas, Marqués de, Joaquin Montserrat, 356, 356n245
Cuba: and corsairs, 46, 299–300; development of, xxiv; and the flota, 107; map of, 102–3; and trade, 76, 84, 106n80, 107n80, 129, 309; and transportation, 96–97; and West Indies campaigns, xxix, 95, 100n72, 134, 313; mentioned, xxx, 17, 22, 36, 49, 56, 65, 72, 94, 132, 135, 138, 271, 276. *See also* Havana
Cubagua, 27
Cubano, El, 366, 372
Cumaná: agriculture of, 24–25; commerce of, 25–27; defenses of, 29–30; earthquakes in, 28; Saavedra describes, 24–30; and smallpox, 28; mentioned, xxix, 23, 31
Cunningham, Mr. (English officer), 35, 36

* li *

Index

Customhouses: and trade, 367
Cyril, Father (vicario over West Florida), 154n107

Daban, Juan (governor of Havana), 234n164
Dalling, John (governor of Jamaica), xxx, 38, 39n43, 42, 45n50, 283
Dalrymple, John (colonel): and the capture of Omoa, 48–49
Danish ships: in French Cape, 308; and slave trade, 309, 310–12; mentioned, 296
Darro River, xxiii
Dauphin, French: birth of, 299, 299n197
Dauphin Island: and British attack on Mobile, 120
Deans, Robert (captain): as hostage, 279, 279n192; and Mobile, 119, 119n88
Decision at Chesapeake. See Larrabee, Harold
Dejabon, 292
Derby (British admiral), 6n9
Descripción de las Indias Occidentales. Historia General de los Hechos de los Castellanos en las Islas y Tierra Firme del Mar Océano. See Herrera y Tordesillas, Antonio de
Destin, 101, 134, 192, 193
Destouches, Chevalier (of the French fleet), 196n138
Devis, Don Nicosás: and gunpowder, 263
Diana, xxix, xxx, 12, 17, 18, 23, 31, 33–35, 36, 38
Diary of Francisco de Miranda, The, Tour of the United States, 1783–1784. See Robertson, William Spence
Dichoso, 313
Digby, Robert (admiral): and Graves, Admiral Thomas, 201, 201n146
Dillon Regiment, 319
Diseases: of Europeans in West Indies, 62, 63, 104, 301, 380. See also Climate, West Indian: effect of

Doctrinas (missionary parishes): and agriculture, 25
Domás, Don José: and *Asís*, 230–31; and cochineal, 265; and Saavedra's Veracruz mission, 234
Domenec (mail-packet captain), 286, 298
Dominica: and Bouillé, Marquis de, 221n154; French capture of, xxv
Doniol, Henri: *Histoire de la participation de la France a l'établissement des Etats-Unis d'Amérique*, 208n149
Dragon, 220, 266, 272
Dragons' Mouths. See Bocas de los Dragos
"Drawbacks": and Britain's trade policies, 81
Duc de Bourgogne: and Battle of the Saintes, 321
Dudley (British general), 66
Dull, Johnathan R.: *The French Navy and American Independence*, 207n148
Duquesne, Chevalier de: and the *Triomphe*, 380n259
Dutch, 75, 226

Earthquakes: and construction techniques, 28; in Cumaná, 28; in Jamaica, 58, 70; in Puerto Real, 60
East Florida: and conditions of peace, 378; proposed invasion of, 310–12, 310n201; and Quesada, Juan Nepumuceno de, 356n244. See also West Indies campaigns
East Indies, 26, 35
Ebro River, xvi
Echevarría y Elguzúa, Santiago José (bishop): and Santiago de Cuba, 101, 101n77; and West Florida, 154n107
École Militaire (of France), 336, 336n222
École Supérieure de Guerre. See École Militaire
Église de Sainte Geneviève, 336, 336n224
Eighteenth-Century Florida and the Caribbean. See Sheridan, Richard B.

* lii *

Index

El bicho: New World disease, 24
El Escoral, 105, 105n78
El Ferrol, xxvi, 12, 13, 15, 357
Elizabeth (sister of Louis XVI): Saavedra meets, 335, 335n218
Encyclopedia of the American Revolution. See Boatner, Mark Mayo, III
Engageante: and Battle of the Saintes, 319, 320
England: agricultural methods of, 71, 73, 77, 90–91; and American colonies, xvii, 3, 51, 54, 54n52, 92–93, 159, 159n113; and Atlantic-Pacific link, 39; capture of Port Mahon, 313, 313n202; colonial policies of, 68, 69, 72–73, 75, 76, 78–79, 80–83, 85, 86, 92, 174, 260; government of, 51, 65, 72, 74, 82, 92–93, 200; and Indians, 175, 177, 257; and Jamaica, xxvi, 65, 66, 67–68, 76, 129, 200, 233; and Jews, 45; and Lake Nicaragua expedition, 39, 39n44, 40, 42–43, 62, 107; maritime supremacy of, 4, 5n7, 6n10, 295, 314, 315, 316–17, 325; navy of, 85, 119n88, 186, 187, 189, 190, 191; and Peace of Utrecht, 38n42; and Pensacola, xxxi, 116, 119, 142, 144n101, 153–73, 174; people of, 50, 251; privateers of, 122; and war with the allies, xxvi, 3n3, 4–5, 31, 118–20, 203, 276, 285, 286, 293, 296, 307, 308, 310, 314, 319–23, 324, 325, 330, 337n227, 351, 352, 353, 356, 357, 357n246, 358, 360, 361, 361n247, 362, 370, 371, 375–76, 378, 379, 380; and war with Holland, 132, 319n204
English Channel, 129, 365
Enríquez, Aaron, 44–45
Ensenada, Marqués de la, Zenon de Somodevilla: and reform in Spain, xxv
Enterprise of Florida, The. See Lyon, Eugene
Enumerated products: and Britain's trade, 79
Escuela Prática de Artillería (Artillery Drill School): of Veracruz, 243, 268

España Regiment: and Battle of Pensacola, 144, 170n118
Espelius, Don José: and the Guadalquivir River, xiv
Esquivel, Juan de: and Jamaican settlement, 64
Essai Général de Tactique. See Guibert, Comte Jacques Antoine Hippolyte de
Estaing, Comte Jean Baptiste Charles Henri Hector d': and the American Revolution, 198n140; in Madrid, 363; and the peace, 380, 380n259; role in the allies' West Indies operations, 198, 198n140, 364, 364n249, 365, 367, 368–69, 370, 371, 372, 373, 374, 375, 375n256, 376, 376n258, 377, 378, 380; and Vaudreuil, Marquis de, 320n205; and Versailles junta, 337n227
Estrada (of French Cape): and supplies from Santiago de Cuba, 294
Etroit de la Paix. See Angostura de Paz
Europa Point: and the *San Miguel*, 360
Europe: merchandise from, 220; and Spanish silver, 252, 253
Europeans: attitude toward New World natives, 259–60; and disease, 62, 234; and Indians, 176, 184, 185; and West Indies' climate, 63, 104
Expérimenté, 319
Ezpeleta, Don José de (colonel of the Regiment of Navarra): career of, 118n85; and Mobile, 118–19; and Pensacola expedition, 127n93, 141n97, 143, 143n100, 154n106, 155, 167n116, 169n118, 171, 171n121; and West Indies operations, 295

Fabian y Tuero (bishop of Puebla), 262, 262n186
Falkland Islands. See Malvinas Islands
Family Pact: and the French and Spanish navies, 101n76, 188n129
Faro, 349

Index

Ferdinand VI (king of Spain): and Sitios Reales, 346n234
Fernán Núñez, Conde de (Spanish ambassador to Portugal), xiv, xvi, xxiii–xxiv, xxv,
Fersain (engineer in Veracruz), 268, 268n188
Figuerola, Don Pablo: and Pensacola expedition, 165, 166
Filibusteros: and French Cape, 195; and Puerto Plata, 287
Fixed Regiment of New Orleans, xxii
Flag-of-truce ships, 118, 215, 222, 273, 275, 296, 298, 298n196, 302, 303, 305, 306, 308, 309
Fleury, André, Cardinal de Fleury: and the French Navy, 188, 188n129
Flores, Don Juan de: and the Alcazaba excavation, xxi
Florida, 5n6, 158, 176, 185, 344n232. *See also* East Florida; Pensacola; West Florida
Floridablanca, Conde de, José Moniño y Redondo: and the American Revolution, 4n4, 9n16, 332n210; and Gálvez, Bernardo de, 344, 344n232; role of, xxiv, 4n4, 9n16; and Saavedra, xxix, 341, 342, 344, 345, 346, 347, 351, 354–55, 358, 362; mentioned, 334
Florida Keys. *See* Northern Keys
Flories, Manuel Antonio: and New Granada, 213n152
Flota (New Spain), 105n79, 107, 108,
Flour, 85, 138, 290, 266, 380
Floyd, Troy S.: *The Anglo-Spanish Struggle for Mosquitia*, 49n51
Foi, 199
Foreign Interest in the Independence of New Spain. See Rydjord, John
Fort Augusta (Jamaica), 37, 60, 61, 63
Fort Charles (Jamaica), 59, 60, 61, 63
Fort Deanes (Pensacola), 155
Fort George (Pensacola), 117n84, 157, 158, 159, 161, 162, 164, 171, 172, 174,
Fort Half Moon (Pensacola), xxxi, 155, 156, 157, 158, 161, 162, 164, 166, 168, 169, 170–71, 173

Fort Panmure (Natchez), 211n150
Fourteenth Regiment: in Jamaica, 314
4th Act of George III, 81
Fox, 300
France: and allied operations against the English, xxiii, xxvi, xxix, 3, 3n2, 3n3, 4, 5, 5n6, 5n7, 6n8, 6n10, 7n11, 8n14, 10n18, 11, 12, 13, 17, 18, 19, 19n26, 31, 32, 100–101, 107n80, 108, 112, 122, 125–26, 130, 132, 134, 135, 139, 140, 144–53, 154–55, 167, 169, 192n132, 193, 194n136, 196, 196n137, 196n138, 197, 198n139, 198n140, 200–203, 206, 207n148, 209–210, 215, 221n154, 226, 227–28, 233, 286, 287–88, 292–93, 296, 300–301, 303, 306, 307, 308, 310–12, 313, 314, 315, 316, 319–24, 325, 342, 350, 350n239, 364, 364n249, 365, 373, 374, 375, 375n256, 376–77; colonies of, 83, 85, 122, 198n139, 200, 226–27, 318; and corsairs, 299; court of, 203, 205, 206, 332; and Gibraltar, 352, 352n241, 361–62; and Gillon, Alexander, 274n190; navy of, 186–91, 197, 198n140, 310, 314, 315, 332n209, 364, 365; and peace, 370, 371, 375–76, 377, 378, 379, 380, 380n259; privateers of, 380n259; relations with Spain, xxxii, 101n76, 340; Spanish aid to, 107n80, 205, 206, 211, 212, 212n151, 221–23, 297–98, 314, 316; and trade, 83, 85, 122, 226–27, 366, 367; treasury of, 208; troops of, and Spanish troops, 123, 288, 297, 298, 304–5, 356
Franciscans: in New Spain, 256, 256n181
Fredericka, Czarina, 333n212. *See also* Nord, Duchesse du
Free trade, 8n14, 13, 13n20, 78–79, 81, 84, 248, 262, 309, 345. *See also* Trade
French Cape: allied troops in, 304; defense of, 195, 202, 203, 212, 214, 217–18, 227–28, 229, 230, 235, 273; governors of, 198–99; Saavedra describes, 194–96; Spanish aid to, 193,

* liv *

Index

204–5, 207, 287, 292, 293, 297–98; theater of, 195; treasury of, 205; weather of, 308; and West Indies campaigns, 101n75, 112, 122, 194n136, 203, 207n148, 232–33, 286, 288–89, 290–91, 292, 298, 306, 309, 311n201, 325, 338, 369; mentioned, 209, 350, 353, 354, 372. *See also* Guarico

French Cays, 215, 229

French in America during the War of Independence of the United States, 1777–1781, The. See Balch, Thomas

French Navy and American Independence, The. See Dull, Johnathan

Gage, Thomas (English general), 306n200
Galera (Point), 23
Galgo, 303
Galicia, 14, 256n181, 351
Gallardo, 192
Gálvez, Antonio de (uncle of Bernardo de Gálvez), 363–64, 368, 370, 371, 372, 373, 374, 375, 377, 378
Gálvez, Don Bernardo de (commandant of Army of Operations): and the Algiers expedition, xx, 98n68; career of, xxii, xxiii, xxviii, 7, 7n11, 98n68, 191, 228, 344n232; illness of, 380; and Louisiana, xxii, xxviii, 98n68, 186, 226–27, 344, 344n232; and Mobile, 7n13, 119; and New Granada, 213n152; and peace, 370; and Pensacola expedition, xxx, xxxi, xxxiv–xxxvi, 7n13, 99n71, 100, 100n72, 113n82, 116–17, 119n88, 123, 123n90, 124–25, 126, 127n93, 141–43, 151–52, 153, 154, 154n106, 155, 155n109, 158–59, 168, 171n121, 172n122, 186, 211n150, 225n157; and the rebellion in Peru, 279; and Saavedra, xxi, 10n18, 98–99; and trade, 312; and West Indies campaigns, 207n148, 211, 212, 212n151, 213, 215, 216, 218, 219, 223, 224, 225, 227–29, 230, 231, 232–33, 234n164, 247, 257, 272, 273, 275, 277, 278, 280–81, 289, 291, 292, 293, 294–98, 299, 300, 301, 302, 303, 305, 306–8, 310–12, 313, 314, 316–17, 324, 325; mentioned, 5n6, 118, 192, 216n153, 235, 268, 276, 322, 343, 345, 349, 353, 357, 369, 372, 378

Gálvez, Don José de (uncle of Bernardo de Gálvez): career of, xxii–xxiii, xxiv, 8, 8n14, 98n68, 249, 249n173, 349n238; and peace, 378; as Saavedra's mentor, xi, xxi, xxii, xxiv, xxvii, xxviii–xxix, xxxiv, 4n5, 8, 8n14, 9n17, 192, 341, 344, 378–79; and West Indies campaigns, 117–18, 125, 125n92, 206, 233, 310–11, 342, 343, 344, 345, 346, 348, 351, 352, 354–55, 362, 373, 376; mentioned, 241n166, 333, 334, 337, 338, 364

Gálvez, Don Lucas (friend of Saavedra), 291

Gálvez, Don Matías de (father of Bernardo de Gálvez), xxiii, xxiv, 11n19, 98n68, 241n166, 253n176

Gálvez, Don Miguel (uncle of Bernardo de Gálvez), xxii–xxiii, xxiv, 224, 224n155, 346, 346n233, 353, 354, 358

Gálveztown, xxxi, xxxv, 142, 142n99, 225n157, 281

Gannon, Michael V.: *The Cross in the Sand*, 101n77

García, Don Ignacio, 24

García Panes, Diego, 242n167

Garden of the Queen: and Columbus, 97n67

Genoa, 17

George III (king of England), xvii, 4n4, 55n53, 81, 323n206

Georgia, 159, 159n113, 171, 173, 185, 311n201

Germans: at Pensacola, 161, 168, 169, 173

Gibraltar: and allied operations against England, xxiin10, 4n4, 5n6, 5n7, 6, 6n8, 6n9, 100n72, 342, 344, 343, 348, 350–51, 352, 352n241, 354, 355–56, 357, 357n246, 358, 359, 360, 361, 362, 365, 371, 372, 374n254

* lv *

Index

Gil, Don Gerónimo (of Mexico): and Academy of Fine Arts, 253, 348
Gil, 216. See also San Gil
Gillon, Alexander, 274n190, 275, 275n191
Ginger, 74–75, 77,
Girón, Don Geronimo: and Pensacola expedition, 144, 155, 155n109, 157, 162, 169, 170n118, 171
Glorieux, 320, 321, 322, 323
Goats, 77
Gold, 83, 254
Golfo Triste, 23
González, Manuel (lieutenant of the Regiment of Spain), 7n12, 17, 24, 35
González (Spanish prisoner in Jamaica), 38, 42, 94
González de Castejón, Don Pedro (Spanish minister of the navy), 17, 17n23, 225, 342, 348
Gotier: and Spanish ship design, 239
Gottschalk, Louis: *Lafayette and the Close of the American Revolution*, 337n227
Grains, 79, 248. See also Wheat
Granada, xi, xv, xxiii, xxv, xxxiii, 90
Granja, La. See Monte Christi
Grasse, Comte François Joseph Paul de, Marquis de Grasse-Tilly: and Chesapeake expedition, 194n136, 196–97, 205–6, 207n148, 212n151, 221n154, 225–26, 227, 232n162, 275; and de Grasse–Saavedra agreement, 206, 207, 207n148, 212, 225, 227–28, 229, 235, 272, 273, 311n201; and West Indies campaigns, 192, 192n132, 197, 199–203, 204, 205, 206, 206n148, 207n148, 208, 208n149, 211, 212, 212n151, 221–23, 230, 232–33, 278, 286, 294–95, 298, 298n196, 307, 308, 314, 315, 319–23, 332, 333; mentioned, 173n122, 210, 299, 310
Graves, Thomas (English admiral), 196n138, 201, 201n145, 226
Great Inagua, 326
Green, Mr. (citizen of Kingston), 50
Greene, Nathaniel, 159n113

Grenada, 198n140, 322, 323
Grimaldi, Marqués de, 8n14, 9n16, 332n210
Guadalquivir River, xiv
Guadalquivir River Company, xxii
Guadeloupe, 30, 260, 308, 319, 321, 323, 371
Gualiquirie Indians, 27, 27n35
Guarico: agriculture of, 78, 91; and corsairs, 299; defense of, 201, 272; map of, 136; and peace, 378; trade of, 85; and West Indies campaigns, 8n14, 10n18, 109, 117, 125, 128, 132, 138, 139–40, 145, 192, 193, 202, 230, 233, 235, 272, 277, 278, 279, 280–81, 283–84, 285–91, 311n201, 350n239, 356, 380; mentioned, 18, 18n24, 194, 216, 216n153, 221, 379
Guarrapiche River, 25, 26
Guatemala, xxix, xxx, 11, 40, 84, 110–11, 112, 121, 140. See also Guatemala expedition
Guatemala expedition, 107, 108, 121, 214, 215, 229, 235, 240n166, 249, 272, 273–74, 279–80. See also Guatemala; West Indies campaign
Guayana, 25–26
Guercía, Gerónimo Enrile, 38n42
Guerrero, 134, 149
Guevara, Don Ramón de , xxi
Guibert, Comte Jacques Antoine Hippolyte de: *Essai Général de Tactique*, xvii, xviin8
Guichen, Comte Luc Urbain du Bouexic de, 101n75, 193n132, 198n139, 301, 306, 308
Guilford Courthouse: Cornwallis's victory at, 159n113
Guipuzcoana Company (of Cumaná), 25
Gulf of Cariaco, 29
Gulf of Las Damas, 22, 22n28
Gulf of las Yeguas, 22n28
Gulf of Mexico, xxviii, 10, 109, 112, 113n82, 129, 138
Gulf of Papaguaya, 39, 43
Gulf of Paria. See Golfo Triste
Gunpowder, 138, 243, 254, 263, 342, 343

* lvi *

Index

Haiti, 192n132, 208n149
Hanxleden, Johann Ludwig Wilhelm von, 119n87. *See also* Waldes
Hargreaves-Mawdsley, W. N.: *Spain under the Bourbons, 1700–1833, A Collection of Documents*, 35n49
Harrington (brother of the Duke of Manchester), 42
Havana: and Bonet, Don Juan, 364; bread shortage in, 115, 345; defenses of, 123, 131–32, 140, 276; disease in, 104; and the flota, 105n79, 107; government of, 100, 100n72, 100n73, 100n74, 345, 380n259; Mexican aid to, 247, 249–51, 257, 266, 268–69, 297–98; and Miranda, Francisco de, 216n153; and Padres Belemitas, 104; and Pensacola, 175; and Saavedra's commission, xxx, 9n17, 49, 98, 191; and the San Juan de Dios, 104; and Spanish aid to the French, 206, 209, 212n151, 208–9, 210–11, 212n151, 316; and trade, 38n42, 230n161, 235, 309, 312, 366; treasury of, xxx, 105–6, 113, 131, 139, 227; and West Indies campaigns, xxviii, 5n6, 7, 7n13, 10, 31n40, 100–101, 104, 106, 107, 108, 109, 112–13, 114, 116–17, 119, 121, 126, 128, 129, 135, 138, 139–40, 143, 144–45, 150, 154, 155, 168, 173, 192, 202, 203, 206, 211n150, 225n157, 234n164, 239, 247, 250, 277, 279, 292, 293, 301, 303, 306, 307, 310n201, 312, 317, 323, 350, 350n239, 365n250, 376, 377; mentioned, 17, 18, 31, 32, 42, 43, 95, 125n92, 147, 149, 217, 238, 281, 295, 358, 379. *See also* Cuba
Hector (French official), 331
Hector, 321, 322, 323
Hemp: and trade, 80
Hercules, tower of, 15–17
Heredia (Spanish colonel), 303–4, 305
Hermosilla, Don Ignacio de, 45
Hernani, 340
Herrera, Miguel de, 74, 141n97
Herrera y Tordesillas, Antonio de: *Descripción de las Indias Occidentales. Historia General de los Hechos de los Castellanos en las Islas y Tierra Firme del Mar Océano*, 74n59
Herring, Hubert: *A History of Latin America*, 349n238
Hides: and Spanish Louisiana, 227
Hispaniola, 18n24. *See also* Saint Domingue
Histoire de la participation de la France a l'établissement des Etats-Unis d'Amérique. See Doniol, Henri
Historia filosófica y política de los establecimientos y comercios de europeos en las dos Indias. See Reynal, Father
Historia General y Natural de las Indias. See Oviedo y Valdés, Gonzálo Fernández de
History of America. See Robertson, William
History of France, A. See Maurois, André
History of Latin America, A. See Herring, Hubert
Holland: at war with England, 132, 198n139
Honduras, 39n43, 48, 76, 121, 214, 215
Honey: and trade, 79
Hood, Samuel, 1st Viscount Hood (English admiral), 198n139, 226
Horder, 339
Horn, Albrecht von, 167n116
Horses: in Jamaica, 77
Hôtel des Invalides, 336, 336n221
Hôtel de Ville, 336, 336n219
Hound, 119n88
House of Burgundy, 51
Howe, Richard, Earl Howe (admiral), 351, 361n247
Howe, William (general), 306n200
Huarte, Don Martín, 345
Huet, Don Luis, 117, 117n84, 121, 234,
Hundred Years War, 336n219
Hurricanes, 18, 30, 32, 37, 40, 70, 71, 167–68, 198n139, 217–18
Hussey, R.: *The Caracas Company*, 26n33

* lvii *

Index

Inagua (Great, La, Little), 36
Inconstante, 18, 190, 207
Indians: as allies of the British, 116, 154, 156, 157, 158, 159, 160, 161, 162, 163, 164, 170, 171, 173; as allies of Spain, 168; ancient histories of, 157, 158; characteristics of, 175–77, 180; of Cumaná, 25, 27, 29; dependence on Europeans, 177; of Jamaica, 64–65, 74, 75; and the Jesuits, 27n35; and Lake Nicaragua, 39; languages of, 176, 177–78; of Mexico, 244, 253; and Mobile, 119; of Peru, 258; political relations of, 178–79; and the Presidios Internos, 256–57; and the Provincias Internas, 256, 256n182; and the Regiment of the Crown, 247; relations with white men, 183–85; and Saavedra, 24, 175–85; Spanish supplies for, 293–94; stereotypes of, 27; temples of, 246; and trade, 175, 176–77, 179–80; as warriors, 178, 176–77, 180–83; mentioned, 107, 153, 174, 257. See also tribal names
Indigo: and contraband trade, 85; in Cumaná, 25; and England's trade policies, 80; and the flota, 105n79; of Jamaica, 73–74; trade monopolies of, 79; trade of, 274n190
Industry: of Jamaica, 86–91
Influence of Sea Power upon History, The. See Mahan, Alfred Thayer
Influenza, 353, 354, 355
Intrépide: catches fire, 190, 205; and Grasse, Comte de, 192n132; and Parscau, Duplessis, 375n257; mentioned, 101, 149, 150, 193
Invincible, 13
Irazábal, Calvo de: and Pensacola expedition, xxxv
Iriarte, Don Tomás de. *See* Iriarte y Oropesa, Don Tomás de
Iriarte y Oropesa, Don Tomás de, xxiv
Iris, 196n137, 315, 315n203, 316, 318
Islas Terceras, xxvi
Isles de Barlovento. *See* Windward Islands

Italian Theater: Saavedra visits, 334, 334n216, 335
Izquierdo (Spanish admiral?), 336, 336n220, 376, 377

Jacmel, 300
Jalapa, 244, 264
Jamaica: agriculture of, 54, 59, 64, 67, 68, 68n58, 69, 71–78, 80, 82, 87–90, 91; and the American Revolution, 50–51; and buccaneers, 67, 76; climate of, 47, 54, 56, 62, 63, 66, 88; and Cuban corsairs, 46–47; defenses of, 37, 47, 59–63, 113n82, 121, 132, 217, 230, 233, 296, 302, 306–7, 314; description of, 54, 55–59, 71; diseases of, 62, 301; and earthquakes, 58, 70; as an English colony, 38, 39n43, 42, 64–69, 72–73, 74, 79, 80, 81, 83, 86, 91–94; and flag-of-truce ships, 118, 216, 275; and hurricanes, 70, 217; Indians of, 64–65, 74, 75; industry of, 86–91; Jews of, 45, 85; and the Lake Nicaragua expedition, 40, 41, 42–43; map of, 52–53; maroons of, 65, 65n56; and Miranda, Don Francisco de, 216n153, 273; mulattoes of, 62; and Pensacola, 116, 144, 144n101, 172n122; population of, 69–71, 77; prosperity of, 67, 68–69; roads of, 42, 71; and Saavedra, xxx, 36, 37, 38–39, 55, 94; slaves of, 65, 68, 69, 76, 77; and Sloane, Sir Hans, 55, 55n53; and the Spanish Islands, 72; trade of, 38n42, 66, 71, 75, 76–86, 92, 129, 223, 291, 299; mentioned, xxix, xxxiii, 19, 31, 44, 130, 138, 214, 283. *See also* Jamaica expedition
Jamaica expedition: allied plans and preparations for, xxvi–xxvii, xxx, 5, 8n14, 10n18, 11, 63, 107–9, 112, 121, 122, 200–203, 207n148, 223, 229, 233, 265, 273–74, 296, 299, 300, 301, 302, 303, 306–8, 309, 310–12, 311n201, 313, 316–17, 323–24, 325, 337n227, 357, 357n246, 374, 376n258. *See also* West Indies campaigns

✳ lviii ✳

Index

James River, 226
Jaruco, 135
Jason, 324, 325
Jesuits, xxxiii, 8n14, 27n35, 195, 249, 249n173, 261, 262, 263
Jews, 45, 45n49, 85
Jitacalco, 253
Joaquina Carlota de Borbón (queen of Portugal), xviii
Johnstone (English captain at Pensacola), 171n119
Jones, Joseph: at Pensacola, 172n122
José de Ezpeleta, Gobernador de la Movila, 1780–1781. See Borja Medina, Francisco de
Journal of an Officer in the Naval Army of America in 1781 and 1782. See Shea, John Gilmary
Journal of the Mission to America. See Saavedra, Don Francisco de
Jovellanos, Gaspar Melchor de, xv, xx
Junta de Generales (of Havana), xxix, xxx, 10, 99–100, 109, 112–13, 114, 116–17, 123, 125–26, 128, 129–30, 131, 132, 133, 138–40, 141, 141n98, 144, 155n109
Junta de Seville, xxxii

Keppel, Augustus (admiral): and the Battle of Ushant, 4n3
Kessel, Baron de (brigadier): in Puerto Plata, 285, 288
King's Inmemorial Regiment: and Pensacola expedition, 144, 154, 154n108
Kingston: compared to Pensacola, 174; and corsairs, 46–47; countryside of, 54; description of, 58, 70; defenses of, 59, 60, 61, 306; entertainment of, 47–48, 49; founding of, 70; map of, 57; and methods of attack, 63; militias of, 62; mulattoes of, 62; port of, 58, 61; and Saavedra, xxx, 38, 55; taxes of, 94; and trade, 37, 58, 81; mentioned, 42, 45, 132, 274
Kingston Bay, 37, 61

Labat (French official or officer), 197, 204, 218
La Borda (French banker), 335
La Cabaña, 130, 131
La Coruña, xxix, 11, 12, 13–15, 16, 125, 376
Lafayette, Marquis de, Marie Joseph Paul Yves Roch Gilbert du Motier: in America 200n142, 201, 201n144, 226; and Jamaica expedition, 375n256; and peace, 380n259
Lafayette and the Close of the American Revolution. See Gottschalk, Louis
La Filipina (watchtower near Havana), 128, 129, 133, 144
Lafrenière (rebel of Louisiana): killed by O'Reilly, Alejandro, xvi
La Guaira, 310
La Idea del Descubrimiento de América. See O'Gorman, Edmundo
Lake Chalco, 246
Lake Nicaragua: and English expedition to, 39, 39n43, 40, 41, 42–43, 62, 94
Lake Texoco, 246
Lalone, M. (commandant of the *Serpent*), 153, 186
La Mexicana (hospital ship of Pensacola expedition), 145
La Motte Piquet, Comte de, Guillaume (admiral), 319, 319n204
Landes, 339
Lángara y Huarte, Don Juan de: background of, 6n8; Saavedra visits, 374, 374n255; and the Spanish fleet, xxvii, 5–6, 6n8
Languedoc, 204
Lara, Don Manuel de, 95
Larizosa (a captain): and Pensacola expedition, 164
Larrabee, Harold: *Decision at Chesapeake*, 196n137
Lasaga (a director of mining in Mexico), 258
Laws of Navigation, 79n61
Le Brasseur (interim intendant of Guarico), 194, 194n135, 197, 204, 227

Index

Lecoutraix, house of (Paris): Saavedra visits, 334, 336
Leeward Islands: and British forces, 8n14
Legion of the Duc de Lauzun: at Yorktown, 201n143
Le Mans, 331
Lencero: and the defense of Mexico, 264
Lentillano (of Guarico), 197
Lerma, Duque de, Francisco Gómez de Sandoval y Rojas, 341
Levrette, 101, 134, 149, 151, 152, 193
Lewis, James A.: *The North American Role in the Spanish Imperial Economy, 1760-1819*, 115-16
Licorne, 101, 146, 147, 149, 150
Liebre, 303
Lillancourt, M. de (interim governor of Guarico), 198, 204, 208n149, 218, 227, 310
Lima: rebellion in, 260; mentioned, 29
Linen: and England's trade policies, 80
Liquor: and taxes, 213n152
Lisbon, 359
Llavador Mira, J. *See* Morales Padrón, F.
Log of H.M.S. Mentor, 1780-1781, 120n88
Logwood: and Jamaica, 76; and monopolies, 79
London: and Grasse, Comte de, 323n206; and trade, 79
London, 232
Long Island: and Cornwallis, 200n141
Longoria, Don Francisco (colonel): and Pensacola expedition, 155, 164
López Carrizosa, Don Felipe Lope (captain): and Pensacola expedition, 155
Lopéz Gonzalez (bishop of Puebla), 262, 262n186
Los Decenios (Saavedra's autobiography), 6n10
Los Jardines (the gardens), 97, 97n67
Louisiana: and arms for the Indians, 256; and Gálvez, Bernardo de, 98n68, 113n82, 186, 226-27, 344, 344n232; O'Reilly, Alejandro, xvi, 368n251; and the Pensacola expedition, 107, 116, 154, 154n107, 164; rebels in, xvi, 158n112, 368n251; and Saint Maxent, Gilbert Antoine de, 334, 334n213; mentioned, 31, 127
Louis XIV (king of France): and the French Navy, 187-88, 188n130
Louis XV (king of France): and the French Navy, 188, 188n130; mentioned 336n224
Louis XVI (king of France): and the American colonies, 3n2; and Castries, Duc de, 334; and the Comédie Française, 334n214; Saavedra meets 331-32, 333, 335n218; and Spanish funds, 222
Louis Stanislaus Xavier, Comte de Provence (Louis XVI's brother): Saavedra meets, 335, 335n218
Lourdes Díaz-Trechuelo, Madame: *La Real Compañía de Filipinas*, xxvn11
Louvre, the, 334, 334n215
Lowndes, Rawlins (governor of South Carolina): and Gillon, Alexander, 274n190
Lucea Harbour, 59
Lucía, 192
Lumber: and trade, 80
Lupac, Marquis de: Saavedra visits, 334
Luxembourg, Chevalier de: and the *South Carolina*, 274n190
Luxembourg Garden, 336, 336n223
Lyon, Eugene: *The Enterprise of Florida*, 370n252

McDonald, John (major): and Battle of Pensacola, 167n116
Machault d'Arnouville, Jean Baptiste: and French Navy, 188n129
Madeira, xxix, 18
Madison, James, Jr.: and Pensacola, 172n122
Madrid: Casa Tócame-Roque of, xiiin6; influenza in, 353; and Jamaica expedition, 296, 306, 307, 337, 337n227; orders for West Indies, 107, 108, 126, 200; and Philip II,

Index

105; and Saavedra, xvi, xxiii, 11, 346, 353, 358–59, 363; mentioned, 29, 31, 99, 245, 245n170, 303, 305, 313, 334, 338, 340n228, 363, 364, 366, 375, 379, 380;
Magnánimo, 192, 313
Magnifique: and Battle of the Saintes, 321
Mahan, Alfred Thayer: *The Influence of Sea Power upon History*, 198n139
Mahon. *See* Port Mahon
Maísí, 36
Málaga, 377
Malagueta. *See* Tabasco pepper
Mallorca Regiment, 357
Malvinas Islands, xv
Manchac: Bernardo de Gálvez captures, 98n68
Manchioneal (bay of), 58
Mangino, Don Fernando José de (superintendent of Mexican mint), 251, 251n174, 257–58, 348
Manila: Mexican funds for, 249
Manzanares River, 25, 29
Mapas, planos y dibujos sobre Venezuela existentes en el Archivo General de Indias. See Morales Padrón, F.
Maracaibo: rebellion in, 213n152, 233; and Trinidad, 30
Margarita, La, 17, 23, 23n31, 24, 27–28, 28n36
María Luisa (wife of Charles, prince of Asturias): Saavedra meets, 342, 342n230
Marie Antoinette (queen of France): Saavedra meets, 335, 335n218, 338
Mariel, 271
Maritime mail service (of Spain), 14, 14n21, 15, 31, 84n62, 286, 295, 296, 297, 298, 303, 309, 343, 349, 357, 372, 379
Maroons. *See* Negroes
Marseilles, 301
Martinique: and agricultural methods, 78; and coffee, 75; and combined fleet 32; and Grasse, Comte de, 230, 278, 294; and Guichen,

Comte de, 101n75, 193n132, 301, 306, 308; hurricane on, 30; and Jamaica expedition, 203, 307–8, 310, 314, 319; and Saavedra's commission, 10n18; and *Saint Esprit*, 323; and Spanish funds for, 221–22; mentioned, 13, 17, 18, 27, 205, 223, 286, 318
Maryland: and American forces, 232n162; and French forces, 350n239
Masserano, Prince: from Gibraltar, 350–51
Matanzas, 141, 193, 209, 211, 301
Matilde, 223, 225, 219, 272, 280
Maurois, André: *A History of France*, 187n127
Maxwell, John (governor of Bahamas): surrender of, 234n164
Mayaguana, 31, 129, 138, 326
Mayáns y Siscar, Gregorio, xv, xvn7
Mayorga, Martín de (viceroy of New Spain): on condition of New Spain, 255–56; and flour regulations, 266; and Mexico during American Revolution, 240, 240n166; and Royal Hacienda, 251 and Saavedra's Mexican mission, 247–48, 257, 268; mentioned, 258
Mazé, Don Nicolás (captain of Mallorca Regiment), 357
Meat: in Cumaná, 26; in Jamaica, 71, 77; in Havana, 345; for Spanish forces, 218; and trade, 79
Media Luna Fort. *See* Fort Half Moon
Mediterranean Sea: and conditions of peace, 357; and siege of Gibraltar, 360, 361, 361n247
Melilla, 64
Mentor, 119n88
Mercury: and silver minting, 252–53; supply of, 253n175
Mérida: rebellion in, 213n152
Mexico: the *Acordada* of, 257, 257n184; agriculture of, 261; and aid to Havana, 106, 131; and aid for West Indies campaigns (Guatemala, Jamaica, and Providence expeditions), 108, 218–19, 229, 233, 247, 249–51, 257, 258, 264,

265, 266, 268, 277, 278, 297–98; altitude of, 244–45; and American Revolution, 241n166; architecture of, 252, 253, 256, 261, 262–63; and character of the people, 247; climate of, 243, 244; compared to Jamaica, 64; and Cortez, 246, 246n172; and Cuba, 310; defense of, 245, 264; discontent in, 247–48, 250–51; employment in, 259; and Guatemala, 121; gunpowder factory of, 263; income of, 260; Indians of, 244, 246, 253, 256–57; and Jesuits, 263; and Louisiana, 227; and Mangino, Fernando José, 251n174; maps of, 236–37; and mining, 249, 252–53, 258, 263–64; and Pacheco y Bobadillo, Diego, 263n187; and Padres Belemitas, 245–46; Saavedra's mission to, 108, 240, 247–48, 272, 273; and situados from, 193, 193n133, 220, 221, 230; taxes of, 248; and trade, 248; treasury of, 29, 249, 250; mentioned, 235. See also Mexico City; New Spain; Veracruz

Mexico City: and Academy of Fine Arts, 253; Cathredal of, 257; cigar factory of, 258–59; and Constanzó, Miguel, 253n178; and gunpowder, 243; plain of, 246; poor of, 261; roads to, 264, 267; Saavedra in, 240, 247, 248, 251–52, 253, 255, 257, 258; wealth of, 261. See also Mexico; New Spain

Middlesex (county in Jamaica), 71

Militias of Granada, xxiii

Ministry of Marine, Spanish: and Ministry of the Indies, xxi; mentioned, 314

Ministry of State, Spanish: and Moniño, José, xxiv

Ministry of the Indies, Spanish: and authority in the Americas, 299–300; and Ministry of Marine, xxi; and Saavedra, xxiv, 9, 9n15, 44; mentioned, 314

Minorca: and Crillon, Duc de, 356n243; and Port Mahon, 313, 313n202; mentioned 5n6

Minor Orders: and Saavedra, xii, xiin3

Miralles, Juan de (Spanish agent to Continental Congress): and declaration of war, 4n5, 5n6; his mission to America, 106n80; in Philadelphia, 225n158, 274n190; and Valle, Antonio Ramón, 100n73

Miranda, Don Francisco de: charges against, 216, 216n153; and Jamaica expedition, 273, 274; and Providence expedition, 234n164; and Saavedra, xviii–xx; and Spanish American independence, 217n153

Mississippi River: and American settlement, 311n201; and arms transportation, 158n112; and climate, 168; and Gálvez, Bernardo de, 98n68; and Indian territory, 176; and Pensacola expedition, 142; and trade, 226–27; mentioned, 119, 150

Mobile: attacked by the English, 118–20; captured from the English, 7, 7n13, 17; and Gálvez, Bernardo de, xxviii, 98n68, 113n82; Indians of, 293–94; and Pensacola expedition, 116, 127n93, 141n98, 142, 143

Mobile Bay, 119, 120, 127n93

Modyfort, Thomas: and Jamaican sugar, 76

Mogarra. See Mayaguana

Moka: and the Dutch, 75

Moniño y Redondo, José. See Floridablanca, Conde de

Monito, 32

Monmoriet, Count of: and Spain's neutrality, 6n10

Monne: of French Cape, 195

Mono, 32

Monte Christi, 194, 291, 289

Montego Bay, 59

Monteil, Chevalier de: and combined fleet, 122–23, 125, 134, 135, 138, 139; and French fleet, xxx, 100, 100n75, 193; on French Navy, 186–91; and Pensacola expedition, 140, 144–45, 150, 375n257; and situado for Puerto Rico, 205; and Spanish fleet, 132, 133; mentioned, 101, 127, 130, 196, 197, 199, 204,

334, 335–36
Monte Pío (Mexican public pawnshop), 254, 254n177
Monterey, 256n182
Montmart, Vicomte de: Saavedra reports West Indies situation to, 331, 332
Montmorin de Saint Herem, Comte de, Armand Marc (French ambassador to Spain): and Gibraltar, 344; and West Indies operations, 341, 341n229, 342, 343, 346, 350, 357, 357n246; mentioned, xxvi
Morales (Spanish naval officer), 222
Morales Padrón, F.: *Mapas, planos y dibujos sobre Venezuela existentes en el Archivo General de Indias*, xxviiin12
Morant Bay, 58, 61
Morant Point, 36–37, 58
Moreno, Don Pedro (of Cumaná), 28
Morfí, Father Juan Agustín: in New Spain, 256n181
Morris, Robert: and trade, 230n161
Morro, the (of Havana), 131, 134
Mosquito Indians: and Lake Nicaragua, 39
Mouchoir Bank, 284
Mulattoes: in Jamaica, 62, 69; and Mobile, 118–19, 120; in Pensacola expedition, 164; in old Veracruz, 243. See also Negroes; Slaves
Mules: in Cumaná, 26; in Jamaica, 77; and Jamaica expedition, 293, 294, 296
Muños, Juan Bautista: and history of the Indies, xxiin10
Muzquiz, Don Miguel (Spanish minister of finance), 342, 378

Nantes, 300, 331
Nassau, Prince of, Prince Charles Henri Nicolas Othon de, 374, 376
Natchez: captured by Gálvez, Bernardo de, 98n68; rebellion of, 211n150
Naval stores: and English trade policies, 80; and monopolies, 79
Navarro, Martin (intendant of Louisiana): and taxes, 226–27

Navarro García de Valladores, Don Diego José: governor of Havana, 4n5, 99, 100n73, 139, 191, 230n161; and Miralles, Juan de, 106n80; Saavedra visits, 358; mentioned, 5n6, 9n17
Navia, Don Victorio de (commandant of the Army of Operations): and Pensacola expedition, 7, 7n11, 105, 112, 116–17, 124–25, 191; mentioned, xxviii, 9n17, 10n18, 99, 99n70
Navigation Act: and trade, 79
Negrillo, 269
Negril Point, 59
Negroes: and agriculture, 80; and the British, 120, 167; and corsairs, 46–47; free, 69, 70; in Jamaica, 8n14, 62, 65; and maroons, 65; in Mobile, 118–19; and Pensacola, 157–58, 164, 173; in Puerto Plata, 290; and rebellion in New Granada, 213n152; and the rum trade, 80; as slaves, 68, 310–12; and slave ships, 309; in the Spanish colonies, 68, 335; taxes on, 93; trade of, 85, 310–12, 345; and the Treaty of Utrecht, 57, 68; in Veracruz, 243. See also Mulattoes; Slaves
Neile, Arthur, 224, 224n156
Nelson, Horace (captain): and Lake Nicaragua expedition, 39n44
Nelson, Thomas (governor of Virginia): and Battle of Pensacola, 172n122
Néréide, 305–6
Neve, Felipe (governor of Provincias Internas), 256n182
Nevis: and Bouillé, Marquis de, 221n154
New Andalusia. See Nueva Andalucía
New England: and horses, 77
New Granada: rebellion in, 213, 213n152
Newil, Mr. (commissioner of prisoners in Jamaica), 38
New Mexico: and Croix, Teodoro de, 256n181
New Orleans: and Campbell, James, 279; and Dalling, John, 39n43; and

* lxiii *

Index

Gálvez, Bernardo de, 98n68, 142, 211n150; and Mobile, 118–19; and Pensacola expedition, 126, 127n93, 141, 143, 143n100, 162

Newport: and the French fleet, 196n137, 196n138, 198n140, 201n143, 201n144

New Spain: and Cagigal, Juan Manuel de, 380n259; condition of, 255–56, 348; and Cruillas, Marqués de, 356n245; discontent in, 250–51; factories of, 86; flota of, 105n79; and funds of, 140, 250; and Gálvez, Bernardo de, 98n68, 344n232; and Gálvez, José de, 8n14; and Gálvez, Matias de, 11n19, 98n68; Indians of, 185, 253, 256–57; and the Jesuit expulsion, 249, 249n173; and mining, 249, 252–53; and the Treasury of Havana, 113; viceroys of, 241n166, 263n187. *See also* Mexico; Mexico City; Veracruz

New World: agriculture of, 71–72, 77, 88–89, 261: and the American Revolution, xxv; and barbarism, 16; climate of, 88–89; colonization of, 24, 66, 67, 69, 82, 83, 259–60; condition of, 251, 342; and conditions of peace, 357; and cotton, 74; criollos of, 259; and Indians, 176; industry of, 86; revenues from, 91–94; and trade, 78, 80, 82; mentioned, 169

New York: and allied forces, 200n142; and British forces, 198n139, 201n145, 207n148, 226, 228, 232, 232n132, 306; and Clinton, Sir Henry, 306n200; and Estaing, Comte d', 198n140; and flag-of-truce ships, 215, 222; and Pensacola, 172n122; and Spain's strategy, 8n14; mentioned, 33, 36

New York Gazette: and Pensacola, 172n122

Nicaragua: and Guatemala, 107; and Huet, Don Luis, 121. *See also* Lake Nicaragua

Noailles, Marquis de, Emmanuel Marie Louis de (French ambassador to England), 3

Nord, Comtes du. *See* Russia, Dukes of

Nord, Duchesse du, 333n212. *See also* Russia, Dukes of

North, Counts of the, 333n212. *See also* Russia, Dukes of

North American Role in the Spanish Imperial Economy, The, 1760–1819. See Lewis, James A.

North Carolina: and Chesapeake expedition, 200; and Cornwallis, 159n113

Northern Keys (Florida Keys), 134, 135

Nra. Sra. de la O, 146, 147, 148, 149, 151. *See also* O

Nueva Andalucía, 25

Nuevo Leon, 245n182

O, 128, 129, 133, 186, 192. *See also* Nra. Sra. de la O

Oaxaca: and Mexican funds for Guatemala, 249; and Palafox y Mendoza, Juan de, 263n187

Ogaban, Don Bernardo, 95

O'Gorman, Edmundo: *La Idea del Descubrimiento de América,* xxiin10

Ohio River: American settlements and the Spanish, 311n201

Olavide, Don Pablo de, x, xx

Old Channel: and shipping routes, 31, 209, 210, 301, 303

Old French Cape, 285. *See also* French Cape

Old Harbour, 58, 63

Old Veracruz, 243. *See also* Veracruz

Ometepe (island of), 39

Omoa, fort of: captured, 48–49

O'Neill, Arturo: and Battle of Pensacola, 170n118

O'Neill, Don Carlos: arrival at French Cape, 292

Only Land They Knew: The Tragic Story of the American Indians of the Old South. See Wright, J. Leitch, Jr.

Ópera (of Paris), 333, 333n211, 335, 336, 338

Index

Opera of Tesco, 335
Orange Bay, 59
Order of Bethlehem. *See* Padres Belemitas
O'Reilly, Alejandro, Conde: and Algiers expedition, xvi–xx; and Louisiana, xv, 368n251; as Saavedra's mentor, xi, xiv, xv, xvi, xvii; and West Indies operations, 368, 369
Orinoco: and fortifications, xxviii
Orinoco River, 23, 25, 26, 27n35, 30
Oristan, 64
Orizaba, 240
Orozco y Berra, Manuel: *Historia de la Dominación Española en Mexico*, 241n166
Orvilliers, Comte d' (admiral), 4n3, 7n11
Orwell, Colonel (of Jamaica), 47, 49
Otte, Enrique: *Las Perlas del Caribe*, 28n36
Oviedo y Valdés, Gonzálo Fernández de: *Historia General y Natural de las Indias*, 22n28
Oxen: and sugar production, 78

Pacheco y Bobadillo, Diego, Duque de Escalona: career in Mexico, 263n187
Pacific Ocean: and canal to Atlantic, 39, 39n45, 43
Padres Belemitas: of Mexico, 246; of Puebla, 245; travel with Saavedra, 260–64; in West Indies, 245, 245n171. *See also* Belemites
Padrón, Francisco Morales: *Jamaica española*, 42n46
Pájara, 147, 192, 221
Palace of Versailles: Saavedra describes, 333
Palafox y Mendoza, Juan de: career in Mexico, 263, 263n187
Palenque: in Jamaica, 58
Pallas, xxx, 35, 36, 38
Palmier, 101, 130, 133, 146, 190, 193, 196
Pampatar, 23
Pancorbo (rocks of), 340
Pan de Daijaban, 238

Pan de Matanzas, 281
Panes, Don Diego: and gunpowder production, 263; and Mexico's copper mines, 163–64; of Perote, 245
Paraguay: and New Granada, 213n152
Pardo, Don Benito: and Battle of Pensacola, 170; and Regiment of the Crown, 247
Paris, 107, 200, 206, 222, 323n206, 331n207, 333, 333n211, 350, 336n219, 336n224
Parker, Peter (admiral): and American Revolution, 200n141; and Grasse, Comte de, 323n206; in Jamaica, 45; mentioned, 45n50, 120n88
Parma, Duke of (father of María Luisa), 342n230
Parscau, Duplessis: and Saavedra, 375, 375n257
Paul, Czarevitch, 333n212
Paula: and Mexican flour, 266
Peace of Paris: and French Navy, 188n129; mentioned 92
Peace of Utrecht: and slave trade, 68; mentioned 38n42
Peace treaty (between the allies and England), 378, 379, 380, 380n259
Pearls: of Margarita, 27
Peñalver, Don Josef, 235, 243–47
Peñalver, Don Ignacio (treasurer of the army), 100
Penn, Sir William (admiral): and British conquest of Jamaica, 65
Pensacola: agreement to spare the city, 158–59; climate of, 166; and Continental Congress, 172n122; and contraband trade, xxviii, 174; and Dalling, John, 39n43; as an English port, xxviii, 119n88, 151; Indians of, 293; and Mobile, 119–20; negroes of, 173; plans of, 117n84; and Saavedra's commission, 10n18, 112; Saavedra describes, 174; Spain cedes to England, 174; in Spain's strategy, xxix, 8n14, 10, 31n40, 106–7, 112; as Spanish territory, xxxii; terrain of, 156, 158; and trade, 174, 175; mentioned, 124n92, 132, 186, 192, 224. *See also* Battle of Pensacola;

* lxv *

Index

Pensacola expedition
Pensacola expedition: accounts of, xxxi, xxxiv–xxxvi; allied forces prepare for, xxviii, xxix, xxx–xxxi, 7, 7n11, 7n13, 10, 99–100, 100n72, 107, 109, 112–13, 114, 116–17, 118, 123–24, 125–30, 131, 132, 133, 138–40, 141, 141n98, 144–56, 158, 160, 167, 168–69; and British defense, xxxi, xxxvi, 116, 119, 142, 144, 144n101, 153–54, 155, 156–57, 158, 159, 161, 163, 167n116, 173, 211n150, 215; British prisoners from, 173; and Cagigal, 152; and Chacón, José María, 365n250; and civilians, 159; and deserters, 161, 162; and Gálvez, Bernardo de, 108, 141–43, 151–52; and Parscau, Duplessis, 375n257; and Spanish conduct, 225, 225n157; and weather, 167–68. *See also* Battle of Pensacola; West Indies campaigns
Pepper: and trade monopolies, 79
Pérdida de la Isla de Trinidad. *See* Pérez Aparicio, Josefina
Perdido River: and Pensacola expedition, 143n100
Pereda, Don José de: and Pensacola expedition, 167
Pérez Aparicio, Josefina: *Pérdida de la Isla de Trinidad*, 31n39
Perlas del Caribe, Las. *See* Otte, Enrique
Permanent Regiment of Havana, 98, 144
Perote, fort of, 244, 245, 264
Peru: factories of, 86; Indians of, 258; and monopolies, 279; rebellion in, 258, 278–79; and taxes, 279; mentioned 64, 251
Petite Anse: and French Cape, 195
Philadelphia: and Miranda, Francisco de, 216n153; and peace, 380n259; and Rendón, Francisco, 230n161, 232, 232n162, 350n239; Spanish agents in, 100n73, 225, 225n158; mentioned, 229
Philip, Duke of Orleans, 188n130
Philip II (king of Spain): criticism of, 105; and El Escorial, 105n78; and the Morro, 131; and Sitios Reales, 346n234
Philip III (king of Spain), 341
Philip V (king of Spain), 45n48, 346n234
Philippine Islands: and Mexican funds for, 249; and Spanish commercial companies, 26n33
Picarones, 46–47. *See also* Corsairs
Picolet, 195
Pinar, 263
Pineda, Don Manuel de (colonel): and Pensacola expedition, 155, 155n109, 163, 168
Piñeres, Juan Francisco Gutiérrez de: and rebellion in New Granada, 213n152
Pirates: and British, 308; and Cuba, 299–300; and Jamaica, 68, 76. *See also* Buccaneers; Corsairs; Privateers
Píritu (missions of), 32, 32n41
Pitch: and trade, 80
Placer of Rota, 378
Plain of Otumba, 246, 246n172, 260
Plan del Río, 243
Plan for Intendants, 349, 349n238
Plantains: in Jamaica, 76–77
Plata, La: reefs of, 37
Plymouth: and companies of trade, 79; and Rodney's fleet, 301; mentioned 197n139
Pointe du Raz, 330
Point Isabel, 289
Point Morant, 129, 138
Poirouse, Monsieur: and the *Astre*, 325
Poitiers, 339
Polson (British officer in Jamaica): and English expedition to Lake Nicaragua, 39n44, 40, 41
Pombal, Marqués de, Sebastião José de Carralho e Mello: and Cantofer, xxv
Pondicheri: captured by British, xxv
Pontchartrain, 331
Porkin, 300
Port Antonio, 61, 63
Port-au-Prince, 190, 313

* lxvi *

Index

Portell Vila, Herminio: *Vidas de la Unidad Americana*, 217n153
Port Maria, 61
Port Mahon: Spanish capture of, 292, 301, 310, 313, 313n202, 356n243; and conditions of peace, 357, 378
Port Morant, 58
Port of Santa María, 298
Port Royal, 37, 44, 45, 57, 61, 63, 64, 69, 70, 94, 119n88
Portugal: and church tithes, 92; and Gálvez, Bernardo de, 98n68; independence of, 263n187; queen of, xxv; relations with Spain, xxiv; and royal revenues, 91–92; and slave trade, 68; and Spain's American dominions, xxiii; mentioned, 299, 330, 352
Posada y Soto, Ramón (fiscal in Mexico City), 254–55, 255n179
Pozuelo, 260
Preci (officer), 292
Presidios Internos, 256, 256n183
Prince of Wales Redoubt, 171n119
Princess Regiment, 216
Privateers: of England, 106; of France, 380n259. *See also* Buccaneers; Corsairs; Pirates
Provence, 221
Providence: and shipping, 274. *See also* Providence expedition
Providence expedition: and Cagigal, 275, 275n191, 307, 312; and Gálvez, Bernardo de, 229, 300 and Miranda, Francisco de, 216n153; plans for, 229, 233, 234, 234n164, 235. *See also* Providence; West Indies campaigns
Provincias Internas, 256, 256n182
"Provisional Rules Governing Maritime Mail," 14
Puebla: architecture of, 262–63; religious of, 262; Saavedra describes, 261–62; and trade, 262; mentioned, 260
Puebla de los Angeles, 261, 263n187
Puerto Cabello: and Jamaica expedition, 357n246, 376n258
Puerto de Santa María: and Estaing, Comte d', 367, 368; Saavedra in,
xx, 374, 375
Puerta de Tierra: merlons of, 356
Puerto Plata: and conduct of campaign troops, 288; defense of, 285, 286, 287; and French ships, 318; and Guarico expedition, 285–91; negroes of, 290; Saavedra describes, 285, 286–88, 289, 290, 291; and Spanish shipping, 317, 321
Puerto Real: and earthquake of 1692, 60; Saavedra in, 363, 368, 369, 373, 374
Puerto Rico: and British fleet, 325; and Cartagena, 272; and free trade, 84; and Guarico, 224; situado for, 193, 193n133, 205, 272, 230, 231; mentioned, xxix, 31, 32, 197, 215, 310
Puerto Santo, 18
Pulques: taxes on, 248
Punta de Agüero. *See* Tartar Point
Punta Delgado, 240

Queen's Redoubt, 155, 171n119
Quesada, Juan Nepumuceno de, 356, 356n244, 366, 372
Quito: and rebellion in, 233, 278–79

Rábago (Spanish naval officer?), 376
Rabie, Monsieur (French commandant of engineers): and art, 301
Railleuse, 302, 305
Ramillies, 48
Randolph, Edmund: and Pensacola's surrender, 172n122
Ravenel, M. de (captain of the *Andromaque*), 151
Rea, Robert R. *See The Log of H. M. S. Mentor, 1780–1781*
Real Academia de La Lengua, 45, 45n48
Real Audiencia de Santo Domingo, 7n11
Real Compañia de Filipinas, La. *See* Lourdes Díaz-Trechuelo, Madame, xxvn11
Red Cliffs (fort in Pensacola): and British defense of Pensacola, xxxi, xxxv, 142, 153, 155, 163, 173

Index

Regiment of Agénois: at Chesapeake Bay, 194n136
Regiment of Aragón: and Pensacola expedition, 168, 170n188; mentioned, 216n153, 302
Regiment of Bourbonnais: at Yorktown, 201n143
Regiment of Cantabria: and Gálvez, Bernardo de, 98n68
Regiment of Dillon, the, 315
Regiment of Flanders: and Pensacola expedition, 161
Regiment of Gatinais: at Chesapeake Bay, 194n136
Regiment of Guadalajara: and Pensacola expedition, 144, 170n118
Regiment of Havana: and Pensacola expedition, 170n118; mentioned, 128
Regiment of Hibernia: and Pensacola expedition, 144, 157, 162, 170, 170n118
Regiment of Louisiana: deserters from, 161
Regiment of Navarra: in Havana, 100n72; and Mobile, 118–19; and the Pensacola expedition, 144, 168, 170n118
Regiment of New Orleans: and Pensacola expedition, 159
Regiment of Royal Deux-Ponts: at Yorktown, 201n143
Regiment of Saintonge: at Yorktown, 201n143
Regiment of Soissonais: at Yorktown, 201n143
Regiment of Soria: and fighting among allied soldiers, 304; and Pensacola expedition, 144, 170n118
Regiment of Spain, 7n12, 17, 374, 120
Regiment of the Crown: aid for West Indies operations, 247–48, 250, 265, 266, 267–68
Regiment of the Prince: in Mobile, 120; and Pensacola expedition, 170n118
Regiment of Touraine: at Chesapeake Bay, 194n136
Regiment of Zamora: and fighting among allied soldiers, 297, 304; formation of, xiii
Regimiento Inmemorial del Rey, xiv
Regla, Conde de, Pedro Romero de Terreros: death of, 258; and Pensacola expedition, 125, 125n91; and the treasury, 249, 249n173
Reglamento al público. *See* Regulation of Free Trade
Regulation of Free Trade, xxiv, xxvii, 13n20, 14n20
Reinaud, M. de (governor of French Cape), 194, 194n134, 198–99
Rendón, Francisco (Spain's man in Philadelphia): and the American Revolution, 106n80; and the British fleet, 232, 232n162; and East Florida, 310n201; and the French fleet, 376, 376n258; and Miranda, Francisco de, 153, 271; and peace, 380n259; and Pensacola, 172n122; in Philadelphia, 225n158; and Smith, Robert, 230n161; and Solano, 350, 350n239; and Valle, Antonio Ramón del, 100n73; and Vaudreuil, 350, 350n239
Rengel (traveling companion of Saavedra), 374
Renombrado, 129, 133, 134, 149, 150, 151, 276
Reparaz, Conde de (owner of the *San Miguel*), 379
Revolution of 1688: and trade, 79
Rey (artillery officer): and Spanish artillery, 294, 318; field tents of, 308–9
Rey, 279
Reynal, Father: *Historia filosófica y política de los establecimientos y comercios de europeos en las dos Indias*, xxiin10
Rhode Island: and the French fleet, 196, 226, 228
Riaño, Juan Antonio de: and Pensacola expedition, 143n99, 225n157
Richelieu, Cardinal de, Armand Jean du Plessis, 337
Richmond, 196n137, 319, 325
Ricla, Conde de (Saavedra's friend), xxi

Index

Río Caribe: port of, 23
Río de la Plata: and the Portuguese, xxiv; and Spanish politicians, xxiii
Río Guainabo, 95
Rivadeneira y Barrientos, Antonio Joaquín: and the *Acordada*, 257, 257n184; and Saavedra, 260–64
Robertson, William: *History of America*, xxi, xxii
Robertson, William Spence: *The Diary of Francisco de Miranda, Tour of the United States, 1783–1784*, 217n153
Rochambeau, Comte de, Jean Baptiste Donatien de Vimeur: and allied plans to defeat Cornwallis, 200n142, 201, 226; in America, 107n80; and American expeditionary force, 196n138; army of, in Newport, 201n144; at Chesapeake Bay, 194n136; and lack of funds, 208n149, 212n151; in Maryland, 350n239; and the Yorktown campaign, 196n137, 201n143
Rockfort, 63
Roda, Marqués de, Manuel (former Spanish minister of state), 348–49, 351, 352
Rodney, George Bridges (admiral), 1st Baron Rodney: and Battle of the Saintes, 319–23; British fleet of, 197–98, 197n139, 296, 301, 306, 307, 308, 310, 315, 316–17; capture of Saint Eustatius, 319n204; engages Grasse, Comte de, 308; and Gibraltar, 4n9, 6n8, 6n9; role in the West Indies, 193n132, 295
Roebuck, 232
Roman Catholic Church: tithes of, 92
Rouhier (French naval minister): and the French navy, 188n129
Royal College of Physicians (of England): and Sloane, Sir Hans, 55n53
Royal Hacienda: and aid for West Indies operations, 266; authority of, 260; of New Spain, 248, 255, 251
Royal Louis, 375
Royal Society (of England): and Sloane, Sir Hans, 55n53

Royal Treasury (of Spain): and the mail-packet charter, 296
Ruby, 232
Ruiz, Don Pedro: and flag-of-truce ships, 118; and Jamaica, 214, 216
Ruiz de Villarías, A. M.: *El venerable Pedro de Betancurt*, 245n171
Rum: and the *Inconstante*, 207; and the *Intrépide*, 205; in Jamaica, 77; monopoly of, 25; and sugar, 76; trade of, 79, 80, 223, 271, 283
Rush, N. Orwin: *The Battle of Pensacola*, xxxiv–xxxvi
Russia, Dukes of, 333, 335, 338
Rydjord, John: *Foreign Interest in the Independence of New Spain*, 241n166

Saavedra, Don Francisco de: career of, xii–xxix, xxxii, xxxiv, 8, 8n14, 9, 9n17, 10–17, 54n52, 112, 121, 125, 154n108, 344, 370, 371, 378–79; as English prisoner, xxx, xxxiii, 33–35, 38, 42, 43, 44, 49, 55, 94; and the de Grasse–Saavedra agreement, 199–203, 205–6, 207, 207n148, 208, 208n149, 212, 212n151, 227–28, 229, 231, 235, 272, 273, 275, 311n201; and Indians, 24, 27, 175–85, 257; *Journal of the Mission to America*, xxxiii–xxxiv; life of, ix–xxixx, 6n10; and Pensacola expedition, xxxi, 116, 124–25, 127, 153, 154, 157, 185–86; and plans and preparations for West Indies campaigns, xxxi, 63, 99, 107–9, 112–15, 116–17, 118, 128, 130, 140, 191, 193, 196, 200–203, 204, 205, 206n148, 212n151, 215, 216, 218–19, 221–23, 224, 225, 228–29, 230, 231, 232–33, 234–35, 238–40, 241n166, 243–47, 249–51, 254, 257, 264–69, 272, 285–91, 297–98, 299, 300, 301, 303, 306–8, 313, 316–17, 323–24, 325, 338, 342, 344, 345, 346, 348, 351, 352, 353, 354–55, 357, 362, 368–69, 370, 371, 372, 373–74, 375, 377, 378, 380; travels and commentaries, xx, xxix–xxx, xxxiii, 13–15, 24, 174–75,

Index

194–96, 213, 213n152, 218, 240–41, 242–43, 248, 251–52, 253, 255–56, 257, 258, 260–64, 325–31, 333–37, 338–45, 346, 351n240, 352, 353, 354–55, 358–59, 362, 363, 368–69, 373, 374, 375, 376, 378–79, 380
Saavedra de Sangronis, Don Francisco de. *See* Saavedra, Don Francisco de
Saba: and Bouillé, Marquis de, 221n154
Sagittaire, 212n151, 319
Saint Ann's Bay, 59, 61
Saint Augustine, 4n5, 8n14, 172n122, 239, 310–12, 378
Saint Christopher, 8n14, 202, 221n154, 286, 298, 298n196, 302, 305, 308
Saint Domingue, M. de (captain of the *Courageuse*), 227, 231, 232, 243–47, 267, 278, 281
Saint Domingue, 18, 18n24, 201n143. *See also* French Cape; Guarico
Saint Esprit, 204, 323
Saint Eustatius, 30, 198n139, 221n154, 319n204
Saint-Jean-de-Luz, 340
Saint Lucia, 8n14, 202
Saint Martins, 198n139, 221n154
Saint Maxent, Félice de (wife of Bernardo de Gálvez), 224n155, 334n213
Saint Maxent, Gilbert Antoine (father-in-law of Bernardo de Gálvez): in Paris, 334, 334n213
Saint Simon, Marquis de, Claude-Anne Maubléru, 194, 194n136, 201n143, 202
Saint Thomas, 62, 308
Saint Vincent, 198n140
Salaverría (a Spanish officer), 192
Salt: trade of, 25, 27
Salt mines, 29
Saltpeter: and Mexican gunpowder, 254
Samaná, 287, 324
San Antonio: fort of, 14
Sanctuary of Guadelupe, 247
San Dámaso, 360–61
San Diego: fort of, 14
Sandwich, 323n206

Sandy Hook, 196n138
San Felipe, 289, 291, 307
San Francisco: hacienda of, 245
San Francisco de Asís, 265, 268. *See also Asís*
San Francisco de Paula, 220
San Gabriel, 145, 313
San Genaro, 276, 280
San Gil, 221. *See also Gil*
San Ildefonso, xxv, 337n227, 340, 340n228, 341, 379
San Juan, 239, 280, 281, 289, 291, 317, 321
San Juan de Dios (in Havanna), 104
San Juan del Norte, 39n44
San Juan de Teotihuacán, 246, 260
San Juan River, 39, 96, 121
San Lorenzo del Escorial. *See* El Escorial
San Luis, 145, 148, 325
San Luis Keys, 197, 207, 210
San Luis Potosí, 254n178
San Miguel (Mexican estate of the Conde de Regla), 258
San Miguel, 360, 379
San Nicolás, 148
San Nicolás Mole, 199, 207n148, 210, 292, 313
San Pedro, 289, 291, 317, 321
San Pío, 128, 365n250
San Quentin, 107n78
San Roman, 113, 113n82, 126, 127, 141–43, 216, 221, 224, 225n157
San Roque, 360
Santa Balbina, 19n26
Santa Catalina, 303
Santa Clara, 225n157
Santa Cruz, 19
Santa Fé: factories of, 86, 254; rebellion in, 213, 213n152, 214, 260, 272, 278; mentioned, 30, 218, 219, 222, 251
Santa Gloria, 59
Santa Lucía, 30, 59
Santa Paula, 19n26
Santa Rosa Island, 119n88, 126, 142, 151, 152, 153
Santiago (of Jamaica), 64n55
Santiago de Cuba: and piracy, 299; Saavedra visits, 130, 130n95; and

* lxx *

West Indies campaigns, 293, 293n194, 294, 295–96; mentioned, 100n72. *See also* Cuba
Santiago de la Vega, 42, 65, 69. *See also* Spanish Town
Santo Domingo: cannons of, 303–4, 305; map of, 136–37; and peace, 371; situado of, 193, 193n133, 205, 206; trade of, 84, 85, 129; and West Indies campaigns, 101, 203, 212n151, 218, 311n201; mentioned, xix, 7n11, 31, 32, 36, 56, 64, 72, 138, 284, 285, 344
Santo Domingo, 307
Sapian, Don N. (captain of the *Carmen*), 151
Saratoga: American victory at, 332n210
Savannah, 8n14, 198n140
Savanna la Mar, 41, 58, 61, 71
Second Cataluña Regiment: and Pensacola expedition, 144
Second Flanders Regiment: and Pensacola expedition, 144
Segovia, 340, 340n228, 346
Sénégal, 17, 320n205
Sepúlveda, 117
Serilly, M. de (treasurer general of the army), 208n149
Serpent, 101, 129, 133, 134, 146, 147, 149, 152, 185, 186, 193
Serrato, Don José, 153
Servies, James A. *See The Log of H.M.S. Mentor, 1780–1781.*
Seven Years War: and the French navy, 188n129; and Jamaica, 69
Sevilla (of Jamaica), 64
Seville, ix–x, xi, xx, xxxii, 256n180
Sèvres factory: Saavedra visits, 337
Shea, John Gilmary: *Journal of an Officer in the Naval Army of America in 1781 and 1782*, 323n206
Sheep: in Jamaica, 77
Sheridan, Richard B.: *Eighteenth-Century Florida and the Caribbean*, 68n58
Siege of Pensacola 1781 in Maps, The. See Coker, William S.

Siguenza Point, 153
Silk: and trade, 79, 80
Silver: from New Spain, 252–53; smelting of, 254; and trade, 83; and West Indies campaigns, 130, 138, 140, 294
Silver Keys, 285
Sitio: Saavedra visits, 346, 346n234, 347–53, 354–58, 359–62
Sitios Reales. *See* Sitio
Situados, 193, 193n133, 230, 231, 272
60th Regiment (English), 171n119
Skins: and trade, 79
Slaves: and Jamaica, 65, 66, 69, 76–77; trade of, 38n42, 68, 68n57, 84, 310–12; and the Treaty of Utrecht, 68n57. *See also* Maroons; Negroes
Sloane, Sir Hans: and Jamaica, 55, 55n53
Smallpox: in the Canary Islands, 19, 19n27; in Caracas, 28; in Cumaná, 28; and Indians, 185; treatments for, 28–29
Smith, Robert: and trade, 230, 230n161
Solano, Don José de: background of, 7, 7n11; promotions of 191, 192; and Puerto Rico's *situado*, 231; role in West Indies campaigns, xxviii, 31, 114, 117, 134, 145, 212, 214, 215, 217, 224, 225, 228, 229, 230, 231, 233, 234–35, 272, 273, 275, 276, 277, 280, 281, 296, 301, 302, 303, 306, 307, 310–12, 313–14, 321, 325, 350, 350n239, 357n246, 375n257, 376, 376n258; mentioned, 99n70, 100, 101, 222
Solano, Francisco de: *Cardinales de Dos Independencias*, 105n79
Soldado, 244
Sonora, 256n182
Sonora, Marqués de. *See* Gálvez, Don José de
Sorbon, Robert, 337n225
Sorbonne, 336, 337, 337n225
Sourris, 147–48
Sousa, Don Miguel de (captain): and the Guatemala expedition, 274, 280

Index

South Carolina: defense of, 274n190; and Gillon, Alexander, 274
South Carolina, 274, 274n190
Souverain, 210
Spain: agricultural methods of, 90; and allied operations against England, xxvi, xxvii, xxviii, xxix, xxx, 3, 4n4, 5n6, 5n7, 6n8, 8n14, 10, 10n18, 11, 17, 19, 19n26, 31, 31n40, 32, 39n44, 101n76, 107–8, 112, 113, 114, 118, 121–22, 123, 125–27, 127n93, 128, 130, 131, 132, 133, 134, 135, 139–40, 142, 143, 144–55, 174, 185, 192, 200–203, 206, 207n148, 216, 216n153, 218, 220, 222, 228, 229, 230, 232–33, 272–73, 276–77, 281, 292, 293, 295, 296, 297, 298, 300, 301, 302, 303, 306, 307, 309, 310–12, 318, 320–21, 323–24, 325, 337n227, 356, 357n246, 360, 362, 375n256, 376–77; and the American Revolution, xxiii, xxv–xxvi, 3n2, 6–7, 202, 332n210; army of, 7n11, 101–2, 104, 105, 106, 277, 318, 342, 380; colonies of, xxiii, 11, 24, 42, 44, 46, 64–65, 68, 72, 86, 91–92, 105–6, 108, 198n139, 200, 217n153, 249, 249n173, 259–60, 279, 310, 311n201, 349n238; and funds for the French, 130, 138, 140, 316, 221–23, 292; maritime mail service of, 14, 14n21, 84n62; navy of, xxvi, 104–5, 122–23, 146, 186, 188, 188n129, 189, 190, 191, 192, 215, 217, 239, 280, 299–300, 313, 364; neutrality of, xxv–xxvi, xxvii, 3–4, 6n10; and peace, 357, 357n246, 370, 371, 375–76, 377, 378, 379, 380; relations with England, xxiin10, xxv–xxvi, xxvii, 4–6, 7n11, 98n68; relations with French forces, 123, 288, 297, 298, 304–5, 356; and relations with Portugal, xxiv, 263n187; trade of, xxvii, 26n33, 38n42, 68, 68n57, 76, 83–86, 106n80, 115, 174, 226–27, 248, 252–53, 262, 274n190, 295; mentioned, ix–x, xv, xxxii, 12, 15–16, 43, 47, 51, 178, 211, 242n167, 279n192, 294, 317, 323, 340, 368n251
Spain under the Bourbons, 1700–1833. See Hargreaves-Mawdsley, W. N.
Spanish Town (Jamaica), 38, 40, 42, 61, 63, 69, 70, 93
Spry, Thomas (captain of the *Pallas*), 35, 38, 45
Starr, J. Barton: *Tories, Dons, and Rebels*, 120n89
Stephenson (English envoy), 158, 159
Stirling Castle, 37
Strait of Tulinger, 331
Strange, Sir Robert, 50
Sugar: in Jamaica, 76, 77, 78, 86, 89–90; and trade, 79, 80, 82, 128, 223, 295
Surinam, 75
Surrey (county in Jamaica), 71
Sweet potatoes: in Jamaica, 76–77

Tabasco pepper: in Jamaica, 54, 75, 77
Tacón, Don Andrés: and Pensacola expedition, 166
Tacubaya: and artillery manufacture, 242n167
Tafia: used in the French Navy, 190; and sugar, 76
Tallapoosas. See Creeks
Tar: and trade, 80
Tartar Point: and Pensacola expedition, 143n100
Taxes: and Casa de Contratación, 370n252; and the French Cape, 196; and Jamaica 81, 86; and New Granada, 213n152; and Peru, 279; and slave trade, 309; in the Spanish colonies, 260
Tea: and contraband trade, 85
Teide, 19, 19n25
Tejera, Eduardo J.: *La Ayuda Cubana en la Lucha por la Independencia Norteamericana*, 208n149
Tellier, Michel Le, Marquis de Louvois: and the French armed forces, 187–88
Temascal, 267
Temperate zone: vegetation of, 156
Tenerife, 18, 19
Tenerife, 17

Index

Ternay, Chevalier de, d'Arnac, Charles-Louis: and the French fleet at Newport, 196n138
Terrible, 232
Texas: and arms for Indians, 256; and the Provincias Internas, 256n182
3d Marine Company: and Battle of Pensacola, 170n118
Tierra Firme, 22, 23, 26, 31, 85
Tigre River, 25
Timber: and the Spanish fleet, 364; and Spanish Louisiana, 227
Tobacco: and monopolies of, 25, 79; and taxes, 213n152
Tobago, xxv, 23, 221n154
Tomasco, Don Juan de, 100, 114, 134, 139, 272
Tories, Dons, and Rebels. See Starr, J. Barton
Tornadoes, 167
Torre, Marqués de la, 99n69
Torrid zone: climate of, 244
Tortoise shell: and Jamaica, 76
Tortosa: and Saavedra's regiment, xvi
Tortuga, 186
Tortuga Sound, 127, 134, 270, 298
Totolingo, 246, 260
Tours, 338
Trade: and the Americans, 107n80, 230n161, 235; and British capture of the Dutch islands, 198n139; and British colonial policies, 78–83, 198n139; in cochineal, 265; and the Cossío Company; and customhouses, 367; and the de Grasse–Saavedra agreement, 227–28, 235, 272, 273, 311n201; of the French, 235; and gold, 83; and Havana, 138, 312; in hides, 227; and Indians, 175, 179; in indigo, 274n190; and Jamaica, 66, 68, 75, 76–77, 78–83, 129, 223, 299; and Kingston, 70, 81; and Louisiana, 226–27; of Mexico, 248; and monopolies, 79–80, 82, 115; and the Navigation Act, 79; and Pensacola, 174, 175; and the Portuguese, 299; of Puerto Plata, 290; restrictions of, 82; and role of silver, 83, 252–53; routes of, 105n79; and rum, 79–80, 271, 283; of silk, 80; of slaves, 38n42, 68n57, 309, 310–12, 345; and the Spanish colonies, 252–53, 259–60, 262; and the Spanish fleet, 216; of sugar, 79–80, 128, 295; of Tabasco peppers, 75, 79–80; and taxes, 81; of timber, 79–80, 227; in wheat, 79–80, 262. *See also* Commerce; Contraband trade; Free trade
Traversai, M. de (captain of the *Iris*), 209, 222, 315, 316
Treasury of Havana, xxix, xxx, 105–6, 113, 131, 139, 227
Treasury of Mexico, 29, 249, 250
Treasury of Paris, 207–8
Treasury of Verazcruz, 268
Treatise on Tactics. See Guibert, Comte Jacques Antoine Hippolyte de
Treaty of Madrid: and slave trade, 38n42
Treaty of Utrecht: and slave trade, 68n57
Tres Siglos de Mexico. See Cavo, Andrés
Trinidad, xxx, 22, 23, 30–31, 31n39, 46, 94, 95, 214, 216
Triomphe, 380n259
Triton, 101, 127, 133, 193
Tropic of Cancer: and climate, 56
Tropics: population of, 262; vegetation of, 156
Tucumán, 17
Tufiño, Don Juan: and Santa Fe rebellion, 219, 222, 278, 279
Tuileries Palace, 334, 334n215, 335
Tupac Amaru: rebellion of, 258n185
Tupac Catari: rebellion of, 258n185
Turk Islands, 194, 284

Ulloa, Antonio de: as governor of Louisiana, xvi; and West Indies, xx
United States: and allied aid to, 201n144; and Miranda, Francisco de, 216n153; and Pensacola's surrender, 173n122; shipping of, 198n139; and Vergennes, Comte de, 332n210. *See also* America; Ameri-

Index

can Revolution
Unzaga y Amezaga, Luis de: governor of Louisiana, 98n68; governor of Havana, 100n72, 380n259
Ursulines: schools of, 195
Urriza, Don Juan de (intendant of the army in Havana): intendant, 100, 100n74; and Miranda, Don Francisco de, 216n153; and supplies for Spanish forces, 114, 122; and the Treasury of Havana, 113
Ushant, Battle of. *See* Battle of Ushant
Ustariz (house of), 379
Utrillo, Juan Francisco Yela: *España ante la Independencia de los Estados Unidos*, 3n2

Valencia: Saavedra in, xv
Valenzuela: and Pensacola expedition, 143n99, 225n157
Valera (of Mexico), 254
Valle, Antonio Ramón del: and Havana's government, 100, 100n73
Vaudreuil, Marquis de, Louis Phillipe de: in the American colonies, 350, 350n239; and French Cape junta, 325; and French fleet, 376n258; and Battle of the Saintes, 320, 320n205, 322–23
Vega, 64
Velázquez (director of mining in Mexico), 258
Venables (British general): and conquest of Jamaica, 65
Venerable Pedro de Betancurt, El. *See* Ruiz de Villarías, A. M.
Venetian ships, 306
Venezuela: and Jamaica expedition, 357n246; and missions of Píritu, 32n41; mentioned, 22n29, 23n31, 216n153
Veracruz: Artillery Drill School of, 268; defense of, xxviii, 242; flota of, 105n79; food stores of, 106; and the de Grasse–Saavedra agreement, 211; and aid for Pensacola expedition, 114, 138, 140; population of, 267; port of, 242–43; and relocation, 266–67; roads to Mexico City, 264; Saavedra's description of, 240–41, 242–43; and Saavedra's mission to Mexico, 219, 224, 234, 238–40; sanitation of, 241, 266, 267; situados from, 220, 221, 230; and Solano's convoy, 312; and aid for West Indies campaigns (de Grasse–Saavedra agreement and the Guatemala, Jamaica, and Providence expeditions), 218, 229, 250, 258, 265, 277, 297–98, 316; mentioned, 17, 264, 280, 379
Vergennes, Comte de, Charles Gravier: and the American Revolution, 5n6, 332, 332n210, 333; and plans for Jamaica expedition, 337, 337n227; and Saavedra, 341; mentioned, 357
Versailles: and Jamaica expedition, 306; Saavedra visits, 331–32, 333, 334, 337; mentioned, 331n207
Versailles junta: and Jamaica expedition, 337, 337n227, 343
Vestal, 310, 316
Viaña, Don Francisco (José ?) de: and the secretariat of the Indies, 358
Victoire (Louis XVI's aunt): Saavedra meets, 335, 335n218
Victoria, 340
Vida en Mexico, La. *See* Calderón de la Barca, Madame
Vidas de la Unidad Americana. *See* Portell Vila, Herminio
Vigas, Las, 244
Village, The: and Mobile, 119, 120
Villages, M. de (French emissary): and Spanish funds for the French, 221–22
Villavivencio (Spanish naval lieutenant): at Pensacola, 153
Ville de Paris: and Battle of the Saintes, 322–23, 323n206; mentioned, 197, 200, 203
Vioménil (French commander): and French forces for Jamaica expedition, 376n258
Virginia, 159, 201n142, 226n159, 227, 232n162, 311n201
Virginia Capes, 196n137

Index

Waldeck Regiment: and English defense of Pensacola, 164, 167n116, 168, 172

Waldes (colonel in the English forces): and English attack on Mobile, 119–20, 119n87. *See also* Hanxleden, Johann Ludwig Wilhelm von

Wall (Antonio?—Spanish officer), 349

Walsingham (English commodore in Jamaica), 47, 62

Wangham, Don Guillermo, 248

War of Succession: and trade, 68

Washington, George (general), 200–201, 200n142, 226, 311n201

Water: and agriculture, 89

Watts (Nathaniel?—of Jamaica), 44, 50, 54, 55

West Florida: and Chester, Peter, 158n112; as English possession, 158, 172; Indians of, 257; and peace, 378; and Saavedra's mission, 10n18; as Spanish possession, xxxii, 172; vicario of, 154n107

West Indies: abuses in, 345; and Barras, M. de, 196n137; and Bouillé, Marquis de, 221, 221n154; and Casa de la Contratación, 370n252; climate of, 88, 108, 269–70, 276, 277, 278, 279–81, 283–84, 296, 300, 307, 318, 313; and La Coruña, 14; and Cuba's place in, 309; and disease, 62, 63, 104, 301, 380; and Estaing, Comte d', 198, 198n140; and Grasse, Comte de, 192n132; industry of, 86; and maritime mail service, 14n21; and Padres de Belemitas, 245n171; and peace, 378; populations of 262; and Saint Simon, Marquis, 194n136; and trade, 78, 90; mentioned 343, 355, 357, 376

West Indies campaigns: allied plans and preparations for, xxix, xxx, 5n7, 7–8, 10, 99–100, 100n75, 109, 112–13, 114, 116–17, 123, 125–26, 128, 129–30, 131, 132, 133, 138–40, 141 141n98, 143, 144, 155n109, 198n139, 200–203, 204, 205–6, 265, 228–29, 279–81, 292, 293, 294, 295, 300, 301, 303, 306–8, 310n201, 331, 337, 337n227, 338, 342, 343, 345, 351, 352, 354–55, 357, 357n246, 362, 372, 373, 374, 375–77. *See also* East Florida; de Grasse–Saavedra agreement; the Guatemala, Jamaica, Pensacola, and Providence expeditions

Whalebone: and trade, 79

Wheat: and trade, 262. *See also* Grains

When the French Were Here. See Bonsal, Stephen

White Plains: and Washington, George, 200n142

Windmills: and Jamaican agriculture, 90

Windward Islands: and allied campaigns, 31, 32, 108, 109, 122, 126, 130, 132, 197–98, 200, 202, 203, 206, 207n148, 222–23, 227, 230, 232–33, 275, 307, 311n201, 345; and hurricanes, 30; mentioned, 23. *See also* West Indies campaigns

Wine: and contraband trade, 85

Wood: and trade, 76, 79

Wright, J. Leitch, Jr.: *The Only Land They Knew: The Tragic Story of the American Indians of the Old South,* 175n125

Xamapa River: and Veracruz, 267

Yamaye: and Jamaica, 64n55

Yams: in Jamaica, 76–77

Yorktown campaign, 196n137, 201n142, 201n143, 225n159, 232n162

Yriarte y Oropesa, Tomás de. *See* Irarte y Oropesa, Tomás de

Yucatán: and Pensacola expedition, 107

Yucca. *See* Cassava

Zacatecas (mint of), 254n178

Zamora Battalion: drill of, 298

Zarala (naval captain): and Battle of Pensacola, 167

Zarate (Spanish officer), 378

Zélé: and Battle of the Saintes, 321–22, 323

Library of Congress Cataloging-in-Publication Data

Saavedra de Sangronis, Francisco, 1746–1819.
 [Journal of the mission to America]
 Journal of Don Francisco Saavedra de Sangronis during the commission that he had in his carge from 25 June 1780 until June 1783 / collated, edited, introduced, and annotated by Francisco Morales Padrón; translated by Aileen Moore Topping.
  p. cm.
 Includes index.
 ISBN 0-8130-0877-8 (alk. paper)
  1. United States—History—Revolution, 1775–1783— Participation, Spanish. 2. Florida—History—Revolution, 1775–1783. 3. Saavedra de Sangronis, Francisco, 1746–1819— Diaries. I. Morales Padrón, Francisco. II. Title.
 E269.S63S23
 973.3' 46—dc19   1988   88-14260
                                                            CIP

WITHDRAWN
FROM
COLLECTION

FORDHAM
UNIVERSITY
LIBRARIES